Man Is
Moral Choice

Man Is Moral Choice

by ALBERT H. HOBBS

ARLINGTON HOUSE·PUBLISHERS
NEW ROCHELLE, NEW YORK

Book design by Pat Slesarchik

Manufactured in the United States of America

Library of Congress Cataloging in Publication Data

Hobbs, Albert Hoyt, 1910–
    Man is moral choice.

    Includes bibliographical references and index.
    1. Man (Christian theology) 2. Conscience.
I. Title
BT702.H62 1979   241   78-27061
ISBN 0–87000–433–6

Contents

MAN IS MORAL CHOICE

PART I

An Apologetic Introduction

Chapter 1

An Apology for My Faith[1]

BRASH IT IS, passing bold to say without let or stint that man is moral choice, and I hasten to soften this hard assertion with a leavening admission that I cannot prove scientifically that moral choice is, more than any other aspect of his nature, the principal feature of man's uniqueness. I hold to this affirmative conviction not as a matter of objective, irrefragable proof, but as a faith: a reflective, examined distillate of many years of study, experience, and wonder.

To support my faith I shall offer evidence, evidence drawn from sources which exceed in quantity and which, I believe, are superior in intellectual quality to those which support contrary descriptions of man, but no matter how large in quantity nor high in quality be such evidence, an assertion such as the one I make can never be scientifically proved, and faith or disbelief will always be an influence in accepting or rejecting it. For this or any meaningful view of man must rest upon qualitative as well as quantitative evidence. In addition, the very nature of an assertion that man can make moral choices in an active, consciously willed manner precludes any prediction of his behavior, and such prediction is the essence of scientific theory.

Choice Implies Responsibility

Having such capacity for conscious choice, man's behavior, though strongly influenced by his heredity and by his environment, is not fully determined by them. Endowed from whence we know not with the capability to play an active, willed role in his moral decisions, he is thereby personally responsible for them.

This interpretation is opposite, for example, to the contention of B. F. Skinner, a prominent representative of the "scientific" view, who insists that man is a puppet, not at all responsible for his behavior. But despite his claims, neither Professor Skinner nor I have scientifically proved our conclusions about the basic nature of man, and the best anyone can do in such circumstance is to provide sufficient evidence to convince reasonable persons of the intellectual credibility of one's hypothesis.

To believe that the most distinctive attribute of man is his capacity for moral choice is to accept the premise that man does have an intrinsic nature; that born in man are potentials for evil as well as potentials for good. This concept of man differs from that of rationalistic scientism which, implicitly if not explicitly (as I shall later explain), rests on an assumption that there is no behavioral aspect of human beings that cannot be readily changed by appropriate scientific techniques. It differs also from the romantic view of man, which is premised on the belief that man is innately good.

Secular and Spiritual Intertwine

I apologize for scanting the role of religion and spirituality in my interpretation of the nature of man. This gross neglect is not because I am ignorant of such influence nor because I disbelieve it, but because my approach is essentially secular. Edmund Burke, prototypical conservative, put the relationship between religion and morality thus:

> Morality does not necessarily include Religion, since it concerns only our Relation with Men. But Religion necessarily includes Morality, because the Relation of God as a Creator

12

is the same to other Men as to us. If God has placed us in a Relation attended with Duties, it must be agreeable to him that we perform those Duties. Hence Moral Duties are included in Religion, and enforced by it.[2]

Yet Burke appreciated this seeming inevitable relationship between religion and morality, warning that "If we should uncover our nakedness by throwing off the Christian religion, which has been . . . the great source of civilization amongst us, . . . we are apprehensive . . . that some uncouth, pernicious, and degrading superstition might take the place of it."[3]

Similarly, Will and Ariel Durant, when they sum up (in *The Lessons of History*[4]) what they learned from the studies that produced their graceful and scholarly ten volumes of intellectual history, say that while morals preceded religion, and religion sometimes promotes orthodoxy independently of morality, and while immorality has, on occasion, flourished in ages of religious domination, yet "there is no significant example in history, before our time, of a society successfully maintaining moral life without the aid of religion."

Conservative philosopher Alexis de Tocqueville pointed out that while despotisms may survive without faith, liberty cannot, and democratic republics are more in need of religion than regimented societies. "I am inclined to think," Tocqueville observed,[5] "that if faith be wanting in man, he must be subject; and if he be free, he must believe." A similar thought is expressed more succinctly and more forcefully in *The Book of Common Prayer*: "In Thy service, perfect freedom."

Whether morality preceded religion and alone can effectively hold together an unregimented society or whether, apart from dictatorship, religion and morality necessarily complement each other is an extremely interesting intellectual question, but it is not the one I address myself to. My stance is similar to that taken by Henry Hazlitt in *The Foundations of Morality*,[6] in that my function is not to maintain the truth of one or another religious doctrine but to insist upon the evidential basis of morality and to show what the rules of morality ought to be. So, while my conception of man's moral nature corresponds to religious ones in that they and I hold that man is defiled from within, not

13

without,[7] I shall stress primarily secular evidence in support of my assertion that man is moral choice.

A View Old, Yet New

I apologize that the evidence which I adduce is drawn mostly from the past two centuries, though I am aware that much was revealed about the nature of man prior to the eighteenth century. I stress evidence and views from the eighteenth century down to the present because it was Edmund Burke's reaction against the rationalistic scientism of his day which forms a philosophical foundation for my intellectual demonstration that man is moral choice.

I am sorry, also, that the philosophical conservatism which was nourished by Burke's views is relatively new to America and most people, including most educated people, are either unaware of its existence or ignorant of its nature. Later on I shall try to describe the essential nature of this philosophical conservatism but for the moment I should like to point out, since the three are so often confused, that it is not the same as nostalgic (or traditionalist, or romantic) conservatism, and it differs distinctively from economic conservatism.

Differing Conservatisms

Conservatism is ordinarily and understandably thought to be traditionalism; a bovine adoration of things past, and a bitterly dogmatic rejection of things new. If it's old it's good; if it's new it's bad! As a meaningful quip has it, "I haven't read it yet, but when I do I'm going to be bitter." Such reactions are an expression of nostalgia for the good old days, conveniently forgetting that the Communist Manifesto is near unto its sesquicentennial. It is glorification of a past when men were men and women were ladies and one readily knew the difference. As their vision of what they might have been dissolves, traditional conservatives replace it with dreams of a past that never was. It is enticingly easy to ridicule traditionalist conservatism and to ignore its palpable virtues, but it is not my purpose to criticize nor to defend this comfortable doctrine.

14

Those who espouse economic conservatism believe that the economic factor is the keystone of the social structure; and if it be properly shaped and set neatly into place, the other elements of society will align themselves harmoniously about it. The year in which I write being 1976, it is meet to note that the mentor for many economic conservatives is Adam Smith, whose *An Inquiry into the Nature and Causes of the Wealth of Nations* was published just two hundred years ago. Smith believed in the strong if not inexorable forces of competition, supply and demand, and other economic principles which some mistakenly took to be scientific laws. His contention that each pursuing his own interest would commonly promote the interests of society —albeit unwittingly, as though guided by an invisible hand— attained widespread and lasting popularity. A central tenet of believers in economic conservatism came to be *laissez-faire*, the desirability if not the essentiality of governmental noninterference with the "laws of economics."

Among better-known economic conservatives are Ludwig von Mises, Frederick von Hayek, and Nobel Laureate and one-time presidential adviser Milton Friedman. Professor Friedman, though, properly insists that he is not at all a conservative, but a true liberal; and he is correct in his contention because the centrality of the economic factor has always been a main tenet of liberalism, and though liberals have drastically remolded their keystone of the social structure from its original *laissez-faire* design (replacing it with the more fashionable Welfare State pattern), their focus of concern on the economic factor as the main determiner of social conditions is still steadfastly held.

I shall describe philosophic conservatism in some detail later but in the meantime I beg you to remember that its central tenet is man's capacity for moral choice, based on his innate and only partially modifiable potential for evil as well as good; hence like traditionalist conservatism it respects the past, but unlike it does not revere it. Similarly, philosophical conservatives agree with economic conservatives (more properly designated eighteenth-century liberals) that economic factors are very important in social affairs and that big government poses a constant and growing threat of despotism, but philosophical conservatives believe that in the social mix morality is a more fundamental ingredient than materialism.

15

Proofs Awkward and Partial

The philosopher Arthur Schopenhauer observed that to preach morality is easy but to give it a foundation is hard, and finding it impossible to establish an intellectually credible basis for man's capability for conscious moral choice by conventional ways of thought, I have created new ways of thinking which, being different, will affright some people and alienate others. I regret this necessity for subjecting readers to the wrenching process needed to lift oneself out of his accustomed and comfortable grooves of thinking, and even more deeply I regret my inability to describe the "proof" that man is moral choice without floundering in some awkwardly pedantic and apparently pretentious phrases.

Please forgive also my resort to Platonic archetypical descriptions; and in this regret I echo the apology of an earlier Hobb(e)s as he admitted that the warfaring conditions that, he hypostatized, prevailed before and made necessary the establishment of society which is the *Leviathan* may never have existed.

The Meanness of Conservatism

Ralph Waldo Emerson insightfully lamented as long ago as 1842 that there is always a certain meanness in the argument of conservatism, and he was certainly prescient in this observation because philosophical conservatism offers no utopia, no pie-in-the-sky, whether the sky be lighted by the twin moons of just-explored Mars or the nostalgic glow of a midwestern sunset. In this view we cannot slough off our faults on others: on our heredity, our environment, or on the absence of untrammeled affection in our childhood. Neither you nor I like this. Praise for our courage in moral choice is fine; we accept that with eyes downcast only to conceal our glee. But blame for our moral cowardice—we all seek something else to explain that.

Emerson, however, continued and concluded his seeming pessimistic comment about the nature of conservatism by saying that the "certain meanness" was joined with a certain superiority in its fact. And this I too shall contend: that while adherence to moral codes does entail suppression of demanding desire and renunciation of immediate pleasure, it also enables us to live fuller lives than we can by ignoring or rejecting moral imperatives.

. . . And the Coldness of Conservatives

My final apology concerns a matter of personal relations with people which, especially in my relations with students, has bothered me for years and which I never had the courage to openly admit. There is a certain coolness in relationships between conservatives and other people. Not only do they fail to be effusive, they are often hardly cordial and more than sometime they are abstractedly impersonal. For many years I tried to excuse reactions such as these by blaming them on the large numbers of students I've taught, on professional absentmindedness, or on a poor memory, but it was not until I learned that Alexis de Tocqueville reacted similarly that I forced myself to admit that simple indifference to most people is also involved. Tocqueville acknowledged that:

> Whenever there is nothing in a man's thoughts or feelings that strikes me, I, so to speak, do not see him. I have always supposed that mediocrities as well as men of parts had a nose, mouth and eyes, but I have never been able to fix in my memory the forms that those features take in each particular case. I am constantly asking the names of these unknown people whom I meet every day and constantly forget. It is not that I despise them, but I have little truck with them, feeling that they are like so many clichés. I respect them, for they make the world, but they bore me profoundly.[8]

With such apologies in mind, let us proceed with the argument that man is moral choice.

Chapter 1. References and Notes

1. The notion for this title is derived from Professor Eliseo Vivas, "Apologia Pro Fide Mea," *The Intercollegiate Review,* October 1965; and from John Henry Cardinal Newman, *Apologia Pro Vita Sua* (1864). Professor Vivas apologizes because he is a secular conservative, one of a "pitiful minority" whose views are ridiculed by an academic world enthralled in liberal orthodoxy. Cardinal Newman's *Apologia* recites an account of his rejection of the religious rationalistic liberalism of the Anglican Church which he ". . . earnestly denounced and abjured" in favor of traditionalist High Church doctrine.

2. H. V. F. Somerset, *A Notebook of Edmund Burke* (Cambridge: The University Press, 1957), pp. 67–74.

3. Will and Ariel Durant, *The Age of Napoleon* (New York: Simon and Schuster, 1975), p. 514.

4. Will and Ariel Durant, *The Lessons of History* (New York: Simon and Schuster, 1968), pp. 43–51.

5. Alexis de Tocqueville, *Democracy in America,* vol. 2 (New York: Vintage Books, 1959), p. 23.

6. Henry Hazlitt, *The Foundations of Morality* (New York: D. van Nostrand Co., 1964).

7. *Mark* 7:21, 22, 23.

8. Alexis de Tocqueville, *Recollections,* trans. by George Lawrence (New York: Doubleday, 1971), p. 103. James W. Muller, "Politics and Philosophy in Tocqueville's *Souvenirs,"* *The Intercollegiate Review,* Winter 1975, p. 40.

Chapter 2

What Is Man?

LIFE'S SURGE, THAT flow and ebb of sea-sourced energy which governs the rhythm of our being, becomes quietest, so they say, between three and four in the morning. And when this insistent throb sinks to a gentle murmur and the distractions of our waking world are damped by quiet night, our spirit sometimes rises through the stilled sea of our desire and surfaces to calm reflection.

It was in such circumstance, now many years ago, that a question which long had plagued me surfaced from my depths of wonderment in a form which provided its own answer. In saying that the answer arose to me as out of a dream, I do not mean that it was a duplication of René Descartes' 1619 dream in which the Spirit of Truth revealed to him the "Universal Science Destined to Raise Our Nature to its Highest Degree of Perfection."[1] Unlike Descartes, I was under no delusion that I had discovered the science of sciences, the universal mechanics in which space and extension were the fundamental reality, motion the point of all departure, and mathematics the language of its revelation which led him to proclaim: "Give me extension and motion, and I will construct the universe."

My comprehension of the real nature of the question "What is Man?" was not an expression of the hubris which scientists uniformly deny and invariably express, nor did it awaken the zeal of a religious prophet, but it more nearly gave me a feeling

20

such as F. Scott Fitzgerald said motivated him to write: a feeling of being ". . . an instrument of something uncomprehended, incomprehensible, unknown."[2]

Man Is Not Simply What He Says

At the time the conviction arose in me that man's essence is his capacity for moral choice, the academic world was tumultuous with excitement as my colleagues in sociology and academicians from many other disciplines fervently proclaimed that one of the deepest hidden areas of human behavior had finally been exposed by the unblinking light of scientific study to reveal its ancient mysteries. A. C. Kinsey, a professor of zoology from the University of Indiana, had published *Sexual Behavior in the Human Male* and soon followed this volume with *Sexual Behavior in the Human Female*.[3] Magazines, newspapers, lawyers, judges, and clergymen as well as professors exulted their conviction that science had now revealed the truth about sex and we should change not only our mores and laws but our religious beliefs accordingly. One prominent religious leader (Rabbi Joshua Liebman, in *Peace of Mind*) informed us that we should rewrite the Ten Commandments to incorporate Kinsey's truths together with the truths of Freud and Marx. My professional skepticism combined with my implicit conservatism to prevent me from joining such believers.

Critical analyses of his sampling techniques, dissection of his statistical methods, and a reflective examination of the prejudice that dominated Professor Kinsey's presentation definitively revealed that his volumes, despite their author's claims to science and contrary to a gullible acceptance by social scientists were, quite clearly and simply, propagandistic.

It was not difficult to demonstrate[4] the skewed sampling, the statistical errors, and the persistent special pleading that characterized both volumes of these supposedly objective, scientific studies. But despite his technical errors, his stultifying humorless prejudice and his unwarranted claims to science, it was apparent that Professor Kinsey was a dedicated man, conscientious and painstaking, who had devoted many years to his study of human sexual behavior. Why then, I asked myself on several four o'clocks of stilled nights, had his years of study led to conclusions that were not only palpably incorrect but which perverted rather than clarified our knowledge of ourselves.

In my waking revery it came to me that Professor Kinsey had erred for the same two reasons that most social scientists err: He had used the wrong methods and, even more importantly, he had asked the wrong questions.

Professor Kinsey repeatedly asserted (more than one hundred times in the first volume alone), and those who read his books firmly believed, that he had used the scientific method to study human sexual behavior. He was convinced that if he could reach definitive conclusions about his life-long specialty—the taxonomy of wasps—by coldly objective methods, he could use similarly strict quantitative methods to reach definitive, unchallengeable findings about the meaning of human sex. He was aware that the scientific method requires controlled observation, meaning that the phenomena being studied must be reduced to quantitative and stable units, and so his investigations reduced all aspects of human sex to an enumeration of orgasms. While a certain degree of objectivity is attained by eliminating sentiments of love and affection, dreams and heartfelt desires from sexual relationships, a great deal of meaning is lost in the process, and the nature of this loss of meaning is amusingly described by astrophysicist Sir Arthur Eddington in his account of the use of a fishing net.[5]

Science Cuts Man to Pieces

In his whimsical parable, Sir Arthur asks us to imagine an ichthyologist (a scientist who studies fish, much as Professor Kinsey, prior to turning to sex during the middle years of his life, studied wasps) who, in his studies of fish, casts a net into the ocean and brings up an assortment of things in his catch. As a scientist, using the scientific method, he cannot help but reach two conclusions:

(1) No creature in the sea is less than two inches long.

(2) All creatures of the sea have gills.

His catch, or, if you prefer, a thousand such catches, stands for the body of knowledge that constitutes the science of ichthyology, and his net represents the intellectual process we use to obtain our scientific knowledge. A layman might reasonably object to the scientist's first conclusion, pointing out that there are many creatures of the sea less than two inches long, saying that this ichthyological "law" existed only because the net which was used to arrive at it, having openings of two inches, cannot catch anything smaller. Our scientific ichthyologist, instead of graciously conceding this obvious relation between cause and conclusion, might scornfully ridicule the layman for pretending knowledge of the universe of fishes which was reached in some way other than by the scientific method, and then proclaim that science has proved: *What my net can't catch isn't fish!*

The second "scientific" conclusion—that all creatures of the sea have gills—involves a psychological rather than a factual fallacy and is reached because the ichthyologist, concerned only with fish, dismisses all the vast array of other forms of sea-life as meaningless waste, simply because they are not included in the field of study which he believes to be most important.

As Sir Arthur Eddington's ichthyologist, conscientiously using the scientific method, would necessarily conclude that there are no baby fishes, so Professor Kinsey, using the sexual orgasm as his net, would, were he rigorously scientific, conclude that there is no relationship between human sexual activity and having babies. Similarly, love, affection, romance, lust, yearning, and the joy of sharing all slip through his net into the drear oblivion of depths unmeasured by science.

In *The Measure of Man,* Joseph Wood Krutch cautions us that we likely have been deluded rather than enlightened by many "scientific" studies because the methods we use for a study of man are for the most part techniques which were originally devised to study machines or rats and are suited, therefore, to detect and measure only those characteristics which machines, rats, and men have in common.[6] By their very nature such methods eliminate most of the things which make us distinctively human. And Arthur Koestler, admitting that scholars in the past often indulged in the anthropomorphic fallacy of imputing human motivations to the behavior of the animals they studied, points out that today, in indiscriminately applying the findings from animal studies to man, we may be guilty of the *ratomorphic* fallacy.[7]

Catherine Roberts, in her analysis of the obligations of scientists when they study man, describes the limits as well as the advantages of applying the scientific method to man, saying:

> A scientific explanation of the essence of human greatness does not exist; no amount of genetic, psychological, chemical, or medical knowledge available today can explain virtue and goodness. It follows that although science possesses the means to direct the further development of man by controlling his propagation, improving his health, and possibly raising his intelligence, it has no means whatever for augmenting his essential humanness.[8]

And the proportions of the role of rationalistic scientism in this context are beautifully but anonymously expressed in the chapel at Stanford University:

No widening of science,
No possession of abstract truth
Can indemnify for an enfeebled hold on the highest and central
Truths of humanity.

It was this "essential humanness" of Catherine Roberts and these "central truths of humanity" referred to in the chapel at Stanford that I sought to explore.

In the interviews which constituted the material for his conclusions about human sexual behavior, Professor Kinsey asked people how many orgasms they had and what form of activity produced them. This substantive basis, though voluminous in quantity, was narrowly limited in its conceptual quality because all of the humanly meaningful qualitative aspects of sex slipped through his orgasmic net. It was also limited in that he obtained merely verbal responses to his questions. For many reasons (faulty memory, exaggeration, cover-up, outright lies) these verbal responses may have been less than true. So no matter how conscientious was his investigation—and he did try to detect discrepancies in the answers of his respondents—he learned only what people *said* they did and could never be sure that what they said they did was what they actually did. In any event he could obtain only verbalizations about orgasms, an important but severely limited aspect of the sexual aspect of life.

His questions at best involved: What man says he does; not what he does do. Even were we to learn all that man does, we would still be far from an answer to the question which has been asked since the memory of man runneth not to the contrary—What is man?

What Is Man?

What is man? What am I, not who am I. Not what is my name, but what is my meaning. What is my meaning as a human being, and what is the meaning which constitutes my uniqueness, my integrity as a person? The Bible puts the question thus:

> What is man that thou art mindful of him? Or the son of man, that thou visitest him? Thou makest him a little lower than the angels. . . .[9]

Centuries later, T. S. Eliot repeated this wonderment, calling it "the question of questions . . . which no political philosophy can escape," and he asks:

> What is man? What is his misery and what his greatness? And what, finally, his destiny?[10]

But a century and a half before Eliot asked his questions, Blaise Pascal[11] felt that he had the answer, putting man indeed far lower than the angels and calling him a chimera, a monster, and a contradiction. Judge of all things, feeble worm of the earth, a sink of uncertainty and error, the glory and shame of the universe. His most frequently quoted reference holds that man is "the weakest reed in nature, but a thinking reed."

Another reedlike metaphor, less mixed than Pascal's and originating in Sir Richard Burton's translation of mid-eastern philosophy, *The Kasidah*, describes man as

> This tube, an enigmatic pipe,
> Whose end was laid before begun
> That lengthens, broadens,
> shrinks and breaks;
> Puzzle, machine, automaton.[12]

25

In his *Essay on Man* in 1792, Alexander Pope repeated the designation of man as a worm. Though part of the "vast chain of being," Pope called man a vile worm, a ". . . chaos of thought and passion, all confused, with too much knowledge for the skeptic side and too much weakness for the stoic's pride; the glory, jest, and riddle of the world."

According to accounts[13] which are likely apocryphal but which in good fun raise some of the difficulties associated with finding an answer to this query, Plato defined man as a two-legged animal without feathers, whereupon Diogenes plucked a cock, brought it into the Academy and said, "This is Plato's man." On which account this addition was made to the definition —with broad, flat nails!

Fyodor Dostoevsky, like Plato, identified man by the number of his limbs, calling him the ungrateful biped.

In the seventeenth century Thomas Hobbes in his *Leviathan* described the life of primitive man as being nasty, brutish, and short; a description which Ambrose Bierce in *The Devil's Dictionary* defines as a form of realism which is "the art of depicting nature as it is seen by toads." In the eighteenth century Rousseau and Diderot reversed Hobbes' version and described man's life as being idyllic, as exemplified in the lives of the Hurons and Tahitians. Voltaire, in *Candide* and elsewhere, ridiculed this notion, and in 1972 anthropologist Colin M. Turnbull[14] told us of the primitive Ik whose children, abandoned by their parents at ages four or five, return, if they live, and laugh as they steal food from their starving mothers. Totally without compassion, Ik parents have no affection or concern for their children, nor do the children for the parents, and the old, the sick, and the crippled are left, without a trace of compunction, to die.

Aristotle referred to *political man*, Adam Smith and the Manchestrians talked with pursed lips about *economic man*, and the improbably named Lionel Tiger and Robin Fox, having impossibly met in the London Zoo, collaborated to give us *Man, The Imperial Animal.*

> It is said that man is the only animal that laughs—and on hearing this the hyena grins.

It is said that man is the only animal that cries—and the crocodile weeps.

It is said that man is the only animal that talks—and the dolphins leap ecstatically as they convey this information to their fellows.

But perhaps all such descriptions of man are pointless because such diverse and renowned authorities as Professor B. F. Skinner and Chairman Mao Tse-tung have insisted that *there is no such thing as human nature.*

The Price Tag on Man

Mayhap we multiply words without knowledge and should discard both the fanciful spiritual and the conflicting intellectual efforts to describe man, limiting our comprehension of him to what is objectively and precisely measurable. According to exact computation, we are informed that the blood serum of an average man could be sold (as of 1972) for some $650, and that his body contains other chemicals worth $3.50, and so we could say, pending further inflation, that a man *is* $653.50.[15] Now this $653.50 man is a magnificent advance over the men of my youth who were described as chemicals worth 98 cents, chemicals which would be worth only $5.60 in inflated 1977 dollars.

In 1976, however, Harold J. Morowitz, a professor of biochemistry at Yale, computed that with hemoglobin at $2.95 a gram, trypsin at $36 a gram, crystalline insulin at $47.50, acetate kinase at $8,860, and a follicle-stimulating hormone a bargain at $4,800,000 a gram, it would take up to $6,000,000,000.00 to synthesize a man![16] With all due respect to quantified values, one wonders if such data contribute more to our understanding of man than Alfred, Lord Byron's description of man as "a sad jar of atoms."

With awesome mechanical precision the designer and reduction engineer R. Buckminster Fuller reduces his analysis of man to:

Man is a self-balancing, 28 jointed, adapter-based biped, an electrochemical reduction plant, integral with segregated stowages of special energy extracts. . . .[17]

With broad, flat nails, I wonder?

Man as an Animal

The "scientific" taxonomic perspective (from which Professor Kinsey studied wasps before he switched his professional interest to human sex) says that in the animal kingdom man is a *vertebrate* in that he has a segmented spinal column; a *mammal* because human young suckle from their mother's mammae, or breasts; a *primate* or one of the top-ranked animals, standing in that rank with monkeys and apes; and being two-legged he would be a *hominoid*; which brings him down (or up) to *Homo*, the species of man, and be he modern, he is also of the wise *sapiens* species as distinguished from now extinct less-wise species which preceded him.[18] Somehow my spirit rebels against this neatly arranged hierarchy, and I would lean with rather more favor to the brilliantly incisive opening statement of Desmond Morris's *The Naked Ape*: "There are one hundred and ninety-three living species of monkeys and apes. One hundred and ninety-two of them are covered with hair. The exception is a naked ape self-named *Homo sapiens*... [who] spends a great deal of time examining his higher motives and an equal amount of time studiously ignoring his fundamental ones."[19]

Neurologically, it can be said that man appeared when the neocortical part of the brain evolved to dominate the palaeocortical and the archicortical divisions.[20]

Man is sometimes particularized as being the tool-making animal, but many animals, including wasps, the brown-headed nuthatch, the black-breasted buzzard, the Egyptian vulture, northern blue jays, sea otters, ants, chimpanzees, baboons, and others use tools for their survival.[21] They use sticks as levers, as whips and as clubs; they use stones for throwing, and leaves as drinking and feeding utensils. And the TWU might be interested in unionizing those ants which use leaves to transport food to their colonies.

As long ago as 1917 the Gestalt psychologist Wolfgang Kohler described in his studies of chimpanzees how they would insert one bamboo pole into another to fashion a tool long enough to gather food that had been placed beyond their reach[22]; and captive Hamadryas baboons have been observed, in a self-taught manner, to cooperate in tool usage.[23] A baboon which cannot use a tool in its cage will altruistically pass it to a fellow baboon in another cage who can use it.

Man and Society

Most commonly man's uniqueness is encapsulated in the expression that he is a social animal, but there is much evidence which nullifies this claim as man's distinction.[24] Indeed, Professor E. O. Wilson in his *Sociobiology* rates human society low on a list of social efficiency (pp. 379–380). Finding that societies are characteristic of four groups of animal types—the colonial invertebrates, the social insects, the nonhuman mammals, and man—he believes that colonial invertebrates (corals, etc.) come closest to producing perfect societies.

Altruistic behavior which, in our conceit, we like to believe unique to man, is actually a marked feature of insect societies, and while such societies function on a basis of impersonal intimacy, ere we sneer at this impersonality let us give thought to how we strive today (through the U.N.; through the concept of one-world) to attain a similar condition of impersonality which Dostoevsky described in *The Grand Inquisitor* as our yearning for a universal ant heap.

Altruism is much less common among nonhuman mammalian societies; members often selfishly exploit the group to gain food and shelter, and ordinarily the sick or injured are left to die—though dolphins, whales, elephants and other infrahuman forms constitute exceptions to this generalization. Human societies cohere, says Professor Wilson, not because we have reduced selfishness but because we have acquired intelligence to consult the past and to plan the future.

In attributing man's capability to form societies and his ability to function within a social structure to his intelligence, Professor Wilson joins a large and distinguished company, for

29

among those who are aware that human society is only one of many forms of society most, by far, credit man's intelligence as being the responsible agency in its creation and its continuance. While being aware of the importance of intelligence in these areas, I would argue that man's capacity for moral choice is even more important, and in this regard agree with the interpretation of Aleksandr Solzhenitsyn, who follows Dostoevsky's reasoning in saying that while the bee has the formula for its hive and the ant the formula for its hill incorporate in its structure, man does not.[25] Man, Solzhenitsyn goes on to say, is free of any formula for his society, and this freedom is not man's "natural" inheritance, but rather the aim of his life and a "supernatural" gift.

We could continue these varied descriptions of man and include others which identify man with his heredity, with his endocrine system, with his environmental influences, with his engrams, his complexes or his toilet training, but obviously man is not solely his brain or his glands or his genes; nor is he simply his political or economic behavior. In *The Lessons of History* Will and Ariel Durant nicely indicate the difficulty in trying to describe man as a function of the many and diverse forms of behavior he engages in.

> Since man is a moment in astronomic time, a transient guest of the earth, a spore of his species, a scion of his race, a composite of body, character, and mind, a member of a family and a community, a believer or doubter of a faith, a unit in an economy, perhaps a citizen in a state or a soldier in an army, we may ask under the corresponding heads—astronomy, geology, geography, biology, ethnology, psychology, morality, religion, economics, politics, and war—what history has to say about the nature, conduct, and prospects of man.[26]

A Need for Poesy

This congeries of different, often competing and sometimes conflicting, roles prevents a total assessment of man from any behavioristic approach, sexual or otherwise; and our attempts to construct him from bits of knowledge gleaned from neurology, endocrinology, reflexology, psychology, psychoanalysis, scientology, economics, political science, sociology or other separate approaches gives us at best a caricature and at worse a delusive belief that we have attained wisdom. To combine these separate disciplines into an "interdisciplinary" approach rests on the assumption that small fractions of knowledge, when multiplied, produce larger totals of knowledge. No matter how many or diverse the aspects of man we compile, ultimately our preference would lead us to accept some and our prejudice to reject others, and when we combine the bits of man which remain we have a mosaic inevitably cemented by the poetic metaphor which alone can go beyond them all.[27]

Following a skimpy survey of pre-Christian views of man and a sketch of the contrasting views among early Christians, I shall argue that our present contrasting conceptions of man are rooted in three differing secular perspectives that emerged during the eighteenth century: the rationalistic-scientistic conception of man, commonly called scientific; the rejection of this view which evolved into the romantic conception of man; and the conservative interpretation of man, which rejects the premises of both.

Chapter 2. References and Notes

1. Floyd W. Matson, *The Broken Image*, (New York: George Braziller, 1964), p. 22.

2. Nancy Mitford, *Zelda* (New York: Avon Books, 1970), pp. 306–307. In a letter from F. Scott Fitzgerald to his wife, Zelda.

3. Alfred C. Kinsey, W. B. Pomeroy, and Clyde E. Martin, *Sexual Behavior in the Human Male* (Philadelphia: W. B. Saunders, 1948); and *Sexual Behavior in the Human Female* (Philadelphia: W. B. Saunders, 1953).

4. A. H. Hobbs and W. M. Kephart, "Professor Kinsey, His Facts and His Fantasy," *The American Journal of Psychiatry*, vol. 104 (1948), and vol. 110 (1954).

5. F. Sherwood Taylor, *A Short History of Science and Scientific Thought* (New York: W. W. Norton, 1963), pp. 348–349.

6. Joseph Wood Krutch, *The Measure of Man* (Indianapolis: Bobbs-Merrill, 1954).

7. Arthur Koestler, *The Ghost in the Machine* (New York: Macmillan, 1967).

8. Catherine Roberts, *The Scientific Conscience* (New York: George Braziller, 1967), p. 66.

9. *Heb.* 2:6, 7.

10. T. S. Eliot, "The Literature of Politics," in "T. S. Eliot and the Critique of Liberalism," by George A. Painchas, *Modern Age*, Spring 1974, pp. 145–162.

11. Blaise Pascal, *Pensées* (1670), Section VII, No. 434.

12. *The Kasidah of Haji Abdu El-Yezdi*, trans. Sir Richard Burton (New York: David McKay, 1931), p. 20.

13. Diogenes Laertius, *The Lives and Opinions of Eminent Philosophers*, trans. Charles Duke Yonge.

14. Colin M. Turnbull, *The Mountain People* (New York: Simon and Schuster, 1972), pp. 121, 131.

15. Philadelphia *Evening Bulletin*, editorial, December 7, 1972.

16. Harold J. Morowitz, "The High Cost of Being Human," *New York Times*, February 11, 1976.

17. Jack Booth, "Bucky's Brilliant . . . but," Philadelphia *Evening Bulletin*, February 28, 1974.

18. Amram Scheinfeld, *Your Heredity and Environment* (New York: J. B. Lippincott, 1965), p. 577.

19. Desmond Morris, *The Naked Ape* (New York: McGraw-Hill, 1967), p. 9.

20. Steven Rose, *The Conscious Brain* (New York: Alfred A. Knopf, 1973), p. 137.

21. Edward O. Wilson, *Sociobiology* (Cambridge, Mass.: Harvard University Press, 1975), pp. 172–173.

22. Wolfgang Kohler, *The Mentality of Apes*, trans. E. Winter (London: Routledge and Kegan Paul, 1927), pp. 135–172.

23. Thony B. Jones and Alan C. Kamil, "Cooperative Tool Use by Captive Hamadryas Baboons," *Science*, vol. 182 (1973), p. 1076.

24. Some recent compilations: Edward O. Wilson, *Sociobiology,*; Edward O. Wilson, *The Insect Societies* (Cambridge, Mass.: Harvard University Press, 1971), Charles D. Michener, *The Social Behavior of Bees* (Cambridge, Mass.: Harvard University Press, 1974).

25. Aleksandr Solzhenitsyn, *From Under the Rubble* (Boston: Little, Brown, 1974), p. 147.

26. Will and Ariel Durant, *The Lessons of History* (New York: Simon and Schuster, 1968), p. 13.

27. Kenneth Burke, *Permanence and Change* (Indianapolis: Bobbs-Merrill, 1965), p. 263.

PART II

Man's Ancient Image

Chapter 3

Reflected from Above

SOON OR LATE all philosophical ideas seem to find their source in Plato, and the belief that man has a positive ability to make moral choices—that while he has potentials for good he also has propensities for evil which he must willfully control to lead a moral life—goes at least as far back as Plato's Phaedrus Myth.[1]

Plato describes the nature of man's soul in a figure which is a composite of a pair of winged horses and a charioteer. The horse on the right is noble, a superb white steed with a haughty neck and an aquiline nose, needing not a whip, only a word for guidance; but on the left its ignoble mate, a dark nag, crooked and lumbering, shag-eared and deaf, can be restrained only by the force of strong reason—the driver. The noble steed, under the governance of shame, refrains from leaping upon its desired, but the shag-eared nag plunges on and would career the chariot crazily into the earth were it not for the steadiness of the noble steed and the control of the driver.

In this myth of the charioteer and in the *Republic* Plato, as did Heraclitus also, described the soul of man as containing higher and lower elements, the lower urging violent action to satisfy pleasurable desire, the higher idealistically restraining the lower in seemingly antithetical but (I would say) actually complementary balance. Our spirit (conscience) provides the balance. The ability to regulate does not, however, give

37

conscience or reason the power to eradicate our lusts.

Centuries later, Martin Luther (1483–1546) used a similar figure of speech, writing that "man's will is like a beast standing between two riders. If God rides, it wills and goes where God wills. . . . If Satan rides, it wills and goes where Satan wills."[2] But unlike Plato, Luther said that the will of man cannot decide which rider shall control; the riders themselves, God and Satan, fight for this control. Thus Luther, in depriving man of ability to control his course, comes much closer to Saint Augustine than to Plato in his beliefs about man's spirit.

Within the Christian religion this dispute about the degree to which man's will can control his destiny is most dramatically conveyed (or so, in view of my limited knowledge, it seems to me) by the differences between Saint Augustine and the British lay monk Pelagius.

Means of Grace, Hope of Glory

According to Saint Augustine (354–430), man brought about his fall of his own accord, that is, by free will, but is not able to rise of his own accord. His ignorance and just condemnation he suffers from birth and from this evil no man is delivered save by the grace of God. God created man good but man corrupted himself by his own choice, and there is no possibility of man's earning a place in God's city by his own merit. The best an individual man can hope for is that, by God's grace, he will turn out to be one of the fixed number of saints with which God will fill His city. Although the number of perfected saints will increase throughout history, this does not mean that secular society will improve correspondingly.[3]

While Augustine promulgated his conception of mankind as a "lump of sin,"[4] unable to save himself and wholly dependent on God's grace, Pelagius (360?–?420), having become a teacher in Rome, there disseminated his quite contrary doctrine of human nature, arguing that in creating man God gave him the unique privilege of being able to accomplish the divine will through his own choice. Thus, it depends on man himself whether he acts rightly or wrongly, and the possibility of freely

38

choosing the good entails the complementary possibility of choosing evil. Grace is an essential element in man's capacity to choose, but by grace Pelagius meant God's gift to us of the possibility of not sinning.

In arguing as he did, Pelagius rejected the doctrine of original sin as it was interpreted by Augustine. As we are procreated without virtue, so also are we procreated without vice. We are born with capacity to improve ourselves or to corrupt ourselves by our exercise of freedom to will in respect of moral issues.

From a philosophical perspective this conflict about the nature of man's will is still very much at issue, but its clerical manifestation seemed to be seriously restrained when Pope Zosimus confirmed the judgment of the Council of Carthage (418) and in unambiguous terms outlawed Pelagianism. Later, the Council of Orange (529) put the quietus of the church on these conflicting views, accepting Augustine's while it anathematized the Pelagian teaching that by the force of nature we can rightly think or choose anything that is good. It temporized, however, by also rejecting Augustine's doctrine of "dual predestination" —the doctrine that some men are predestined to be saved and others to be damned.

Despite this ostensible silencing of disputation at the Councils of Carthage and Orange, the question of the degree to which man had freedom of will in respect to moral issues continues to be argued within the church as well as in secular history. Though the Council of Orange modified Augustine's stance as well as rejecting the teachings of Pelagius, a thousand years later John Calvin (1509–1564) patterned his beliefs after Augustine (as had Luther) in proclaiming predestination[5] and the utter inability of man to work out his own salvation; that while God's grace is freely given it can neither be earned nor refused.

But this long, fascinating and continuing controversy on its religious level is not our principal concern and, leaving such disputation with the theologians to whom it properly belongs or, better yet, to God, for only He knows, let us descend to the mundane levels on which such skirmishes now more commonly occur, though being often fought by ignorant armies which clash by night.

Augustine's religious conception of man as a "lump of sin" totally dependent on God's grace for his redemption and incapable of exercising moral choice so as to determine his fate was essentially reiterated by Luther and Calvin (among others) and continues to exert strong religious influence now, some fifteen hundred years later; and Plato's spiritual (though non-Christian) conception of man's soul as a charioteer who controlled his urges for evil and complemented them by his propensity for good was soon under serious attack and by the second century A.D. Galen (Claudius Galenus, A.D. 130–200) complained of such behavioristic attacks which cut man in pieces, saying:

> Some of these people have even expressly declared that the soul possesses no reasoning faculty, but that we are led like cattle by the impression of our senses, and are unable to refuse or dissent from anything. In their view, obviously, courage, wisdom, temperance, and self-control are all mere nonsense, we do not love each other or our offspring, nor do the gods care anything for us.[6]

Secular Perfectibility

As between Pelagian and Augustinian views of man, the issues were quite clear: man could perfect himself through the exercise of his own capacity to will or he could be perfected only by the infusion of God's grace. In either case, human perfection was spiritual in nature. But beginning in the seventeenth century,[7] coming to general intellectual attention in the eighteenth, and dominating our lives today, two new concepts began to grow in appeal: (1) a belief that man's improvement of himself would be brought about not by exercise of his own free will, nor by God, nor by any combination of the two, but by social programs; and (2) a stress on secular improvement so strong that it virtually expunged earlier notions of man's spirituality.

In the seventeenth century John Locke rejected Augustine's contention that man's corruption by birth is so deep that it cannot be removed by human means. Though Locke was aware of his exaggeration when he used the figures of the "blank tablet," or "the white paper" to refer to the human mind at birth, he did reject the doctrine of inexculpable original sin, and held that man's mind was modifiable, for good or for evil, through education. With the passage of time, and wider acceptance of ideas of secular perfectibility, lesser minds interpreted Locke's temperate doctrines in the extreme forms which were later found in progressive education, J. B. Watson's behaviorism, and B. F. Skinner's totally puppetized, limitlessly malleable man.

Contrary to such advocates, Locke was not talking about unlimited malleability, nor about the educationist's faddish gimmickry, nor Skinnerean conditioning, but about *moral* education. Locke advocated a type of education exemplified by *McGuffey's Readers* and diametrically opposite to that advocated by progressive education's Frontier Thinkers. Far from stressing educational practices such as B. F. Skinner's contingencies of positive reenforcement, Locke's child would be moulded by shame and by appeal to his honor—his good character. He would not be trained to adjust his personality to the level of those around him, in life-adjustment educationist programs, but led to maintain high moral standards, to be "in love with all the ways of virtue." And in the long run it is the law of God which determines what is virtue and what is not.

There is no more question about Locke's brilliance and insight than there is about Plato's, but philosophical arguments such as theirs, no matter how insightfully conceived or cogently presented, had only a small audience, and, as revealed by Galen's complaint about the behaviorist believers of his day, one philosopher's argument was then usually balanced by equally persuasive contrary arguments.

. . . Becomes Scientific Perfectibility

Even though, during the seventeenth century, some intellectuals began to refer to themselves as natural philosophers, rather than calling themselves moral philosophers, it was only with the introduction of science that the major change in thinking about man's moral make-up occurred. This new way of thinking—so potent in its results, many believed, that its conclusions were unassailably beyond argument—shifted beliefs about man overwhelmingly toward those which many people now uncritically accept: that man has no human nature; that man is completely malleable; and that man's meaning is not at all spiritual, only secular.

Chapter 3. References and Notes

1. J. A. Stewart, *The Myths of Plato*, 1905, pp. 336 ff., in Herschel Baker, *The Image of Man* (New York: Harper Torchbook, 1961), p. 45ff.

2. Martin Luther, *On the Bondage of the Will*, II, viii (Weimarer Ausgabe, 635–8), trans. Johnstone and Packer, pp. 103–4. In John Passmore, *The Perfectibility of Man* (New York: Charles Scribner's Sons, 1970), p. 115.

3. *Augustine: Early Writings*, trans. John H. S. Burleigh (Philadelphia, Pa.: The Westminster Press, n.d.). Saint Augustine, *City of God*, ed. Vernon J. Bourke (New York: Doubleday, Image Books, 1958).

4. J. N. D. Kelley, *Early Christian Doctrine* (New York: Harper and Row, 1960), p. 357; and John Passmore, *The Perfectibility of Man* (New York: Charles Scribner's Sons, 1970), p. 99.

5. Rod W. Horton and Herbert W. Edwards, *Backgrounds of American Literary Thought*, 3rd ed. (Englewood Cliffs, N.J.: Prentice-Hall, 1974), pp. 24, 25.

6. J. W. Reeves, *Body and Mind in Western Thought* (Baltimore: Pelican Books, 1959), p. 243.

7. Passmore, *The Perfectibility of Man*, p. 149ff.

Chapter 4

Seen Through a Microscope

OUR BELIEFS ABOUT man did not change from sacred to secular, from spiritual to temporal, from a credulous belief in religious doctrine to an equally credulous belief in science overnight, nor did such change occur in a straight line or affect everyone equally. But it did take place and it now constitutes the most profound influence in our beliefs about ourselves, about education, crime, alcoholism, and our governance.

Though, in 1619, René Descartes was convinced that he had discovered the science of sciences, the universal science destined to raise our nature to its highest degree of perfection, which made of nature a machine that needed no purpose or spiritual significance to operate, he still believed in the human spirit, and thought that he had located the soul in the pineal gland.

Life as Seen by a Deductive Toad

Influenced by Descartes' reduction of the universe to matter and motion, Thomas Hobbes, in his introduction to *Leviathan* (1651) applied the same interpretation to man, reasoning:

> For seeing life is but a motion of limbs, the beginning whereof is in some principal part within; why may we not say, that all *automata* (engines that move themselves by

springs and wheels as doth a watch) have an artificial life? For what is the heart, but a spring; and the nerves, but so many strings, and the joints, but so many wheels, giving motion to the whole body, such as was intended by the artificer.[1]

From such assumptions it was but a simple step to conclude further that imagination is nothing but the motion of corporeal organs and our minds nothing but the motions of certain parts of other organs.

But the artificer who made nature and man a part of it was still, to Hobbes, God, and presumably he could make windup man run slow or fast, to march in measured time or to gyrate to some lunatic disrhythm. Furthermore, though he borrowed his metaphor for man from Descartes, the technique which Hobbes employed to demonstrate the nature of the great Leviathan (the state, which was ". . . but an artificial man," with sovereignty its artificial soul) was geometric-axiomatic; its conceptualization arrived at deductively rather than inductively by the methods which later were to distinguish science from philosophy.

He acknowledged that the state of war . . . in which there would be no arts, no letters, no society . . . in which the life of man would be solitary, poor, nasty, brutish and short . . . peradventure never existed, and was never generally so, over all the world. And it was from this hypostatized, this nonexistent axiomatic, this platonically archetypal condition, that he reached his conclusions, not through induction or purportedly scientific experiment. So it was Hobbes, philosopher, not Hobbes, scientist, who gave us, in *Leviathan,* the "art of depicting nature as it is seen by toads."

How Many Molecules Make a Soul?

Francis Bacon (1561–1626), Baron of Verulam, Viscount Saint Albans, Lord Chancellor of England, influenced by his contemporary Galileo (1564–1642), by his predecessors Leonardo (1452–1519), Copernicus (1473–1543), and by William Gilbert (1540–1603)—a physicist sometimes called the "father of electricity"—attempted, in his *Novum Organum* (New Organon) "... a total reconstruction of science, arts, and all human knowledge, raised upon the proper foundations."[2] The new structure, this restoration of sound knowledge he called The Great Instauration, and the new organon was the system of thought upon which it would be built.

To demonstrate the need for new ways of thinking and a sounder structure of knowledge, Sir Francis felt that he first had to show what was wrong with the ways of thinking which produced the received wisdom of his day, so he criticized the popular intellectual beliefs, most of them having been handed down from Greeks.

Having been exposed at Cambridge to the peripatetics, Bacon criticized Aristotle, and then Pythagoras, Heraclitus, Plato and others, because he felt that they had incorrectly constructed universal systems of knowledge based on nothing more substantial than a few abstract ideas. In his *Natural and Experimental History for the Foundation of Philosophy* (1622) he complained that with the older philosophers, "... one catches at one thing, another at another; each has his own favorite fancy; ... everyone philosophizes out of the cells of his own imagination, as out of Plato's cave; the higher wits with more acuteness and felicity, the duller, less happily but with equal pertinacity. ... Authority is taken for truth, not truth for authority ... these volatile and preposterous philosophies held experience captive, and triumphed over the works of God. ..."

Knowledge which had been derived from the Greeks, Bacon averred, was like the boyhood of knowledge, and had the characteristics of boys: it can talk, but it cannot generate, for it is fruitful of controversies but barren of works. In Aphorism LXXIII, Book I, he complained that from all these systems, after all these years, one could find hardly a single experiment which tended to relieve and benefit the condition of man.

These fragile webs, preposterous wispy universals, these empty and unproductive boyish mouthings of Greek philosophy Sir Francis believed he could sweep away by replacing such deductions (which rested on nothing but imagination) with inductive conclusions built on a hard, enduring foundation of positive (a word to be, two centuries later, used in a similar way by Auguste Comte, founder of sociology) facts from nature.

46

Bacon's new principle of thought, induction, would democratize science. Brilliance would no longer be needed; it would be replaced by patience and plodding thoroughness. His approach was to be systematic, naturalistic, and materialistic, with no place in it for metaphysical ontology.

Sir William Dampier, in his authoritative *History of Science,*[3] Alfred North Whitehead, dean of philosophers of science, and Stephen Mason in his history of science, among others, acclaim the influence of Francis Bacon on the fellows of the Royal Society, on the Paris Academy of Sciences and on the French Encyclopedists of the eighteenth century. Dampier wrote that Bacon's ideas were far in advance of his time, while Whitehead said that by the nineteenth century the prophecy of Francis Bacon had been fulfilled. Man, once considered a little lower than the angels, had by then submitted to becoming the servant of nature.

Jacques Barzun, an acutely perceptive interpreter of intellectual history, extols Bacon as the great theorist of materialistic science, indeed the prophet of our scientific culture.[4] And Theodore Roszak, modern romanticist, says that in Bacon's work we find the moral, aesthetic and psychic materials of the scientific worldview—the bright hopes and humanitarian intentions, obscurely mingled with hidden forces of dehumanization —the promise and the curse of the New Philosophy.[5] He quotes the poet William Blake (1757–1827) as saying that Bacon gave good advice for Satan's Kingdom, and insisting that people must choose: Blake or Bacon.

But in Aphorism LXIV of Book I, Sir Francis issued a warning that is now commonly ignored—that empiricism (the doctrine which we now embrace) "gives birth to dogmas more deformed and monstrous than the Sophistical or Rational school." And he foresaw that though men reject sophistical doctrines and limit themselves to experiment, they are still in danger of prematurely leaping to universals.

Though social sciences now generally insist upon the inductive approach that Bacon recommended to arrive at totally secular conclusions, he contended that man belongs to three kingdoms: the Kingdom of God, where through divine Grace he is saved from his sins; the political kingdom in which God gives power to those who rule; and it is only to the third kingdom—

the kingdom of nature over which man at the Creation has been given dominion—that his inductive principles of knowledge apply. Ethics, having to do with that part of man which is made in the Divine Image, comes under the jurisdiction of revealed knowledge, not scientific knowledge.

Despite all his references to induction based on positive experimental evidence, Bacon, as the Greeks he criticized, produced no solid findings, and in that context he would today be accredited as an outstanding social scientist; for now, as Bacon did more than three hundred fifty years ago, social scientists talk much about their methods but fail to produce any significant results.

Man's Spirit: Explicitly Accepted; Implicitly Rejected

The power of man's spirit to guide him, through reason, between the voracious appetite of the dark shag-eared nag of lust and the unrealistic upward straining of the noble white steed to maintain a calm steady pace toward the idealism endowed by Plato's Gods was taken away by Augustine, restored (with the aid of God's grace) by Pelagius, again taken away by the church, secularized by John Locke, and unwittingly steered into oblivion by Francis Bacon. For though the Lord Chancellor excluded ethics—that part of man which is made in the Divine Image—from this new method of experimental induction, his attempt to relegate ethics to the jurisdiction of revealed knowledge while all else of man was parcelled into pieces by the very nature of his techniques was an arbitrary device. His exclusion of ethics was no more than a nostalgic departing wave at principles which his new organon inescapably led away from. Descartes made a similar nostalgic gesture in contending that while the entire universe, including man, functioned solely in terms of matter and motion, his soul could be neatly secreted and totally insulated in the pineal gland.

While both Bacon and Descartes insisted that man had a soul and was guided explicitly through his conscience by God's grace and revelation, their methods of study, if pursued, would eliminate soul, conscience, and the possibility that God's grace could interfere with their secular deterministic processes.

What Hath Newton Wrought?

Though Bacon, Descartes, Locke and others had considerable influence upon the thinking of intellectuals in the seventeenth and eighteenth centuries, it was not until Isaac Newton (1642–1727) described his magnificent laws of motion that the climate of general intellectual opinion became saturated with the intoxicating notion that science would provide answers to all aspects of man's behavior, mind as well as body, soul as well as mind.

Prior to Newton, science was thought to be limited to practical arts and to inorganic matter (it is wisely observed that man studied first the stars and last himself) but with Newton's breathtaking, seemingly simple descriptions which encompassed the motion of every particle of matter in the entire universe, the root sense of science meaning simply knowledge was broadened first to include and later to exclude *conscience*.[6] Gradually the term "science," which had been limited to physical and experimental studies, came to include theological and metaphysical areas of knowledge, and then spread to include everything about man.

People were convinced that Newton had explained the universe; and if the movements of the farthest planet as well as the motions of the tiniest bit of matter could be explained, how easy it would be to explain everything about man. Though Newton insisted that while he could show that every particle of matter in the universe behaved as though it attracted every other particle with a force which is proportional to the product of their masses and inversely proportional to the square of the distance between them, he could not say *why* this is so.[7] To name this attractive force gravity is no explanation and, he said, ". . . it is enough to know that gravity does really exist." He referred to this force of attraction as ". . . a certain most subtle *spirit* which pervades and lies hid in all gross bodies; by the force and action of which *spirit*. . . . Nor are we furnished with that sufficiency of experiments which is required to accurate determination and demonstration of the laws by which this electric and elastic *spirit* operates [my emphasis]."

Again and over again, Newton insisted that he described how motion occurred, but he could not explain *why*, and he insistently referred to the unknown force as *spirit*. He refused to speculate as to what this spirit of matter might be, saying "I have not been able to discover the cause of those properties of gravity from phenomena, and I frame no hypotheses."

Newton's attitude was consistent. Not only did he disclaim knowledge of the nature of gravity, he also depreciated his contribution to science by comparing himself to a boy who played with pretty pebbles on the beach "while the great ocean of truth lay all undiscovered before me."

But as is commonly the case with those investigators who openly disavow hypotheses, their procedures belie their protestations, and Newton, pious, believing Christian that he was, honestly admitted that ". . . gravity may put the planets in motion, but without the divine power it could never put them into such a circulating motion, as they have about the sun."[8]

As history measures its time it was only a brief span until others of lesser genius, excited by Newton's discoveries but lacking his prudence and devoid of his reverence, proclaimed that science would provide exact answers to everything, not only including man but especially man.

Though Alexander Pope (1688–1744) described the purpose of his *Essay on Man* as an effort to vindicate the ways of God to man, in his epitaph to Newton he exulted:

> Nature and nature's laws lay hid in night:
> God said, Let Newton be! and all was light.

Sir Francis Bacon's gallant effort to erect a wall to protect ethics and the spirit of man from his inductive experimental methods, his sincere attempt to post such preserves as being the province of divine revelation, was soon breached. Matthew Tindal (1657–1733), a fellow of All Soul's College, Oxford, convert to Catholicism, and then renegade from it to rationalism, brushed aside Bacon's arbitrary obstacles and proceeded from theism to deism, giving man a personal God, based solely on

50

reason and rejecting the supernatural revelation which Bacon sought to preserve.

In *Christianity as Old as the Creation*, Tindal asserted that "the real revelation is in Nature herself, and in man's God-given reason; the real God is the God that Newton revealed, the designer of a marvelous world operating majestically according to invariable law, and the real morality is the life of reason in harmony with nature. This is the true morality, this is the true Christianity, as old as reason."[9]

By 1793 the Cathedral of Nôtre Dame was renamed the Temple of Reason, where hymns were sung to glorify liberty rather than God, and the Gregorian calendar was replaced by The Calendar of Reason. Unreasonably, The Calendar of Reason lasted only twelve years.

David Hartley left the clergy and, as a physician, founded physiological psychology. In his *Observations on Man* (1749) he attempted to duplicate Newton's success by finding a single principle which governed relationships between ideas.[10] He extended the mechanization of man's functioning from the limited areas encompassed by Hobbes and Locke to include emotion and moral sense as well.

In France, in 1754, the clergyman Etienne Bonnot de Condillac also enlarged upon and distorted Locke's secular, but moral, conception of man and approached the position of today's B. F. Skinner by insisting that all judgment, reflection, desire, and passion result from sensations.[11] Man is nothing, said the priest, but what he smells, sees, hears, touches and tastes. Even earlier, in Italy, Giambattista Vico proclaimed that science could determine the laws of history and thereby control human destiny. Thus did rationalistic scientism spread and become ever more extreme as it replaced God and revelation to interpret the meaning of man.

David Hume, in his 1739 *Treatise of Human Nature* (which he advertised as "An Attempt to Introduce the Experimental Method of Reasoning into Moral Subjects"), in effect abolished freedom of will by asserting that our minds are nothing but a heap of different relations.[12] Our reasonings concerning cause and effect are derived from nothing but custom.

Heaven on Earth

Gradually, attacks from a variety of intellectuals gnawed at the edifice from which God was believed to control human beings. This weakened structure was shaken to its foundations when Joseph Priestley (1733–1804), convert from clergyman to chemist, discoverer of oxygen (who also described its relation to combustion and its necessity for respiration), joined with Erasmus Darwin (grandfather of Charles) to secularize the earlier theological idea of progress, Darwin applying it to biology and Priestley to human affairs.[13]

Priestley reduced everything, including the soul, to matter. He closed the circle which began with denial of The Fall, and arced through Divine Revelation by rejecting all belief in life after death. Thus Priestley's noose strangled Saint Augustine's Heavenly City of God. He replaced man's search for God's Grace with a utilitarian philosophy that made the highest aim of life the secular pursuit of the greatest happiness for the greatest number of people. His Utopia, his heavenly city on earth, as he described it in *The First Principles of Government* (1771), was one in which

> ... men will probably prolong their existence in it, and will daily grow more happy and more able to communicate happiness to others. Thus whatever was the beginning of this world, the end will be paradisiacal beyond what our imaginations can now conceive.[14]

Having, to their satisfaction, choked Augustine's heavenly city to extinction with the strands of their logic, the scientistic philosophes believed they could reconstruct it on earth, themselves being the architects to design it, and the council for its governance. Having changed from moral philosophers to natural philosophers, they then became philosophers by abandoning their search for universal truths in order to pursue programs for human betterment.

Perspectives Toward Life

The mental processes of man are malleable, and the intellectual perspective of any epoch emerges from the view of the world which is dominant among the learned of the time. Overall views from science, aesthetics, ethics or religion will, at any given time, either alone or merged with others, captivate the beliefs of the learned for reasons which are many and unknown; and through their propagation, they sway the beliefs of people in general. Philosopher of science Alfred North Whitehead called this phenomenon where one kind of thinking dominates other possible overviews of life at a given time "the climate of opinion" (a phrase derived from a seventeenth-century writer whom Whitehead doesn't identify and I don't know).[15] In an effort to describe the basis of my belief that *Man Is Moral Choice*, I call these different perspectives toward life rationalistic-scientistic, romantic, liberal, and conservative.

Rationalistic Scientism

The first perspective, with its early manifestation described in this chapter and its contemporary shape described in Chapter 8, I designate rationalistic-scientistic rather than scientific because when natural philosophers began to call themselves scientists, their attempts to apply the methods of physics and chemistry and the philosophy of mathematics to human behavior and social concerns always failed (and still do); and their conclusions about these matters were based, not on valid scientific procedure, but on processes which, as I shall explain later, have only a superficial resemblance to science. Their methods, seeming scientific were actually pseudo-scientific; their conclusions, scientism.

My contention is that one either accepts his view of life on faith because the climate of opinion makes such belief fashionable or, cantankerously, rejects the conventional view. I shall try to show that neither acceptance of the "scientific" view of human affairs nor its rejection is primarily based on accurate, repeatable experiment or provable hard evidence,

53

though like the romantic, liberal, or conservative views, it is a legitimate way to think about life.

To my knowledge no one has described the origin of the rationalistic-scientistic view of man and his concerns with such sharp insight and simple clarity as Carl Becker in *The Heavenly City of the Eighteenth-Century Philosophers.*[16] Despite loud protestations about their search for knowledge, writes Becker, the main objective of the eighteenth-century philosophes was "to measure and master the world rather than to understand it." "They denied that miracles ever happened, but they believed in the perfectibility of the human race." ". . . having denatured God, they deified nature." They were positive that they had abandoned faith, and they did reject faith in God and all else that is holy, but in the vacuum which resulted they deified nature, and this became their faith, and, unadmittedly, their religion became a method of studying man. Writes Becker:

> The essential articles of the religion of the enlightenment may be stated thus: (1) man is not natively depraved; (2) the end of life is life itself, the good life on earth instead of the beatific life after death; (3) man is capable, guided solely by the light of reason and experience, of perfecting the good life on earth; and (4) the first and essential condition of the good life on earth is the freeing of men's minds from the bonds of ignorance and superstition, and of their bodies from the arbitrary oppression of the constituted social authorities.

This transformation of man as well as of the life he lived; this reconstruction of the Heavenly City of God on earth could be accomplished through the malleability, the perfectibility of man because:

> . . . it was self-evident that man was the product of his environment—of nature and the institutions under which he lived—and that by reshaping his environment in accord with the invariable and determinable laws of nature, his material and spiritual regeneration might be speedily accomplished.

This abiding scientific faith in environmental determinism became the core of communism, the central prop (implicit if not explicit) for socialism and its cousin the welfare state and, as I shall later show, the principal tenet of sociology, psychology, and psychiatry. I should like to present two examples to illustrate how the pseudo-scientific beliefs of the eighteenth century have descended, almost verbatim, into the twentieth century.

Scientism's Past Is Prologue

Pierre Simon Laplace (1749–1827), later the Marquis de Laplace, was born into a devoutly religious farm family and wrote theological essays in school but later became one of the most confirmed atheists in France.[17] E. A. Burtt credits (or blames) him for bringing to a climax the process of elimination of the providential elements in the world order.[18] As a teacher of mathematics, one of his students was Napoleon, who as emperor made Laplace his minister of the interior.

In his five-volume major work, *Mécanique Céleste*, published between 1799 and 1825, Laplace presented his nebular hypothesis which explained the origin of the solar system by postulating a primeval, slowly rotating body of hot gases extending to its farthest reaches. In completely mechanistic fashion he believed he could reduce to a single mathematical formula the present and future motion of all elements of the system; to such a formula nothing would be uncertain.[19] When Napoleon asked him why he had made no mention of God in the origins and evolution of the solar system he said, "I had no need of that hypothesis." Truth, with Laplace, was no longer discoverable by induction of natural facts, but by probabilities.

Laplace was by no means the first to claim that he could explain the entire universe by one mathematical system; some five centuries before the birth of Christ, Pythagoras contended that numbers were the essence of all things, attributing to them a real existence which constituted the elements out of which the universe was constructed.[20]

Nor was he the last, and to illustrate how eighteenth-century beliefs persist into the present, Laplace, born in 1749, was convinced that he could reduce the entire universe to a single mathematical system. Two centuries later, a group of scholars meeting at the University of Chicago changed the expression "social sciences" to "behavioral sciences."[21]

In 1949, as Laplace had done almost two centuries before, and as Descartes had done in 1619, the behavioral scientists proclaimed that "all behavior can be conceived of as an energy exchange within an open system or from one such system to another,"

> We envisage a far-off scientific utopia in which we can re-
> duce to comparable dimension the Oedipus complex, repres-
> sion, submissiveness, physiological traces, acculturation,
> the pH of blood, and every other factor related to behavior.

Sociology as Rationalistic Scientism

Sociology, perhaps more than any other of the social (now behavioral) sciences, has served to propagandize the rationalistic-scientistic view of man and society; and sociology today is substantially the same as it was in the eighteenth century: still claiming that its methodology (meaning its methods) can ascertain the truth about human affairs, and that its conclusions should be the basis for guiding our lives and establishing our future; but still, now as then, unable to substantiate its claims with a single validated theory.

In *The Spirit of Laws* published in 1748, Charles Louis de Secondat, Baron de la Brede et de Montesquieu (1689–1755) tried to establish what is now called scientific sociology, but it was not until 1838 that Montesquieu's countryman, Auguste Comte, coined the term "sociology."

Since the roots of the term sociology come from *socius* (L) meaning companion or associate, and *logos* (G) meaning word, the combination could be taken to mean talking about our companions or associates—whence sociology would mean, simply, gossip. *Socius,* when capitalized, also relates to God as a friend or companion of man, and *Logos* capitalized means the creative word of God; so sociology could mean the friendly words of God to man. Another interpretation of the word, which amuses me because it comes so close to the realities of sociology, evolved from a court case in 1948 in which the legitimacy of a child was at question. Despite sound evidence to the contrary, the judge

56

found the child legitimate, saying: "This court will not lend itself to making any child illegitimate. It would be . . . contrary to the highest precepts of sociology." From which decree we may reasonably conclude that no matter what be the evidence to the contrary, sociologists never call anyone a bastard!

Isidore Auguste Marie François Comte (1798–1857) illiterately ignored these and other possible conceptualizations of sociology and bombastically enthroned it as The Queen of Sciences. Sociology, he asserted, was not only a science, it was at the apex of the hierarchy of the sciences. While eschewing hypotheses, he hypothesized that each field of knowledge necessarily passed through three states: the theological or fictitious state; the metaphysical or abstract state; and the scientific or positive state. Astronomy, physics, and chemistry had by 1822 (when Comte wrote his *Plan of the Scientific Operations Necessary for Reorganizing Society*[22]) already entered the positive state; but physiology, especially in its moral aspects, still had not fully emerged from its theological or metaphysical origins.

Conscience, which Comte ridiculed as "the dogma of unlimited liberty of conscience," was useful only as a means of combatting the theological system. Once theology was vanquished liberty of conscience not only lost its value but became an obstacle to the scientific reorganization of society. The dogma of the sovereignty of individual reason was also destined to vanish. The dogma of the sovereignty of the people which was useful to combat the principle of the divine right of rulers, once having effected its negative aim, would also be expunged.

In Comte's scientific society the rulers, of course, would be the scientists themselves. Not because they were egomaniacal, or greedy for power—of course not—but because they alone were invested with the necessary moral (an interesting use of the term) force. Only they, Comte went on to say, were capable of overthrowing the negative prejudice which held that individuals had an inborn right to freedom from dictatorship—whether such dictatorship be called scientific or not.

A hundred and fifty years later our most widely acclaimed behavioral scientist, B. F. Skinner, repeated, almost verbatim, Comte's degradation of man, his repudiation of conscience, and his scorn for the concept of freedom from scientific dictatorship. In a fashion even more extreme than that of the messianic bohemian Comte, Professor Skinner proclaims:

> I propose to abolish autonomous man, the man who believes in freedom and dignity. His abolition is long overdue. He has been constructed from our ignorance and as our understanding increases, the very stuff of which he is composed vanishes. To man qua man we readily say good riddance. "How like a god!" said Hamlet. Pavlov, the behavioral scientist, emphasized "How like a dog!" That was a step forward.[23]

Skinner (how like Isidore Auguste Marie François Comte you are, Burrhis Frederic!) parrots Comte further in saying:

> The hypothesis that man is not free is essential to the application of the scientific method to the study of human behavior.[24]

After the eighteenth century, this rending of human dignity with words and riddling it with mathematical symbols became the compulsive fashion in all of the social sciences. In psychology, in 1862, Wilhelm Wundt reduced, he believed, the soul, the spirit, and the psyche to precise mathematical relationships, stating that he had scientifically proved that:

> . . . where two psychic functions are in immediate dependence on one another, the dependent function always increases proportionally to the logarithm of the independently variable one.[25]

Eager to join this parade of inchworms, the new *Historische Zeitschrift* announced in 1859 that ". . . this periodical should, above all, be a scientific one."[26] And in 1902 J. B. Bury, in his inaugural lecture as Regius Professor of Modern History, reaffirmed this goal, announcing that "erudition has now been supplemented by scientific method."

In 1882, William Graham Sumner, the first professor of sociology in America, informed his Yale audience that:

We have now acquired the method of studying sociology scientifically so as to attain the assured results. We have acquired it none too soon. The need for a science of life in society is urgent, and it is increasing every year.[27]

Yale's president, Noah Porter, said that while he didn't object to Professor Sumner teaching Herbert Spencer's scientific sociology to graduate students, he did object to its general use because:

The freedom and unfairness with which it attacks every theistic philosophy of society and of history, and the cool and yet sarcastic effrontery with which he assumes that material elements and laws are the only forces which any scientific man can recognize, seem to me to condemn the book as a textbook for a miscellaneous class in an undergraduate course.[28]

Woodrow Wilson, a later (1896) president of Princeton, also pointed out the harm being done by excessive stress on rationalistic scientism, saying,

This is the disservice scientific study has done us: it has given us agnosticism in the realm of philosophy, scientific anarchism in the field of politics. It has made the legislator confident that he can create, and the philosopher sure that God cannot. Past experience is discredited and the laws of matter are supposed to apply to the spirit and the make-up of society.[29]

Saint Augustine took control over our own fate from us and placed it entirely in God's hands. Pelagius and Locke, from differing perspectives, restored at least some power for moral choice to mankind. All of the earlier scientists, Descartes, Newton, and Bacon among them, reserved for man's soul a special status independent of the mechanistic functioning which controlled the rest of the universe. But gradually secular environmental determinism first encroached upon, then engulfed all of man and, the new cycle completed, he was again totally without control over his destiny. The original sin which according to Saint Augustine made all men bad by their very nature was temporarily modified to make, under Pelagius and Locke, man's nature a combination of potentials for good and for evil. But then rationalistic scientism, by contending that all behavior is externally determined, in effect eliminated human nature. In theoretic principle, if not yet in actual practice, we are puppets, and "scientists" jostle each other for the power to pull our strings.

Chapter 4. References and Notes

1. Thomas Hobbes, *Leviathan*, Part I (Chicago: Harry Regnery Co., 1956), pp. 9, 119.

2. Francis Bacon, *The New Organon*, ed. Fulton H. Anderson (Boston: Bobbs-Merrill, 1960), p. 4, pp. xiv-xv, 71.

3. William Cecil Dampier, *A History of Science*, 3rd ed. (New York: Macmillan, 1946); Alfred North Whitehead, *Science and the Modern World* (New York: New American Library, 1948); and Stephen F. Mason, *A History of the Sciences* (New York: Collier Books, 1962).

4. Jacques Barzun, *Science: The Glorious Entertainment* (New York: Harper and Row, 1964), p. 90.

5. Theodore Roszak, *Where the Wasteland Ends* (New York: Doubleday, 1972), p. 145.

6. Raymond Williams, *Keywords* (New York: Oxford University Press, 1976), p. 232.

7. Isaac Newton, *Principia* (Berkeley: University of California Press, 1962), vol. 2, p. 547.

8. *Isaaci Newtoni Opera quae exstant Omnia. Commentariis illustrabat*, Samuel Horsley, LL.D., 5 vols., London 1779–85, vol. 4, 436 ff. Edwin Arthur Burtt, *The Metaphysical Foundations of Modern Physical Science* (New York: Doubleday, Anchor, 1954), p. 291.

9. M. Tindal, *Christianity as Old as the Creation*, 1730. In

Leslie Stephen, *History of English Thought in the Eighteenth Century,* 2 vols., London, 1902.

10. Will and Ariel Durant, *The Age of Voltaire* (New York: Simon and Schuster, 1965), p. 581.

11. Ibid., p. 582.

12. David Hume, Treatise of Human Nature, Everymans Library (1957), Book I, Pt. IV.

13. Stephen F. Mason, *A History of the Sciences* (New York: Collier Books, 1962), p. 328.

14. Mason, *A History of Science,* p. 329.

15. Whitehead, *Science and the Modern World,* p. 3.

16. Carl L. Becker, *The Heavenly City of the Eighteenth-Century Philosophers* (New Haven, Conn.: Yale University Press, 1932), (in order of their presentation), pp. 16–17, 31, 63, 102–3, 138.

17. Will and Ariel Durant, *The Age of Voltaire,* p. 546.

18. E. A. Burtt, *The Metaphysical Foundations of Modern Science* (New York: Doubleday, Anchor, 1954), p. 298.

19. Will and Ariel Durant, *The Age of Voltaire,* pp. 546–549.

20. Thomas Bulfinch, *The Age of Fable,* ed. Rev. J. Loghran Scott, D. D. (New York: David McKay, 1898), p. 357.

21. Leonard D. White, *The State of the Social Sciences* (Chicago: University of Chicago Press, 1956), pp. 29, 32, 38.

22. Auguste Comte, *Plan of the Scientific Operations Necessary for Reorganizing Society,* 1822, in *On Intellectuals,* ed. Philip Rieff (New York: Anchor Books, 1970), pp. 369–305.

23. B. F. Skinner, *Beyond Freedom and Dignity* (New York: Alfred A. Knopf, 1972), pp. 200–1.

24. B. F. Skinner, *Science and Human Behavior* (New York: Macmillan, 1953), pp. 447–8.

25. Wilhelm Wundt, *Contributions to the Theory of Sensory Perception,* 1862, in *Classics in Psychology,* ed. Thorne Shipley (New York: Philosophical Library, 1961), pp. 70, 75.

26. Hans Meyerhoff, *The Philosophy of History in Our Time* (New York: Anchor Books, 1959), pp. 13, 14.

27. William Graham Sumner, *The Forgotten Man and Other Essays* (New Haven, Conn.: Yale University Press, 1919), p. 402.

28. Richard Hofstadter and Wilson Smith, *American Higher Education* (Chicago: University of Chicago Press, 1961), vol. 2, p. 850.

29. Ibid., vol. 2, p. 693.

Through Rose-colored Glasses

NEWTON'S THIRD LAW of motion as commonly stated holds that for every action there is an equal and oppositely directed reaction. And although in our human affairs this is true in only a figurative sense, the second of the secular ways of thinking about man, romanticism, did arise as a revulsive reaction against the cold objectivity of eighteenth-century rationalistic-scientism.

To focus on eighteenth-century romanticism is not to imply that this way of viewing the moral nature of man originated then any more than my focus on eighteenth-century rationalistic-scientism should lead one to infer that such notions about man did not exist before. As Pythagoras attempted to explain the entire universe in mathematical symbols more than two thousand years before Laplace, and as the physician Galen found need to complain about rationalistic advocates of the "nothing but" philosophy of man more than fifteen hundred years before Priestley rent man with his words in the eighteenth century, so also the romantic conception of human nature goes back so far that the memory of man runneth not to the contrary.

It begins, of course, with the Garden of Eden in its serene sinlessness; and eight hundred years before the birth of Christ, the Greek poet Hesiod sang of the Golden Age when men had lived in idyllic harmony like bees.[1] Farther north, at about the same time, the mysterious Druids huddled over their fires in the dark forests, and told of an ancient time when lived noble savages, the Hyperboreans, a peaceful, happy, virtuous people, beloved of Apollo. "No discord knew they, no sicknesses are they acquainted with."[2] Their lives were eulogised by Tennyson in *The Passing of Arthur*:

> The Hyperboreans lived in their valley of Avelion:
> Where falls not hail; or rain, or any snow,
> Nor ever wind blows loudly.

And in the idyllic romanticism of Arthur's Camelot, the thirteenth place at Merlin's round table was never sat upon, until Lancelot and Guinevere changed that perfect circle into a sordid triangle.

But of all the descriptions of a past in which man was happily free, perhaps Euripides gives us the best in *The Bacchae*, as he dramatizes the rebellion, latent in all of us, that throws off all restraints on what we are certain is the precious uniqueness of our subjective selves.[3]

At a time when most of the Greek states were trying to order the lives of their subjects according to reason, an ordering which had deprived the people of much liberty and joy and seemed to give nothing in return, they turned to a worship of Dionysus, the spirit of life which liberates us from pain and fatigue, from tedium, from the bonds of responsibility and law. They found release from their tensions and surcease from care in their shared emotion as they surrendered themselves to the primitive supernatural. Depart from civilization and your mind will become sound; commune with nature and attain wisdom. Civilization is ugly and malicious; nature is beautiful and gentle.

Thus Euripides some five centuries before the birth of Christ described many features of the romantic movement which flared up in the eighteenth century as a reaction against the cold objectivity of rationalistic-scientism. This latter romantic movement is nicely described by Will and Ariel Durant in *Rousseau and Revolution*. It was, they wrote:

> The rebellion of feeling against reason, of instinct against intellect, of sentiment against judgment, of subjectivism against objectivity ... of youth against authority, of democracy against aristocracy, of man versus the state.[4]

Romanticism: Reaction Against Rationalism

Jean-Jacques Rousseau (1712–1778) left his native Switzerland and settled in France (meanwhile switching from Calvinism to Catholicism, then back to Calvinism, and then to Unitarianism) and, without benefit of wedlock, sired five children, all of whom he put in foundling homes; then he wrote one of the world's most influential books on the education of children declaiming that reason was impotent in the teaching of virtue, and denouncing science. His philosophy, prototypically romantic, was based on a belief that man is innately good—there is no original sin in the human heart—and if man does bad things it is because evil social institutions (mostly economic institutions) restrain or corrupt his naturally good instincts. The "fatal accident" (Rousseau, *Social Contract*, Second *Discourse*, p. 214) that perverts man's innate goodness is the establishment of private property, from which comes most of the evils of life.

Rousseau taught that the Huron Indians of America exemplified the naturally good men who lived in the ideal state of nature but, like Hobbes whose "natural" man had an opposite sort of life—nasty, brutish and short—Rousseau admitted that this ideal state of nature and his intrinsically good man ". . . perhaps never existed, and probably never will."

Rousseau's romanticism became for many a fad which replaced the previously fashionable belief in science. His educational ideas in *Emile* led upper-class mothers to breast-feed their infants, even at the opera; to free them from swaddling clothes; and (except for Rousseau) to bring them up themselves instead of relying on tutors. Progressive education and the kindergarten system came to us from Rousseau, filtering down through Pestalozzi, Basedow, Maria Montessori, Friedrich Froebel and finally seeping painfully through the turgid prose of John Dewey to dominate the frontier thinkers of education in America for several decades. Since there is no badness in children, they can do nothing wrong. Let them run, jump and shout to their hearts' content, and learn by actions rather than by books.

Rousseau's influence on literature was, and is, enormous, strongly tincturing the work of Pushkin, Kropotkin, Words-

worth, Coleridge, Godwin, Byron, Shelley, Hawthorne and Tho-
reau. Count Leo Tolstoy believed he could attain natural goodness in his personal life as well as in his writing by renouncing
his aristocratic heritage, by wearing a peasant blouse and boots,
and replacing his crucifix with a medallion of Rousseau. But
though Fyodor Dostoevsky took direct aim in his novels at the
rationalistic scientism which promoted socialism, in *Crime and
Punishment* and in *The Possessed* his shots ricocheted to strike
at least glancing blows at romanticism such as Rousseau's.

Rousseau's compatriot, Denis Diderot (1713–1784) selected
the Tahitians as the intrinsically good children of nature, and he
so persuaded Europeans of the pristine virtue of these islanders
that Captain James Cook brought one of them, a youth named
Omai, back to England with him to become a pet of London
society, painted by Sir Joshua Reynolds and introduced to King
George.

"No, dear friend," Diderot explained to Sophie Volland, "nature has not made us evil; it is bad education, bad models, bad
legislation that corrupt us."[5]

In Germany, the young Johann Wolfgang von Goethe
(1749–1832) incorporated such romantic sentiments in *The Sorrows of Young Werther* (1774), while in England, romanticism
found its chief exponent in Percy Bysshe Shelley (1792–1822).

Shelley and Byron

While at Oxford Shelley wrote a pamphlet which he titled
The Necessity of Atheism and was expelled when he refused to
repudiate it. At eighteen, though convinced that "marriage was
a tyrannical and degrading social institution,"[6] he eloped with
Harriet Westbrook. Much influenced by the writings of the radical William Godwin (of whom, more later), he began his long
prophetic essay, *Queen Mab; A Philosophical Poem*, which he
published at age 21, in 1813. In it he portrayed formal religion
("How ludicrous the priest's dogmatic roar . . . what palpable
deceit. . . ."[7]) and codified morality as the causes of social evil.
In his vision of the future all institutions would wither away, to
enable man to return to his natural state of goodness and felicity. But before that "brighter morn" free of injustice and suffer-

ing can dawn, we must have external revolution to wipe out existing social, political and religious institutions.

Typically romantic, Shelley stresses that man's innate goodness is corrupted by materialistic greed: ". . . yet every heart contains perfection's gem" but "the iron rod of penury compels her wretched slave to bow the knee to wealth" so that "many a Newton" has been compelled to labor at tiresome useless tasks and ". . . the very light of Heaven / is venal . . . and every liberty is bought and sold as in a public mart."

Part of young Shelley's mental adoration of William Godwin flowed over into an emotional attachment to his daughter, Mary Wollstonecraft Godwin, and since he felt that cohabitation without love was immoral, he left his wife Harriet and their two children and eloped with Mary to France, taking with them Mary's stepsister (by Godwin's second wife and her previous husband). Mary's half-sister, Fanny Imlay, born outside the bonds of matrimony to Mary's mother, Mary Wollstonecraft, had committed suicide, and to add to this unsimple arrangement, Shelley invited wife Harriet to join them and live with them as a sister. Harriet declined, sensibly choosing suicide instead.

After Harriet's death, Shelley married Mary Godwin, and her half-sister, Claire Clairmont, became one of Byron's numerous mistresses.

Though the marital and cohabitational mix-ups in the lives of Shelley and Byron would seem, even by today's loose standards, extreme, the sexual and familial affairs of Auguste Comte and Rousseau would make Shelley and Byron, by contrast, seem appropriate subjects for Grant Wood's "New England Gothic."

George Gordon, Lord Byron (1788–1824) enunciated his romantic credo in several places. *Childe Harold's Pilgrimage* includes his adoration of nature (Canto IV, verse 178) "I love not Man the less, but Nature more," and he condemns rulers and their dictates (Canto III, verse 43) calling them "The madmen who are Conquerors and Kings, the founders of sects and systems"; and declares (Canto VIII, lines 50–51) that he ". . . perceived that revolution / Alone can save the earth from hell's pollution." Such sentiments, together with the moralistic nihilism of *Don Juan*, earn Byron credentials as a romantic, but his romanticism seemed to be more in his looks and lifestyle than in his literary expression. He was Romanticism's showman, not sire.

But it is outside the focus of my analysis to argue as to which of the many romantics was prototypical in the context of the rubrics which here apply. Suffice it to say that it was a form of emotional expression which had as its core a belief in the intrinsic goodness of man; a conviction that man, innately good by nature, is corrupted by wrong education and by bad social institutions, particularly institutions which establish and protect private property. And man can be returned to his natural goodness only by overthrow of such established forms. Such beliefs flourished in the eighteenth century and sporadically recur as short-lived but colorful and appealing fads throughout history.

In recounting some of the marital entanglements associated with Shelley, I do not mean a recital of certain aspects of his private affairs to constitute an attack on the merits of his philosophical position or his poetry. His "romantic" mix-ups, as I have noted, were simple compared with those of Auguste Comte, the founder of sociology. As to what manner of man he was, I neither know nor care. Byron, for instance, said Shelley was "as perfect a gentleman as ever crossed a drawing-room . . . the *best* and least selfish man I ever knew. I never knew one who was not a beast in comparison."[8] I cite some of the complications of Shelley's relationships because they relate to a complicated interweaving of intellectual ideas which, to me, is one of the most fascinating webs ever woven.

William and Mary

The Mary Godwin that Shelley left wife Harriet for was the daughter of William Godwin and Mary Wollstonecraft, each a formidable intellectual and fascinating personal figure in his (Forgive me, Mary!) own right. (Mary Wollstonecraft must have spun like a top in her grave when she was listed in *Webster's Biographical Dictionary* as Godwin, Mary nee Wollstonecraft [1759–1797] because she was, in her day, a most extreme advocate of what was then called women's rights, now women's lib.) Her *A Vindication of the Rights of Women* was a disorganized, hastily (six weeks) written, but impassioned and strident shriek for equal rights for women, many of whom would be, she was sure, eminent statesmen, inventive scientists, prominent barristers or brain surgeons, had they not been denied educational opportunities equal to those of men, and had not men treated them as sex toys before marriage and as decorative ornaments, obedient servants, and maternity machines afterward.[9] In her new and better world the sexes would be educated together under the same curriculum and engage in the same or equivalent sports.

While in her publicized role as agitator for equal rights for women, Mary despised men because they treated women unjustly; in her private life she avidly sought their favors. Early in her life, she engaged in an affair with a bisexual painter named Henry Fuseli, and begged his wife to allow her to live with them as a "spiritual partner."[10] She then had a less than spiritual, more than theoretical relationship with Gilbert Imlay, a former aide to General George Washington, who left her with the illegitimate daughter who later committed suicide, an act which Mary herself attempted to emulate by jumping off Putney Bridge in 1795.

She was, however, saved and became the common-law wife of William Godwin. Though both she and Godwin excoriated the institution of marriage in their writings and held it anathema to their beliefs, they submitted to a religious ceremony in 1797 for the sake of their expected child, conceived several months prior to their marriage. Ashamed of such abasement to unpagan rituals they tried to persuade their friends that they still lived in the freedom which others called sin. A few days after the birth of her daughter Mary Godwin, Mary Wollstonecraft died from septicemia acquired from the dirty hands of her delivery doctor.

The father of Mary Godwin, Mary Wollstonecraft's husband on her (at least) third try at husbandry, was William Godwin (1756–1836), acclaimed by many as the most influential English philosopher of his generation, whose ideas were later wafted on wings of song by his son-in-law Shelley.[11]

In Augustine's heritage, William Godwin's parents were devout Calvinists; his father a minister, and himself educated in clerisy. In his major work, his *Enquiry Concerning Political Justice and Its Influence on General Virtues and Happiness*

(1793), he proclaimed that his ideas would lead people to a utopia, indeed a super-utopia, in which

> There will be no war, no crimes, no administration of justice, as it is called, and no government. Beside this, there will be neither disease, anguish, melancholy, nor resentment. Every man will seek, with ineffable ardour, the good of all.[12]

But how to get there? How instil this seeking, and how insure it? Now, there's the rub! Please note that William Godwin had abandoned, as an aery ascension to utopia, the predestination of his Calvinistic parents; nor was he, in his spiritual rejection, railroaded into the determinism of mechanistic scientism. Rousseau's romantic idea of the native goodness of man appealed to him but (for whatever reason) he shied away from a revolutionary upset of institutions as the way to restore man to this idyllic state of nature. Anarchism was his ideal, but he feared it, and instead of violent revolution to overthrow the established institutions of state, property and religion, he prescribed a revolution of opinion as the way to uplift man to his utopian condition. "Make men wise," he counselled—convinced that education would do this, instead of merely enabling them to conceal their ignorance with bigger words—and you will set them free: without war, crime, anguish, melancholy. . . . As for morality, he anticipated B. F. Skinner by almost two hundred years in contending that morality is nothing but a calculation of the consequences of behavior. Morality, he thought, was the science of human happiness, and he followed Helvetius, Priestley, and Bentham in defining good as that which promotes individual or group happiness.

So Godwin's beliefs were an amalgam, a mixture, a hodgepodge, a disquieting and unintellectually annoying mélange of rationalistic scientism and romanticism. But no matter which diverse winds he set his sails to, and unpredictably reset them, the course he announced promised to land mankind upon the shore of the never-never land of total human happiness. No wonder, then, that he was acclaimed the most influential English philosopher of his generation.

The Doubting Thomas

Daniel Malthus, correspondent with and intellectual admirer of Jean-Jacques Rousseau, was also close, both personally and intellectually, to William Godwin. He believed that his son, Thomas Malthus (1766–1834), favoured by such an intellectual environment, would similarly develop into a comfortably disturbing-but-legal radical. But Thomas became a renegade from rationalism and entered the Anglican ministry in 1797. Having thought much about Godwin's *Enquiry Concerning Political Justice and Its Influence on General Virtues and Happiness,* Thomas tried to formalize his doubts about rationalism into print, and in 1798 published *An Essay on the Principle of Population, as it affects the future Improvement of Society, with remarks on the speculation of Mr. Godwin, Mr. Condorcet, and other writers.* Since so many people, including if not especially students of population (who call themselves Scientific Demographers), blissfully overlook the basic theme of Malthus' essay, I shall give a likely interpretation of Malthus' meaning in the context of his background.

Malthus, it seems to me, was not simply trying to prove, as he is so often interpreted as doing, that population, increasing geometrically while the supply of food increases only arithmetically, will first overtake and then exceed available food to produce widespread starvation.

His "positive checks"—those things which increase the death rate—on the growth of population included epidemics, famines, and wars. His "preventive checks," which slow the rate of population growth by decreasing the birth rate, include vice in sexual practices, and under a rubric of "moral restraint" he includes postponement of marriage and sexual restraint within marriage.

We are misled about the meaning which Malthus attempted to convey by ignoring his background and overlooking his title and the context that led him to produce his monumental work. Most references to Malthus reduce his title to *An Essay on Population,* making it sound as though it were a study written for publication in *The New York Times Magazine* by an Assistant Professor of Demography who, beneath a pedantic facade, was making a plea for legalized abortion, birth control, and zero population growth.

His full title, commonly ignored, is a needed frame for his hypothesis. His father and William Godwin had tried to convince Thomas of Godwin's proof that man's reason alone, properly directed through correct educational channels, can unerringly lead us to a utopia where there will be "neither disease, anguish, melancholy, nor resentment, and every man will seek, with ineffable ardour, the good of all." Malthus, appropriately given-named, doubted that the Heavenly City could be so easily established on earth and he gave expression to his doubts in his title, referring in it, not to the mathematical relation between the growth of population and increase in the amount of arable land (which he believed to bear a constant ratio to the amount of food produced), but to the principles of population. And as the title also indicates, his principal concern was not with resources of food as such, but with the future improvement of society. In his title he also specified that he was questioning the philosophic speculation of Mr. Godwin.

As an aside, it should be noted that Malthus' assumption of constancy between arable land and the supply of food needed much modification as new fertilizers, pesticides, and more prolific breeds of plants were discovered, but such modification does not seriously affect his thesis. In stressing the principles of population Malthus was using population to illustrate a much broader and profoundly deeper contention: that immutable principles govern our lives and these, much more than our vaunted reasoning or our educational techniques, have shaped them and will, for good or ill, also shape our future.

Population growth, the phenomenon which Malthus chose to illustrate his broader thesis, always has and always will depend on two basics: sex and food. While one of these principles (food) in its very nature is limited in its potential for increase, the other (the sexual production of babies) is not. While it is true that the recent discoveries noted above have increased the supply of food far beyond limits which Malthus thought possible, in principle his premise is still sound.

The role of sex, the second of his principles, is much more complex, but now as then, once properly understood, needs no modification of Malthus' enunciation. Even the most extreme critics of Malthus must grant that, in humans, sex is still essential to birth and, so far as we know, the nature of the sexual component has changed not a whit. Among the preventive factors which would reduce the birth rate by affecting the casual factor of sex Malthus included, under the heading of "moral restraint," postponement of marriage and sexual restraint within marriage. The population growth of Ireland, once explosive, has long been minimal, as the age of marriage rose to become the highest in the world. In America also, the age of marriage is rapidly increasing, but here as in Western European civilization generally, the rate of population growth has slowed primarily because of Malthus' other preventive check, vice.

Malthus considered vice to be any sexual act other than those designed to fulfill the natural purpose of sex: reproduction. Most people today, and practically all those who are educated, would not only reject such an interpretation, but ridicule it; but having done so, they would then find difficulty in reaching an historically more meaningful definition. As gluttony is the vice of eating when it becomes an end in itself; as hubris or pride is the vice of ungoverned self-esteem, so sex when willfully performed in any way which prevents the natural end result (which is, unarguably, procreation) is a vice. So, with good justification, sayeth the Very Reverend Thomas Malthus.

Now while practice of sex as a vice (condoms, the pill, etc.) may act as an effective preventive check and, incidentally, encourage the practitioners of the vice to applaud themselves as performing a new (and higher, they will modestly admit) form of morality—homosexuals have preened themselves for helping to avoid a population explosion—it is no solution to problems of population.

Such vice, once it becomes common and is even applauded as a virtue, contributes not only to a decrease in the rate of population growth but to its cessation. Even now we are reproducing at a rate below that necessary to maintain a stable population. While an actual decline in population has not yet occurred here, it will, and it is already taking place in several European countries. Historically, such declines have led not to utopia but to disintegration of the societies where they occur.

Writing when he did, at a time when better sanitation and housing were being spun off as incidental benefits of the industrial revolution and were drastically reducing the death rate with consequent large increase in rates of population growth, Malthus assumed that the main problem that was evolving was too rapid population growth. In this assumption, his religious training probably joined with the native skepticism which he directed at Godwin's bargain-basement utopia as he remembered: "When goods increase, they are increased that eat them. . . ."[13]

Though "warmed and delighted" by the enchanting portrayal of the perfectibility of man and society held by Godwin and Condorcet, Malthus' thesis was that the very immutable nature of the basic factors associated with population were such that the rate of population growth, whether too high or too low, would give rise to problems which would seriously affect the improvement of society.

Twenty years later Godwin attempted to rebut Malthus in *Of Population, An Answer to Malthus* (1820), but he relied for his rebuttal mostly on a repetition of his hopes, and complaints that Malthus had converted the liberal "friends of progress" into "reactionaries."[14] In 1838, Charles Darwin, reading Malthus for amusement,[15] was struck by the idea that excessive numbers of any species, plant or animal, would lead to struggles for the limited supply of food and that in such struggles, the fittest would most likely survive: "Here then," he said, "I had at last got a theory by which to work."

Thus we have relationships between Rousseau and Daniel Malthus and William Godwin; between Godwin and Thomas Malthus; between Malthus and Darwin; between Godwin and Mary Wollstonecraft; between their semi-legitimate daughter, Mary Godwin, and Shelley; and between Godwin's second wife's daughter by her first husband, Claire Clairmont, and Byron. As a concluding note to these interrelated people and interwoven ideas, during 1816, while Shelley and Byron with their entourages were summering on the shores of Lake Geneva, Byron suggested that each member of the group write a ghost story. None of these stores amounted to much, but Mary Godwin Shelley produced a lasting allegorical tale called *Frankenstein, or The Modern Prometheus*. Others, I am sure, as well as myself, have wondered if her story of the scientist who created a monster that ultimately destroyed him was stirred up in Mary's mind by the visions of man-made utopias she had been born among and lived with.

Romanticism has a heartwarming appeal, but it usually fades with youth, and Shelley's later works such as *Prometheus Unbound*, which followed the frenetic *Queen Mab*, viewed the evils of society as due to man's own moral failure. Real reforms will come, he said in his later years, not through cataclysmic overthrow of all the bad institutions but through reform of man's moral nature. And in prototypical conservative style, Shelley warned that even if such a victory took place the price of its continuance would be an unremitting vigilance lest the serpent which lies deep in all human nature break loose and tempt us away from our Eden.

Jean-Jacques Rousseau also gradually shifted his philosophical view of the innate goodness of man personified in the Hurons, Iroquois, Tahitians, or the inhabitants of Madagascar. Criticism of his views mounted and even his friends and intellectual superiors such as Voltaire, while granting the effectiveness of Rousseau's felicity with words and the justice of many of his criticisms of society, reminded him that social evils arise from the "insatiable cupidity and indomitable pride of men." When he was sixty, advising the Poles with suggestions for a new constitution, the savant who once declared that "man is born free, and is everywhere in chains" warned them of the necessity for self-discipline, saying he laughed at those who imagine that, to be free, it is enough to be a rebel.[16]

As for the noble savages, apart from Hiawatha and Robinson Crusoe's Friday, primitive peoples seem, by-and-large, to have all of the evils and few of the comforts of civilized folk. For each tribe idealized by Rousseau or Diderot, or by contemporary anthropologists, another can be found living lives which, in civilization, would be called totally evil or bestial.

Colin Turnbull, who had previously described a tribe of Congo pygmies who were "without evil," more recently described another tribe, the Ik of Uganda, whose practices are such that it would be an insult to animals to call them bestial. Though on occasion food may be plentiful, parents will gorge themselves while denying their children. During scarcity, the young will pry open the jaws of the old and steal the food they are eating. The misfortune of others, including the anguish of parents or children, gives rise to joy. Their only conception of goodness is a full stomach.

From his studies of the Ik, Turnbull concludes that ". . . our much vaunted human values are not inherent in humanity at all, but are associated only with a particular form of survival called society."[17]

Romanticism with its idealization of nature as something to feel and enjoy, not to study, and its conception of the innate goodness of man, with his corruption caused only by bad materialistic institutions, is certainly a refreshing contrast to the cold sterility of objectified rationalistic-scientism. But it may be that the very nature of romanticism condemns it to a short life and fences it in as a preserve of the young. There is a vision incorporate in it which deserves a sigh as it fades, as it always soon does. But it vanishes only to arise, its new devotees once again convinced that they know truths so deep that they cannot be explained to others, especially to their elders. And again the radiance of the vision will shine through youth's acne, lighted by an inner conviction that no one ever possessed such beautifully unshareable thoughts.

Chapter 5. References and Notes

1. Robert Graves, *The Greek Myths* (Baltimore: Penguin Books, 1955), p. 36.

2. Stuart Piggott, *The Druids* (New York: Praeger, 1968), pp. 94–96.

3. Euripides, *The Bacchae and Other Plays*, trans. Philip Vellacott (Baltimore: Penguin Books, 1971), pp. 26–31.

4. Will and Ariel Durant, *Rousseau and Revolution* (New York: Simon and Shuster, 1965), p. 887.

5. Denis Diderot, "Correspondence," III, 226, in Peter Gay, *The Enlightenment* (New York: Alfred A. Knopf, 1969), vol. 2, p. 5.

6. *The Norton Anthology of English Literature*, revised, (New York: W. W. Norton Co., 1968), Vol. 2, p. 400ff.

7. Percy Bysshe Shelley, *Selected Poems*, ed. Edmund Blunden (London: Collins, 1970), Canto VI, p. 99 and Canto V, pp. 94–95.

8. Byron, *Selected Verse and Prose Works*, ed. Peter Quennell (London: Collins, 1969), "Childe Harold's Pilgrimage," Canto IV, verse 178, Canto III, verse 43; and Introduction, p. 48.

9. Will and Ariel Durant, *The Age of Napoleon* (New York: Simon and Shuster, 1975), p. 366.

10. Claire Tomalin, *The Life and Death of Mary Wollstonecraft* (New York: Harcourt Brace Jovanovich, 1974).

11. Will and Ariel Durant, *The Age of Napoleon* (New York: Simon and Shuster, 1975), p. 397.

12. William Godwin, *Enquiry Concerning Political Justice, and Its Influence on Morals and Happiness* (3rd ed., London, 1798), vol. 2, pp. 527–528 in Gertrude Himmelfarb, *Victorian Minds* (New York: Alfred A. Knopf, 1968), p. 84.

13. *Ecclesiastes*, 5:11, King James. *The New English Bible* (New York: Oxford University Press, 1970), replaces "food" with "riches."

14. Will and Ariel Durant, *The Age of Napoleon* (New York: Simon and Shuster, 1975), pp. 402–403.

15. Marston Bates, *Man in Nature* (Englewood Cliffs, N.J.: Prentice-Hall, 1961), pp. 57–58.

16. Will and Ariel Durant, *Rousseau and Revolution* (New York: Simon and Shuster, 1965), p. 884.

17. Colin Turnbull, *The Mountain People* (New York: Simon and Shuster, 1972), p. 294.

In Reality's Harsh Glare

EVERY BODY AT rest remains at rest and every body in motion continues in uniform motion in a straight line unless it is compelled to change by external forces acting on it.

This paraphrase of Newton's first law of motion might seem to be an oblique description of conservatives who obdurately resist change until forced to accept it and then, once moved, proceed grudgingly and unimaginatively wherever they are pushed. This is a popular and partially justified interpretation of conservatism, but it applies only to traditionalist conservatives who constitute fair game for ridicule as they solemnly dole out clichés and platitudes as though they were freshly minted gold. But philosophical conservatism is not the same as traditionalism. It first arose in the seventeenth century and did not assume a clear shape until its principles were enunciated by Edmund Burke in the eighteenth century; and it first arose as a reaction against the excesses of dessicated rationalism.

Ridicule of Minute Philosophers

Even as the practice of giving unstinting credence to any pronouncement labelled scientific became the intellectual fashion, there were those who were skeptical, especially when the "scientific truths" were applied in areas other than physics or chemistry. Some philosophers felt that attempts to apply the mechanics of Descartes or Laplace or the induction of Bacon to human affairs and social conditions simply would not work. They felt that the many non-measurable qualitative variables involved in human circumstances prevented the use of such techniques, and that the truths proclaimed were not at all scientific truths but merely rationalistic plausibilities. So, after science became a popular intellectual plaything, but before Burke fleshed out the meaning of philosophical conservatism, there were those who criticized or even ridiculed the notion that the new popular technique of scientific investigation could be applied to human affairs.

As early as 1651, Thomas Hobbes pointed to the risks inherent in an easy acceptance of "scientific" answers, arguing:

> But yet they that have no "science," are in better and nobler condition, with their natural prudence; than men, that by misreasoning, or by trusting them that reason wrong, fall upon false and absurd general rules. For ignorance of causes, and of rules, does not set men so far out of their way, as relying on false rules, and taking for causes of what they aspire to, those that are not so, but rather causes of the contrary.[1]

In *Alciphron, or the Minute Philosopher* (1733), George Berkeley (1685–1753) carries on a platonic dialogue between Alciphron, the minute, or inchworm, scientistic philosopher and Euphranor, Berkeley's protagonist. Gently, patiently, Alciphron is led to concede that deism could lead to atheism and atheism could bring about a collapse of morality, and Euphranor wonders why skeptics of religion shouldn't be skeptics of science, too, for many of the postulates (frictionless motion, total vacuums, anti-matter and quarks) of scientists are quite as far beyond our comprehension as, for example, The Trinity.

Euph. You have then a passion for truth?
Alc. Undoubtedly.
Euph. For all Truths?
Alc. For all.
Euph. To know or to publish them?
Alc. Both.

Euph. What! Would you officiously set an enemy right that was making a wrong attack? Would you help an enraged man to his sword?

Alc. In such cases, common sense directs one how to behave.

Euph. Common sense, it seems then, must be consulted whether a truth be salutary or hurtful, fit to be declared or conceded.[2]

Thus the good Bishop of Cloyne, in addition to raising doubt about the efficacy of pure reason, interjects one of the tenets of conservatism; the necessity, after all the facts are in and all hypotheses tested as best reason can, to resort to prudent judgment.

In *Gulliver's Travels* (1726) Jonathan Swift (1667–1745) also whets the cutting edge of his satire on the extremes of theoretical and speculative reasoning, whether in science, politics, or economics, and in his final voyage Lemuel Gulliver encounters a race of horses, Houyhnhnms, who live entirely by reason, have no word in their language to express anything that is evil, and who have as their slaves the proto-human Yahoos, who are creatures of appetite and passion.[3] In true conservative style, Dean Swift declared man to be not a rational animal but an animal *capable of reason,* and his satires were a recital of creatures who refused to live up to this capability.

Swift's French counterpart in satire, François Marie Arouet (Voltaire—1694–1778) in *The Ignorant Philosopher* denounced the ideas of Descartes saying,

> ... he has built such an imaginary world; his whirlwinds and three elements are so prodigiously ridiculous, that I ought to suspect everything he says upon the soul, after he has imposed upon me with respect to bodies.[4]

He mocked Rousseau's romanticism in *Candide*; and Professor Pangloss' (all-tongue) proclamation that "all the events in this best of possible worlds are admirably connected. If a single link in the great chain were omitted, the harmony of the entire universe would be destroyed," can reasonably be interpreted as a thrust at the mechanistic causality of Laplace and Descartes. In one of the greatest put-downs of all time, Candide admits that all of this rationality may be true "... but let's cultivate our garden."

Theist Voltaire declared that the showpiece of the Enlightenment, the massive French Encyclopedia, was a vehicle of liberal propaganda.

To Rousseau's request for comment on his *Discourse,* Voltaire responded by disagreeing with Rousseau's romantic thesis, saying, "That which has made and will always make this world a vale of tears is the insatiable cupidity and indomitable pride of men," not institutions or bad education. As for the nature of morality, in *The Ignorant Philosopher* he stated:

> Morality appears to me so universal, so calculated by the universal Being that formed us, so destined to serve as a counterpoise to our fatal passions, and to solace the inevitable troubles of this short life, that from Zoroaster [sixth century B.C.] down to Lord Shaftsbury [eighteenth century], I find all philosophers teaching the same morality, though they have all different ideas upon the principles of things.

Burke Proposes Philosophical Conservatism

Edmund Burke (1729–1797), Lord Beaconsfield, is generally recognized as the founder of philosophical conservatism and his *Reflections on the Revolution in France* (1790)[5] is commonly taken to be analogous in its relation to philosophical conservatism with Adam Smith's *Wealth of Nations* and economic conservatism.

Reflections was written when Burke was in his sixties, and some contend that he had been a romantic in his earlier years. This contention, however, is primarily based on a pamphlet entitled *A Vindication of Natural Society, or a View of the Miseries and Evils Arising to Mankind from Every Species of Artificial Society. A Letter to Lord — By a Late Noble Writer* (1756). This essay, a criticism of scientific rationalism and of abstract, geometrical reasoning, was a vigorous condemnation of all government and was more anarchistic than Rousseau's *Discourse on the Origin of Inequality,* but whether Burke meant it to be taken literally, or whether the essay was, as most suppose,[6] a

83

satire of romanticism meant also to parody the excesses of rationalism of one Lord Bolingbroke, we cannot know for certain. William Godwin, for one, took Burke's burlesque attack on institutions seriously. Likely, though, Burke was criticizing excesses of rationalism at the same time that he drew a parody of the extremes of romanticism.

In politics, Burke vigorously opposed efforts of George III to extend his power in England and in America. He was a staunch supporter of the rights of Americans and was one of the first to plead for abolition of the slave trade.

Burke objected both to rationalism and to romanticism. He held that politics ought not to be adjusted to abstract human reasonings but to human nature, of which reason is but a part and by no means the greatest part. "The nature of man is intricate; the objects of society are of the greatest possible complexity; and therefore no simple disposition or direction of power can be suitable either to man's nature, or to the quality of his affairs" (p. 92). He thoroughly distrusted "this mechanic philosophy." No matter how brilliant the reasoning of any individual, it is to be viewed skeptically if it conflicts with the experience of the race. Our liberties, he said, are not "natural rights." "From Magna Carta to the Declaration of Right it has been the uniform policy to claim and assert our liberties as an *entailed inheritance* derived from our forefathers and to be transmitted to our posterity" (p. 52).

Burke decried the excesses of the French Revolution, and of the attacks on the royal family he lamented:

> ... The age of chivalry is gone. That of sophisters, economists and calculators, has succeeded; and the glory of Europe is extinguished for ever. [p. 111]

> ... now all is to be changed. All the pleasing illusions, which made power gentle and obedience liberal, which harmonized the different shades of life, and which, by a bland assimilation incorporated into politics the sentiments which beautify and soften private society, are to be dissolved by this new conquering empire of light and reason. All the decent drapery of life is to be rudely torn off. All the superadded ideas, furnished from the wardrobe of a moral imagination, which the heart owns, and the understanding ratifies, as

necessary to cover the defects of our naked, shivering nature, and to raise it to dignity in our own estimation, are to be exploded as a ridiculous, absurd, and antiquated fashion.

On this scheme of things, a king is but a man, a queen is but a woman; a woman is but an animal, and an animal not of the highest order . . . that sort of reason which banishes the affections is incapable of filling their place. [pp. 112–113]

But power, of some kind or other, will survive the shock in which manners and opinions perish; and it will find other and worse means for its support. [p. 114]

To me the above passages are the most lucid, lyrical and prophetic description of the effects of unbridled rationalism ever written. In them Burke points out that morality is not the product of reason, it is something that "the heart owns and the understanding ratifies." And be it remembered that understanding is a much broader concept than knowledge.

These principles of morality are not discovered through scientific experiments, nor are they derived from abstract theories, no matter how elaborate or impeccably logical:

The lines of morality are not like ideal lines of mathematics. They admit of exceptions; they demand modifications . . . not made by the process of logic, but by the rule of prudence.[7]

And it is the degree to which we incorporate moral principles into our lives that will, soon or late, determine the degree of liberty which we enjoy.

Society cannot exist unless a controlling power of will and appetite be placed somewhere; and the less of it there is within, the more there must be without. It is ordained in the eternal constitution of things that men of intemperate minds cannot be free. Their passions forge their fetters.[8]

It may be that in restraining our desires within the guiding lines of moral principle we sacrifice some pleasure or profit but, says Burke, such sacrifice is worthwhile.

It is better to cherish virtue and humanity by leaving much to free will, even with some loss to the object, than to attempt to make men mere machines and instruments of a political benevolence. [p. 149]

Burke, deeply religious himself, believed that by his very constitution "man is a religious animal"; that atheism is against not only our reason, but our instincts; and that it cannot long prevail. We know and, what is better, we feel inwardly, that religion is the basis of civil society, and the source of all good and all comfort (p. 130). He believed that priests should not be politicians:

... politics and the pulpit are terms that have little agreement. No sound ought to be heard in the church but the healing voice of Christian charity. The cause of civil liberty and civil government gains as little as that of religion by this confusion of duties. . . . Wholly unacquainted with the world in which they are so fond of meddling and inexperienced in all its affairs, on which they pronounce with so much confidence, they have nothing of politics but the passions they excite. Surely the church is a place where one day's truce ought be allowed to the dissensions and animosities of mankind. [p. 23]

Amen, Brother Burke! What was said in 1790 applies even more broadly today, and with minor paraphrase should, with equal justification, be applied to many college professors.

Burke distinguished between the American Revolution and the French Revolution by pointing out the obvious differences that, unfortunately, many people ignore. The American separation from England was "a revolution not made, but prevented." It preserved, rather than destroyed, the traditional framework of life in America. The French Revolution, on the contrary, was intended to uproot the entire delicate growth called society, and it would end (as in fact, it did) in either tyranny or despotism. In this process, the real rights of people, their entailed inheritance, would be lost in their fanatic scramble for delusive abstract rights.

Burke is prototype and mentor for philosophical conservatism because the theme which binds his thoughts into an harmonious whole is his conception, always present, though more often implicit than explicit, of the moral nature of man. He rejects the romantic vision of man's innate natural goodness, and he repetitively rejects with equal vigor the dessicated rationalism of the "sophisters and professors" whose nothing-but rhetoric would make of man "an animal, and an animal not of the highest order."

He was sure that science would produce no simple formula for society, nor could romanticism explain our social affairs by asserting and reiterating the existence of human rights. He was convinced that society was an infinitely complex structure full of hidden relationships, checks and balances, a synthesis of opposing forces and tendencies, a congeries of conflicting principles founded on compromise and barter. In its very nature neither it nor man is perfectible.

Man's rights are not abstractions created by fiat, but earned, entailed inheritances, loaned to us with the obligation that we transmit them to posterity.

Science cannot provide us with sound guides to life because the lines of morality are not the ideal lines of mathematics, and while man must use his reason he must also look to the wisdom of civilization to arrive at prudent judgment. This need to contain his reason within the confines of personal experience framed in a background of the wisdom of civilization—this capability of man consciously to combine reason and experience to form prudent judgment, "the first of all the virtues"—constitutes man's uniqueness; and this is the short-term weakness of conservatism as it is its long-term strength.

Lacking the seeming certainty of irrefutable logic, the exactness of scientific experiment, and the dogmatic comfort of prescribed natural rights, conservatism relies on judgment; and judgment, though it may be the first of virtues, is always arguable and often fallible.

Thus, it was no surprise that conservative British intellectuals greeted Burke's attack on the French revolutionaries with delight. The poet Samuel Taylor Coleridge having, unlike many, matured as he grew older, discarded his youthful radicalness and declared that he could not conceive of a time when the writings of Burke would not have the highest value. In Burke's writings, he enthused, there was not one word he would add or withdraw.

But there were many, including Burke's close friend the prominent clergyman Charles James Fox, who admired the changes brought about by the French Revolution, and Burke's attack on rationalism and romanticism was soon challenged by those who disagreed with his interpretation of it, especially those who, having had Burke as an ally in their defense of the American Revolution, railed at him as a turncoat when he attacked the French revolutionists.

Paine's Rebuttal of Burke

Within the year, Thomas Paine (1737–1809), in *Rights of Man*, responded vigorously to *Reflections*, ridiculing the moral and religious abstractions which Burke had used to question the validity of abstract natural rights and the reasoning which had led to their adoption.[9]

Some fifty thousand copies of Paine's *Rights of Man* were sold in England within a few weeks and more than 200,000 by 1793 to attest to the popularity, then as now, of the conviction that man can be endowed with rights which he has not earned.

Quaker Tom Paine, though born in England, emigrated to America in 1774, and his pamphleteering contributed much to arouse feeling in favor of the independence of America from Britain.[10] General Washington credited his 1776 pamphlet *Common Sense* with having brought about a powerful change in the minds of many men, and *The Crisis*—"These are the times that try men's souls"—did much to uplift the spirits of both soldiers and citizenry. After we succeeded in separating our governance from the power of George III, Paine returned to Europe to support the French Revolution, and there, in 1794, "second year of the French Republic, one and indivisible," he published *Age of Reason*, prefaced by his assertion that "The most formidable weapon against errors of every kind is Reason. I have never used any other, and I trust I never shall."[11]

Early on, while an apprentice staymaker in London, Paine attended a course of scientific lectures and became intrigued with Newtonian mechanics in which the universe, once set in motion, behaved eternally in accordance with natural law, and it occurred to him that the political universe might be susceptible to the same analytical techniques (*Rights of Man,* p. 12).

Burke's distrust of unfettered reason, his doubt that science could be applied to human affairs, his devotion to religion, and his refusal to endow man with a pocketful of abstract natural rights, were all anathema to brilliant pamphleteer and polemicist Paine. Paine venerated science, was obsessed by reason, worshipped nature, and hated religion. As Carl Becker observed of other eighteenth-century philosophers, he denatured God only to deify nature. He insisted that he was not an atheist, but a deist. Perhaps so, but if so, his deism was a non-Christian dualism of reason and nature. He stated flatly:

> I do not believe in the creed professed by the Jewish church, by the Roman church, by the Greek church, by the Turkish church, by the Protestant church, nor by any church that I know of. My own mind is my own church. [p. 6]

In *Rights of Man,* after attacking Burke's criticism of the practices and aims of the French Revolution, Paine went on to describe the new world which could be attained once people replaced the "fabulous mythology" of religion and the outmoded beliefs and customs of society by reason and science.

The French Revolution, he was sure, was just a first step toward utopia. It would, he asserted, be followed by world revolution, and all Europe would be under one government. War would be abolished, armies and navies disbanded, and there would be abundance for all. Wretchedness would be vanquished by pensions for the aged, guaranteed employment and extensive welfare programs. The new rational state would give generous subsidies for births, education, marriages and funerals, while at the same time taxes for lower-income persons would be eliminated.

Such frabjous wonders would result as society, compelled in a process similar to that hypostatized by Auguste Comte, changed from rule by superstition, through rule by power, to a new form of society governed by no belief other than reason, that would ineluctably promote both the common interests of the society and the common rights of man.

Paine ridiculed the seriousness of any difficulties which might arise as society was forced to abandon its bad old ways and warmly embrace cold, dry reason. The bloody Terror and the placental assassinations which, in the French Revolution, accompanied the birth of his utopia, Paine dismissed as "so few sacrifices," saying that "Among the few who fell there do not appear to be any that were intentionally singled out. They all of them had their fate in the circumstances of the moment. . . ." (*Rights of Man*, pp. 72, 73) Burke's criticism of the Terror arose, said Paine, because "He pities the plumage, but forgets the dying bird." What matters the loss of a few frills and a few people.

Paine, English born and American bred, who found his real love in the French Revolution, bears a likeness to Oregon-born, Harvard-educated, expatriate to Russia John Reed, whose *Ten Days That Shook the World* (1919) apotheosized the Russian Communist Revolution in similar fashion. And in manner parallel to Paine's dismissal of the victims of the Terror as being only a few whose deaths, far from being caused by fanatic viciousness, reasonably resulted as "their fate in the circumstances of the moment," some American intellectuals airily dismissed millions of Kulaks and Ukrainians who were sacrificed to promote "reasonable, scientific" communism and the victims of Stalin's purges with the giggling quip that "after all, you can't make an omelet without breaking a few eggs."

Second in popularity only to his *Rights of Man*, which became for many years of the nineteenth century the agitator's handbook, was his dogmatic attack on organized religion, *Age of Reason*, and a 1967 study of the biographies of 150 secularists who lived between 1850 and 1965 reported that forty-eight of the fifty secularists who specified books that most influenced their beliefs, indicated either the Bible or *Age of Reason*. (*Rights of Man*, p. 39) In it Paine attempted to bring religion into conformity with the spirit and discoveries of science, and his scientific, reasonable assessment of revealed religion was:

It has been the most dishonorable belief against the character of the Divinity, the most destructive to morality and the peace and happiness of man, that ever was propagated since man began to exist. [p. 6]

He summarized his feelings about Christianity, the worst of all religions, thus:

Of all the systems of religion that ever were invented, there is none more derogatory to the Almighty, more unedifying to man, more repugnant to reason, and more contradictory in itself, than this thing called Christianity. Too absurd for belief, too impossible to convince, and too inconsistent for practice, it renders the heart torpid, or produces only atheists and fanatics. [p. 181]

Paine insisted that he was not an atheist, but he fitted Burke's description of one, being the sort of man who aims at dominion, and his means are the words he always has in his mouth—the natural equality of man and the sovereignty of the people.

Paine concludes his reasonable scientific diatribe by revealing that revealed religion became the abomination it is because it wandered from the immutable laws of science, and the right use of reason.

Melville's Rebuttal of Paine

It was in surrebuttal to Paine's *Rights of Man* rebuttal of Burke's *Reflections on the French Revolution* that Herman Melville wrote *Billy Budd, Sailor (An Inside Narrative),* which, though written during the 1880s, was not published until 1924.[12] I trust that readers will forgive what seems to be a pedantic excursion as I try to show how Melville, in *Billy Budd,* rejected perfectionist, utopian views such as Paine's while subtly conveying his belief in the conservative view of man and society. I embark upon this tack because most interpreters of *Budd* ignore this, to me, obvious message; because it is a valid interpretation; and primarily, of course, because it supports my theme.

Stripped to the planking of her keel and ribs, Melville's tale has a young lad, Billy Budd, foretopman, taken from a merchantman and impressed on a man-of-war. Billy performs his duties full and well and is liked by all of his mates except John Claggart, master-at-arms, who develops an immediate antipathy toward him and ultimately tells Captain Vere that Billy is fomenting mutiny. In a confrontation before the captain, Claggart repeats his accusation and Billy, unable to defend himself verbally because of a speech defect, strikes out physically in his mute anguish and kills Claggart.

Farfetched though it seems, this drama of young innocence betrayed into a murderous assault that led to his hanging, was a vehicle which Melville used as an allegorical expression of his beliefs about man and society.

Rights of Man was the merchantman from which Billy was impressed and this name was given the ship because:

> The hardheaded Dundee owner was a staunch admirer of Thomas Paine, whose book in rejoinder to Burke's arraignment of the French Revolution had then been published for some time and had gone everywhere. [p. 48]

In addition to this obvious jointure of Melville's theme to Paine and Burke, it is likely that Melville was aware that Paine used nautical terms in referring to his schooling under his master, Reverend William Knowles, and also refers in *Rights of Man* to going to sea in a privateer. Captain the Honorable Edward Fairfax Vere is the master of the *Indomitable* on which Billy was impressed, and Melville may have made one of his many plays upon words to relate the master Knowles to the master Vere (veritas, verily, verism—meaning either truth or realism).

The *Indomitable* had engaged a French ship of the line which Melville at first called the *Directory*, then assigned it variously as Athée, Atheiste, and ended calling it *Atheist*, in likely reference to Paine.

The time of the tale was 1797, a few months after "the Great Mutiny" at Nore; a mutiny in "a fleet the right arm of a Power than all but the sole free conservative one of the Old World." (p. 54) Some mutineers ran up the red flag on their ships, thereby "... transmuting the flag of founded law and freedom defined, into the enemy's red meteor of unbridled and unbounded revolt.

Reasonable discontent growing out of practical grievances in the fleet had been ignited into irrational combustion as by live cinders blown across the Channel from France in Flames." (p. 54)

Here Melville not only draws a close analogy between the mutiny and the French Revolution, but in describing the Union Jack as "the flag of founded law and freedom defined" he describes England in the manner of Burke. Melville's descriptive "Reasonable discontent growing out of practical grievances . . . had been ignited into irrational combustion" is not only typically Burkean in thought, but also in style. Compare it, if you please, in its meaning and in its rhythm, with Burke's observation on the course of the French Revolution:

> But you, who began with refusing to submit to the most moderate restraints, have ended by establishing an unheard-of despotism. [*Reflections,* p. 217]

Billy Budd, Melville's protagonist, was a naive youth of phenomenal natural innocence, "a certain musical chime in his voice seemed to be the veritable unobstructed outcome of the innermost man." He was a foundling, but "noble descent was as evident in him as in a blood horse." There was just one thing amiss, a vocal defect which, during emotional stress, caused Billy to stutter or to go mute, "a striking instance that the arch interferer, the envious marplot of Eden, still has more or less to do with every human consignment to this planet of Earth . . . one way or another he is sure to slip in his little card, as much as to remind us—I too have a hand here." (p. 53) Thus Melville indicates that even saintly Billy is flawed, as is all mankind, with an immutable combination of potential for evil as well as good.

Master-at-arms John Claggart, antagonist to foretopman Billy Budd, was evil, darkness, "the direct reverse of a saint."

> Now something such an one was Claggart, in whom was the mania of an evil nature, not engendered by vicious training or corrupting books or licentious living, but born with him and innate, in short "a depravity according to nature." [p. 76]

Mediating protagonist and antagonist is Captain the Honorable Edward Fairfax Vere, who loved books and whose

> ... settled convictions were as a dike against those invading waters of novel opinion social, political, and otherwise, which carried away as in a torrent no few minds in those days, minds by nature not inferior to his own. While other members of that aristocracy to which by birth he belonged were incensed at the innovators mainly because their theories were inimical to the privileged classes, Captain Vere disinterestedly opposed them not alone because they seemed to him insusceptible of embodiment in lasting institutions, but at war with the peace of the world and the true welfare of mankind. [pp. 62–63]

If Melville, in the full passage devoted to Captain Vere of which the above is a part, is not portraying Lord Beaconsfield, he is at least describing Burke's conception of Burke!

As previously related, Billy, falsely accused by Claggart of fomenting mutiny, and due to his affliction unable to defend himself verbally, mutely strikes at his accuser and kills Claggart, later saying "could I have used my tongue I would not have struck him." Despite his affection for Billy and an appreciation of the circumstances in which he killed a superior, Captain Vere decrees that he shall be hanged, and he is "hung and gone to glory," and his mates collect pieces of the spar on which Billy was hanged, for "to them a chip of it was as a piece of the Cross."

Several interpreters have followed this part of the allegory in their interpretations, accounting Billy as Christ, Claggart as the Devil, and Captain Vere as God; but I believe an interpretation somewhat less obvious to be intellectually credible: that in *Billy Budd, Sailor,* Melville was disputing Paine's belief that the natural goodness of man, if unhampered by superstition, customs, and mythological religious cant, would overflow to cover all mankind with its beneficence. Melville was saying that evil as well as good is part of man, and no matter what be the political system, they will clash, and when Captain Vere sentenced Billy to hang it was symbolic of Melville's feeling (and Burke's, too) that neither perfect good nor complete evil can be allowed to exist on earth any more than they can at sea, leaving, in their absence, us alone with our compromising selves, forever faced with the necessity for seeking the virtue of prudence to govern our lives.*

*An attempt to show that Melville's *Moby Dick*[13] is, like his *Billy Budd*, an allegorical espousal of the conservative belief in the unperfectibility of man, was unsuccessful. That *Moby Dick* can be interpreted allegorically as well as being enjoyed as a cracking good seafaring tale is supported by Melville's reference (in the extracts about whales which preface the tale) to Thomas Hobbes' *Leviathan*, called a Commonwealth or State—which is but an artificial man. He also refers to Edmund Burke's figure of speech which describes Spain as a great whale stranded on the shores of Europe, and one of the passages in *Moby Dick* is "The world's a ship. . . ." And the seamen on Ahab's ship, the *Pequod*, in a manner almost painfully contrived, are drawn from many countries.

In addition to its apparent universality, it is tempting to draw from *Moby Dick* an allegory with romanticism. In the editor's introduction he refers to Captain Ahab as the type of romantic hero ready-to-defy-the-world made popular by Byron. Ahab's peg-leg seems an obvious parallel to Byron's club-foot, and in the text Melville refers to Byron's *Childe Harold* and quotes from it the familiar "Roll on, thou deep and dark blue ocean, roll!" Melville's text also refers to romanticist Percy Shelley's revolutionary poem *Queen Mab*, and mentions Edmund Burke.

Moby Dick also contains references to the Hypoboreans, the peaceful, happy, virtuous noble savages, beloved of Apollo, whom the Druids romanticized as the people of a gone golden age.

A pointed reference to romanticism would seem to exist in that the three harpooners, whose job it is to attack the whale (Leviathan, the state) are all Indians who are referred to as noble savages; and Queequeg comes from Rokovoko, "which is not on any map," that is not-a-place, which means utopia.

A long passage obviously relates to Billy Budd and master-at-arms Claggart, though in *Moby Dick* the comparable names are Steelkilt and Radney and their ship the *Town-Ho* instead of the *Indomitable*. Steelkilt is "a tall and noble animal with a head like a Roman, and a flowing golden beard, and a brain and a heart and a soul in him, gentlemen, which made Steelkilt Charlemagne." Radney is ugly as a mule and as stubborn and malicious.

Radney orders Steelkilt to perform unreasonable and degrading tasks which are beneath his station, and when Steelkilt refuses to obey,

Hannah Arendt interprets Paine in a fashion similar to Melville in *Billy Budd*, contending that the absolutes inherent in *Rights of Man* spell doom when incorporated into the political system, and that Burke's "lasting institutions" break down not only under the onslaught of elemental evil but under the impact of absolute innocence as well.[14]

---

strikes him with a hammer. In self-defense, Steelkilt strikes back, and Radney falls to the deck "spouting blood like a whale." Radney is later killed by Moby Dick, and Steelkilt abandons the ship which is corrupted society to stay on an island "where no civilized creature resided."

Revellers on *The Bachelor*, "a full ship and homeward bound," are described as sounding as though they were pulling down the Bastille, and Captain Ahab, as he smashes his quadrant on the deck, says: "Science! Curse thee thou quadrant . . . no longer will I guide my earthly way by thee."

Thus a moderately credible case could be made that *Moby Dick*, like *Billy Budd*, is allegorically a depiction of excesses of romanticism and reason; but such threads of relationship seemed stretched so far as to be ravelled, and Melville's allegory in *Moby Dick* seems more biblical than ideological.

From the Bible we learn that Omri, warrior captain, became King of Israel and Ahab, his son, succeeded him to reign for twenty-two years as the wickedest and most powerful ruler the Israelites ever had. Ahab wed the alien Jezebel and through her influence tried to abolish the worship of Jehovah, God of Israel. In *Moby Dick*, Ahab says of God: "Thy right worship is defiance."

Moby Dick—the title—seems likely derived from Moab, son of Lot's daughter, sire of the Moabites, who fought Ahab, wicked king of the Israelites, who was killed in battle.

The name of the good ship *Pequod* may have its derivation from the land of Pekod, which the Lord said should be utterly destroyed; and the *Pequod* was destroyed.

Ishmael, the narrator, has the name of the son of Abraham by Hagar, the bondwoman. Being "born of the flesh, not of the spirit," Ishmael was cast out of the house of Abraham, but the Lord promised that his lineage would extend forever. And Ishmael is the only survivor of the *Pequod*—he survives because he is kept afloat by a coffin, lined with pitch and tightly closed to make it buoyant, the making of which led Ahab to ask: "Can it be that in some spiritual sense the coffin is, after all, but an immortality-preserver?" And Ishmael is rescued by a ship whose captain lost his two sons at sea; and the ship was *Rachel* (who wept for her lost sons).

And thus again we have this interweave of clashing political views which all, soon or late, reduce themselves to differing conceptions of the nature of man: Burke versus Rousseau, Paine versus Burke, Melville versus Paine, as it was with Godwin (whom Paine entrusted with the manuscript for *Age of Reason*) versus society, Wollstonecraft versus men, Mary Shelley versus her parents, and, among many others, Malthus versus Godwin and Rousseau. Such is the necessary essence—too long submerged by the naive notion that our human problems have been, or are about to be, solved by rationalistic-scientism—of intellectual disputation which I hope in some small way to bestir.

Unlike our robust disputatious yesterdays, our belief in today's scientism has oiled the sea of our intellectual discontents; but this pleasant seeming-calm may be fetid stagnation and to bestir it we need more of Melville's waves to test our mental balance against their roll and pitch, more of Dylan Thomas' "rage, rage" against the smoothness of our good journey as we glide into intellectual senescence, thinking it maturity.

Romanticism Matures into Conservatism

As Shelley discarded his romantic revolutionary views in *Queen Mab* for the conservatism of *Prometheus,* and as even the prototypical Rousseau modified his romanticism in his later years, so Samuel Taylor Coleridge (1772–1834), in his earlier years a student of and ardent supporter of science, later repudiated this associationist philosophy that had earlier fascinated him, rejecting the notion that all thought is the mechanical product of sensations.[15] In the conservative fashion, he rejected rationalistic-scientism and came to believe that evil is so inborn in us that human intelligence alone is inadequate to the office of restoring health to the will.

William Wordsworth (1770–1850) whose youthful rhapsodical acclaim of the French Revolution,

> Bliss was it in that dawn to be alive;
> But to be young was very Heaven,

was often repeated, and who, like Paine, praised the Revolution as the liberation not of one nation only, but potentially of all mankind;[16] and who was much taken with William Godwin's *Enquiry Concerning Political Justice*, later repudiated the excesses that both rationalism and romanticism led to and became an ardent conservative.

In Germany, Johann Wolfgang von Goethe's romantic *The Sorrows of Young Werther* (1774) inspired youths to *Sturm und Drang* in an ecstasy of moral and social revolt, with Rousseau as their god and Goethe as his prophet. They eagerly responded to Rousseau's appeal for naturalness and freedom, and rejected materialism, naturalism and determinism.[17] They identified nature with God and felt that to be natural was to be divine. Society alone corrupted man's innate goodness.

In his masterwork, *Faust* (begun in 1798, but not published until 1808), Goethe turned, as have so many others, to the conservative interpretation of the meaning of life.[18] His "Prologue in Heaven" makes clear that the fate of Faust is not a particular life dramatized, but man's fate. And this universality of the theme is further underscored as Mephistopheles dubs Faust's desire, "Sir Microcosm." The Lord believes that Faust is one man not debased by reason; that he will be guided by it to truth. Man's innate will for good and his groping intuitions will lead him along the paths of righteousness, despite some detours. Mephistopheles, representing eighteenth-century rationalism, disagrees and makes a pact with Faust, promising "miracles of every fashion," (line 1752) to Faust who wants to close his mind to sorrow and ". . . feel down to my senses' core." (line 1771) Mephistopheles promises to give him more than any man has ever seen before. Faust, in return, agrees to surrender his soul to the devil if he ever, even due to the lies of Mephistopheles, fully satisfies his secular dreams:

> If I to any moment say:
> Linger on! You are so fair!
> Put me in fetters straightaway,
> Then I can die for all I care! [lines 1699–1702]

Prior to making his pact with Faust, Mephistopheles has an encounter with a scientist, Wagner, who has created a minature of man, Homunculus, which bears the semblance of life but is not real flesh and blood. While Faust seeks to overcome his physical nature and find peace on a spiritual level, Homunculus, the epitome of pure reason, expects to find fulfillment through enhanced physical existence. He is confident that he can do this because he possesses none of the emotions that lead real human beings into false impressions or aspirations. Homunculus, specifically so-called but not related to Goethe's Faust, is also created as an ideal for mankind by B. F. Skinner, more than one hundred and fifty years later. The real Skinner, like the fictional Wagner, is grimly serious about his creation.

After the pact is signed in blood, Faust gluttons on the ripest of the fruits of life; indulges all possible lusts of the flesh; wallows in luxury and strides in power; then finally settles on the secular purpose for which he agrees to consummate the pact by giving his soul to Mephistopheles. The project which, to him, is eternally good, the thing for which he bids time to: "Linger on, thou art so fair," is what today we would call urban renewal, complete with forced evacuation of an aged couple "for their own good." Struck blind by Care, Faust hears sounds which his mind envisions as land being cleared, the sea diked, swamps drained, flowers brought instantly to life, and buildings built for the utopia, "a land like paradise" for which he willingly will surrender his soul to the devil. In fact, the sounds are made by Mephistopheles' minions (Lemurs) who are digging his grave. Mephistopheles gloats that the clock has stopped for the poor wretch who wanted to hold it fast; that "Time masters him who would withstand / My power. . . ." (11, 590–94)

Before Mephistopheles can wisk away Faust's soul, however, angels swoop down and bear away his remains, and Goethe's closing lines (12, 110–1) are similar to the passage in which Dante has Virgil (reason) replaced by Beatrice as man's guide through purgatory:

> The Eternal Feminine
> Draws us onward.

Rationalism Rejected for Conservatism

Fyodor Dostoevsky (1821–1888), as many other youths, had his fancy taken by socialism and its scientistic view of man's malleability and perfectibility until, in 1849, he was arrested as a member of a socialist discussion group (the Petrashevskys), imprisoned for eight months, sentenced to be shot, reprieved at the last moment (in what may have been a staged performance), and banished to Siberia for nine years. His brush with death and his long Siberian association with non-intellectual man as he is, rather than as Saint-Simon, Fourier, and other socialist theoreticians insisted he should be, convinced Dostoevsky that man is not innately good—nor, for that matter, innately bad. He found man capable of anything—in either direction.[18]

Much of what he wrote during and after his Siberian banishment (*Notes from House of the Dead, Notes from the Underground, Crime and Punishment, The Possessed,* and *The Brothers Karamazov*) inveighs against the socialistic-scientistic view of man and espouses his newly acquired conservative belief. He particularly criticized the views of man and society contained in N. G. Chernyshevsky's *What Is To Be Done?,* a book much studied and greatly admired by Lenin.

Chernyshevsky argues that there is no essential difference between a mineral, plant, animal, or man.[19] All "special natures" assigned to man are fantasies of a pre-scientific era; religion is a fairytale; free will makes as much sense as saying: "The plate broke because the plate broke." Reason, Chernyshevsky implied, could perceive the law of human nature, reconstruct society according to its dictates, and usher man into a life of perpetual bliss.

This liberal view of man, spread by many others in addition to Chernyshevsky, "held that man is good; that he will seek everyone's communal advantage as he becomes more enlightened; that a new golden age, a new Eden will dawn as soon as man behaves according to rational, scientific principles. The truths of science are unquestionable and final, and lead inexorably to a recognition of doctrines of determinism and necessity."[20]

By the time he wrote *The Possessed,* Dostoevsky was reacting angrily against these scientistic views:

> This has been the special knack of pseudoscience, that terrible scourge of mankind, a scourge worse than plague, famine and war, an evil that didn't exist until this century. Half-knowledge is a tyrant without precedent, one that has its own priests and slaves; a tyrant that is worshiped with unprecedented awe and adulation and before which science itself fawns and cringes.[21]

The peasant, for Dostoevsky, was a carrier of ideals but should not be idealized. The idealized peasant that the liberals loved was a peasant that had never existed, and could not exist, except in the abstractions of the liberals. . . . They refused to accept the real peasant: the peasant who was ignorant, slothful, greedy, sadistic, drunk " . . . but the peasants know when they are sinning and in knowing, they acknowledge a judgment and law beyond their judgment and law."[22]

"Dostoevsky believed in God; in the organic processes of social change; the glory of the Russian state and the glories of the Orthodox faith; in personal freedom and responsibility; and in the impossibility of altering man's nature and situation by abstract rational and external manipulation."

Our Conservative Heritage

Though America prior to and during the revolution had its ideologues such as Thomas Paine with his idealization of reason, basically the American Revolution was, as Burke pointed out, intrinsically different from the French Revolution which was soon to follow, and from the Russian Revolution of 1917.

At the time of America's revolution, her political practices (except, of course, for the domination of George III) and her legal principles were firmly and deeply embedded in English history, and there was no intent or effort to shatter or even to shake this bedrock. Our first constitution, that of Virginia in 1776, was drafted by George Mason and can readily be traced back to Magna Carta of 1215, the Petition of Right in 1628, and the English Bill of Rights of 1689.[23] Our laws, almost always in

101

principle and usually in practice, were derived from Sir Richard Blackstone's *Commentaries* with their roots fixed deeply in precedence and divine sanction; not from Jeremy Bentham's ideological rationalism. Leaders of the American Revolution were not coffee-house messianic intellectuals such as Paine, the Jacobins, Comte, Marx, and Lenin, but men of substance and practical political experience. Their credo was enunciated by lawyer John Dickinson: "Experience must be our only guide, reason may mislead us."

Crane Brinton, in his well-known study of revolution, also indicates that unlike the French and Russian Revolutions ours was not a social revolution, nor even, basically, a political one.[24] While the French believed that immutable forces of nature and reason foreordained their destiny, and the communists put similar blind faith in economic determinism, Americans mostly put their trust in God.

Hannah Arendt, in her *On Revolution*, points out that "most manifest" in the French Revolution was the inability of the participants to control its events, which seemed to occur independently of their purposes.[25] In America "the exact opposite took place," and the Revolution seemed to proceed as though man were in control of his destiny.

M. Stanton Evans lists the differences between the American Revolution and others, characterizing ours as being opposed to innovation; reverent of traditions such as those embodied in the common law and British custom; suspicious of all centralized governments; respectful of property rights; particular and legalistic rather than universal or arbitrary in respect of rights; and, finally, aimed at a single limited objective, independence from Great Britain.[26]

Once freed from the tyranny of George III, the sovereign colonies were loathe to surrender more of their hard-won independence than they had to, and were suspicious of any attempt to establish a strong central government. To soothe their fears and to persuade the colonies that a federal government could be established to their advantage and without unduly encroaching upon their independence, John Jay, James Madison, and Alexander Hamilton wrote eighty-five essays which collectively were titled *The Federalist* 1787–88.[27]

To calm one fear, the three writers assured their colonial

102

readers that no matter what form the federal government might take, it would never be a democracy. They, as well, presumably, as most of their readers, feared the encroachment of mob rule at least as much as they feared the monarchy from which they had recently escaped. These were men of substance, practicing politicians rather than theoreticians, and, distrusting the unfettered reason which was rapidly building up to the revolution in France, they relied on experience handed down from the past, and referred over and over again to their respect for the lessons of history. Like Burke, they gave little credence to abstract natural rights or to the innate goodness of man. They rejoiced in the variety of human conduct while insisting on the unity of human nature.[28]

Using virtually the same words and certainly expressing a conception of the relationship between man's nature and social order virtually identical to that of Burke, the authors of *The Federalist* insisted that history teaches us that men need institutions to master their passions. Man is not all bad, but has a mixture of tendencies toward depravity and a capability to express qualities which inspire esteem. But on balance, Hamilton repeatedly warned, man's rapacity, avarice, animosity, and vindictiveness will outweigh his virtues (Nos. 1, 6), and such bad traits, said Madison, are "sown in the nature of man." (No. 10) He summarizes the necessity for government in terms of man's mixture of potentials for good and evil:

> What is government itself but the greatest of all reflections on human nature? If men were angels, no government would be necessary. If angels were to govern men, neither external or internal controls on government would be necessary. In framing a government which is to be administered by men over men, the great difficulty lies in this: you must first enable the government to control the governed; and in the next place oblige it to control itself. [No. 15]

In accord with the promises of the Hamilton, Jay, and Madison essays in *The Federalist*, and in deference to the justified fears of the colonies that a federal government would deprive them of their sovereignty, the Constitution provided that the legislative, executive, and judicial branches of the federal government would prevent each other from attaining excessive power. Most importantly, the powers of Congress were rigidly restricted:

> To lay and collect taxes to pay the debts and provide for the common defense and general welfare of the United States . . .
>
> To borrow money.
>
> To regulate interstate and foreign commerce.
>
> To establish uniform rules of naturalization and uniform laws of bankruptcies.
>
> To coin money; to regulate its value; and fix the standard of weights and measures.
>
> To punish counterfeiters.
>
> To establish post offices and post roads.
>
> To grant copyrights and patents.
>
> To establish courts inferior to the Supreme Court.
>
> To punish piracies and felonies on the high seas.
>
> To declare war.
>
> To raise, support and regulate an army and navy, and militia. [Article 1, Section 8]

Except for the reference to the general welfare in the first of these enumerated powers, the restrictions placed upon the makers of our laws and thereby upon our federal government are clearly delineated and rigidly limited.

I am sure that others as well as myself have puzzled over the seeming contradiction between the romantic conception of man which introduces the Declaration of Independence and the conservative conception of man which is expressed in *The Federalist* and codified in the Constitution.

How, I often wondered, could one reconcile the "self-evident" truth "that all men are created equal" and "inalienable rights" to "the pursuit of happiness" expressed in the Declaration with *Federalist* interpretations that argued that avarice

104

and animosity are "sown in the nature of man" and therefore he needs institutions to master his passions? Because men are not angels they need government; and since those who govern are also unangelic the power of government must itself be controlled. From such convictions evolved the restrictions on the Federal Government which were incorporated into the Constitution.

In *Inventing America: Jefferson's Declaration of Independence* (New York: Doubleday, 1978), Garry Wills describes the meaning that Jefferson intended to convey by phrases such as all men being created equal and having an inalienable right to pursue happiness so as to resolve this seeming contradiction. With thorough documentation and credible inference, Wills shows that Jefferson meant that all men possess the highest attribute of mankind—a sense of moral responsibility, conscience. He did not mean that they were equal in other respects, and he described at great length the differences between slave and free, colonist and native. But no matter how extensive the ethnic differences which he believed to exist, he steadfastly insisted that all men equally possessed the faculty for moral responsibility.

Jefferson's conception of moral responsibility was essentially the same as the meaning which I have stressed. He wrote:

> Man was destined for society. His morality, therefore, was to be formed to this object.

> It would have been inconsistent in creation to have formed man for the social state, and not to have provided virtue and wisdom enough to manage the concerns of the society.

> Morals were too essential to the happiness of man to be risked on the uncertain combinations of the head. She [Nature] laid their foundation therefore in sentiment, not in science. That she gave to all, as necessary to all; this [science] to a few only, as sufficing with a few. [Wills, p. 187]

Nor did Jefferson imply that an inalienable right to the pursuit of happiness signified his approval of a hedonistic questing for personal pleasure. Together with Francis Hutcheson,

105

Adam Smith, Adam Ferguson, and others, Jefferson conceived true happiness to be serving others within a social context; that only through consideration for others and for the society is the greatest happiness and the perfection of the larger system attained. His was not an endorsement of individuation but, as Adam Ferguson indicated, a reciprocal relationship with others within the context of the social structure (Wills, p. 253); one which I have described as functional complementarity.

As for the "welfare clause," Jefferson, in his *Opinion on the Constitutionality of the Bank* (1791) said that this clause did not in any way imply that it gave power to Congress to levy taxes for any purpose it pleased; nor to do anything it pleased to provide for the general welfare, but only to levy taxes to pay for things Congress could legally do (as spelled out in the enumerated powers).[29] To infer otherwise—which almost everyone now does— ". . . would render all the preceding and subsequent enumerations of power completely useless. It would reduce the whole instrument to a single phrase—that of instituting a Congress with power to do whatever would (in its often biased judgment) be for the good of the United States; and as they would be the sole judges of the good or evil, it would be also a power to do whatever evil they pleased."

This blanket power, which we now accept as part of our Orwellian rewritten history, together with the mistaken notion that the Constitution, which never mentions the word, established the United States as a democracy, have effectively expunged the remainder of the Constitution, leaving us naked victims to those expressions of human avarice which the founders warned against.

In his First Inaugural Address (1801), Jefferson indicated the proper limits to functions which should be performed by our Federal government. We had been endowed by Providence with many blessings, he said, and these could be further enhanced by:

> . . . a wise and frugal Government, which shall restrain men
> from injuring one another, shall leave them otherwise free
> to regulate their own pursuits of industry and improve-
> ment, and shall not take from the mouth of labor the bread
> it has earned. This is the sum of good government, and this
> is necessary to close the circle of our felicities.

Which, as Tocqueville Foresaw, We Now Abandon

But Jefferson's hope was not our fate, and it was left to a conservative French aristocrat, Count Alexis Charles Henri Maurice Clérel de Tocqueville, to describe, with astonishing prescience, what the future of America was to be a century before it happened. In 1835 and 1840 Tocqueville's two volumes of *Democracy in America* were published, and while Tocqueville was favorably impressed by many aspects of American customs and institutions, he foresaw that despotism would encroach upon American life because the people would become a multitude of men, equal and alike, "incessantly endeavoring to procure the petty and paltry pleasures which glut their lives."[30] Each would become a stranger to the fate of all the rest, and his children and his private friends would, for him, constitute the whole of mankind.

> Above this race of men stands an immense and tutelary power, which takes upon itself alone to secure their gratifications and to watch over their fate. That power is absolute, minute, regular, provident, and mild. It would be like the authority of a parent, if, like that authority, its object was to prepare men for manhood; but it seeks on the contrary to keep them in perpetual childhood: it is well content that the people should rejoice, provided they think of nothing but rejoicing. For their happiness such a government willingly labours, but it chooses to be the sole agent and the only arbiter of that happiness: it provides for their security, foresees and supplies their necessities, facilitates their pleasures, manages their principal concerns, directs their industry, regulates the descent of property, and subdivides their inheritances: what remains, but to spare them all the care of thinking and all the trouble of living?
>
> Thus it every day renders the exercise of the free agency of man less useful and less frequent; it circumscribes the will within a narrower range, and gradually robs a man of all the uses of himself. The principle of equality has prepared men for these things. It has predisposed them to endure them, and oftentimes to look upon them as benefits.
>
> It covers the surface of society with a network of small

complicated rules, minute and uniform, through which the most original minds and the most energetic characters cannot penetrate, to rise above the crowd. The will of man is not shattered, but softened, bent, and guided; men are seldom forced by it to act, but they are constantly restrained from acting. Such a power . . . compresses, enervates, extinguishes, and stupefies a people, till each nation is reduced to nothing than a flock of timid and industrious animals, of which the government is the shepherd.

Much that Tocqueville foresaw has already happened, and if we continue to succumb to a government that provides for our security, supplies our necessities, facilitates our pleasures, manages our principal concerns, regulates the descent of property and subdivides our inheritances, the exercise of our will, being further softened, bent and guided, becomes less useful and less frequent. The safeguards that were promised in *The Federalist* and incorporated into the Constitution have not been shattered by the brute force of dictatorship, they have been gently dissolved by the soothing balm of promised security.

Despite Jefferson's sound logic and the clear intent of the Constitution, we expanded the welfare clause so much that it now smothers the Constitution under the Welfare State. As Tocqueville foresaw, we not only fail to resist the growth of the welfare state with its small myriad complicated rules, minute and uniform, but we applaud it and gaze upon it with pride as a product of civilized maturity. And it is a pretty thing—as pretty as a leaf on which the frost has touched.

As we have refused to control our will and appetites from within, we find in accordance with the lesson so long taught, so often repeated, and so seldom learned, that we are increasingly being controlled from without.

Having, I trust, described sufficient aspects of our ancient images of man to indicate how the contrasting views of rationalism, romanticism, and conservatism emerged from their status as abstract ideas to influence not only our thinking about ourselves, but our literature, our education, and our politics, I should now like to argue in greater detail what I have already hinted at: that our current beliefs are little else than reflections of these perspectives on the nature of man which first became clearly delineated in the eighteenth century.

Chapter 6. References and Notes

1. Thomas Hobbes, *Leviathan; or The Matter, Form and Power of a Commonwealth, Ecclesiastical and Civil,* 4th ed. (London: George Routledge and Sons, 1894), p. 30.

2. G. N. Wright, *The Works of George Berkeley,* vol. I (London: Thomas Tegg, Cheapside, 1843), p. 381.

3. *The Norton Anthology of English Literature,* revised, vol. I (New York: W. W. Norton, 1968), p. 1507.

4. Voltaire, *The Best-Known Works of Voltaire* (New York: Blue Ribbon Books, 1927), p. 435, p. 185, p. 461.

5. Edmund Burke, *Reflections on the Revolution in France* (Chicago: Henry Regnery Co., 1962).

6. Peter J. Stanlis, "The Modern Social Consciousness," *The Occasional Review,* February 1974, p. 89.

7. Edmund Burke, *An Appeal from the New to the Old Whigs,* 1791, in Peter Viereck, *Conservatism* (New York: D. van Nostrand, 1956), p. 30.

8. Edmund Burke, "A Letter to a Member of the National Assembly," 1791, *Edmund Burke's Works,* 1871, in *Edmund Burke on Revolution,* ed. Robert A. Smith (New York: Harper Torchbook, 1968), p. 150, p. xiv.

9. Thomas Paine, *Rights of Man* (Part I, 1791; Part II, 1792), ed. Henry Collins (Baltimore: Penguin Books, 1976).

10. Will and Ariel Durant, *The Age of Napoleon* (New York: Simon and Shuster, 1975), pp. 394–397.

11. Thomas Paine, *Age of Reason: Being an Investigation of True and Fabulous Mythology*, (New York: Thomas Paine Foundation, n.d.), pp. 6, 47, 186.

12. Herman Melville, *Billy Budd, Sailor (An Inside Narrative)*, ed. Harrison Hayford and Merton M. Sealts, Jr. (New York: Phoenix Books, 1966).

13. Herman Melville, *Moby Dick, or, The Whale*, ed. Leon Howard, (New York: Modern Library, 1950).

14. Hannah Arendt, *On Revolution* (New York: Viking, 1963), p. 79.

15. Will and Ariel Durant, *The Age of Napoleon* (New York: Simon and Schuster, 1975), pp. 440–447.

16. Ibid., pp. 420–421.

17. Will and Ariel Durant, *Rousseau and Revolution* (New York: Simon and Schuster, 1967), p. 520.

18. Johann Wolfgang von Goethe, *Faust*, trans. Charles E. Passage (Boston: Bobbs-Merrill, 1965).

19. Edward Wasiolek, "Dostoevsky: A Revolutionary Conservative," *Modern Age*, Winter 1964–65, pp. 62–68.

20. Fyodor Dostoevsky, *Notes from the Underground and the Grand Inquisitor*, preface by Ralph E. Matlaw (New York: E. P. Dutton, 1960), pp. x, xi, xii.

21. Fyodor Dostoevsky, *The Possessed*, trans. Andrew R. MacAndrew (New York: New American Library, 1962), p. 237.

22. Fyodor Dostoevsky, *Notebooks for The Brothers Karamazov*, ed and trans. Edward Wasiolek (Chicago: University of Chicago Press, 1971), p. 8, p. 2.

23. Samuel Eliot Morrison, *The Oxford History of the American People* (New York: Oxford University Press, 1965), pp. 270–272.

24. Crane Brinton, *The Anatomy of Revolution* (Englewood Cliffs, N.J.: Prentice-Hall, 1952), pp. 52–53.

25. Hannah Arendt, *On Revolution* (New York: Viking, 1963), pp. 44–45.

26. M. Stanton Evans, *The American Revolution: A Study in Conservatism* (Bryn Mawr, Pa.: Intercollegiate Studies Institute, 1962), pp. 28–29.

27. Alexander Hamilton, James Madison, and John Jay, *The Federalist Papers* (New York: Mentor, 1961).

28. Peter Gay, *The Enlightenment*, vol. 2, *The Science of*

Freedom (New York: Alfred A. Knopf, 1969), p. 565.

29. Henry Steele Commager, *Documents of American History,* 7th ed., vol. 1 (New York: Appleton-Century-Crofts, 1963), pp. 159, 188.

30. Alexis de Tocqueville, *Democracy in America,* ed. Phillips Bradley (New York: Vintage Books, 1959), vol. 2, pp. 336–337.

PART III

Man's Current Reflection

From Plato's Chicken to Skinner's Pigeon

NOTHING HAS EVER been more insupportable for a man and a human society than freedom. . . . Did you forget that man prefers peace, and even death, to freedom of choice in the knowledge of good and evil? Do you know that centuries will pass, and humanity will proclaim through the mouth of their wisdom and science that there is no crime, and therefore no sin, there is only hunger?[1]

Thus, in Dostoevsky's allegory, the Grand Inquisitor admonished the risen Christ before he burned him at the stake because Christ had refused to succumb to the temptations of Satan and thus provide people with what they really want—miracle, mystery, and authority—instead of freedom to choose between good and evil. Christ had refused to turn stones into bread, though by doing so he would have promised man the miracle of materialistic security, and mankind would have followed him like a flock, fearful only that he would withdraw this miraculous manna (this secular and permanent food, so contrary to the temporary manna which God had sent to the Israelites) from them. He refused to cast himself from the pinnacle of the temple as later, though reviled by the gawkers, mocked by the chief priests, and gibed by the thieves, He refused to prove Himself the Son of God by descending, unmarked and unharmed, from the cross. These twin refusals to demonstrate his mastery of the mystery of life indicated that man's love must be

115

freely given to God, not expressed as the rapture of an awe-struck slave. And He refused, also, to accept the sword of Caesar, representing the authority before which mankind yearns to kneel.

Above all, admonished the Inquisitor, man seeks someone to worship, someone to keep his conscience, and some way to unite all mankind into one universal ant hill.

Dostoevsky's theodicy is one in which the essential relationship between God and man is love, freely given, not enticed through seductive temptations of miracle, mystery, and authority, though this freedom of choice between good and evil often entails loss of pleasure, loss of security, and much suffering.

As Dostoevsky rejected the clerical utopia of the inquisitor, he also scorned the "scientific" utopia of his contemporary Chernyshevsky and the "scientific socialism" of Saint-Simon. In *The Possessed* he inveighed against the pseudo-science incorporate in such schemes which promised man secular miracle, mystery, and authority, calling it ". . . that terrible scourge of mankind, a scourge worse than plague, famine and war, an evil which didn't exist until this century."[2]

Our reluctance to accept our human responsibility in freedom of choice between good and evil led us, as we repudiated the authority of the established church represented in the figure of the Grand Inquisitor, to place our credulous faith in science. Increasingly we look to what we believe to be science to keep our conscience as we worship its miracles, gape in awe at its mysteries, and humbly bow to its authority.

Scientific Utopia: Once Clear, Now Confused

Many eighteenth-century philosophers were convinced, as Carl Becker astutely observed, that science was soon to reveal the "constant and universal principles of human nature," and they believed that they would bring Saint Augustine's City of God down to earth as they persuaded man to accept the few simple scientific formulas which they were on the verge of discovering.[3] Despite their failure, during the past two hundred years, to verify scientifically a single theory about human nature, many behavioral scientists (earlier called moral philosophers, then social scientists) are still convinced that they are giddily teetering on the verge of such miraculous discovery of life's mystery while educated people accord them authoritarian homage.

Real scientists, such as physicists, have long recognized that the dreams of the eighteenth-century philosophers were whimsical fantasies, and at the 1976 joint meeting of the American Physical Society, the National Academy of Sciences, and other scientific groups, several of our most prominent physicists admitted that their knowledge of the laws which control even the most elementary natural phenomena is much less certain now than it was a century ago, and they wondered if the assumption of simple and uniform natural laws on which physical sciences had been based for more than two centuries were justified.[4] They wondered if their present state of knowledge was analogous to that of those pre-Copernican astronomers who constructed epicycles within cycles within epicycles to "prove" that the universe revolved around the earth; and Dr. John A. Wheeler, one of the architects of modern physics, said:

> We can well believe we have not understood the first thing about what physics is, not the first thing about who we are and what the world is.

As an illustration of this loss of certitude about even the simplest form of matter, the atom was for many years thought to be the irreducibly smallest possible particle. John Dalton, a founder of atomic theory, wrote: "We have endeavoured to show that matter, though divisible in an *extreme* degree, is nevertheless not *infinitely* divisible."[5] But then Lord Ernest Rutherford described the atom as being, in fact, divisible and made up of a nucleus surrounded by electrons. Rutherford's description was more complicated, but was still a tidy construction in that the negatively charged electrons travelled, as did the planets in their uniform paths about the sun, in orderly fashion around the positively charged proton nucleus which, physicists were then convinced, was solid and irreducible.

Now, in addition to electrons and protons, the atom is believed to contain neutrons, nucleons, positrons, mesons, pions, muons, hadrons, leptons, baryons, antibaryons, neutrinos, color forces, color, gluons, charms, charmonium, charmed hadrons, and antimatter. *Antimatter?* Are we asked to believe that matter is in part made of antimatter which is composed of antiparticles? Yes; and we haven't even mentioned the quarks: the up quarks, down quarks, strange quarks, and, possibly, charmed quarks! The designation "quark" is taken from a line in James Joyce's *Finnegan's Wake*, in much the same manner that Sir Arthur Eddington (whose parable of the fishing net was referred to in Chapter 2 to illustrate some of the limitations of scientific method) took the term "jabberwocky" from Lewis Carroll's *Alice in Wonderland* to describe an arcane process in physics.

Perhaps, with such distinguished precedent, I will be forgiven if I turn to the same source to describe the meaning of science as it is currently used in the behavioral sciences.

Behavioral Science Is Glory

Humpty Dumpty chided Alice for celebrating her birthday, which came only once a year.[6] Instead, he said, she should celebrate her un-birthdays, because there were three hundred and sixty-four of them. To replace a single birthday present with three hundred and sixty-four un-birthday presents—that would be *glory*, announced Humpty Dumpty, and when Alice said that she didn't know what he meant by "glory," he informed her that glory meant a nice knock-down argument. When Alice objected that "glory" doesn't mean "a nice knock-down argument," Humpty Dumpty scornfully pronounced:

> "When I use a word, it means just what I choose it to mean—neither more nor less."

> "The question is," said Alice, "whether you *can* make words mean so many different things."

> "The question is," responded Humpty Dumpty, "which is to be master—that's all."

Americans especially make a fetish of science and, as chemist Anthony Standen put it some years ago, it is our modern version of the sacred cows which others worshipped in the past.[7] Though the idea of a value-free science in studies which describe

118

the vital aspects of human social behavior is absurd, it is quite commonly held in this society which indiscriminately worships science and has all but canonized scientists.

Science, the Humpty Dumpty word in question, means simply "to know" in its root sense, but since most of the things we know (our name, our street address, our height and weight, and numerous other discrete items), while useful, are clearly not at all scientific, and we should feel foolish if someone acclaimed us as a scientist simply because we knew our own telephone number or zip code. So it is not the root sense of the word science which is important, but its connotation.

Most Americans seem to believe that science connotes a procedure that infallibly leads to answers that are true—permanently true—and entirely devoid of prejudice; answers which once arrived at must be accepted, not further argued. But to reach such objective seeming-truths, a specific procedure must be followed.

Controlled Observation: Each item of data in a scientific study must be transformed into a variable which every competent person, no matter what his bias, can accept. Such agreement can be attained only when all the data have been reduced to quantitative, uniform, stable units. Thus the subject matter of science is found in the measurement of weights, heights, distances, pressures, velocities, and other quantitative units that can be recorded on speedometers, odometers, altimeters, scales, gauges, and similar instruments.

All of the many sentiments and emotions, hates, fears, loves, preferences, and prejudices that are so vital to us as persons and so important in our relations with others are qualitative and unpredictably variable. None of these and other qualities so essential to our conception of ourselves and so prominent in our feelings toward others has ever been reduced to quantitative, uniform, and stable units, and hence they are quite unsuitable for scientific investigation.

Hypotheses also constitute an integral element in the indivisible—it is risky to accept a conclusion which is *partly* scientific—code of scientific procedure. Since even the simplest act and the most elementary mental process involves literally billions of facts, the eminent philosopher of science, Alfred North Whitehead, described the collection of facts—which many pe-

119

dantic persons extol by prefacing the approach to every social problem with "let's get the facts . . ."—as a method which, if pursued consistently, will leave science exactly where it found it.

The collection and the statistical manipulation of facts by themselves have little meaning unless the data are carefully contained within an hypothesis which can be tested. Hypotheses should be explicitly stated so that other investigators, critical of the findings, can also test them. They should be so described that it is not possible to derive contradictory conclusions from the same data. They should be so formulated that it is possible, through controlled observation, to prove them wrong.

Virtually all of the so-called scientific conclusions described by behavioral scientists involve facts without hypotheses or are based on hypotheses (such as all of the major assumptions that constitute the foundation for psychoanalytic conclusions) which cannot possibly be verified by controlled observation. In neither case do such procedures meet the standards and tests which are essential to reach a valid scientific conclusion.

Verification is the crux of scientific procedure, and one of the more common tests of it is prediction. Unless predictions can be made, unless they are consistently accurate, and unless their accuracy is based on a stated invariable and immutable relationship between natural phenomena, the hypothesis needs to be reexamined and likely replaced by another. Prominent among the areas in which social scientists have attempted predictions are economic trends, opinion polls, and population forecasts. In all of these areas the results have been repeatedly and grossly wrong.

Even when all of these necessary procedural steps are followed and other safeguards are employed to assure objectivity, there is no guarantee that scientific conclusions are true in any but a temporary and special sense, as was amusingly pointed out by Dr. Alexander Calandra, a teacher of science.[8]

Scientific Fetishism

To show that we can make a fetish of "proper scientific procedure," and that we sometimes use it though other methods

120

may be better, Dr. Calandra told of a student who took an examination in an elementary course in physics. One question was: "Show how it is possible to determine the height of a tall building with the aid of a barometer." Instead of giving the pedantically desired answer, derived from the formula that relates changes in atmospheric pressure as indicated by barometric readings to changes in altitude, the student gave a simpler but more accurate answer: "I would," he said, "take the barometer to the top of the building, attach a long rope to it, lower the barometer to the street, and then pull it up, measuring the length of the rope. The length of the rope is the height of the building."

When the student received a zero for his correct but unwanted answer, he proceeded to show that the height of the building could be ascertained, also, in other ways; most of them more nearly accurate than the "scientifically correct" way. He told how one could drop the barometer from the top of the building and by timing its fall with a stopwatch determine the height of the building by applying the law of falling bodies; or one could measure the length of the barometer, measure the length of the shadow it cast and the length of the shadow cast by the building at the same time, and by the use of simple geometric proportions ascertain the height of the building.

His best answer, simplest and most nearly accurate, ignored scientific procedure entirely. He said he would ". . . take the barometer to the basement and knock on the superintendent's door. When he answers say 'Here, I have a very fine barometer. If you will tell me the height of this building, I will give you this barometer.' "

Science Can Add to Ignorance

Scientific procedure, undoubtedly the finest technique available to reach conclusions about some kinds of problems, should not be applied blindly and automatically to all problems. However excellent, it must be used with imagination, discrimination, and prudence. Even in its most appropriate and very best usage the limitations which Sir Arthur Eddington illustrated in his parable of the ichthyological interpretation of the catch of a fishing net apply. As cited in Chapter 2, there is a factual weak-

121

ness in every scientific conclusion because, no matter how precise the technique (exemplified by the fishing net), most facts associated with the phenomenon will slip through into oblivion. The psychological fallacy is perhaps even more important than the factual weakness in those studies which deal with human beings and their relationships. Here, especially, we "see" only what our bias leads us to believe important. In these areas of study this psychological tendency is a much graver limitation than it would be to an ichthyologist who, despite the array of other forms of life caught in his net, "sees" only the fish because they are the focus and limit of his interest.

Since the psychic and emotional parts of our lives, our inmost thoughts and deepest feelings, our fears and loves, our likes and dislikes, our preferences and prejudices, are qualitative rather than quantitative, and unpredictably variable rather than stable, the techniques of controlled observation cannot sensibly be used to collect data about them, to verify hypotheses or to rebut them. Nor can predictions be made from the conclusions we reach.

How Many People Can Be Swept Under a Rug?

If behavioral scientists were able to make predictions about any aspect of human beings, they should have no difficulty at all predicting how many people there will be at some given time in the future. All other aspects of human behavior and social relationships are much more complex than this, and if scientists encounter difficulty on this simple level, their difficulties on all other levels will be multiplied many times over. So, rather than elaborate on the difficulties of predicting complicated aspects of human behavior, I shall limit my illustration of the impossibility of predicting human behavior to some of the failures to predict on the simplest level the number of people who will inhabit these United States in the future.

As a basic difficulty, the Bureau of the Census admits that its count in the latest (1970) census was likely at least 5,000,000 short. This factor alone—not knowing the base from which one begins—makes predictions of future populations suspect.

In 1936 the U. S. Bureau of the Census predicted that the

122

ultimate upper limit of our population would be 143,000,000 people and it would be reached in 1955.[9] In 1955, the population was 166,000,000, and not only still increasing but rising in a manner which many writers described as a "population explosion."

In 1953, by this time properly changing its estimate of the future population from "prediction," the Bureau of the Census *projected* a population of 221,000,000 by 1975. It was 213,000,000 in 1975. In 1958 the Bureau of the Census projected 244,000,000 by 1975. Our population was 213,000,000.

Whether grandiosely designating its forecasts "predictions" as it did in the past, or more properly calling its estimates of the size of future populations *projections*, the Bureau of the Census has, in all of its estimates of twenty years or more into the future, been seriously incorrect. To compensate for its inability to forecast the size of future populations with any high degree of accuracy, the Bureau of the Census now makes four projections into the future, and we are now informed (in the *Statistical Abstract of the U.S.* for 1976) that according to 1974 projections our population in the year 2050 will be somewhere between 227,000,000 and 499,000,000—a difference of 272,000,000 people!

So consistent are the errors and so great is the difference between projections that it seems clear we cannot even come close to accurate prediction of even the simplest aspect—numbers of people—of human life.

These erroneous population projections are not presented as a criticism of the Bureau of the Census, but only to make the point that if prediction is not possible on this simplest level, how very far away we are from being able to do it on much more complicated levels such as sex, family life, criminality, politics, economics, and all of the other significant aspects of human concern. To its credit, the Bureau of the Census did abandon the term "prediction," with its connotation of accuracy, for the more modest (and more nearly apt, though perhaps "estimate" would be even better) term "projection."

By contrast, the authors of some sociology textbooks have boasted that their scientific knowledge about race relations, population, criminology, the family, group behavior, the evolution of institutions, the process of social change, and other areas is as enduring as the Rock of Gibraltar and will be as true centuries hence as now![10]

Such claims by sociologists, anthropologists, psychologists, political scientists, economists, and other behavioral scientists are, of course, empty bombast, but unfortunately they are believed by many people, especially many educated people, to be the objective truth about the nature and the future of man. Many more such claims could be cited,[11] and numerous articles and books have been written to show the fallacies in such assertions of scientific certitude about human affairs,[12] but it is not my responsibility, nor that of anyone else, to disprove such claims; it is the positive and intellectually inescapable responsibility of those who make them to prove their case beyond reasonable doubt. But since the eighteenth century when such claims were first made down to the present not a single instance exists where this has been done.

This is not to say that accurate forecasts about human beings and social events are impossible. One may be correct in forecasting economic trends, or war, or the winner of the World Series or the Superbowl, but such accurate forecasts are the result of astuteness, luck, knowledge of the phenomena, a good sense of how people will react, and other qualitative elements that may be summed up as being good sense and good judgment, not science.

Benjamin Franklin was remarkably accurate in forecasting the growth of population in the United States and in 1840, with eerie prescience, Alexis de Tocqueville forecast what is happening to our society today. But the methods of behavioral sciences serve more to detract from long-range accuracy than to contribute to it, and in relation to major issues of the future an intelligent layman or an intuitive novelist is more likely to be accurate in his forecasts than a behavioral scientist.

In addition to assuring us that we were faced with a potentially disastrous "population explosion" just before our birthrate plunged to its all-time low, behavioral scientists have "predicted" that crime rates would decrease once the level of employment and wage rates rose; when we adopted the prescriptions of criminologists in the form of indeterminate sentences, probation, parole, and psychiatric counselling; and as public housing replaced slums. Instead, crime rates rose to unprecedented heights. Behavioral science experts assured us that divorce rates would decline as we adopted their recommendations, whereupon divorce rates rose to all-time highs, and marriage rates which, we were assured, would increase, have now decreased to a dangerously low level. Similarly, a decline in the rates of mental disorder was forecast as wage levels increased, as competition decreased, as economic and social security in the form of public assistance, unemployment compensation, old-age pensions, Medicare, and Medicaid made our lives less worrisome, and courses in mental hygiene were introduced into schools. The incidence of mental disorder thereupon rose astronomically.

The Falseface of Science

Claims of objective and permanent truths about human behavior do not evolve out of real scientific procedure (controlled observation; hypotheses which can be proved or disproved by controlled observation; and verification as evidenced by prediction), but they arise from false science, scientism, and only by rare chance do they happen to be correct.

There are many ways to make people believe that conclusions about human behavior are scientific when they are not, ways which I have described in *Social Problems and Scientism* and which are related in the several other sources cited in the references appended to this chapter. Here I shall give just one illustration of such intellectually misleading devices: the use of a soft definition of science.

Soft definitions of science are widely used by authors of books which claim to contain scientific conclusions about personal and social behavior. The authors of one prominent sociology textbook, for instance, contend that a scientific conclusion can be reached merely by (1) gaining knowledge through one of our senses, (2) relating such knowledge to other facts, and (3) finding someone else who agrees with our conclusion.[13] Any time, therefore, that you (1) stick out your hand and feel water drop on it and then (2) conclude from previous experience that when this happens it must be raining, and (3) confirm your hypothesis with someone else, you have reached a scientific conclusion.

You could extend this scientific conclusion into the far reaches of metaphysics by inferring that if it is raining and if

125

you stay out in it, you will get wet. You could then make a daring inferential quantum leap to the conclusion that if you don't want to get wet you'd best go inside. Ergo, by such soft definition a scientist is anyone who knows enough to come in out of the rain!

There is no law which requires that everyone must use a rigorous rather than a loose or soft definition of science, but it seems likely that unless this term is described with a fairly high degree of intellectual discipline its deserved prestige will soon be eroded. One should especially limit one's use of the term if there is any likelihood that people might apply one's "scientific" conclusions, erroneously believing them to be totally objective and permanently true, to their own lives. A good standard, it seems to me, is to use the term "scientific" only if one is content to have others use it similarly to reach conclusions which one thoroughly dislikes.

In one of the chapters of a sociology textbook,[14] for example, its editors strongly assert that their conclusions are scientific, using as their authority for the scientific status of their sociological conclusions a book titled *Can Science Save Us?*, written by Professor George A. Lundberg.[15] In another chapter of their textbook these authors flatly claim that science has proved that no significant differences between races exist. The paradox in this instance lies in the circumstance (apparently unknown to the authors of the textbook) that the authority for their claims to scientific validity (including their purported proof about the absence of significant racial differences) was for many years a prominent member of an organization (the International Association for the Advancement of Ethnology and Eugenics) devoted to finding "scientific" proof that significant racial differences *do exist*. One can't have it both ways.

Among the many books claiming to present a scientific description of man, I should like to select two which have received high acclaim and broad support for their claims, to show how this pseudo-scientific, scientistic approach, today as in the eighteenth century, inevitably reduces man to a puppet.

In 1964 a book titled *Human Behavior: An Inventory of Scientific Findings* was published.[16] On the jacket and in widespread advertising,[17] the publishers claimed that this book contained 1,045 scientific answers to questions such as what causes divorce, how extensive is sexual activity, and how effective is

126

psychotherapy. These 1,045 findings were an inventory of conclusions derived from the best research done in the behavioral sciences (anthropology, economics, history, political science, psychology, and sociology) to that date.

An elaborate but pitifully loose definition of science introduced these 1,045 findings, and they were summed up by describing the kind of man that the "science" of the 1960s produced. The image of man produced by the best findings from all of the behavioral sciences is acknowledged to be the "Big Question," ... "the most fundamental question of all." "If this were all we knew about man, what would he appear to be?" The answer:

> ... behavioral science man is social man—social product, social producer, and social seeker. ... Our man seeks virtue through reason far less than he seeks approval through the people around him; his evil comes from frustration, not from inherent nature. ... The traditional images of man have stressed, as prime motivating agents, reasons or faith or impulse or self-interest; the behavioral science image stresses the social definition of all these. Here, the individual appears less "on his own," less as a creature of the natural environment, more as a creature making others and made by others.

Authors Berelson and Steiner admit, rather sorrowfully it seems, that behavioral science has little to say about nobility, moral courage, ethical torments, the delicate relation of father and son or of the marriage state, life's way of corrupting innocence, the rightness and wrongness of acts, evil, happiness, love and hate, death, even sex. They should have anticipated the absence of these most vital elements of life in their findings because such attributes are impossible to catch in the nets which behavioral scientists use.

In the very nature of its methods of study, scientism can produce only a hollow man, a looking-glass man, a culturally conditioned puppet.

What Profiteth Skinner's Man?

Burrhus Frederic Skinner attended Hamilton College in Clinton, New York, and according to several accounts he had a flair for writing in addition to a good deal of mechanical ability. He hoped to become a novelist but, failing in this, he became a professor of psychology at Harvard. In a 1968 survey of chairmen of psychology departments at American universities, he was overwhelmingly chosen as the most influential figure in modern psychology. The magazine *Psychology Today* predicted that "when history makes its judgment, he will be known as the major contributor to psychology in this century." In 1971, the American Psychological Association gave him its annual award and hailed him as "a pioneer in psychological research, leader in theory, and master in technology, who has revolutionized the study of behavior in our time. A superlative scholar, scientist, teacher and writer." Also in 1971, he was runner-up to attorney William M. Kunstler for the Senior Fellow Award of the University of Notre Dame.

These and other honors which have been so abundantly showered upon Professor B. F. Skinner provide a gilded frame for a man who is rich in academic awards and ranked high in the esteem of his intellectual peers, but perhaps they obscure rather than reveal Skinner the man who says "yet, yet, I am unhappy."

Despite his personal unhappiness, or mayhap because of it, he is convinced that we shall perish if we do not follow his scientistic prescriptions and we are guaranteed contentment if we do.

In his 1971 *Beyond Freedom and Dignity,* Professor Skinner warns us that we are faced with "terrifying problems" involving a "population explosion," "nuclear holocaust," "world famine," and "ghettos." "Things," he sepulchrally intones, "grow steadily worse," and "new horrors" arise which we must resolve or "all is lost."[18] But Professor Skinner follows his doomsday pronouncements by consoling us that wonderful possibilities are within our reach. We can have a world in which people can live together without quarreling, they can maintain themselves by producing all of the food, shelter and clothing they need, they can enjoy their own lives and contribute enjoyment to the lives of others in art, music, literature, and games. These undemanding Skinnerian products consume only a reasonable part of the resources of the world and, considerately, they add as little as possible to its pollution. They bear no more children than can be raised decently. Having been conditioned to know themselves accurately, they manage themselves effectively.

Which Way to Utopia?

All we need do, not only to avert our imminent catastrophes, but to whisk ourselves into utopia, is to grasp the significance of operant conditioning, which means that when behavior is followed by a certain kind of consequence it is more likely to occur again, and a consequence having this effect is called a reinforcer.[19] Food, for instance, is a reinforcer to a hungry organism and anything that the organism does which is followed by the receipt of food is likely to be done again whenever the organism is hungry. Some stimuli are called negative reinforcers; any response which reduces the intensity of such a stimulus—or ends it—is likely to be repeated if the stimulus recurs. Thus, if a person escapes from a hot sun by moving under cover, he is more likely than not to again move under cover if he finds himself in an unpleasantly hot sun. The reduction in temperature attained by moving under cover to avoid the direct rays of the hot sun reinforces the behavior it is "contingent upon"—that is, the behavior it follows. Operant conditioning also occurs when a person simply avoids a hot sun—when, roughly speaking, he escapes from the threat of a hot sun. (Whether this applies to mad dogs and Englishmen is not clear.) Negative reinforcers are called "aversive" in the sense that they are things that organisms, in a temporal sense, turn away from. The really important good things in our lives are positive reinforcers, and the really bad things are negative reinforcers.[20] What is ultimately good or bad are things, not the feelings of people.

129

All of this, while not very clearly expressed by Professor Skinner, sounds simple enough, being strongly reminiscent of trial and error learning; of Jeremy Bentham's Felicific Calculus; and of the ages-old observation that you can catch more flies with molasses than with vinegar. And when Professor Skinner's simple sounding ideas are coupled with trivial and ambiguous illustrations and presented in language which is wondrous to behold but difficult to decipher, one cannot help but recall H. L. Mencken's comments about Thorstein Veblen, who seems to be one of Skinner's mentors. About Veblen's writing, Mencken said: "Words are flung upon words until all recollection that there must be a meaning in them, a ground and an excuse for them, is lost. . . . Worse, there is nothing at the bottom of all this strident wind-music—the ideas it is designed to set forth are, in the overwhelming main, poor ideas, and often they are ideas that are almost idiotic."[21] Professor Skinner's writing is not so bad as that described by Mencken, but it is often awkward and frequently ambiguous.

A Compass Without a Needle

In *Beyond Freedom and Dignity* and in Professor Skinner's fictional version of utopia, *Walden Two*, we are asked to believe that profound scientific principles about human behavior can be deduced from children being compelled to wear a lollipop around their neck without licking it (the lollipop being powdered so that any licks taken on the sly can be detected); and from children being compelled at mealtime, for reasons unknown to them, and at the whim of their director, to stand and wait long past their accustomed time for eating. We are expected to derive scientific principles of human behavior because sheep stay within an enclosure which was once electrified to condition them against escape, but now no longer is. All such instances would seem to represent simple examples of negative Class One conditioning rather than of operant conditioning or of the uses of contingencies of positive reinforcement. In simpler terms, since a sheepdog acts as the deterrent to the escape of the sheep, and a director of the children sneaks his looks at their powdered lollipops and whimsically compels them to wait before dining, Skinner seems to more nearly describe authoritarian control and regimented obedience than operant (Class Two conditioning) or instrumental conditioning.

Despite these and many other evidential limitations, Professor Skinner insists that his conclusions are scientifically proved, asserting that *Walden Two* was founded on specific behavioral and cultural laws and precise ("Give me the specifications, and I'll give you the man") techniques.[22]

Unfortunately, Professor Skinner fails to supply substantive evidence or convincing examples to show that his operant conditioning actually works with even a semblance of the effectiveness he claims for it and, lacking such evidential support, he explains his failure to provide a sensible intellectual rationale for it by asserting that it cannot be explained in customary language.

Professor Skinner admits that a science of human behavior is by no means as advanced as physics or biology, but he says that the science of human behavior has an advantage in that it may throw some light on its own difficulties. He says that science *is* human behavior, and so is the opposition to science. He asks us to ponder on what has happened in man's struggle for freedom and dignity, and what problems arise when scientific knowledge begins to be relevant in that struggle? He assures us that these issues will be discussed "from a scientific point of view," but this does not mean that the reader will need to know the details of a scientific analysis of human behavior; a mere interpretation will suffice. We can reject traditional explanations if they have been tried and found wanting in an experimental analysis and then press forward in our inquiry with unallayed curiosity. Those instances of behavior which are cited (we are informed) are not offered as proof of the interpretation. The proof is to be found in the basic analysis—which is to remain secret. We are told that the principles used to interpret the instances of behavior which are cited have a plausibility which would be lacking in principles drawn entirely from casual observation. The text, Professor Skinner admits, will often seem inconsistent because English is full of prescientific terms. Though critics have argued that the apparatus used in the operant laboratory misrepresents natural behavior because it introduces an external source of power, we are reminded by Professor Skinner that men also use external sources of power when they fly kites, sail boats, or shoot bows and arrows.

Here, virtually verbatim, we have the core of Professor Skinner's contention that he has made scientific discoveries about human behavior which, when understood, will save us from destruction and steer us to utopia.[23] And here we have abundant illustration of language wonderful to behold but difficult to decipher. Rarely has linguistic confusion been so compounded.

How can a science of human behavior throw light on its own difficulties, and in what way would it be an advantage to know that the difficulties associated with a science of human behavior are insurmountable, both now and in the foreseeable future, and then to pretend that such difficulties do not exist?

What sense does it make, and how does it advance our understanding, to be told that "Science *is* human behavior, and so is the opposition to science." The same can be said of smoking cigarettes, eating spinach, spitting in public places, and picking one's nose.

New Myths for Old

Much additional criticism could be directed at the non-sequiturs, the linguistic barbarisms, and the syntactical assassinations (just how does one shoot a bow?) through which Professor Skinner heaves, grunts, bellows, and groans in his attempt to surround and smother the fact that no appreciable scientific evidence supports his grandiose claims.

Lacking solid evidence, Professor Skinner carefully avoids telling us what he means by "science," "scientific analysis," "behavioral science," "behavioral engineering," and similar terms, and the only examples which he cites have as their gamut the trivial and the absurd. He asks us to accept plausibility instead of evidence, and he rests his case on a strident repetition of claims that neither he nor anyone else can prove. In his tiresomely repetitive incantation of "science"—a science which, in the areas where he meanders, is without evidential support—

Professor Skinner, while renouncing the myths of freedom and dignity, asks us to replace them with his own myth—the myth of science.*

*Opposite the editorial page of the *New York Times*, August 11, 1972, under the lead "Freedom and Dignity Revisited," Professor Skinner attempted to rebut his critics. Strangely indeed, Skinner cites Fyodor Dostoevsky's assertion (in *Notes From the Underground*) that he would go mad rather than perform as a puppet pulled by the strings of false science as an example of scientific prediction, apparently believing that any statement in the future tense, if correct, is such a prediction! Many of his critics, says the professor, have patterned Dostoevsky in having ". . . shown a taste for destruction and chaos, some of it not far short of madness." And ". . . a kind of hysterical blindness" afflicts those who question his conclusions about the nature of man and the source of our salvation.

In further effort to answer criticism and to clarify the position he took in *Beyond Freedom and Dignity* and in other works, Professor Skinner published *About Behaviorism* in 1974. Again, he failed to supply any solid evidence to support his conclusions, merely repeating as incantations that "Thinking is behavior," "Discrimination is a behavioral process: The consequences, not the mind, make discriminations," "Human thought is human behavior," and "Thinking has the dimensions of behavior."

Professor Joseph Weizenbaum, reviewing Skinner's *About Behaviorism* in the *New York Times*, July 14, 1974, concluded that "One need not be against behaviorism, nor be a philosopher of science or a logician, one need only have respect for the English language to be disheartened, to say the very least, by the abuse language and logic are made to suffer in this book."

Despite his lack of proof and his inability to express clearly his negation of the old saw: "What is mind? Never matter. What is matter? Never mind," Skinner, by accident if not by evidence, may be correct. For those who believe, as did his predecessor, J. B. Watson, that thinking is nothing but subvocalized speech, and who can read without moving their mind but not without moving their lips; for those who believe that there is no such thing as abstract thought and who, in so believing, reject all mathematics; for those who are convinced that *all* the causes of behavior lie outside the individual and that man is totally lacking in responsibility, deserving neither praise nor blame and who, in so believing, reject all notions of capacity for choice, dignity, character, conscience, and integrity, Professor Skinner is an admirable leader, I think.

Professor Weizenbaum's *Computer Power and Human Reason*

133

Science, Falsely So-Called

Professor Skinner asserts his purpose thus:

> I propose to abolish autonomous man, the man who believes in freedom and dignity. His abolition is long overdue. He has been constructed from our ignorance and as our understanding increases, the very stuff of which he is composed vanishes. To man *qua* man we readily say good riddance. "How like a god!" said Hamlet. Pavlov, the behavioral scientist, emphasized "How like a dog!" That was a step forward.[24]

It is the positive responsibility of writers such as Professor Skinner who claim to have reached scientific truths about the deepest aspects of our lives to prove their claims with impeccable tested evidence as well as with irrefragable argument. Remembering this, and keeping in mind that one does not have to *disprove* a claim to scientific truth, I should like to analyze Professor Skinner's contention that "Pavlov, the behavioral scientist, emphasized 'How like a dog!' "

The term "behavioral science" was coined at the University of Chicago in 1949. Ivan Petrovich Pavlov died in 1936. Pavlov was a physiologist, and physiology was not included in the so-called behavioral sciences. I. P. Pavlov, a conscientious researcher, always stressed the many exceptions to his findings: that some dogs could easily be conditioned; some only with difficulty; and that it was virtually impossible to condition some dogs. He stressed the capacity of the dog, through its cerebral cortex, to modify (will to change) this process, and above all he stressed—exactly contrary to what Skinner would have his readers believe—that

> Obviously even greater caution must be used in attempting similarly to apply our recently acquired knowledge concerning the higher nervous activity in the dog (to men)—the more so, since the incomparably greater develop-

---

(W. H. Freeman, 1976) is an excellent analysis of the limits which pertain to attempts to equate computer calculations with human reason.

ment of the cerebral cortex in man is pre-eminently that factor which has raised man to his dominant position in the animal world. It would be the height of presumption to regard these first steps in elucidating the physiology of the cortex as solving the intricate problems of the higher psychic activities in man, when in fact at the present stage of our work no detailed application of its results is yet permissible.[25]

Similarly, W. H. Gantt, Pavlov's American translator, in his *Physiological Bases of Psychiatry* reminds us that:

Pavlov never described the classical conditional [Please note the use of the word "conditional" rather than "conditioned." "Conditional" more aptly stresses the tentative and temporary nature of the conditioning process, avoiding the connotations of "once make; never break": of the permanent-sounding "conditioned"] reflex as a law of nervous activity, but rather a central phsyiological phenomenon that was an aspect of the general law of temporary nervous connections and associations. Pavlov did not state that the classical conditional reflex was the law governing these phenomena, but was an extremely simple and crucial phenomenon that was itself governed by the same processes that control the other phenomena.[26]

Gantt also emphasizes, as does Pavlov, that man has capacities for speech, ideas, and the ability for conceptual learning which are either nearly or totally impervious to the conditioning process, so it would be interesting to learn where Professor Skinner derived his interpretation that Pavlov considered man to be like a dog.

Likewise, Pavlovian neurologist M. Jean-François Le Ny states flatly that:

It would be ridiculous to claim that human action, conduct and thought are "reflexly conditioned in the same sense as the salivation of Pavlov's dogs."[27]

Additionally, Jerzy Konorski, student of Pavlov and professor of neurophysiology at the Nencki Institute in Warsaw, Poland, in his authoritative *Integrative Activity of the Brain* repeatedly warns of the dangers inherent in attempting to apply the findings of infra-human conditioning to man, and seriously questions both the assumptions and the techniques used by Professor Skinner.[28]

To the degree that the process of conditioning relates to human beings in their societal relationships (whether it is designated reflexive conditioning, classical conditioning, Class One conditioning, Class Two conditioning, instrumental conditioning, or operant conditioning), much of the evidence conflicts with Professor Skinner's overly simple contentions about environmental determinism; but even if such conflict did not exist, Skinner has still failed to provide us with substantial, testable proof for his assertions, and this is the inescapable responsibility which he evades and tries to obscure with fractured syntax and flamboyant protestations about some hypostatized "basic scientific analysis" which he refers to repeatedly but never describes.

Vintage Vinegar

In *Beyond Freedom and Dignity*, we are warned that all kinds of epidemics still prevail and death stalks the land while hunger dehumanizes people. But we are given solace by the thought that: "Science will convert earth into a paradise. Hunger, let alone starvation, will be unknown; 'none will be rich, and none poor.' More than that: man will conquer his own nature. He will subdue not only 'the forces of evil which are without,' but, much more importantly, 'the base instincts and propensities which he has inherited from the animals below.' " What God had been in man's imagination, man will become in reality. Man will then be a creator.

This statement, which encompasses the essence of Skinner's 1971 contention that we must turn to science to save us, is a paraphrase only slightly changed from Winwood Reade's *The Martyrdom of Man*, first published in 1872.[29] In other words, Skinner is trying to sell vintage vinegar in plastic champagne bottles.

In essence, Professor Skinner's position can also be stated thus: My supreme object is to measure and master the world rather than to understand it. Since my object is to measure and master the world, I can make relatively little use of theology, philosophy, and deductive logic, and in their place I have enthroned science, and the technique of observation and measurement.[30] Here, with the only significant change being the one in which the single subject (Skinner) replaces the plural which related to the convictions of many of the eighteenth-century philosophers, we have the rancid taste of a thirst for dictatorial control disguised as a humane wish to spread scientific truth that has persisted for two centuries.

Skinner would seem to view himself as endowed with godlike powers that destine him to direct men into a reformed world of his creation. The scenario of *Walden Two* has as its narrator one Professor Burris, an obvious alter ego of Burrhus Frederic Skinner. The director of this scientifically engineered community and protagonist in this fictional utopia is T. E. Frazier, while the antagonist is one Professor Augustine Castle, an obvious reference to Saint Augustine's castle in the sky, *The Heavenly City of God.*

In colloquies between Frazier and Castle, narrator Burris describes Frazier as being relaxed, casual, calm, composed, humorous, understanding, and graceful. Castle is a fat, awkward, petulant clown who slams doors in pique, fulminates and growls as various husky noises issue from his throat, and his eyes pop when he incoherently harangues Goodman Frazier.

Toward the end of *Walden Two*, Burris describes Frazier, reclining on a hillside, ". . . lying flat on his back, his arms stretched out at full length. His legs were straight but his ankles were lightly crossed. He allowed his head to fall limply to one side, and I reflected that his beard made him look a little like Christ. Then, with a shock, I saw that he had assumed the position of crucifixion."[31]

Skinner repeats this godlike theme in an article in *Psychology Today.*[32] In ponderous rhetorical style, Skinner refers to Michelangelo's depiction of the creation of man in the Sistine Chapel and says:

> It is possible that we have misread Michelangelo and have reversed the roles of creature and creator. Is it not man who has created God? And will Adam not awake at last to an intelligent existence when the soporific virtues of Life and Mind have crossed the gap in the other direction?

137

Utopia: A Playground for Puppets

Assuming that, despite his dubious evidence and tenuous rationale, we do trust Skinner, and by following his prescriptions attain his promised utopia, thereby preventing our otherwise imminent destruction, at what cost do we gain this our profit?

We shall have to discard totally the conceptions of man which most people now hold. Man becomes a puppet, pulled by the strings of environmental stresses manipulated by Skinner and his behavioral engineers. Praise and blame, punishment and reward, must go.

> *The hypothesis that man is not free is essential to the application of the scientific method to the study of human behavior.* The free inner man who is held responsible for the behavior of the external biological organism is only a prescientific substitute for the kinds of causes which are discovered in the course of a scientific analysis. All these alternative causes lie *outside* the individual. ... These are the things which make the individual behave as he does. For them he is not responsible, and for them it is useless to praise or blame him.[33] [my emphasis]

Away, at once and for all time, with patriotism, devotion, bravery, and sin. We support our government only because it has arranged special contingencies for us; we support our religion only because of the contingencies arranged by the religious agency. We are brave only when environmental circumstances compel us to be, and what we believe to be sin is only an anomaly in our history of reinforcement.

Skinner gives us a scenario in which man, up to now, has been a mere child in respect of knowledge and, in consequence, of virtue; now, as a result of the development of science, man can determine what is the best thing to do; once he knows this he will constantly improve his condition. The development of science is bound to carry with it the constant improvement of the human condition, to a degree which will be, like the growth of science itself, unlimited.

Skinner's contentions might, to many, seem to constitute a new, daring, scientific hope for our future, but the preceding paragraph, which so succinctly describes Skinner's supposedly modern discoveries, actually refers to the dreams of philosophers of the eighteenth century![34]

Skinner's viewpoint on man has some legitimate predecessors, such as those who were criticized by the physician Galen (Caludius Galenus, A.D. 130–200) who said:

> Some of these people have even expressly declared that the soul possesses no reasoning faculty, but that we are led like cattle by the impression of our senses, and are unable to refuse or dissent from anything. In their view, obviously, courage, wisdom, temperance, and self-control are all mere nonsense, we do not love each other or our offspring, nor do the gods care anything for us.

Professor Skinner can also find support in some of the minor philosophers of the eighteenth century such as Pierre Nicole, and in more recent pseudo-scientific works exemplified by Professor George Lundberg's *Can Science Save Us?* (second edition, 1961), Professor Robert S. Lynd's *Knowledge for What* (1939), or the more recent *Chance and Necessity* (1971) by French biologist Jacques Monod.

But Professor Skinner's real, though unacknowledged mentors are neither scientists, pseudo-scientists, nor utopian analysts of man's estate, but Dystopians such as George Orwell (whose *1984* was published in the same year, 1948, as Professor Skinner's *Walden Two*) and the younger Aldous Huxley, whose *Brave New World* parodied the cynical approach of behaviorist John B. Watson, the psychologist who anticipated his successor, Professor Skinner, by pronouncing that:

> The behaviorist, in his efforts to get a unitary scheme of animal response, recognizes no dividing line between man and brute.

In Orwell's lucid and frighteningly prescient *1984*, the arch-villain O'Brien contends, as does Skinner, that men are infinitely malleable, and in *Brave New World*, the Controller nicely anticipates the Director of *Walden Two* and the promises of *Beyond Freedom and Dignity* by alleging that his people are happy because they get what they want and don't want what they can't get. They are not bothered by mothers or fathers or wives or children or deep-felt love; and they are so conditioned that they can't help behaving as they ought to behave. "Why," he asks, in precise anticipation of Skinner, "should anyone throw all this away in the name of liberty?"

God's Mercy Strained Through a Fishnet?

When we have attained Skinner's utopia, when, as advised by Dostoevsky's Grand Inquisitor, we have conquered freedom and made men happy, what manner of man remains? Our remnant may be content with his materialistic lot, but is he then superman or Nietzsche's last man—mass-produced and so despicable that he is no longer even capable of despising himself? Perhaps in his craven zeal to avoid the nuclear holocaust predicted by geopolitical military expert Skinner, our projected man will become T. S. Eliot's hollow man, dying not with a bang but with a whimper.

Our future Skinnerian man will, in any case, be Herman Melville's

> Man, disennobled, brutalized
> By popular science—atheized
> Into a smatterer.

And what now of our future man's creator? What of Professor Burrhus Frederick Skinner who insists upon making of himself a graven image?

May God have mercy on his external contingencies of positive reinforcement!

Chapter 7. References and Notes

1. Fyodor Dostoevsky, *Notes From the Underground and The Grand Inquisitor*, trans. Ralph E. Matlaw (New York: E. P. Dutton, 1960).

2. Fyodor Dostoevsky, *The Possessed* (New York: Signet, 1962), p. 237.

3. Carl Becker, *The Heavenly City of the Eighteenth-Century Philosophers* (New Haven, Conn.: Yale University Press, 1959), p. 103.

4. "Physicists Now Confront Possibility That Natural Action Is Ever Complex," *New York Times,* April 28, 1976.

5. Sheldon L. Glashow, "The Hunting of the Quark," *New York Times Magazine,* July 18, 1976.

6. Lewis Carroll, *The Annotated Alice*, with notes by Martin Gardner (New York: Clarkson N. Potter, 1960), pp. 268, 269.

7. Anthony Standen, *Science is a Sacred Cow* (New York: E. P. Dutton, 1950).

8. Alexandra Calandra, "Science Teacher Chides Teachers," *New York Times,* March 8, 1964.

9. In, among other places, *Philadelphia Public Ledger,* October 29, 1936.

10. William F. Ogburn and Meyer F. Nimkoff, *Sociology,* 3rd. ed. (New York: Houghton Mifflin Co., 1958), p. 19.

11. A. H. Hobbs, *The Claims of Sociology* (London: Stackpole, 1951).

141

12. Stanislav Andreski, *Social Sciences as Sorcery* (New York: Andre Deutsch, 1972); Jacques Barzun, *The House of Intellect* (New York: Harper and Row, 1959); Jacques Barzun, *Science: The Glorious Entertainment* (New York: Harper and Row, 1964); Ludwig von Bertalanffy, *Robots, Men and Minds* (New York: George Braziller, 1968); Jacob Bronowski, *Science and Human Values* (New York: Harper Torchbook, 1959); Har, Kyung Durk, *Social Laws* (Chapel Hill: University of North Carolina Press, 1930); A. H. Hobbs, *Social Problems and Scientism* (Harrisburg, Pa.: Stackpole, 1953); A. H. Hobbs, *The Vision and the Constant Star* (New Canaan, Conn.: Long House, 1956); Joseph Wood Krutch, *The Measure of Man* (Boston: Bobbs-Merrill, 1954); C. S. Lewis, *The Abolition of Man* (New York: Macmillan, 1950); C. S. Lewis, *That Hideous Strength* (New York: Macmillan, 1969); Floyd W. Matson, *The Broken Image* (New York: George Braziller, 1964); Catherine Roberts, *The Scientific Conscience* (New York: George Braziller, 1967); P. A. Sorokin, *Fads and Foibles in Modern Sociology and Related Sciences* (Chicago: Henry Regnery, 1956); Anthony Standen, *Science is a Sacred Cow* (New York: E. P. Dutton, 1950); J. W. N. Sullivan, *The Limitations of Science* (New York: Mentor, 1949); and F. Taylor, *A Short History of Science and Scientific Thought* (New York: W. W. Norton, 1963).

13. Raymond W. Mack and Kimball Young, *Sociology and Social Life*, 4th ed. (New York: American Book Company, 1968), p. 5.

14. Edward C. McDonagh and John E. Simpson, eds., *Social Problems: Persistent Challenges* (New York: Holt, Rinehart and Winston, 1965), pp. 513–523.

15. George A. Lundberg, *Can Science Save Us?* 2nd ed. (New York: David McKay, 1961).

16. Bernard Berelson and Gary A. Steiner, *Human Behavior: An Inventory of Scientific Findings* (New York: Harcourt Brace and World, 1964), pp. 662, 666.

17. A. H. Hobbs, "The Falseface of Science," *The Intercollegiate Review*, January 1965, pp. 17–22.

18. B. F. Skinner, *Beyond Freedom and Dignity* (New York: Alfred A. Knopf, 1971), p. 3.

19. Ibid., p. 27.

20. Ibid., p. 107.

21. George B. de Huszar, *The Intellectuals*, (New York: The Free Press, 1960) p. 144.

22. B. F. Skinner, *Walden Two* (New York: Macmillan, 1948), pp. 277, 292.

23. B. F. Skinner, *Beyond Freedom and Dignity* (New York: Alfred A. Knopf, 1971), pp. 22–23, 202–203.

24. Ibid., a condensation of statements from pp. 200–201.

25. I. P. Pavlov, *Conditioned Reflexes*, trans. G. V. Anrep, M.D., D.Sc. (New York: Dover Publications, 1960), p. 395.

26. W. H. Gantt, *Physiological Bases of Psychiatry* (Springfield, Ill.: Charles C. Thomas, 1958), p. 97.

27. Hilaire Cuny, *Ivan Pavlov: The Man and His Theories* (Greenwich, Conn.: Fawcett, 1962), p. 93.

28. Jerzy Konorski, *Integrative Activity of the Brain* (Chicago: University of Chicago Press, 1967), pp. 2–5.

29. John Passmore, *The Perfectibility of Man* (New York: Charles Scribner's Sons, 1970), pp. 262–263.

30. Carl L. Becker, *The Heavenly City of the Eighteenth-Century Philosophers* (New Haven, Conn.: Yale University Press, 1959), p. 17.

31. B. F. Skinner, *Walden Two*, p. 295.

32. B. F. Skinner, "The Machine That is Man," *Psychology Today*, April 1969.

33. B. F. Skinner, *Science and Human Behavior* (New York: Macmillan, 1953), pp. 447–448.

34. John Passmore, *The Perfectibility of Man*, p. 208.

Chapter 8

In Pink Neon

AS ROUSSEAU IN France, Goethe in Germany, Shelley in England, and many other youthful eighteenth-century intellectuals erupted in romantic rebellion against the cold objectivity of the scientistic rationalism of the philosophes, so, roughly between 1960 and 1970, many youths railed against the unpersonal way they were being treated in bureaucratic universities (please do not fold, tear, or spindle!) that prepared them only, they were convinced, to be fitted as insensate cogs in the Orwellian machine which society was becoming.

With touching sentiment and enviable elegance, such feelings were expressed in "Theodicy of 1984":

> Our ideal is a university, a community of scholars bound together by the search for knowledge and truth and feeling a sense of responsibility to their society. That ideal declares that teaching and learning are more important than economic self-interest, and where that ideal has been a reality, men have been able to face the future with self-confidence and hope. We believe in the defense of this ideal, but this vision of the university is being extinguished by a general social process of which Kerr [Clark Kerr, then President of the University of California] is both analyst and advocate.[1]

Bruce Payne, David Walls, and Jerry Berman, the Berkeley students who expressed these ideals and this fear, subtitled their article "The Philosophy of Clark Kerr," and they described the society of which president Kerr was both analyst and advocate as one which is fundamentally identical with the managerialism of Saint-Simon and the militarized capitalism of Edward Bellamy; all of these being societies in which a government of persons is replaced by the administration of things—because under their beneficent ægis persons are reduced to things. And in Kerr's new society the university would be handmaiden to this industrial state, with higher education centered around the production of technicians and managers to minister its needs.

These students were aware that it would be difficult to prevent the degradation of universities into knowledge factories, but they proposed to resist this trend, hoping thereby to postpone Kerr's Orwellian 1984 to perhaps 2025, rather than having it established by 1975, which they accused Kerr of attempting to do.

Within two years, the activities of a student Free Speech Movement at Berkeley had attracted nationwide attention, and student Mario Savio's widely publicized interpretation of the situation, "An End to History," paralleled that of "Theodicy," similarly pointing to president Clark Kerr as being largely responsible, saying that students of the University of California, in their efforts to attain free speech, had come against ". . . what may emerge as the greatest problem of our nation—depersonalized, unresponsive bureaucracy." Such bureaucracies, said Savio, begin as tools, means to certain legitimate goals, but they end up feeding on their own existence. He argued that the classical Christian formulation of the university was one in which it was in the world but not of the world, while "The conception of Clark Kerr, by contrast, is that the university is part and parcel of this particular stage in the history of American society; it stands to serve the need of American industry; it is a factory that turns out a certain product needed by industry or government."[2]

Many others joined in this protest about the manner in which American universities were being depersonalized, bureaucratized, and becoming creatures of the state, as administrators ignored the injunction of anarchist Bakunin (Mikhail Bakunin, rival of Karl Marx), and plunged mindlessly toward their own extinction as they sought to incorporate their universities into the communities in which they found themselves.

. . . Versus Technological Objectivity

Rather than attempting to describe these issues in their complexity, I shall limit the evaluation of the romantic criticisms of these students to the target of their attack, Clark Kerr, president of the University of California, who, ironically, received the American Association of University Professors' Meikeljohn Award for the manner in which he had liberalized faculty and student rights in the very year during which the Free Speech Movement erupted at Berkeley. I also wish to say that, unlike the student authors of "Theodicy of 1984," I feel that while Clark Kerr was an analyst of the "general social process" which they rebelled against, he was not an advocate of it.

Kerr described the course which he believed society will take in his *Industrialism and Industrial Man,* and while his interpretation leads to conclusions which are as repulsive to me as they are to the authors of "Theodicy," I feel that his analysis is dispassionate as well as intellectually perceptive.

Kerr contends that as the industrialization of societies proceeds, the conflict of ideologies (e.g., communism versus capitalism) will become blunted, and as this conflict fades a consensus society will emerge wherever industrialization is successful, and thus the cultural patterns of the world will intermingle, blending together harmoniously.

Class differences will vanish and other elites will be submerged as the inhabitants of industrialized societies become divided into the managers and the managed; and as distinctions between private and public enterprise diminish, the differences between private and public managers will dissipate.

The state, far from "withering away," will be all-powerful and will regulate conflict. Such conflict will not be class warfare but bureaucratic gamemanship wherein persuasion, pressure, and manipulation will take the place of face-to-face combat. In a memorable phrase, Clark Kerr foresees a time when "the

146

battles will be in the corridors instead of in the streets and memos will flow instead of blood."[3]

Workers will be increasingly regimented but they will accept greater restrictions on their activities at work because the increased efficiency of the new industrial state will give them higher standards of living, more leisure time, and their ". . . leisure will be the happy hunting ground for the independent spirit, during which they can practice [by the numbers, I suppose] a new bohemianism as a reaction against the restricted nature of their working life." "Utopia never arrives, but men may well settle for the benefits of a greater scope of freedom in their personal lives at the cost of considerable conformity in their working lives. . . ."[4]

Since intellectuals and students are volatile, with shifting opinions and no steady commitment to any single institution or philosophic outlook, they are not fully to be trusted in fostering the creation of this managerial society, but they must be used in its development.[5]

This reference to intellectuals and students being *used* is also found in Clark Kerr's 1963 Godkin Lectures at Harvard, later published in book form as *The Uses of the University*, and in this work also, it is difficult to determine whether Kerr is advocate or dispassionate analyst.[6]

Kerr does describe the university as something to be used, and he confesses that the multiple and often inconsistent characteristics which have attached themselves to American universities—British-oriented undergraduate life, German-modeled graduate studies, and American-style service to the state—should be kept as confused as possible for the preservation of the whole balance, thus describing (endorsing?) the hypocrisy which invariably characterizes university administrators as they exercise their "ready versatility of conviction."

As for the increasing reliance of universities on a growing variety of ever-expanding Federal grants, and the inescapable loss of academic independence associated with them, Kerr expressed the attitude of many university presidents in this limerick:

> There was a young lady from Kent
> Who said she knew what it meant

147

When men took her to dine,
Gave her cocktails and wine,
She knew what it meant—but she went.

Professor Kerr's description of the society of the future in *Industrialism and Industrial Man* is in the utopian tradition, and there are some interesting parallels between Kerr's career and that of Sir Thomas More, who first designated the ideal society "utopia." After publishing his *Utopia* in 1516, Sir Thomas became High Steward of Oxford in 1524. Clark Kerr, co-author of *Industrialism and Industrial Man*, was president of the University of California. More's thinking about the future was much influenced by the scientific theories of Copernicus, while Kerr was captivated by a belief in the inevitable governance of society by scientific technology. Both were fired from their university posts!

But there is a basic difference between the nature of the society envisioned by More and that forecast by Kerr. Sir Thomas stressed that society would only improve in the measure that men improved themselves; his utopia arose from the inner resources of men, while Kerr's evolved from impersonal forces imposed on men from without.

Edward Bellamy, whose 1887 projection of utopia, *Looking Backward*, which was translated into every important language and sold more than a million copies,[7] is much more nearly Kerr's mentor than is Sir Thomas More.

Bellamy's *Looking Backward* typified the utopias of the nineteenth and twentieth centuries in that he shifted the focus for the improvement of society from reform of the individual to reform of institutions; he assumed that inefficient and inequitable practices in economic production and distribution gave rise to most social ills; and he stated that the happiness and well-being of men will be attained primarily through economic efficiency.

While the asserted goal of Bellamy and Kerr was the happiness and well-being of men as individuals, both seemed to believe that economic efficiency was so essential to the attainment of these goals that the sacrifice of other human values was justified. Hence, it is understandable that students at the University of California were soon joined by many other students and intellectuals in romantic rebellion against the coldly mechanical materialistic determinism embodied in Kerr's future society, and that they rebelled also against the notion that the university was to lose its integrity as it was *used* by being relegated to the role of a factory which had as its primary function the production of technicians and managers to operate the new industrial state.*

Much more evidence could be offered and elaborated on to show how nicely the protests of the mostly middle-class college students of the 1960s paralleled the romantic rebellion of sensitive, youthful intellectuals against the dry objectivity of scientistic rationalism in the eighteenth century.

But the more recent student rebellion soon came to be principally associated and often identified with a single group, The Students for a Democratic Society (SDS), and as the abstract humanistic idealism exemplified in "Theodicy" merged with and then was absorbed into the concealed political aims of SDS, an

*As an illustration of the manner in which the idea of a university is changed from its conception as an independent center for the independent study of universal issues to one in which it is thought of as a creature of and for the state, Barbara Crossette describes ("Dispute Over New British College Reflects Nation's Ideological Split," *New York Times,* July 18, 1977) some of the objections encountered when the University College at Buckingham was established in 1973 as a private institution. The president of Britain's National Union of students complained that "The whole attempt in higher education has been to make universities more responsive to society as a whole ... education is a social good, not a private good."

Tudor David, editor of *Education,* a publication for school administrators, described what I believe to be a stronger argument in the effort to make man as well as the university a creature of the state by pointing out that "The bureaucrat believes the system he has created and is working for is perfect...." Thus fortified with the self-righteous conviction that he is laboring to perfect mankind, the bureaucrats who now run the things that are in the saddle can feel that their system constitutes "An End to History" and conscientiously resist any changes in it.

So the Government refuses to grant degrees to the graduates of the private college, refuses to permit them to take civil service examinations, and refuses them postgraduate grants.

illogical jointure of romanticism and scientistic rationalism evolved much as Dostoevsky anticipated it would.

A Mesalliance with Rationalism

In the introduction to *Notes From the Underground and The Grand Inquisitor,* translator Ralph E. Matlaw points out how Dostoevsky perceived that while Hegel's dictum "all that exists is rational, all that is rational exists" constituted a logical basis for scientistic rationalism, it also, less logically, became attached to Rousseau's romanticism, and the natural rights of man became translated into scientistic, psychological verities, absolving the individual and placing all blame on the environment.[8] And as such apparently antithetical concepts became entangled in Chernyshevsky's utopia of the nineteenth century, they entwined themselves also in the student movements of the twentieth.

Thomas Hayden, president of SDS, in "A Letter to the New (Young) Left," stressed that "radicalism as a style involves penetration of a social problem to its roots, its real causes. Radicalism presumes a willingness to continually press forward with the query: Why?" ". . . radicalism of style demands that we oppose delusions and be free."[9] In the "Port Huron Statement," issued at their first national convention (1962), SDS expressed its feeling that the new left must include liberals and socialists, the former for their relevance, the latter for their sense of thorough-going reforms in the system, so that people may see the political, social, and economic sources of their private troubles and organize to change society. Thus SDS stressed rationalism more than romanticism.

An excursion into the background of this seemingly romantic student movement of the 1960s may reveal some of the reasons why its inherent inconsistencies quickly became associated with bombast and bombs rather than with an idealistic improvement of man's estate.

In 1960 a socialist-oriented (but non-communist) organization of Social Democrats, called the League for Industrial Democracy, sponsored the organization of Students for a Democratic Society, to be supported by funds drawn principally

150

from the United Automobile Workers union and the Amalgamated Clothing Workers Union. SDS was successor to a previous student branch of the LID, the Student League for Industrial Democracy, established in 1928 by the LID in opposition to the communist-dominated National Student Union.

SLID, in turn, was successor to the Intercollegiate Liberal League of 1921, which succeeded the Intercollegiate Socialist Society, founded by socialist muckraker Upton Sinclair and novelist Jack London in 1905.

All of these student organizations were intellectual heirs to the American Fabian Society of 1895, which was the direct descendant of the British Fabian Society, established in 1883.

Prominent British intellectuals, such as playwright George Bernard Shaw, historian H. G. Wells, philosopher Bertrand Russell, historian Graham Wallas, and playwright John Galsworthy joined together in the British Fabian Society to "Remould the World Nearer to their Heart's Desire" by establishing a socialist state through the strategy employed by Quintus Fabius Maximus, called "the Delayer" because he avoided pitched battles, content to wear down his opponents through delay and harassment until they succumbed of their own weakness. Thus the Fabians, who adopted the slogan "The Inevitability of Gradualism," avoided an outright pitched battle (a vote) with their enemy (capitalism) and within some sixty years converted Britain into a socialist state.

The Fabians accomplished their goal through pamphleteering, heckling at meetings, and intellectual gnawing at the roots of capitalism. While the story of their success is interesting in its own right, I shall not further digress by a recital of it, instead narrowing the issue down to the manner in which they, and all who pursue a similar intellectual course, invariably not only change their conception of the relation between man and the state, but reverse it.

While many prominent and brilliant intellectuals participated in the British Fabian Society, the steady and prime movers were Beatrice and Sidney Webb, she the aggressively capable daughter of wealthy parents, he head of the fountainhead for the intellectual propagation of socialism, the London School of Economics.

In their early attempts to destroy capitalism and establish socialism, the Webbs exalted the supreme worth of the individual, saying:

> The essence of British socialism lies . . . in its determination to apply moral principles to social life . . . , insisting that the individual human personality is an end in itself. . . .
> Fabianism as a doctrine began with the conviction of the value of the human person and a belief that all men and women have an equal right to live their lives in a manner which seems to them morally good. The state exists for the individual, and the maintenance of his rights is its first duty.[10]

But as they approached nearer to an attainment of their goal, Sidney Webb changed his interpretation, now reasoning:

> Though the social organism has itself evolved from the union of individual men, *the individual is now created by the social organism of which he forms a part* [my emphasis]; his life is born of the larger life; his attributes are moulded by the social pressure; his activities, inextricably interwoven with others, belong to the activity of the whole.

This jointure of romanticism with the supposition that the innate goodness of man would emerge once the evils of the economic institution were eliminated shifted insensibly to the "rationalistic" assumption that man is not naturally good, but his goodness (or badness) is solely the product of his environment. The circle is completed as rationalism embraces scientism, and it is easy for those who trace this curve to ignore their jump from one plane of reasoning to another.

An account of the Webbs' 1932 visit to Stalinist Russia indicates their pleased discovery that:

> . . . the administrators in the Moscow Kremlin believe in their professed faith, and this professed faith is science.[11]

Here was a country where their dreams had come true. Russia was not, they admitted, a democracy. But was that, after all, so important? Was not free thought and speech a mockery of human progress, wrote Beatrice, ". . . unless the common people are taught to think, and inspired to use this knowledge in the interests of their commonwealth"?

This inherent inconsistency ultimately perplexes all social planners who try to blend the water of innate human goodness with the oil of socialist economic determinism. Influential political analyst Walter Lippmann, when president of the Harvard chapter of the Intercollegiate Socialist Society (ISS), youthfully proclaimed his adherence to the Fabian doctrine by describing the objectives of ISS thus:

> In a general way our object was to make reactionaries standpatters; standpatters, conservative liberals; conservative liberals and liberals, radicals; and radicals, Socialists. In other words, we tried to move everyone up a peg.[12]

However, with advancing years, pundit Lippmann realized that

> It's not possible by Government action or any other action I know to create a perfect environment that will make a perfect man.[13]

Ignorant of the history of movements such as theirs, unaware of the inconsistency inherent in thinking that they could combine the romantic concept of the natural goodness of man with the scientistic economic determinism of socialism, which is necessarily (though often unadmittedly) premised on the assumption that there is no such thing as human nature, their youthful zeal untempered by age and lacking the prudent judgment derived from practical experience, the ostensibly romantic students of the sixties were not only accepted at their own high opinion of themselves but often lauded as the brightest, most honest, and most courageous youths of any generation.

Certainly there was much justification for the issues raised in "Theodicy of 1984," "An End to History," the "Port Huron Statement," and many other reasoned as well as romantic objections to the bureaucratization of the university and of society in general, to the conversion of the university into the multiversity and creature of the state, to the injustices inflicted upon minori-

153

ties, and to the callous pointlessness of the Vietnam War. And thus many who sympathized with the student arguments and protests romantically portrayed them not only as a generation in revolt against the evils of the system but also as somehow endowed with virtues denied to others.

Millions of Americans accepted, at least for a time, the eulogy of youth in *The Greening of America* by Yale professor Charles A. Reich, who ecstasized that the unconventional clothing of youth expresses an affinity with nature being like architecture which does not clash with its natural surroundings, but blends in. Reich contended that jeans express freedom and nudge the wearer into deep questions—that they demonstrate a significant new relationship between man and technology and express profound democratic values.[14] The new generation, Reich said, though idle, is not lazy because most work is meaningless, degrading, and inconsistent with self-realization. Their music is a repository of fantastic energy, telling of a tranquil and fresh closeness to nature while it expresses the staccato experience of modern American life. Drugs establish a blood-brotherhood relationship with musicians and add a whole new dimension to creativity and to experience. Rock, the professor enthused, had achieved a height of knowledge, understanding, insight and truth concerning the world and people's feelings that is incredibly greater than what other media have been able to express.

Through their life-style, their denim jeans, their loafing, and their music, said Reich, youths of the sixties emerged from Consciousness I and II, which subordinated man's nature to his role in the economic system—Consciousness I on the basis of economic individualism, II on the basis of participation in its organization; both subordinating man to the state. Youth of the 1960s attained Consciousness III, which transcended science and technology, liberated man, freed him from linear and analytical thought, enabled him to build his own philosophy and life-style, his own culture in which he "rediscovers a childlike, breathless sense of wonder; this is the quality that Consciousness III supremely treasures, to which it gives its ultimate sign of reverence, vulnerability, and innocence, 'Oh wow!' "[15]

To which the only appropriate response would seem to be "Good Grief!"

In further support of such romantic interpretation, *The Times* of London referred to the SDS seizure ("liberation," the students called it) of five buildings at Columbia University in 1968 as "The Ruddite Rebellion." The immediate reference was to Mark Rudd, the publicized leader of the illegal seizures and the accompanying vandalistic destruction: and the inferential association was to Ned Lud, the eighteenth-century Lancashire workman whose destruction of factory equipment initiated much smashing of labor-saving machinery by other workmen who feared that developing technology would eliminate their jobs. This outbreak was called "The Luddite Rebellion." Since the universities had often been referred to as factories which were stripping students of their independence to make them cogs in the machinery of the state, the analogy seemed to have an appealing aptness.

Since most of the rioters who seized university buildings and sought to control these institutions became incoherent when asked what they would do if they did attain power, I half seriously stretched the figure into the Ruddite, Luddite, Buddite Rebellion to include in it Melville's Billy Budd, who was unable to express the totality of his intrinsic goodness because of his speech defect.

The Romantic Vision Fades

Gradually, even some of the more ardent supporters of the student rebellion began to feel that this was not really a new romantic movement, that neither its sources nor the expression of its discontent were unique. How meaningful, we began to wonder, really was the life-style? Was the long hair romantic or greasy, tangled, unkempt, and dirty? What was the significant difference between students who tie-dyed their jeans to discolor them, tore the bottoms of their slacks to make them look ragged, and sewed on patches where none were needed, and students of an earlier era who paid to have their white bucks dirtied and plucked threads in the elbows of their Cashmere sweaters to make them seem worn? Was rock, with all of its deafening electronic amplification, actually an expression of naturalness; were the "messages" con-

155

veyed by Bob Dylan's lyrics profoundly meaningful; were universal secrets to be learned by playing Beatles' records at varying speeds, and if so, did such messages make any more sense than Charles Manson's conviction that the Beatles' use of the phrase "helter-skelter" was proof that Armageddon in the form of racial war was nigh upon us?

I mean, was the language, y'know, like simple and—y'know what I mean—like honest or, I mean, like dumb, y'know what I mean, man, huh man? Was the profanity earthy and strong or were popular phrases such as "Fuck the draft!" and "The CIA sucks!" (involving syntactical rape as well as physiological absurdities) as banal as eighth-grade locker-room expressions? Was the constant "rapping" an effort to get to the roots of meaning or an attempt to avoid systematic study and disciplined analysis? Was the aggressively assertive passion for peace an expression of idealistic conviction or did they mistake their fear for virtue?

While newness is not a necessary adjunct to verity, much of the appeal of the highly publicized "romantic" protests of the sixties emerged from a belief that in their generational revolt youths had discovered daring and dashing forms to express ideas not only contrary to those of their parents but entirely fresh and new.

Yet centuries before the birth of Christ, Plato in his *Republic* described conditions in Athens wherein:

> Insolence they term breeding, and anarchy liberty, and waste magnificence and impudence courage. . . . The father gets accustomed to descend to the level of his sons and to fear them, and the son to be on a level with his father, having no shame or fear of his parents. . . . The teacher fears and flatters his scholars, and the scholars despise their masters and tutors. . . . The old . . . imitate the young . . . nor must I forget to tell of the liberty and equality of the two sexes. . . . They chafe impatiently at the least touch of authority, and at length . . . they cease to care even for the laws, written or unwritten.[16]

Russian student nihilists of 1862 are described as:

Young men and women in slovenly attire, who called in question and ridiculed the generally received convictions and respectable conventionalities of social life, and who talked of reorganizing society on strictly scientific principles. . . . Their appearance, manners and conversation were apt to shock ordinary people, but to this they were profoundly indifferent, for they had raised themselves above the level of so-called public opinion, despised Philistine respectability, and rather liked to scandalize people still under the influence of what they considered antiquated prejudices.[17]

As students of the sixties participated in Civil Rights marches, in the thirties students at Oxford and Cambridge participated in hunger marches.[18] British students sought to abolish Officers' Training Corps from their campus; American students tried to get rid of ROTC; both were against fascism, a favorite gimmick of the sixties being to spell America "Amerika." British students grew beards à la Lenin; American students emulated the beard of Che Guevera. Students at Cambridge had a Free Speech Movement thirty years before that at Berkeley; students of both eras and both countries protested strongly against social conventions, especially those relating to sex. While American students of the sixties chanted Ho, Ho, Ho Chi Minh, British students of the thirties lyricized "Stalin is My Darling." The British student left-wing socialist organization which dominated the thirties movement, the Federation of Socialist Societies, was infiltrated by Stalinist Communists. The American left-wing socialist organization which dominated the sixties movement, the Students for a Democratic Society, was infiltrated by Maoist (Progressive Labor Party) Communists.

Radical students of the sixties proclaimed that they were not obscene, the Vietnam War was obscene; they were not immoral, the Vietnam War was immoral. When asked if World War II was also obscene and immoral they expostulated, "No, it wasn't—it was completely different!"

Again their ignorance of the past condemned them to repeat it because in the late thirties pacifism among university students was vigorously expressed. The sixties' vulgar "Fuck the Draft" and "Hell, no, I won't go," was balanced by such pre-World War

II anti-war slogans as "The Yanks are *not* coming," and "This time, let God save the king!" Future Widows of America, shrouded in black and bearing coffins, paraded before the White House, and students at Princeton organized the Future Veterans of America, demanding, tongue-in-cheek, that their veterans' benefits be paid before they entered military service, so they might better enjoy them.

As the SDS was infiltrated by PLP (Maoist) Communists, the Student League for Industrial Democracy had been infiltrated by Stalinist Communists. Since Stalin and Hitler, at that time, had formed a non-aggression pact while they divided Poland between them, it was in the communist interest to keep America from entering into what was then called an imperialist, immoral war. Many of the demonstrations for nonentry, among the public as well as among students, were (unknown to most of the participants) engineered by communist-oriented groups. When Hitler attacked Russia, the propaganda reversed itself overnight. The American Peace Mobilization, designed to keep us out of this imperialistic, immoral European war, immediately became the American People's Mobilization dedicated to speeding our entry into this moral crusade to protect civilization from fascist beasts. The switch was so sudden and the adherence to the communist-line so obvious that SLID lost its intellectual credibility.

Another aspect of the romantic student movement which was at first sentimentally appealing but which later lost its attractiveness was the strident anti-establishment nature of the protests. While the faults of both the university and the societal establishment are many and certainly need correction as well as attention, more and more people became reluctantly, then painfully, aware that these young rebels of the sixties were not interested in ushering in a new life; they were merely obsessed with assailing the old.

Also, without being aware of the premises in which their thinking was rooted, they entrapped themselves in an old fallacy: the assumption that if the establishment is bad, all that is anti-establishment must be good; if the aristocracy is bad, the peasants must be good; if the wealthy are bad, everything associated with the poor must be good.

In her *On Revolution*, Hannah Arendt describes this pro-

158

cess during the French Revolution. ". . . Having seen the vices of the rich and their incredible selfishness, they concluded that virtue must be 'the appanage of misfortune and the patrimony of the poor.' " Since "the charms of pleasure were escorted by crime," they assumed that the torments of misery must engender goodness.[19]

College students should have been aware of this fallacy and avoided it because many have warned of its superficiality. Dostoevsky, as I indicated previously (Chapter 6), granted that the peasant was a carrier of ideals but insisted that the peasant beloved of romantic-rationalistic liberals was an hypostatized abstraction; that the real peasant, ignorant, slothful, greedy, sadistic, and drunken, yet retained that virtue of which romanticists were bereft—knowing when they sinned, and in their knowing acknowledging a higher law.

Many years later, Dostoevsky's countryman, Nobel award winner and indomitable foe of the communist suppression of human integrity, Aleksandr I. Solzhenitsyn, in his modern version of the level of purgatory which Dante reserved for intellectuals, *The First Circle*, describes how the intellectual Nerzhin, when forced to live among and be treated as a peasant in a prison camp, discovered that the supposedly sensitive and idealistic members of the intellectual elite who shared his fate often turned out to be cowards, quick to cave in, adroit in excusing their own vileness as they degenerated into beggars and hypocrites. And the peasants who represented The People had no homespun superiority, no greater stature, were no firmer of spirit than others.[20]

Milovan Djilas, a Yugoslav, but also an indomitable protester against those aspects of communism which denigrate the human spirit, similarly admits that, as youths coming from prosperous families he and his fellow revolutionaries had a romantic conception of The Worker but learned to their surprise that on the whole workers were no more courageous than others, and most of them had precious little interest in revolution.[21]

Despite these and many other indications that virtue is no more implicit in poverty than it is in wealth, youths of the sixties aped the mannerisms, the speech, and the clothing of the Underprivileged as British university students of the thirties wore corduroy trousers and workers' caps, dropped their aitches, and ate peas with a knife. Christopher Isherwood devoured enormous quantities of chocolates to ruin his teeth because he identified rotten teeth as a trait of the workers.

From Vision to Ego-shriek

Other factors contributed to a growing realization that student activists were not quite the innocent idealistic romanticists that they were first assumed to be.

A second look at Berkeley revealed that the university had a record of a greater degree of freedom of speech than most other universities, and that under the deceptive slogan of a Free Speech Movement a small group of political activists were attempting to establish the campus as a center of political action —a condition which would have destroyed its reputation as an educational institution.

The romanticism of the Ruddite, Luddite, Buddite conception of student revolt was considerably tarnished as Mark Rudd, leader of the seizure and vandalism of the buildings at Columbia University, admitted to the editors of *The Columbia Spectator* and at a speech at Harvard that the ostensible reasons for the seizure of buildings at Columbia were merely pretexts; they were, in his expression: "Bull." The real reason for inciting students to protest to the extent that it would necessitate a confrontation with the police was to radicalize them; this technique being a grotesque parody of Walter Lippmann's earlier attempts as president of the Harvard chapter of the Intercollegiate Socialist Society to radicalize students step by gradual step.

When a fellow-student asked Mark Rudd if he would carry vandalistic defacement so far as to destroy a Rembrandt in Columbia President Grayson Kirk's office, he replied, "There's nothing I wouldn't do."[22]

Zeal for pacifism was seen more and more clearly as a function of the nearness of the draft. At Harvard it was not until the draft directly affected college students that ". . . the war became *the* dining hall topic. . . . Now everyone, up to and including the Young Republicans, was against the war."[23]

When the Communist Progressive Labor Party members took control of the SDS at Harvard the agitation for peace and an early end to the war became a militant program for continuing it until the Vietcong were victorious. The SDS Anti-war Committee of November 1968 attacked the very idea of peace negotiations. In astonishing repetition of the Communist Party U.S.A. (Stalinist) take-over of the SLID in conjunction with World War II, the entire sixty-man Harvard delegation to the 1969 SDS convention were members of the Progressive Labor Party (Maoist) faction of the Communist Party.

Even more people began to wonder about the legitimacy of the idols acclaimed by the SDS. Ho Chi Minh could be respected for the doggedness of his patriotism, and perhaps some could derive more than Kahlil Gibran banalities from the thoughts of Mao Tse-tung, and Che Guevera certainly cut a dashing figure, but it was astutely observed that he needed the (Cuban) revolution more than the revolution needed him. And most rioters actually knew very little about these or others of their heroes, so it seemed that, lacking personal integrity and even idealistic goals, the students of the sixties selected as their heroes those who were far away or dead—preferably both.

Most of their swamis and gurus and drug-induced revelations had all of the depth of meaning of the conviction of Winston Churchill who, having wakened in the middle of the night convinced that he had discovered the secret of the universe, wrote it down and learned in the morning that all of life's problems can be resolved by a realization that "the whole is pervaded by a strong smell of turpentine."[24]

Unaware that they were hopelessly entangled in ideological confusion wherein their romantic conception of the innate goodness of man was interwoven with rationalistic socialist and communist doctrines of environmental determinism, and failing to attain Utopia Now! despite their unshakeable certitude in their own pure righteousness, student radicals became frantic, engaging in actions which increasingly were at variance with the attainment of any sensible goal.

By 1966 a campus survey indicated that formerly sympathetic professors, as well as many students, were becoming alienated from The Movement:

> At Wisconsin and Berkeley . . . radicals of the left shout down opposition, stifle debate over the war, or student

161

power, or faculty power, and call for the destruction of the "corporate-military system," which, they say, includes the university.

The editor of the *Wisconsin Daily Cardinal* said: ". . . the extremists have broken down, intellectually and psychologically. Instead of asking themselves 'What is the problem? What can be done about it?' they're asking, 'What is the most radical thing to do?' "

On all five campuses visited, the new leftists were beginning to argue that the "Higher Morality" of their protest against an unjust war superseded individual rights such as free speech. The most radical among them displayed total scorn for individual liberties.

Professor John Silber, a liberal philosopher from the University of Texas, described them as "The New Fascisti" and said: "They are undistinguishable from the far right. They share a contempt for rational political discussion and constitutional, legal solutions. . . ."

At Wisconsin, Professor Williams, a socialist whose stinging critiques of American foreign policy are read eagerly by new leftists, said of them: "They are the most selfish people I know. They just terrify me. They are acting out a society I'd like to live in only if I were an orangutan."[25]

During the spring of 1968 there were 10 bombings on college campuses; that fall there were 41; next spring, 84 on campus and 10 off campus and, according to documented accounts, during the fall of 1969, violent demonstrations occurred on at least 73 campuses and 26 of them were marked by brutal clashes between students and police.

The nation witnessed the spectacle of the government forced to occupy its own campuses with military troops, bayonets at the ready and live ammunition in the breeches, to control the insurrection of its youth; the governors of Michigan, Ohio, Kentucky and South Carolina declared all campuses in a state of emergency, and the National Guard was activated twenty-four times at 21 universities in sixteen states. [In the month of May 1970 there were] . . . no

162

fewer than 169 incidents of bombings and arson, 95 of them associated with college campuses and another 36 at government and corporate buildings . . . in the first week of May, 30 ROTC buildings on college campuses were burned or bombed. . . .[26]

The SDS was smashed by the Progressive Labor faction at the national convention of the summer of 1969, and the activist fragment which remained designated itself the Weathermen (with increased popularity of women's liberation movements Weathermen was changed to Weather Persons, then to Weather Bureau) faction.

In November 1969 members of the Weathermen faction attempted to blackmail a legitimate peace demonstration in Washington, D. C. demanding $20,000 under threat of disrupting and discrediting the demonstration by hooliganism; when their extortionate demand was refused, they carried out their threat. The coup de grâce of the SDS as a legitimate organization came with the explosion of a townhouse in Greenwich Village, March 6, 1970, where several members of the group blew themselves up as they were making killer bombs. Thus the Movement ended, not with a whimper but a bang.

In focusing my description of the youthful disruptions of the sixties on those aspects which relate to the conception of man, I have slighted or omitted numerous other factors which were associated with it, not, thereby, meaning to imply that such factors may not be, in other contexts, of equal or greater significance.

There were many and good reasons for romantic outburst against our increasingly bureaucratized, stultifyingly mechanized society in the sixties and, together with many others, I hoped for its success. But its sentimental vision became a raucous ego-shriek and its radicalism, which in the beginning meant intellectual probing down to the roots of society's problems, soon translated itself into fanatic bombing; disgustingly cowardly as well as completely dissociated from the attainment of any sensible purpose.

Whether because of the weakness of its basic premise in the innate goodness of man, or due to the inconsistency of attempts to intertwine this premise with the implicit economic determinism of socialism, or as a function of the inexperience and youthful impatience of its principal adherents, romanticism, as it seems always destined to do, quickly burned itself out.

With romanticism being only a sporadic and brief—though certainly appealing and undeniably dramatic—interlude in the ways of thinking that lead us to believe in one or another conception of man, and with naked scientism of the Skinnerian variety being too unpalatable for all but an unfeeling, isolated pedantic few, we turn now to the ways of thinking about man which for two centuries have dominated our thinking and, thereby, our doing—liberalism and conservatism.

Chapter 8. References and Notes

1. Bruce Payne, David Walls, and Jerry Berman, "Theodicy of 1984: The Philosophy of Clark Kerr," in *The New Student Left*, ed. Mitchell Cohen and Dennis Hale (Boston: Beacon Press, 1966). First published in *The Activist*, vol. 2, 1962.

2. Mario Savio, "An End to History," *Humanity*, December 1964. Also in *Revolution at Berkeley*, ed. Michael V. Miller and Susan Gilmore (New York: Dell, 1965).

3. Clark Kerr, John T. Dunlop, F. Harbison, and Charles A. Myers, *Industrialism and Industrial Man* (New York: Oxford University Press, 1964), p. 235.

4. Ibid., p. 238.

5. Ibid., p. 62.

6. Clark Kerr, *The Uses of the University*, (Cambridge, Mass.: Harvard University Press, 1963).

7. Glenn Negley and J. Max Patrick, *The Quest for Utopia* (New York: Henry Schuman, 1952), pp. 76–77.

8. Fyodor Dostoevsky, *Notes From the Underground and The Grand Inquisitor*, trans. Ralph E. Matlaw (New York: E. P. Dutton, 1960), pp. xii, xiii.

9. Thomas Hayden, "Letter to the New (Young) Left," in *The New Student Left*, ed. Mitchell Cohen and Dennis Hale (Boston: Beacon, 1966), pp. 2–9.

10. Anne Fremantle, *This Little Band of Prophets* (New York: New American Library, 1960), pp. 24, 260.

11. C. Northcote Parkinson, *Left Luggage* (Boston: Houghton-Mifflin, 1967), p. 95.

12. M. Stanton Evans, *Revolt on the Campus* (Chicago: Regnery, 1961), p. 163.

13. *Time*, April 9, 1973.

14. Charles A. Reich, *The Greening of America* (New York: Bantam, 1970).

15. Ibid., p. 285.

16. Will and Ariel Durant, *The Lessons of History* (New York: Simon and Schuster, 1968), p. 74.

17. *Encyclopaedia Britannica*, 1911 ed., as cited by Douglas D. Goodheart in *The Pennsylvania Gazette*, April 1973, p. 3.

18. Stuart Samuels, "English Intellectuals and Politics in the 1930's," in *On Intellectuals*, ed. Philip Rieff (New York: Anchor Books, 1970), pp. 213–269.

19. Hannah Arendt, *On Revolution* (New York: Viking, 1963), p. 76.

20. Aleksandr I. Solzhenitsyn, *The First Circle* (New York: Harper and Row, 1968), pp. 388–389.

21. Milovan Djilas, *Memoir of a Revolutionary* (New York: Harcourt Brace Jovanovich, 1973), as quoted in Walter Jaquer's review, *New York Times*, April 1, 1973.

22. James Simon Kunen, *The Strawberry Statement* (New York: Avon Books, 1969), p. 157.

23. Steven Kelman, *Push Comes to Shove* (Boston: Houghton-Mifflin, 1970), pp. 108–109, 118–119.

24. Steven Rose, *The Conscious Brain* (New York: Alfred A. Knopf, 1973), p. 268.

25. Nan Robertson, "The Student Scene: Militant Anger," *New York Times*, January 20, 1967,.

26. Kirkpatrick Sale, *SDS* (New York: Random House, 1973), pp. 636–637.

Chapter 9

Liberal Vision, Conservative Star

Liberals were firmly convinced that their body of doctrine was eternally true. They believed that they had, like the incomparable Newton before them, discovered the secrets of nature formerly buried in the confusion of men's minds. . . . Nothing remained, they were convinced, but to make existing society conform to the laws of nature they had discovered.

The assumption behind this liberal view of man, of course, is that he is a thoroughly rational being. . . . Liberals admitted the existence of evil and injustice and irrational action, but all these shortcomings in the individual they attributed to ignorance. Educate a man, they believed, and he will become both rational and good. Man, they insisted, was infinitely perfectible and perfectly good.

THUS THOMAS P. Neill, in his historical survey of liberalism, equates eighteenth-century liberalism with scientistic attempts to discover and apply scientific laws (such as Newton's) to mankind.[1] Education in these laws would fill the void left by the absence of innate characteristics and malleable man would thereby attain perfection.

Arthur A. Ekirch expresses a parallel interpretation of eighteenth-century liberalism in *The Decline of American Liberalism.* Inspired by the magnificent discoveries of Newton, liberals believed that similar scientific laws, applying to supernatural as well as natural phenomena, would soon be discovered and a new natural religion, based on the evidence of science, would be accepted through reason instead of by faith.

> Assuming that man would use his reason and obey the natural law, the philosophers of the Age of Enlightenment envisioned a steady progress on the part of society toward the ultimate goal of the perfectibility of mankind.[2]

In *The Heavenly City of the Eighteenth-Century Philosophers* (referred to in Chapter 4), Carl Becker, having described how the eighteenth-century philosophes shifted their endeavors from a philosophic quest to ascertain the nature of universal truths to pragmatic efforts to master the world as well as measure it, then spelled out their premises for the perfectibility of man.[3] As described by Becker, their assumptions were identical with those which liberals implicitly if not explicitly accept today: That man is the product of his environment, and that his spiritual as well as material regeneration will be attained by reshaping his environment in accordance with the invariable and determinable (scientific) laws of nature.

Contemporary liberals would object to any contention that liberalism of the eighteenth century was the same as, or even significantly similar to, the form which liberalism takes as it approaches the twenty-first century. To begin with, many would question the accuracy of the interpretation of eighteenth-century liberalism, and others would insist that the conception of man embodied in it is not only very different from theirs, but is abhorrent to them. There would be much merit in their objections. In its raw state the rationalistic conception of man as devoid of human nature, a totally malleable, environmentally determined creature, is an unpalatable dose for sensitive folk, and as an illustration of liberal objection to it Arthur Schlesinger, Jr., who comes closer than most to being a prototypical liberal intellectual, objects to B. F. Skinner's view of man.

While Professor Schlesinger admits[4] that Professor Skinner pursued the logic of the behavioral approach to an ultimate conclusion with admirable candor when he applied the method of science to human affairs, he deplores this ultimate conclusion in which:

168

. . . the contribution which may be claimed by the individual himself appears to approach zero. Man's vaunted creative powers, his original accomplishments in art, science and morals, his capacity to choose and our right to hold him responsible for the consequences of his choice—none of these is conspicuous in this new self-portrait.

Professor Schlesinger argues that Skinner's totally deterministic scientific conception conflicts with the democratic view of man which assumes at least some capacity for freedom of choice and some degree of individual responsibility, and he contends further that Skinner, having neglected to provide scientific proof that man is merely a puppet, asks us to accept his assertions as a substitute for conclusive proof, thus reducing his purported science to a myth which must be accepted on faith.

Many liberals in addition to Professor Schlesinger reject conceptions such as the totally predetermined, puppetized homunculus which is stamped out by scientistic Skinnerian machines; and they also contend that the similar silly-putty creation of the eighteenth-century philosophes described by O'Neill, Ekirch, and Becker no longer characterizes their belief about man. Therefore, my contention that twentieth-century liberals accept, implicitly if not explicitly, assumptions about man's perfectibility which are patterned after those of the eighteenth century would seem highly dubious.

A Description, Not a Definition

Definition, here as in so many areas of disputation, is the source of such wide differences in interpretation. So far as I know, neither liberalism nor conservatism can be clearly defined, but I hasten to add that this difficulty is not limited to these terms, not does it preclude an analysis of these concepts as vital influences in our thinking.

If we ponder the meanings of things we soon realize that many of the words which shape our beliefs about society and man cannot be defined in any precise statement so as to include all of the essential qualities inherent in the concept while excluding all other qualities. Most meanings of words which we accept as definitions of the ideas inherent in them are soon seen to

169

involve terms which themselves need clear definition, or they are arbitrary or tautological.

I described earlier how Newton refrained from attempting a precise definition of the meaning of gravity by referring to it as the *spirit* of matter—whatever that may mean. Examples were given to show that the term "society," which we commonly use to refer to the circumstances and structures involved when humans live in interrelatedness, also applies to coral formations, insects, and so forth. Similarly, the word "culture" can be applied to a variety of conditions and its usage as it pertains to differing patterns of human behavior has never been clearly defined. For that matter, the present treatise is an explication of the many differing conceptions of the word "man."

Even the simplest and commonest terms, such as "life," defy unambiguous definition, and the term "death," which until recently had a meaning so simple that it was understood by all, is now shrouded in uncertainty. Directors of the American Medical Association in 1973 ruled out all attempts to set a precise definition of the word, concluding that "Death shall be determined by the clinical judgment of the physician." In so doing, officials of the AMA recognized that the test of most meaning ultimately becomes one of prudent judgment.

Thus the absence of a precise definition of liberalism or conservatism does not make these concepts unique or even unusual; nor does it preclude description of their nature or analysis of their influence.

In the present usage, liberalism and conservatism are attitudes toward life; not merely political views. Neither is new; the principles which shape these attitudes being much the same as they were in the eighteenth century, even though the application of such principles has changed in many details. Neither is in any absolute sense true; and neither view is scientific. Both are intellectually legitimate ways of thinking about life, but they are not the only legitimate ways, nor is either life-outlook provably the best.

Usage of the term "conservatism" is further complicated by the circumstance which was described in the "Introduction" where I pointed out that many people believe conservatism to be traditionalism, a bovine adoration of things past, and a bitterly dogmatic rejection of things new. Others, mistakenly but understandably, equate a conservative philosophy of life with economic conservatism; based on the assumption that the economic factor is the keystone of the social structure, and if it be properly shaped and set neatly into place, the other elements of society will align themselves harmoniously about it. Conservatism as it is described below is neither the nostalgic conservatism which expresses itself in traditionalism nor economic conservatism, but philosophic conservatism with its central tenet being man's capacity for moral choice, a capacity which is based on his innate and only partially modifiable potential for evil as well as good.

Usage of the term "liberalism" is complicated because, as Professor Schlesinger's rejection of Skinner's man indicates, liberals balk at acceptance of the scientific projection of their rationalistic conception of man and, as Dostoevsky foresaw, they illogically inject romantic notions of the intrinsic goodness of man into the absence of human nature which is implicit in the limitless malleability of rationalistic man.

My description of the contrasting perspectives which characterize liberalism and conservatism is in terms of Platonic archetypes—ideal conceptualizations of which things are only approximate copies. Few people fit perfectly into these archetypes, and during our lifetimes many of us change from tendencies in one direction to tendencies toward the other, as did Rousseau, Shelley, Goethe, and many others. Even at a given moment of time, most of us are inconsistent, leaning toward the liberal view on some issues and toward the conservative on other.

Liberals and the Perfectibility of Man

Within this context the basic distinction between liberalism and conservatism focuses on the perfectibility of man. Implicitly if not explicitly, embodied in their programs though it may be denied by their words, liberals believe that man is readily malleable; it follows as a corollary that human nature is at best a minor element in our behavior. Today as in the eighteenth century, liberals believe that secular (scientific) formulas have been or soon will be found to mold malleable man into a better being— not yet perfect, to be sure, but definitely and surely progressing in that direction. Contrariwise, conservatives believe (as they

171

have for more than two centuries) that the mixture of potentials for good and for evil which is man can be modified in only limited degree. They grant that both internal and external forces—heredity and environment—affect man but insist that in relation to moral issues he is an active, determining factor, and hence a responsible agent. Strong though such pressures be, man is the final arbiter of choice. They are convinced that no scientistic formula has or will change this immutable core of man's meaning.

Similar to the manner in which Ekirch, O'Neill, and Becker depicted the eighteenth-century liberal conception of the malleability and perfectibility of man, Jeffrey Hart in *The American Dissent* describes the twentieth-century liberal conviction that human nature is changeable and plastic with enormous if not infinite potential for improvement.[5] In this view, evils do not arise from any defect in human nature but from defective social institutions.

Formulas for Perfectibility

Scientific formulas to create perfected man have changed in their details over the years, but the belief in their effectiveness persists as part of liberal doctrine. In the twentieth century, Professor B. F. Skinner believes that by isolating infants from happenstance environmental effects in Skinner Boxes and limiting their experience to contingencies of positive reenforcement he can create people whose freedom from qualms of conscience and indifference to questions of character would make them totally adjusted. In the eighteenth century Jeremy Bentham and James Mill tried to create Mill's son, John Stuart Mill, into the "Saint of Rationalism" whose faculties of reason and critical analysis would be cultivated to the exclusion of all else, ". . . on the premise that the thoroughly rational and analytic man would be the consummate utilitarian."[6]

The brilliant Bentham, mentor of so many liberals in a variety of intellectual areas, believed that as Newton had invented calculus to measure the motion of inorganic objects, so he had discovered in his "Felicific Calculus" the precise way to measure happiness, and that this calculus could be applied through his

Deontology: The Science of Morality (published posthumously in 1834). Bentham believed what Skinner was to claim to be a new scientific finding two hundred years later—that rationality would rid man's mind of such stultifying notions as duty and honor—these and similar abstractions being "nonsense on stilts."

In his *Autobiography* the remarkable similarity between John Stuart Mill's indoctrination by his father and Jeremy Bentham and that which Professor Skinner would like to inflict upon us is described:

> My course of study had led me to believe that all mental and moral feelings and qualities, whether of a good or of a bad kind, were the results of association; that we love one thing, and hate another, take pleasure in one sort of action or contemplation, and pain in another sort, through the clinging of pleasurable or painful ideas to those things, from the effect of education or of experience.[7]

As the Skinners of today attempt to persuade us of the efficacy and the drastic need to apply contingencies of positive reenforcement to our children, so his tutors convinced John Stuart Mill that ". . . the object of education should be to form the strongest possible associations of the salutary class."

Despite his indoctrination, Mill came to realize that, contrary to the doctrines of Utilitarianism and its pleasure-pain calculus, ends are best attained indirectly rather than directly, this being especially so in respect of one's own happiness. Mill also came to appreciate, and to assign it as a prime necessity of human well-being, "the internal culture of the individual. I ceased to attach almost exclusive importance to the ordering of outward circumstances." Having thus renounced the omnipotence of environmental determinism, which in one form or another has always dominated liberal thought, Mill, in conservative fashion, came to seek "The maintenance of a due balance among the faculties. . . ."

Ultimately Mill wrote a critique of Benthamism, expressing contempt for any philosopher who failed to recognize conscience or the sense of duty as a human motive, and he expressed his fear of the effects of Benthamite doctrine, saying:

173

By the promulgation of such views of human nature, and by a general tone of thought and expression perfectly in harmony with them, I conceive Mr. Bentham's writings to have done and to be doing very serious evil. . . . It is difficult to form the conception of a tendency more inconsistent with all rational hope of good for the human species, than that which must be impressed by such doctrines upon any mind in which they find acceptance.[8]

Whether it be Jeremy Bentham in the eighteenth century or Burrhus Frederic Skinner in the twentieth, the liberal doctrine of the virtually limitless malleability of man through environmental determinism remains intrinsically the same, the minor difference being in the manner of its presentation; be it the elegantly expressed rationalism of Bentham or the pedantic assertions of Skinner, mumbled through the falseface of science.

As indicated above in Arthur Schlesinger's expression of his abhorrence of Skinner's man, liberals are revolted by the scientistic or rationalistic view of man in its naked form and adamantly refuse to extend the implications of their programs to the inference about man which is, in the nature of the case, inherent in them. Instead of accepting the conception of man which is implicit in their programs, they arbitrarily (and inconsistently, I should say) endow man with the innate goodness of romanticism, but in so doing find it difficult to distinguish at what point their "humanitarian" endeavors, designed to do things *for* man, begin to do things *to* him.

Godson to John Stuart Mill was philosopher Bertrand Russell—Fabian socialist, militant pacifist and iconoclast of marital mores, sometimes called "The Lord of Reason"—who raised his son John according to the "scientific" behaviorism of American professor of psychology John Broadus Watson. Philosopher Russell plunged his terrified three-and-a-half-year-old up to his neck in the sea day after day to properly condition him, and when in later years son John exhibited severe mental problems pacifist Russell contended that they arose because his son was a member of the post-World War I generation.

Bertrand, Earl Russell, was far from alone in his credulous belief that science, in the form of J. B. Watson's behaviorism, had discovered the formula to produce a higher order of mankind and in foolishly inflicting his belief upon his child. So many thousands of educated and mostly liberal parents in America raised their children according to Watson's "laws of conditioning" that the years between 1925 and 1940 became known as "The Era of Stop-Watch Motherhood."

Watson promised, as Bentham had before and Skinner would later, that:

> . . . these children in turn, with their better ways of living and thinking [will] replace us and in turn bring up their children in a still more scientific way, until the world finally becomes a place fit for human habitation.[9]

Once we freed ourselves from our foolish customs and conventions the science of behaviorism would be the foundation of all future ethics and every child would be a rich and wonderful individual.

Having begun his behavioristic studies in 1912, Watson was cited by the American Psychological Association in 1957 for having ". . . initiated a revolution in psychological thought," much as B. F. Skinner was cited by the same organization in 1971 for having ". . . revolutionized the study of behavior in our time."

Since Skinner's behavioral approach is intrinsically the same as Watson's behavioral approach, it seems that it doesn't take much to produce a revolution in psychology. The mental orbit of those who follow this discipline must be quite wobbly for such a minor nudge to change its circuitry.

Neither Watson's nor Skinner's ideas were new, Galen having complained about such "nothing-but" practitioners more than two thousand years ago. In the standard manner which is inescapable in a scientistic study of man, Watson reduces man first to a beast (". . . If you are to remain scientific, you must describe the behavior of man in no other terms than those you would use in describing the behavior of the ox you slaughter. . . ."[10]). He then further reduces humankind to a primordial glob ("The behaviorist finds that the human being at birth is a very lowly piece of unformed protoplasm, . . .").[11]

The behaviorist, in an "utterly mechanistic" way, can, through conditioning, transform this glob of protoplasm into perfected man.

In short, the cry of the behaviorist is, "Give me the baby and my world to bring it up in and I'll make it crawl and walk; I'll make it climb and use its hands in constructing buildings of stone or wood; I'll make it a thief, a gunman, or a dope fiend. The possibility of shaping in any direction is almost endless.[12]

The only difference between the process of thinking and playing tennis ". . . is that we use the muscles of our throat, larynx, and chest instead of the muscles of our arms, legs, and trunk. We learn to think by learning to do."

Intrigued by the heady notion that science had proved that they could condition their children to be anything they wished—doctor, lawyer, Indian chief—educated parents, eager to renounce the wisdom of ages in favor of the latest "scientific truth," dutifully raised their children according to what they took to be the most recent dictates of science. Since science had proved that children could be conditioned to respond automatically if they were fed, put into bed, pulled out of bed, put on potty and shoved off potty, at specific times each day, mothers raised children according to a rigid stop-watch regimen.

Though Watson (as Skinner) talked much about the scientific proof on which he based his hypotheses, he failed to provide any evidence which held up under even moderate skepticism, but this did not dissuade the many people to whom the world "science" is magical assurance. Nor did Aldous Huxley's brilliant satire of conditioning (*Brave New World*) lead people to see the dangers as well as the absurdity of their beliefs. Emancipated (i.e., indoctrinated by scientistic hypotheses) people renounced Watson's absurd regimented child-rearing practices only to adopt the equally absurd, equally unproved scientistic "permissiveness" of Freud.

Since children soon acquire a realistic sense of things which their gullible parents have abandoned, probably most of them were not harmed by this nonsense, soon learning to tolerate their parents' silliness. Some may have been physically hurt, though, for Watsonian doctrine held that physical fondling was the only "natural" stimulus which gave rise to the "emotion" of love. Therefore, if an infant cried it should never be picked up and fondled else this would condition the child forever to associate crying and love. Thus it is quite likely that many babies, shrieking their blasted heads off because a diaper pin was sticking in their bottoms and not giving a damn about either love or their parents' obsession with conditioning, may have injured their larynges.

Another aspect of Watsonian "scientific truth" was neatly riposted by a *New Yorker* cartoon which also affirmed the native good sense of children. At the same time that many people believed in Watson's hypotheses about raising children, "science" had informed parents that children should eat spinach. "Why should children eat spinach?" The few who dared inquire about the basis of this scientific dictum were squelched by the indubitable information that "Spinach has iron in it." No one then dared ask "Who wants a rusty kid?" So parents dutifully tried to feed spinach to their children, but many children, not liking the taste, balked at eating it. Some children, with their uncontaminated sense, felt, as was later shown to be the case, that spinach wasn't especially good for them and certainly not essential to their health.

Parents were faced with a problem: Science proclaimed that they must feed their children spinach, but children resisted eating it. Remedy: Watson's conditioning. Associate the eating of spinach with a pleasant experience (a technique later glorified to become the Skinnerian contingency of positive reenforcement) and the child will be conditioned to love spinach—as in school, you were led to believe that if you gave a pupil ice cream when he was first exposed to arithmetic, he would soon become a whiz at differential equations. So, the way to reconcile the two scientific imperatives on the child's life was to make eating spinach a festive occasion, pretending that it is not that despised vegetable but, say, green ice cream.

The *New Yorker* cartoon shows Mommy, Daddy, and Junior seated at a dining table with smiling Mommy and Daddy gulping down their "green ice cream," but the child sits back in his chair, refuses to eat, and says, "I still say it's spinach, and I still say to hell with it!"

Thus the conditional reflexes which Ivan Petrovich Pavlov (together with those who followed his scientific precedent) insisted could be applied only to some animals under some circumstances and could not in any strict sense be applied to humans

177

at all was seized upon by pseudo-scientists to degrade man to a glob of protoplasm while claiming that conditioning is a panacea for our problems.

The scientifically valid bases of Pavlov's *conditional* physiological reflexes were distorted by Watson to become permanently fixed *conditioned* reflexes and unconscionably stretched to apply to human emotions and sentiments. Skinner carried the process further and, substituting proclamations for proof, asserted that only hollow man, emptied of freedom, conscience, and all else which dignifies life, was worthy of the future.

Environmental Determinism

Cultural anthropologists stretched and distorted Pavlov's basically valid idea to its logical (but not thereby either scientific or truthful) conclusion with their doctrine of cultural conditioning. Among the most extreme claims about cultural conditioning were those made by Margaret Mead and Ruth Benedict; consequently their writings quickly became the most acclaimed and the most popular.*

Many cultural anthropologists hold, as certain doctrine, that man's beliefs about himself and about life are nothing but a reflection of the culture in which he happens to live, that "personality is merely the subjective aspect of culture." By far the most effective spreaders of this dogma have been the students of Franz Boas, particularly the two indicated above, Margaret Mead and Ruth Benedict.

Dr. Ruth Benedict's book, *Patterns of Culture*, originally published in 1934, went through more than twenty printings in

*At this point it seems advisable to remind the reader that the theme of this book is the differing beliefs which people have about the secular nature of man; where they originate, how they are spread; why they are accepted, and what are their implications. Consequently wide areas of all of the disciplines (psychology, anthropology, sociology) referred to are omitted in order to emphasize those which have had—whether intellectually justified or not—the greatest impact upon people's beliefs about man.

sales of more than a million copies. While pleasantly readable, *Patterns of Culture* was not, by even the widest stretching of the word, scientific, being a second-hand study of three primitive (now underdeveloped) groups. But, in standard fashion, Dr. Benedict asserted that her findings were scientific and most readers, being college students whose professors had failed to educate them properly, accepted this baseless claim, and believed that Dr. Benedict had provided scientific anthropological proof to bolster the scientific psychological proofs from Watson and Skinner, all of these supporting the contention that man, devoid of human nature, is molded by external forces of which he has no knowledge and over which he has no control.

Dr. Margaret Mead, in her preface to *Patterns of Culture*, says that Dr. Benedict's special contribution in her book is her view of human cultures as "personality writ large," but this is not at all the point which Dr. Benedict stresses. Much more than culture being "personality writ large" in *Patterns of Culture*, its theme is that the human person is nothing but "culture writ small," and is expressed thus:

> If we are interested in human behavior, we need first of all to understand the institutions that are provided in any society. For human behavior will take the forms those institutions suggest, even to extremes of which the observer, deep-dyed in the culture of which he is a part, can have no intimation.[13]

Intertwined with and reenforcing the psychological and anthropological conceptions of natureless, malleable, environmentally determined man is the psychoanalytic conception of man, with the Freudian interpretation dominating all others.

> In America today, Freud's intellectual influence is greater than that of any other modern thinker. He presides over the mass media, the college classroom, the chatter at parties, the playgrounds of the middle classes where child-rearing is a prominent and somewhat anxious topic of conversation; . . . It is a good omen that he is being treated as a culture hero.[14]

179

Though somewhat dated, and couched in the hyperbole of an adoring disciple, Professor Philip Rieff's description of Freudian influence indicates the emotional impact which the psychoanalytic conception of man had upon educated, liberal Americans. Thousands of articles in popular magazines, and millions of copies of hundreds of books told people not only how to raise their children, what to think and do about sex and marriage, and how to understand and cure alcoholism, drug addiction, mental disorder and allergies, but also what to do about education, how to treat criminals, what causes wars; and they offered "scientific" answers to just about every other question which man has ever asked about himself, mankind, society, history, religion, art, and chess.

Professor Rieff refers to Freud's writings as ". . . the masterwork of the century," and ". . . perhaps the most important body of thought committed to paper in the twentieth century," which ". . . has contributed as much as doctrine possibly can to the correction [sic] of our standards of behavior." And Professor Rieff confers upon this moral prince who was morally upright to the last ". . . a kind of secular sainthood."

We are told that to comprehend the new scientific Freudian morality, it is essential to expose the whole rotten empire of the family, to recognize that "To be religious is to be sick," and to smash the past.

Acclaim such as that gushed by Professor Rieff, while shamelessly exaggerated, yet represents the widespread enthusiasm which greeted this additional thread that "scientists" could pull to make puppetized man dance.

Since psychoanalytic dogma warned parents and teachers that if they inhibited the "natural" urges of children neurosis might result, its permissive doctrines replaced the strict regimen and conditioning of Watsonian behaviorism.

When my children were young, I took notes from one of the more scholarly of the hundreds of books which advised parents how to raise their children according to psychoanalytic "laws." The subtitle of this book was *How to Avoid the Neurotic Pattern*, so I jotted down the things which every parent should take into consideration if he wished his children to become emotionally stable adults.[15] By implication, if not by direct statement,

parents were warned that complexes or neuroses might result
if:

During the oral stage:

The infant is fed too much—or if the infant is fed too little.
The infant is fed too fast—or if the infant is fed too slowly.
The infant receives insufficient affection—or too much affection.
The infant is weaned too soon—or too late.
Anyone is unpleasant to the infant—or if too much affection
is shown.
The mother goes on a vacation.
The parents move from one house to another.
The mother dies.
The child feels hostility.

During the anal stage:

The process of toilet training is begun too early—or too late.
The mother is too busy.
The mother becomes impatient.
She scolds or nags.
The child feels tensions.

In the unlikely event that the child survives these hazards
of the oral and anal stages, he reaches the genital stage when
male children between the ages of four and six have as their
primary urge the desire to kill their father and mate with their
mother, while girls between three and five—being more preco-
cious than boys—feel that their principal goal in life is to kill
their mother and have a baby by their father. The scholarly
authors of the book informed me that the existence of these
"instinctual drives" had been amply proved by careful studies
over a long period of time. During this genital stage complexes
may originate:

If the boy's father is absent.
If the boy's mother is absent.
If the girl's father is absent.
If the girl's mother is absent.
If either the boy's or the girl's mother or father is absent.
If the father dies.

181

If the child is ill.

If another child is born.

If the parents are too restrictive—or too indulgent.

If the child is rejected—or if the child is overprotected.

If the child has a traumatic experience, such as being sent to nursery school.

Having completed my notes from the book, I spanked each of my children with it and gave it to a nervous neighbor whom I didn't like.

Of the many such books which threatened parents with all manner of future calamity if their children were not raised according to the permissive dictates of the "science" of psychoanalysis, the chiefest in influence was Dr. Benjamin McLane Spock's on baby and child care which, first published in 1946, sold more than twenty-one million copies.

These scientistic formulas from behavioral psychology, cultural anthropology, and Freudian psychoanalysis coalesce in the liberal view of man as a being or creature devoid of human nature, whose malleability can be shaped toward perfection by deterministic formulas.

Perfectible Man

Since sociology, apart from intellectually unimportant specialties (such as demography and penology), is the academic expression of liberalism, the sociological perspective of man is one in which his personality—the term "character" is seldom found in sociology books—is formed through a combination of cultural conditioning and psychoanalytic mechanisms. While all of us, obviously, are *influenced* by the culture in which we live, sociologists give the impression that our culture not only influences, but virtually *determines* our personality.

Since, according to the dictates of cultural conditioning doctrine, all members of the same sub-culture (region, class, or family) would believe and behave identically, it is necessary to supplement the doctrines of cultural determinism with psychoanalytic interpretation to account for the obvious differences which exist, even between members of the same family. Such differences, sociologists contend, arise from a variety of compulsions, rationalizations, complexes, fixations, tensions, and a host of other psychoanalytic mechanisms.

Since our lives are shaped by the external pressures of cultural forces and by the internal imperatives of "universal" psychoanalytic drives we do not, as individuals, deserve either praise or blame for our conduct.

Having neither conscious awareness nor willful control over the forces which shape us, we lack integration, consistency, and character and our behavior is little more than a reflection of specific social situations to which we have been exposed. Differing associations and experiences create most of the differences between men and women, between criminals and the lawabiding, between heroes and cowards, between the chaste and the profligate.

To improve such waxily flexible personalities, experts must change the social situations to which they are exposed. Change the culture and thereby change the people; improve the culture and hence improve the people; perfect the culture and ultimately perfect the people. This is the vision of liberalism—a future in which man, freed from guilt, lives in a society freed from want.

The Constant Conservative Star

Conservatism, in stodgy contrast to liberalism, can offer no appealing promise; no utopia, no easily applied formula to eradicate our sins, excuse our failures, compensate for our weakness or salve our conscience. A conscientious conservative must admit that it cannot be scientifically proved that man has an intrinsic nature which entails potentials for evil as well as good. Though he can adduce much evidence to support this interpretation of man, an inferential leap is required in order to accept it and, understandably, many prefer to avoid this upsetting mental and emotional hurdle.

If man can, by act of will, choose between good and evil in the very nature of the case, his behavior in this regard cannot be predicted. Since a crucial test of science is the ability to predict, the conservative conception of man automatically excludes large and vital areas of human life from scientific study —at least from the sort of study which most people believe to be scientific. To academicians who sorely need the support of scientific authority to buttress their assertions about man and society, this is an unacceptable alternative to the liberal assumption of natureless, malleable, hence predictable man.

The "meanness" which Emerson ascribed to the arguments of conservatism also detracts from its appeal. For conservatives hold

> ... that evil exists independently of social or economic maladjustments; that we must search for the source of our discontents in defective human nature rather than in a defective social order; and that man, far from being malleable; is subject to cultural alteration only slowly and to a limited degree. The conservative therefore considers it his stern duty to call attention, as did John Adams, to the "general frailty and depravity of human nature" and to the weakness of reason as a guide to personal conduct or collective endeavor.
>
> The man who has rights also has duties. Rights are at bottom simply claims on other men, and the law of equilibrium commands those who make claims to be ready to pay for them. In return for the chance to enjoy his rights in a community, a man has the obligation to use these rights responsibly. The right to life carries with it the duty to live morally. Freedom of conscience is matched by the duty to think wisely and worship decorously.[16]

The conservative view of human rights as earned, not given, as entailed, not spendable, contrasts with liberal notions which seem to hold that rights can be created by fiat, endowed by decree, poured forth by pulling levers on voting machines as though they were gum-ball machines.

In addition to this central difference about the nature of man, liberals and conservatives differ on other issues such as the role of economics in society; the relative importance of personality and character; and the time dimension in which social problems should be viewed.

As their conception of perfectible man has in principle remained the same since the eighteenth century, so liberals have consistently held that the economic factor is the most important element in social life. If this keystone be properly designed and fitted all other elements of the social structure will fall symmetrically into place about it. Though the particular form which such economic determinism takes changes over the years much as the scientistic formulas for human perfectibility change, the principle persists as an identifying characteristic of liberalism.

As described in Chapter 1, Adam Smith was mentor for the eighteenth-century form of liberal economic determinism, and the stress which Smith and his interpreters put upon the strong if not inexorable forces of competition, supply and demand, and other valid economic factors led some of the more enthusiastic liberals to believe that these were scientific laws. Smith's contention that if each would pursue his own economic interest he would thereby promote the general social interest—albeit unwittingly, as though guided by an invisible hand—was translated into the doctrine of *laissez-faire*, the desirability if not the essentiality of governmental non-interference with the "laws of economics."

John Maynard Keynes became prototype of the twentieth-century form of liberal economic determinism, and though the Welfare State economics which he and his interpreters espoused involved a doctrine opposite to *laissez-faire*, requiring that government exert ever greater control over economic factors, the principle of the centrality of the economic aspect in society persisted as a major tenet of liberalism.

Liberals would protest, with justification, that it is not economics as such which is their concern; certainly it is not an obsession with financial profits nor with the crass materialism at which they sneer. But their programs—to be described in Chapter 10—seem premised on the assumption that if people are assured of economic welfare they will be better people and we shall have a better society.

This tenet of liberalism is not naked economic determinism, but it leans in that direction, which explains, in part at least, why liberals often slide over into socialism. Only a very small percentage ever plunge into membership in the Communist Party, because they balk at the ugly practices of Communists much as they avert their eyes from the grotesque man created by Skinnerian behaviorism. But beneath their specific rejection of Communism they seem to sense, in the economic determinism which they share, a family resemblance. Communism, to liberals, is an ugly cousin. One certainly has no desire for a close relationship with such a relative and may even ridicule her, sometimes indulging in public snubs. But if a member of one's family is attacked by an outsider, the thrust of the attack, though indirect, hurts us too, and is resented.

I know of no conservatives who abhor wealth or who shun material comfort; but in principle philosophic conservatism—unlike economic conservatism, which actually clings to the tenets of eighteenth-century liberalism—does not hold that the economic factor is the most important social element. While respecting the great importance of material well-being, philosophic conservatives would contend that public morality and personal integrity are more basic to social well-being. All of our economic arrangements, all of our paper currency and all of our cheap clad coins, have value only to the degree that we place our trust in debt-engulfed government—Heaven help us!

Believing as they do in the plasticity of human nature and the malleability of man, liberals tend to stress personality and adjustment rather than character and integrity. Thus progressive education was aptly referred to as a program to promote life-adjustment. "He is a *warm* person." "Be nice to people." "There is no such thing as a bad boy." "I never met a man I didn't like." "Smile." These accolades contrast with the reserve and sometimes coldness of conservatives who believe that respect for persons does not necessitate demonstrations of affection.

Convinced that people and social affairs can be changed by use of scientistic psychological or economic formulas, liberals stress speed in coping with problems, favoring a short-term approach. Conservatives, convinced that no person nor any generation or formula can successfully solve the problems of man, tend to view them from a long-term perspective.

Differences between the liberal and conservative conceptions of man are conveyed not only through academic studies but also, and perhaps even more effectively, through fiction, essays, and trade books addressed to the general public. Usually such fictional or thematic literature rests upon one or another of the three conceptions of man, and it often arises from academic sources.

186

Spread of Liberal Doctrine

Chernyshevsky, whose novel *What Is to Be Done* (1863) (so admired by Lenin, so despised by Dostoevsky) was based on "The Anthropological Principle of Philosophy," which holds that there is no essential difference between a mineral, plant, polyp, animal, and man. Each obeys the same law of nature, and all differences are merely differences of complexity. Free will makes as much sense as saying that "the plate broke because the plate broke." Reason, Chernyshevsky implied, could perceive this law of nature, construct society according to it, and usher man into a life of perpetual bliss.

One hundred and fourteen years later, in 1977, in a summary of the influence of anthropology, a leading anthropologist quotes Professor Lionel Trilling, for many years mentor of intellectual liberalism, as saying "No book has had so decisive an effect on modern literature as *The Golden Bough.*"[17]

Sir James George Frazer, author of *The Golden Bough*, states that science must replace religion as an explanation of natural phenomena—including, of course, man, he being the subject of anthropological study. Frazer, in characteristic scientistic fashion, contended, without proof, that:

> The order laid down by science is derived from patient and exact observation of the phenomena themselves. The abundance, the solidity, and the splendour of the results already achieved by science are well fitted to inspire us with a cheerful confidence in the soundness of its method. Here at last, man has hit upon a golden key that opens many locks in the treasury of nature.[18]

A dramatic illustration of the manner in which different conceptions of man find their way into novels of great influence is found in the contrast between J. D. Salinger's *The Catcher in the Rye* and William Golding's *Lord of the Flies*.

More than seven million copies of *Catcher* were sold since 1951, most of them to college students. Salinger portrayed sixteen-year-old Holden Caulfield, who at the time of the story had flunked out of three prep schools, as sensitive, innocent youth wracked by the cruel conventions of a corrupt society. Golding's

187

fantasy describes English schoolboys stranded on a South Sea island where, independent of all social institutions and with their youthful innocence unalloyed by the cynicism and evil of older folk, they quickly become involved in theft, physical assault, bestiality, and murder. They are on the verge of cannibalism when they are rescued—by a warship!

Golding describes his purpose thus:

> The theme is an attempt to trace the defects of society back to the defects of human nature. The moral is that the shape of a society must depend on the ethical nature of the individual and not on any political system however apparently logical or respectable. The whole book is symbolic in nature except the rescue in the end where adult life appears, dignified and capable, but in reality enmeshed in the same evil as the symbolic life of the children on the island.[19]

Interestingly, while making a movie of Golding's *Lord of the Flies,* the children who enacted the parts of the stranded English schoolboys threatened each other with violence and, even while offscreen, created a situation much like that in the book. Their director, Peter Brook, summed up his reaction to the rapidity with which the real-life breakdown of morals and manners paralleled the fictional one by saying:

> The only falsification in Golding's fable is the length of time the descent to savagery takes. I believe if the cork of continued adult presence were removed from the bottle, the complete catastrophe could occur within a long weekend.[20]

Thus we find the differing liberal and conservative versions of the nature of man competing for the loyalty of masses of people today in contrast to eighteenth-century conditions when the low level of literacy made such intellectual notions the concern of only a few, and the uneducated, nonreading masses relied on their religion, their experience, their heritage, and their differing judgments as to what man was and what life should be.

188

A Summing Up

Neither liberalism nor conservatism is new, nor in any absolute sense, true. Both are intellectually legitimate ways of looking at life, and adherents can find much evidence to support either but neither can be proved to be scientifically valid. Neither is totally good nor bad and faulty interpretations can arise from either perspective.

Conservatives may mistake false and arbitrary conventions for the timeless star of moral guidance; nostalgia or self-interest may outweigh the evidence which supports their conclusions; their long-term view may turn out to be too long and issues which might have been settled simply if attacked early may be permitted to fester into serious social sores.

Liberals, bemused by their vision of perfectibility, may mistake newness for truth; scientism for science; they may discard valuable traditions for shoddy novelties; their precipitous action may be based on expedience in which principles are ignored so that bad means are used to achieve good ends.

In any representative society both the liberal vision of perfectibility and the conservative star of tested experience are needed and danger arises if either view is dominant for long. As Emerson said: "Each is a good half, but an impossible whole. . . . In a true society, in a true man, both must combine."

Why Liberalism Dominates

Our conservative heritage is described in Chapter 6 where I point out that despite ideologues such as Thomas Paine, the founders of America were for the most part men of practical affairs whose credo was expressed by John Dickinson: "Experience must be our only guide, reason may mislead us." This rich time-tested experience went back to Magna Carta of 1215, and came down to us through the Petition of Right, the English Bill of Rights, and the Virginia Constitution of George Mason.

Our legal heritage rested on the precedence and divine sanction of Sir Richard Blackstone's *Commentaries* rather than hanging on the fine but thin threads of Jeremy Bentham's rationalism, and the authors of *The Federalist* which persuaded our forefathers to adopt the Constitution stressed the evil which is "sown in the nature of man."

Since it is a primary function of intellectuals to analyze their society critically, it was meet and right that American intellectuals, who developed in numbers and grew in influence as the country grew, should level their liberal barbs at their conservative host. As education increased in scope and prestige the role of liberal rationalism grew to outweigh the role of prudent reason anchored in experience to a degree that our intellectual heritage came to be dominated by liberalism.

In 1950, in his preface to *The Liberal Imagination*, Lionel Trilling, deservedly the dean of intellectual liberals, lamented that:

> In the United States at this time liberalism is not only the dominant but even the sole intellectual tradition. For it is the plain fact that nowadays there are no conservative or reactionary ideas in general circulation. This does not mean, of course, that there is no impulse to conservatism or to reaction but . . . the conservative impulse and the reactionary impulse do not, with some isolated and some ecclesiastical exceptions, express themselves in ideas but only in action or in irritable mental gestures which seek to resemble ideas.[21]

Conservative Peter Viereck cites a newspaper of 1950 which listed charges against a prisoner accused of creating a public disturbance. One of the charges was: "He was using abusive and obscene language, calling people conservatives and all that."[22]

A survey of reading preferences of successful applicants to the college of Columbia University in 1966 indicated that author John Steinbeck was the pronounced favorite, getting 23 percent of the votes, compared with Shakespeare's 9 percent. When Steinbeck was awarded the Nobel Prize for literature in 1962, he stated that "a writer who does not passionately believe in the perfectibility of man has no dedication nor any membership in literature."

Liberalism grew to influence academic life in most of its branches, and to dominate the social sciences and other disciplines which relate to the nature of man and to the role of man's

190

nature in social affairs. In 1969 the Carnegie Commission on Higher Education surveyed a sample of 60,447 faculty members in American universities. Unfortunately, no question which related directly to the liberal-conservative conceptions of the nature of man was asked, so the attitude of university faculty members on this matter can only be inferred from the responses to the question closest to this issue.

Answers to the question "How would you characterize yourself politically at the present time?" were separated into the categories "Left," "Liberal," "Middle-of-the-Road," "Moderately Conservative," and "Strongly Conservative." Faculty members representing 29 academic disciplines were surveyed and, to take responses to the extreme positions first, the highest percentage who considered themselves "Strongly Conservative" were from engineering faculties at 4.5 percent. The highest percentage who considered themselves "Left" were from sociology, at 19.4 percent.

Among the 29 academic disciplines surveyed, the faculties of those most directly involved with study of the nature of man and its implications for society, the social (now behavioral) sciences showed the highest percentage of left-liberal leaning, with sociologists being the most (81 percent) biased and faculty members from the allied area of social work being next highest with 79 percent. Philosophy, at 77 percent, was third, and anthropology, psychology, and history showed 69 percent left-liberal bias.

University departments of religion, thought by many laymen to hold to a conservative stance on most issues, actually have been, for several decades, a branch of behavioral sciences in the same reciprocal way that the behavioral sciences are major outlets for liberal doctrine. Sixty-eight percent of the faculty members of university departments of religion considered themselves to be left-liberals; only 11 percent considered themselves to be conservative.

Only 5 percent of the sociologists and 6 percent of social work faculties considered themselves to be conservative, and about 10 percent of university professors of anthropology, psychology, philosophy, and history considered themselves to be political conservatives.

I believe that if the liberal-conservative leaning were

191

derived indirectly, by asking questions related to beliefs about the nature of man and his malleability instead of couching the question in terms of political beliefs, the liberal leaning would be even stronger than the extreme bias found in this Carnegie survey. Professor J. B. Watson, for example, whose conditioning doctrines equated man with beast and totally malleable, was, in political and economic affairs, conservative. I further feel that if a study were limited to the more prestigious and influential universities, the findings would show an almost absolute monopoly of liberalism.

University students, believing that they are attending a university which is similar to Cardinal Newman's conception of a place of higher and universal education, actually attend Clark Kerr's multiversity dominated by narrow technical training. Such students are further deluded in believing that they are being given a liberal education when, more nearly, they are receiving an indoctrination in liberalism.

A questionnaire designed by Professor David Reisman of Harvard was distributed by the editors of *National Review* in 1961–63 and again in 1969–70.[23] Both surveys found that the beliefs of college students become more liberal as a function of the duration of their attendance. Sophomores are more likely to accept liberal doctrine than freshmen, seniors more likely than juniors, with, as expected, graduate students tilting further left than undergraduates, and faculty, especially in social science departments, being almost entirely made up of liberals.

A majority of students at the twelve institutions surveyed (Sarah Lawrence, Williams, Yale, Marquette, Boston University, Indiana, South Carolina, Howard, Reed, Davidson, Brandeis, and Stanford) accepted liberal doctrine on most issues, except at Reed, where the highest percentage was radical.

Those who took a conservative position on social and political issues declined from 27 percent in 1961–63 to 15 percent in 1969–70, while liberals increased from 51 to 59 percent and student radicals increased from 7 to 17 percent.

As an illustration of the change between 1961–63 and 1969–70, "Full socialization of all industries" was opposed by 62 percent of the students polled at the earlier date but only 8 percent in the later survey. Support for "National Health Insurance" increased from 54 to 74 percent.

192

Of the students polled during 1969–70, 77 percent said that their political attitudes had changed in a leftward direction since they entered college, while only 9 percent had moved to the right. In the earlier poll, while 48 percent of the students surveyed felt that they had moved leftward, a smaller but significant 23 percent felt that they had moved toward the right of the political spectrum.

The 70 most prestigious American intellectuals who figured in a survey which covered the period 1964–68[24] were divided, according to my assessment, between liberals and conservatives in about the same proportion as professors of social science, more than 70 percent being liberals.

From this and other evidence it is reasonable to conclude that the doctrines of liberalism have dominated intellectual circles and social science faculties for a long time. Scientifically unfounded but appealing and persuasive scientistic doctrines from anthropology, psychology, social work, sociology, psychoanalysis, and other disciplines were spread by non-academic intellectuals not only to influence our beliefs about man in general, but to persuade us as to how we should raise our children; how children should be educated; what to do about criminals, alcoholics, and drug addicts; how to be happily married; what caused war and how to prevent it and just about every other aspect of our lives.

When Franklin Delano Roosevelt was elected President in 1932, many people believed that through the "New Deal" he had created a new way of thinking about life in America which then had been incorporated into new laws and institutionalized through new federal agencies. In fact, as even a cursory study of the situation reveals, it was neither President Roosevelt nor the Democratic Party which brought about the programs which institutionalized our change from a society governed—in principle at least—by conservative doctrine to a welfare state created by intellectuals and dominated by liberal doctrine.

To describe the manner in which Roosevelt, the superb politician, was influenced by the academics and intellectuals who made up the Brain Trust which he appointed is an interesting excursion but it branches away from the theme here presented. Those interested in learning how academic doctrines of economic liberalism were conveyed to President Roosevelt and then incor-

193

porated into the laws which govern us can learn much of it by reading Rexford Guy Tugwell's *The Brains Trust* (New York: Viking, 1968), or Raymond Moley's *The First New Deal* (New York: Harcourt Brace, 1966).

For present purposes, suffice it to say that our laws as well as our manners and morals came to be dominated by the doctrines of liberalism and if there is any merit to my contention that it is a proper function of intellectuals to criticize their society, whatever form it may take, then as our society came to be more and more dominated by liberal doctrine it became the obligation of at least some intellectuals to criticize it, much as intellectuals earlier had taken up the responsibility to criticize our society when conservatism was the dominant doctrine.

A Modest Upsurge of Conservatism

As a reaction to the liberal dominance in social and political as well as academic and intellectual aspects of our life, during the 1950s an increasing number of books and articles were written to criticize the welfare state created by liberals. Unfortunately, many of these publications were critical of specific practices, mostly economic, and in presenting the limited views of economic conservatives they reflected eighteenth-century liberal doctrine more than philosophical conservatism. Other authors sought to equate collectivistic liberal doctrines with communism and the extreme and blunderbuss nature of their attack alienated many persons who otherwise would have joined them to criticize the liberal system. Many of the publications, also, were merely nostalgic complaints of the sort which Lionel Trilling properly dismissed as essentially irrelevant to serious argumentation about principles.

Most of the early criticism of the new liberal society attacked only its surface aspects; its results, not its causes; its tendrils, not its roots. But in manner similar to that in which the Fabians gnawed at the roots of capitalism several intellectuals —some of whom were also academics—began to hack away at the scientistic roots of liberalism.

Many people were first made aware that university students were being indoctrinated with liberal scientism through *God*

194

and Man at Yale (1951) wherein William F. Buckley, Jr., forcefully and in high literate style described how his Yale professors had, by insisting that the pseudo-scientistic approach to religion was the only valid one, promoted agnosticism if not atheism. Buckley also revealed the degree to which liberal bias in favor of collectivism dominated courses in economics. From inside the academic world, Professor D. R. G. Owen similarly depicted the pernicious influence of false science on religious belief in *Scientism, Man, and Religion* (1952).

In a series of analyses designed to progress in depth and scope, I published *The Claims of Sociology* (1951), *Social Problems and Scientism* (1953), and *The Vision and the Constant Star* (1956), the first to show that sociologists, despite their claims to scientifically proved objectivity, presented a biased view of man and society; the second to illustrate the manner in which pseudo-science not only influenced, but increasingly determined our response to life's problems; the third to argue that our comprehension of the meaning of man and our efforts to shape our future were not at all an issue of science versus non-science but a choice between the vision of personal emancipation combined with collectivistic utopia implied in liberalism and of personal responsibility guided by the constancy of moral principle inherent in philosophical conservatism. *Man Is Moral Choice*, fourth in this series, is designed to contribute historical and intellectual breadth to this same issue and to describe the ways of thinking which make the conservative view intellectually credible.

In 1956, Professor Pitirim A. Sorokin similarly attacked the pseudo-scientific pretensions of sociologists in *Fads and Foibles in Modern Sociology and Related Sciences.* Sociologist Robert A. Nisbet tried in 1953 to nudge his colleagues toward an awareness of other than liberal interpretations in *The Quest for Community,* and from the field of cultural anthropology Professor Dorothy Lee dared charges of academic heresy by presenting a thoughtful, perceptive, and exceptionally literate interpretation, *Freedom and Culture,* which fitted anthropological findings into a context of the integrity of the individual rather than the usual plasticity of the personality.

F. A. Hayek edited *Capitalism and the Historians* in 1954, a book which portrayed the persistence of anti-capitalist, procollectivist bias by historians, and Jacob Burckhardt, in *Force and Freedom* (1955), contributed a favorable description of a conservative approach to history. Poet and Professor E. Merrill Root in *Collectivism on the Campus* (1955) not only described the prevalence of liberal doctrine in academic life but made an impassioned plea for surcease of the penalties which liberal professors imposed upon their colleagues who questioned their dogma.

In England, Dr. H. J. Eysenck published *Uses and Abuses of Psychology* (1953) to question the validity of using "scientific" psychological findings in human affairs; and C. S. Lewis, who as early as 1946 had brilliantly fantasized a future controlled by social scientists in *That Hideous Strength,* forecast in 1950 that the doctrines of cultural conditioning were leading us toward *The Abolition of Man.* Naturalist Joseph Wood Krutch described the limitations of conditioning and psychoanalytic interpretations as instruments when used in *The Measure of Man* (1954).

These and many other works attacked the scientistic academic foundations of liberalism and numerous publications showed that science was not so easily applicable, nor so certain in its findings as sociologists, psychologists, and many others thought it to be. To mention only a few: chemist Anthony Standen published his amusing *Science is a Sacred Cow* in 1950, pointing out among other things that if we applied the same statistical procedures which many social scientists rely on to reach scientific truth to our ordinary life we would necessarily conclude that a man who on Sunday night got drunk on whiskey and soda; on Monday on Scotch and soda; and on Tuesday on bourbon and soda was made drunk by the soda!

No matter what their ideological conviction, no perceptive professor could fail to appreciate—and all should have been humbled—by the graceful way Jacques Barzun scalpeled through the puffery of academic pretentiousness in *The House of Intellect* (1959); and the assertion that "The social sciences today have yet to show one universal element or controlling 'law,' one unit of measurement, one exactly plotted variable, or one invariant relation," which he made in *Science: The Glorious Entertainment* (1964), has yet to be successfully disputed.

Of all the many books which describe the nature of science,

its method, its implications, and the limited degree of its applicability to man and society, I was particularly impressed by Stephen C. Pepper's *World Hypotheses* (1957). My own hypothesis that our conception of the nature of man is, more than anything else, the basis of our world outlook; whether it be the rationalistic-scientism on which liberalism rests, romanticism, or conservatism led me to a deep appreciation for the intellectual rigor with which Pepper insisted that no matter what our hypothesis, we should be aware of the metaphor in which it has its roots. Hypotheses which hold that man is so highly malleable that he can be conditioned in virtually limitless degree must have as their root metaphor, whether admittedly or not, the assumption that man is little more than Watson's glob of protoplasm.

More than any other work, the book which brought philosophical intellectual conservatism to respectful public attention was Russell Kirk's scholarly and gently persuasive *The Conservative Mind,* published by Henry Regnery in 1953.

In addition to these developments, an upswell of conservatism was indicated by the appearance of magazines such as *National Review* with its sprightly newsiness, *Modern Age* with its somber conservative essays, and *The Intercollegiate Review* designed primarily for distribution to students through the Intercollegiate Study Institute. ISI was founded in 1952 by a vigorous and fiercely independent liberal of the old fashion, Frank Chodorov, as the Intercollegiate Society of Individualists. Chodorov hoped that the ISI would be the obverse of the Intercollegiate Socialist Society which set out in 1905 to convert students to liberal collectivism.

Another indication that the upswell of conservatism was more than a minor ripple was the publication of *Making It.* Author Norman Podhoretz was editor of *Commentary* (considered to have more influence on the thinking of intellectuals than any other magazine except *The New York Review of Books* and *The New Yorker*) and he declared that he and other prominent intellectuals had, during the mid-fifties, turned to a new way of looking at things, which he designated "The Age of Revisionist Liberalism." He described this revision in thinking as:

> . . . the effort to purge the liberal mentality of its endemically besetting illusions regarding the perfectibility of

197

man and the perfectibility of society, and to purge it as well of the particular illusions regarding the Soviet Union to which so large a part of its constituency had fallen prey in the thirties.

> . . . the anti-utopianism of the revisionist liberals—their Niebuhrian stress on human imperfection as the major obstacle to the realization of huge political dreams—jibed beautifully with the "tragic sense of life" which, in common with all students barely out of their diapers, I was certain I shared with Shakespeare.[25]

The "tragic sense of life" which Norman Podhoretz included as an essential ingredient of revisionist liberalism had also been referred to by William Faulkner in his 1949 acceptance of the Nobel Prize. A writer, said Faulkner, must relearn the lessons of the human heart; teaching himself that the basest of all things is to be afraid; and having learned that, forget it forever, removing fears for self and holding only to the old verities and truths of the heart. Failing this, said Faulkner:

> He writes not of love but of lust, of defeats in which nobody loses anything of value, of victories without hope and, worst of all, without pity or compassion. His griefs grieve on no universal bones, leaving no scars. He writes not of the heart but of the glands.

Saul Bellow, one of the most esteemed of the small group of intellectuals who have been called ". . . the Diors and Schiaparellis of intellectual fashion design. What they think today, you're apt to find yourself, in a Sears Roebuckish sort of way, thinking tomorrow,"[26] on receiving the Nobel Prize for literature in 1976, referred to Conrad in saying that an artist should appeal "to that part of our being which is a gift, not an acquisition, to our sense of pity and pain." To do this the artist must attempt to find in life ". . . what is fundamental, endearing, essential."

And in *Mr. Sammler's Planet*, Mr. Bellow had his protagonist question scientistic rationality as he wondered,

> . . . whether the worst enemies of civilization might not prove to be its petted intellectuals who attacked it at its

weakest moments—attacked it in the name of proletarian revolution, in the name of reason, and in the name of irrationality, in the name of visceral depth, in the name of perfect instantaneous freedom.[27]

As Bellow's Nobel acceptance speech contrasted (and as Faulkner's had earlier) with John Steinbeck's insistence that all writers pay obeisance to the liberal doctrine of the perfectibility of man, so his 1949 novel, *The Adventures of Augie March,* contrasted with J. D. Salinger's *The Catcher in the Rye.* Holden Caulfield, endowed with wealth and breeding, blamed his dissatisfaction with life on the cruel conventions of corrupt society, but Bellow's fatherless, broken-familied, slum-housed, poverty-ridden, minority-statused Augie March, educated in pool rooms rather than prep schools, proclaimed in the opening paragraph: "I am an American . . . and will make the record in my own way. . . . a man's character is his fate."[28]

And in the final chapter Augie, despite the knocks which he took, repeats his conviction that a man's character is his fate, and if he turned out to be a flop, well, Columbus, when sent back from his voyages in chains, must have thought that he, too, was a flop. "Which didn't prove there was no America."

Another of our foremost authors, Arthur Miller, rejected scientism dramatically in his address to the Thirty-fourth International Congress of P.E.N. (a society of poets, playwrights, essayists, editors, and novelists). After reciting some of the distorted aspects of scientific interpretations of human life, Miller recalled a speech he had given to a congress of American psychologists in 1963. To dramatize his contention that without an appreciation of human values one doesn't even produce good science let alone good art, Miller cited experiments in which Nazi doctors fastened electrodes to people before deliberately drowning them in order to obtain an objective recording of their reactions as they died.

Afterwards, about twenty-five people, all professional psychologists, gathered round me. "Why isn't it science?" they asked.[29]

Playwright Miller sharply criticized the effects of scientism on writers, saying that they are:

> . . . face to face with a devilish and false ideology running rabid in the world: the ideology of scientism, which would have us believe that the instinct of a writer to create a synthesis of meanings for life is false and trivial, and that the only truth is the truth that can be documented in statistics or an empirical experiment. It is the triumph of the pettifogger, the triumph of the lover of minutiae. It is the defeat of that kind of mind which tries to make of knowledge a unified and moral whole.*

Liberals, understandably, did not take kindly to these conservative incursions which, though ever so slightly, encroached upon a domain which they felt to be theirs by right of long tenure, and they did what, I am sure, conservatives would have done were the positions reversed.

Conservative scholars found it difficult to secure academic posts and, once appointed, tenure was hard to come by and promotions were withheld if they seriously questioned liberal doctrine. Much of this discrimination is not vindictiveness, but results from a cocoon of self-righteousness which enshrouds some liberals so thickly as to be impenetrable to contrary thought. Those who disagree are not so much guilty of wrong thoughts as of non-thought. Many social scientists have so long told each other that they are scientists and thereby objective— though they know not a whit of science—that they thoroughly believe it. Those who question such unquestionable truths are so

---

*A parallel criticism of ideological formulas occurred in France, as some younger intellectuals, several of them former Marxists or Maoists, disparagingly designated the "new right" by their critics, now not only oppose Marxism but properly carry their criticism of systems back to the eighteenth-century philosophes and their obsession with remaking the world, describing as "arrogance" the enlightenment conception that intellectuals should dominate (measure and master) the world rather than study it. In place of such intellectual scientistic-rationalistic formulas "what is needed and useful is a persistent, detailed, practical and unremitting effort to patch things up and keep them from getting worse."[30]

mentally confused that they can be best helped by seeking a career elsewhere. Invariably, discrimination is practiced by liberals not from jealousy or vindictiveness; it is done to help the misguided recipient of misunderstood kindness. It is done for his own good, and in a wonderfully ironic way, this is correct, because the sooner a conservative social scientist realizes the impenetrability of academic liberals to contrary views the better off he is.

Conservatives have difficulty in having their works published, and when published they commonly are ignored, ridiculed, or reviewed hypercritically. Despite his prominence as an intellectual of superior ability, when Norman Podhoretz announced abandonment of the liberal doctrine of the perfectibility of man, *Making It* was subjected to many vitriolic reviews.

The techniques of such reviewing are simple and standardized: (a) you misstate the premises of the argument and distort its implications—this, currently, is being widely done with the emerging discipline of sociobiology. (b) If a literary work, you attack the style, but since most social science writing is not at all literary there is no style to attack. (c) If you can find nothing wrong with content or style, attack the author. I was called a Metternich, a Machiavelli, an enemy of progress, a foe of progress, a reactionary and a member of the party of the past, not a member of the party of the future, when I questioned the scientific validity of the claims of sociology.

Such resistance to ideas contrary to liberal doctrine is not confined to America. It took years for George Orwell to find a publisher for his delightful *Animal Farm*, and playwright John Braine, growing up in England as a Socialist when "... virtually every living writer of any consequence was a Socialist,"[31] couldn't imagine that there were any innate aspects of man which would prevent Socialists from creating, not simply a better society, but a perfect society in which there would be no war, no crime, no poverty, no neuroses, no racism, no class division, and only the irreducable minimum of ill health. Having renounced socialism, he found his once-praised work now scathingly criticized and concluded that:

> The Socialist Establishment is so firmly in control of
> the mass media, in England as in the United States, that any

professional writer who has publicly rejected socialism will almost inevitably suffer for it.[32]

Braine's countryman, novelist Kingsley Amis, having been, with Braine, one of England's praised "angry young men," renounced liberalism as he realized that many of the ills of life are not solvable by political means and sometimes the attempts to so eradicate them are harmful.[33] Brotherhood could not be legislated, he felt, because if you try to compel brotherhood you soon find yourself enforcing something different, and worse than the mere absence of brotherhood. He acknowledged that the vision of constructing the Just City cannot be discarded without a sense of loss, but some things work better without a planned program than with one.

In Russia, when socialist intellectuals dominated literary life under the Tsar, Dostoevsky sardonically contributed this advice to a new writer.

> Henceforth, you must adopt our tactics and follow them unconditionally. You must respect, screen and protect all those who declare themselves to be *progressives*. Even if they are not worth it . . . or if they have contributed in two years some little couplet, say even one like
>
> > Bek and Bek and Lev Kambek,
> > Lev Kambek and Bek and Bek,
>
> . . . we must consider them sacred.[34]

Though liberal discrimination has slowed the spread of conservatism, other factors also keep it below the level which it should attain to constitute a healthy intellectual balance to liberalism in academic life, literature, and national affairs. As I indicated previously, some expressions of conservatism have been nit-picking querulousness and some have been eighteenth-century economic liberalism, limited in appeal as well as confusing to those who try to understand what the real issues are. In relation to the moral nature of man—to me the fundamental difference—there is much exhortation but, until now, no intellectually credible affirmative explanation of the conservative position. In addition, there is the understandably greater appeal of

202

a form of liberalism which promises freedom from guilt and want in contrast to a conservatism which insists on unending need for conscientious responsibility in making judgments which exclude panaceas. Such factors make liberalism by far the dominant element in the thinking of academicians who teach about man and society, intellectuals who write about them, and clergy who preach about them.

Since one of the principal characteristics of liberals is that they are as biased as conservatives and seem to be objective primarily because they have the values of society upside down, the view we tend to get from them, while rationalistically plausible, is in terms of our traditional values, not only inaccurate, but inverted. This upside-down conception of morality is described in the following chapter.

Chapter 9. References and Notes

1. Thomas P. Neill, *The Rise and Decline of Liberalism* (Milwaukee: Bruce Pub. Co., 1953), p. 182, p. 172.

2. Arthur A. Ekirch, *The Decline of American Liberalism* (London: Longmans, Green and Co., 1955), p. 3.

3. Carl L. Becker, *The Heavenly City of the Eighteenth-Century Philosophers* (New Haven, Conn.: Yale University Press, 1932), p. 138.

4. Arthur Schlesinger, Jr., "The Humanist Looks at Empirical Social Research," *American Sociological Review*, December 1962, p. 771.

5. Jeffrey Hart, *The American Dissent* (New York: Doubleday, 1966), pp. 54–55.

6. Gertrude Himmelfarb, *Victorian Minds* (New York: Alfred A. Knopf, 1968), pp. 116–117.

7. John Stuart Mill, "Autobiography," in *The Norton Anthology of English Literature*, revised, vol. 2 (New York: W. W. Norton, 1968), pp. 1274–1282.

8. *Early Essays of John Stuart Mill* (1897) in Gertrude Himmelfarb, *Victorian Minds*, pp. 122–123.

9. John B. Watson, *Behaviorism* (Chicago: The University of Chicago Press, 1930), p. 304.

10. Ibid., p. v.

11. John B. Watson, *The Ways of Behaviorism* (New York: Harper & Brothers, 1928), p. 28.

12. Ibid., pp. 35–36, p. 84.

13. Ruth Benedict, *Patterns of Culture* (New York: Mentor Books, 1960), pp. 206–207.

14. Philip Rieff, *Freud: The Mind of the Moralist* (New York: Anchor Books, 1961), preface.

15. O. Spurgeon English and G. H. J. Pearson, *Emotional Problems of Living: Avoiding the Neurotic Pattern* (New York: W. W. Norton, 1945).

16. Clinton Rossiter, *Conservatism in America: The Thankless Persuasion* (New York: Vintage, 1962), pp. 22, 38, 17.

17. James W. Fernandez, "Anthropology, A Discipline About Man Himself," *New York Times*, July 17, 1977.

18. Sir James George Frazer, *The Golden Bough* (New York: Macmillan, 1942), p. 712.

19. William Golding, *Lord of the Flies* (New York: Capricorn Books, 1955), pp. 250–251.

20. Lionel Tiger, *Men in Groups*, (New York: Random House, 1969), p. 163.

21. Lionel Trilling, *The Liberal Imagination* (New York: Anchor Books, 1953), p. 5.

22. Peter Viereck, "The Philsophical 'New Conservatism' " in *The Radical Right*, ed. Daniel Bell (New York: Anchor Books. 1963), p. 187.

23. *National Review*, "Opinion on the Campus," June 15, 1971, pp. 635–650.

24. John Leonard, "The Top 70 Intellectuals," *New York Times Book Review*, October 29, 1970.

25. Norman Podhoretz, *Making It* (New York: Random House, 1967), pp. 88–89.

26. By novelist George P. Elliot, in "Notes on Cult; or, How to Join the Intellectual Establishment," by Victor S. Navasky, *New York Times Magazine*, March 27, 1966.

27. Saul Bellow, *Mr. Sammler's Planet* (Greenwich, Conn.: Fawcett, 1970), p. 34.

28. Saul Bellow, *The Adventures of Augie March* (New York: Viking, 1953), pp. 3, 536.

29. Arthur Miller, "The Writer as Independent Spirit," *Saturday Review*, June 4, 1966, pp. 16–19.

30. Flora Lewis, "A New Philosophy in France Finds Marx-

ism 'Monstrous,' " *New York Times*, July 31, 1977.

31. John Braine, "Why One British Socialist Turned Conservative," *New York Times Magazine*, March 2, 1969.

32. John Braine, "On Leaving the Herd," *National Review*, July 29, 1969.

33. Kingsley Amis, "Why Lucky Jim Turned Right," *National Review*, October 17, 1967.

34. Fyodor Dostoevsky, *Notes From the Underground and The Grand Inquisitor* (New York: E. P. Dutton, 1960), pp. 217–218.

Chapter 10

In De Quincey's Mirror

REJOICE! REJOICE ALL ye who live in the beneficent shadow of the ivory tower, for in the circle of its shade there is no sin. Look you as you might, you people of this Brave New World, you shall find neither sin nor evil nor lust nor envy. Nowhere among these circles of shade is there hate nor greed nor deceit nor wrongdoing. Nor is there covetousness nor perversion nor laziness.

Through your civilized veneer some ancient urge may rise to seek the sun behind the tower's cast penumbra and make you wonder: If there be no bad, can there be good? If I am never to be judged lazy, why should I work? If I have only personality, where is my character, for if I am only what people think me to be, beyond their thinking what am I? But these be primitive emotional stirrings, soon stilled by the rationality spread from the tower.

As I was about to describe how our manners and morals have not only changed but have been inverted, I picked at random five recently published textbooks on social problems and studied their indices—as, previously, I have studied scores of others—and found that the most recent texts (1975–1977) are identical with all others published in the past twenty-five years in that none of them mention sin, evil, lazy or laziness, lust, envy, bad or badness, deceit, hate, covet or covetousness, wrong or wrongdoing, greed, perversion, or character. Since, historically,

207

these concepts are associated with most of the social problems of mankind, we now seem to have attained the perfect society. We can be further assured of this our progress toward utopia because virtually all of the authors of these many texts claim that their conclusions are based on science.

But perhaps we have merely traded our spiritual weakness for secular ills, because in this knowledge which descends on us from the tower we find that while there is no sin, there is much sickness. We learn that criminals, formerly sinful, now are sick; that drug addicts and alcoholics suffer not from spiritual weakness but from sickness. Neurotics and those who pervert the uses of sex are sick; and those who shun laziness by working long or hard are sick workaholics; and the cause of most of these separate sicknesses is our collectively sick society.

It is not difficult to demonstrate that violations of all of our codes of social conduct—our manners and morals (which in the jargon of sociology are called folkways and mores)—whether they involve simple civility, crime, pre-marital sex, adultery, homosexuality, alcoholism, or dope addiction have for some forty years increased much faster than our increase in population. But this is now so commonly known that even some of the experts admit it, so in this chapter I shall concentrate on the ways our beliefs about these former social ills have changed so as to eliminate the element of evil from our feelings.

Thou shalt not steal; thou shalt do no murder. Once we were sure that crime was spiritual sin as well as social evil; now we are increasingly uncertain, and I shall relate some of the steps which have led us to our bewilderment.

In 1899, in Chicago, the first juvenile court was established so that delinquent youths would be treated like neglected children. The philosophy was that, whatever the charge which brought the youth into court, the procedure was to be oriented around understanding, guidance, and protection of the youth rather than criminal responsibility, guilt, or punishment. Such courts, operating under a doctrine of *parens patriae*, act as a parent should, no longer performing as agencies established by the society, paid for by the society and existing for the protection of the society from criminal activity.

Originally these juvenile courts handled only children, but as time went on the age of those legally qualified to come before them increased, rising to eighteen years. Originally most of the children brought before these courts were truants, waifs, mischievous boys, runaways, or at worst, children involved in petty thievery. Now many of them are rapists, drug peddlers, muggers, and other serious offenders. Originally the concept of the juvenile court arose from warm-hearted humanitarianism, but now the practices as well as the philosophy are mired in scientistic psychoanalytic doctrine, and the only prisoners associated with the practices of the juvenile court are the judges, chained to scientism.

To protect muggers and rapists from embarrassment, the public and press are barred from the hearings, a measure which, while certainly humanitarian, is chillingly reminiscent of the star-chamber secrecy which Anglo-Saxons fought for centuries to remedy.

Rules governing the presentation and admissibility of legal evidence are abandoned, and the interests of society are no longer protected by a prosecuting attorney. A youth is brought into court through a "contact," not an arrest, and a "fact-finding session" replaces a trial. Youths are not found guilty, but the "finding" may be against them in which case they are "placed," not sentenced. While awaiting a "finding," most young criminals are free to commit further crime; those who are held to await a "fact-finding session" are not remanded to a jail but placed in a Youth Study Center. Only a small percentage of young criminals, no matter how serious the crime or how mountainous the evidence, ever appear before the court, their cases having been "adjusted" before a court appearance.

Now more than half of all serious crime is committed by youths below the age of eighteen, and since 1960 serious crimes by such youths have increased more than twice as fast as adult crimes, which, in turn, have increased four times as fast as the population. But such complaints about increases in crime, especially in youthful crime, seem, in our new dispensation, the veriest sort of nit-picking pettifoggery which totally ignores the progress we are making.

Because, you see, the records of all crimes committed by juveniles are expunged. No matter how many or heinous his actual crimes, when a juvenile graduates to the adult courts he is a first offender. Thus, in a fashion that even George Orwell, with his superb skill at describing the imagined machinations of power-corrupted utopianists could not conceive, we re-write history and eliminate guilt.

There is significance for the conception of morality also in changing the word "criminal" to "delinquent." While a criminal has willfully broken laws which we need for our social survival, the delinquent has committed no positive wrong; he has merely failed to fulfill a duty or obligation. As all of us fail in one way or another to live up to our religious obligations, our obligations as husbands or wives or parents or employers or dutiful children or otherwise; we are all delinquent; so what's all the fuss about? There is in this no sin, no evil, no guilt, no threat to society, no need for punishment or blame.

In similar fashion criminologists have removed the connotations of badness, evil, sin, and guilt from adult criminals. Instead of looking upon criminals as evildoers, students are taught to envision them as "incompletely socialized personalities," or as persons "who are making a normal response to an abnormal situation." A recent way which our sociological scientists have found to eliminate the evil of crime is to designate criminals "deviants." A blurb for a 1977 social problems textbook describes the meaning thus:

> Your students usually think of deviants in the usual categories—prostitutes, drug addicts, radicals, criminals, juvenile delinquents—but in a study by J. L. Simmons the respondents included as deviant: liars, career women, Democrats, reckless drivers, atheists, card players, straights, hippies, conservatives, divorcees, motorcycle gang members, bearded men, and Christians.

There is nothing inherently deviant in any human act.

Well, that gets Jack the Ripper, Son of Sam, Stalin, Hitler, and Attila (Scourge of God, King of the Huns) off the hook; not to mention the Marquis de Sade and all necrophiliacs! Small wonder that George Orwell felt that "Who controls the language controls the people!"

As for the treatment of crime, the best thing to do is nothing at all, for psychoanalysts have informed us that people commit crimes because they want to be caught and punished in order to

210

relieve the guilt feelings they have about sexual urges. This being the case, it is best to turn our backs and refuse to arrest or punish criminals. Failing to receive the punishment which is their basic motive for their criminal acts, their frustration will soon make them law-abiding.

The psychoanalytic interpretation has lost some of its appeal, but the liberal establishment still holds staunchly to the environmental (slums cause crime, bad housing causes crime, poverty causes crime, unemployment causes crime) causes of crime despite much evidence that such putative "causes" ignore many exceptions, discount numerous related variables, and have never been proved. There is, of course, some merit to this liberal contention, and it is not my purpose here to argue it, but merely to cite an extreme illustration of its application to show: (a) how scientistic doctrine reaches into our highest areas of governance; and (b) how neatly such contention is the obverse of both religious and societal doctrine.

On July 13, 1977, a disruption of the supply of electrical power resulted in a blackout in New York City. Looting, arson, and vandalism, beginning with the blackout and continuing into the following day, resulted in millions in losses by both black and white merchants and between three and four thousand arrests. In contrast to earlier lawless rampages which had been associated with racial issues and in which looting was much less, there was no racial issue involved. Looters, mostly black, stole indiscriminately from stores, with no concern as to whether they were owned by black or white. Indeed, from a relative point of view, black merchants likely suffered more than white. The pillage was not carried out by a hungry mob. Some food was taken, but the principal targets were jewelry, televisions, record players, liquor, furniture, and, in one incident, fifty new cars were driven out of a showroom. Much of the looting was done by children who were being provided, during the summer, with free meals through a school program.

Predictably, most of the experts, despite much evidence to the contrary, blamed the looting on poverty; but saddest of all, the President of the United States, who had so often proclaimed himself a deeply religious man, immediately attributed it to lack of governmental housing programs and insufficient jobs, and as I read the statement of this sincere man I could not help but

211

contrast his interpretation with a biblical one:

> For out of the heart proceed evil thoughts, murders, adulteries, fornications, thefts, false witness, blasphemies. [Matthew: 15, 19]

There isn't much difference in the words involved—all one need do is substitute "belly" for "heart"—but there is a vast difference in the meaning of these interpretations.

Orwell's Reversal

Since we have transformed all criminals into either delinquents or deviants, and since all of us are delinquent and all are deviant, there is no difference between criminals and others. But an additional step remains in a process that I call Orwell's Reversal.

In 1954, Bertram M. Beck, director of the Juvenile Delinquency Project of the United States Children's Bureau, asserted that the absence of aggressive behavior on the part of non-delinquent children may be a greater danger signal than the violence of delinquents; that delinquents therefore might have "greater emotional health" than youths who obey the law. Conformity, he implied, may be a greater social problem than crime. This is the process of Orwell's Reversal rounded into completion.

In his insightful and prescient novel, *1984*, George Orwell described the world created by Ingsoc (English Socialism), where techniques of Newspeak ("Newspeak is Ingsoc and Ingsoc is Newspeak") were used to convince people that:

> War is Peace!
> Freedom is Slavery!
> Ignorance is Strength!

Such outrageous slogans were made to seem credible by the Ministry of Truth (Minitrue in Newspeak), which based its propaganda on the premise: "We create human nature. Man is infinitely malleable." In *1984* the heresy of heresies was common sense.

Our ivory towers are not so physically impressive as the

212

glittering white tower which soared three hundred meters into the air to house Minitrue, nor are the purportedly scientific truths which issue from them as rigidly doctrinaire as the propaganda conveyed through Newspeak by Minitrue, but the similarities in the process of inverting beliefs, of persuading people that good is bad, up is down, day is night and wrong is right are interesting if not disquieting.

In outline, the process of Orwell's Reversal develops thus:

(a) There is a social problem which social scientists contend they can solve.

(b) Their remedial measures are put into effect. In the case of crime: changing names of jails to Youth Study Centers, penitentiaries to reformatories, then to Correctional Centers as convicts became clients; changing determinate sentences to indeterminate; increasing use of probation, parole, psychiatrists, psychologists, social workers. In general, shifting the emphasis from punishment to techniques of remaking (reforming) the criminal, and from protecting the interests of society to re-educating the criminal. Slums are cleared, public housing built.

(c) The problem persists, and commonly gets worse.

(d) The experts deny that it is getting worse.

(e) Finally the "scientists" admit that the problem is not being solved, but they re-define it—"crime is a normal response to an abnormal situation"—to lead people to believe that the problem is not so bad as it seems and that the behavior which causes it is normal—delinquency or deviance—and shared by all.

(f) As the problem continues to grow, it is proclaimed as a new dispensation that the activities which produce it are better than normal and the condition is good rather than bad.

Scientism Delivers Us from Sexual Evil

As the Levites caused the people to understand the law—the law that told them of the sexual sins which were punishable by death and of others which were unclean and made the land unclean—so "science" led the people to reject it. And whereas the people wept when they heard the words of Levitical law, the people rejoiced when they were told that they should ignore the law—that no form of sex was evil nor unclean nor an abomination to be punished.

The new law seemed to proclaim that any form of sexual behavior, by or with any one or any thing, at any time, under any circumstances was normal; except that some forms (homosexuality) were more normal than others (sexual relations between husband and wife, especially if performed in the conventional "missionary" position).

Loudly were the people told that "traditional concepts of what is normal and abnormal, natural and unnatural in sexual behavior" had been exploded; that they had been revealed as myths and delusions by a soberly documented report whose findings were so contrary to what civilized man had been taught for generations, that *they would be unbelievable but for the impressive weight of scientific agencies backing the survey.*[1]

The report was A. C. Kinsey's *Sexual Behavior in the Human Male,*[2] and the foundations which funded the Kinsey surveys withdrew their financial support when several studies clearly revealed that their conclusions were based more on Professor Kinsey's bias than on scientific evidence.[3] But the conclusions were what people wanted to hear because they offered apparently scientific support for the sexual licentiousness which people gleefully descended into.

Leviticus says (XX, 12): If a man has intercourse with his daughter-in-law, they shall both be put to death. Kinsey says (4, II, 121) that parents object to adult molesters of their female children primarily because they have been conditioned against such acts. Children are adversely affected by adult sexual molestation primarily because their parents, due to improper conditioning, make a fuss about it. Otherwise, says Kinsey, an adult molester may contribute favorably to the later socio-sexual development of the child. Adult molesters, according to the new giver of the law, are educators without portfolio.

Most of Kinsey's conclusions are based on an assumption that malleable man can be limitlessly conditioned, in this contention holding much the same view as Watson and Skinner. But

214

neither of these, despite their extreme and unwarranted claims, would go so far as Kinsey, who contends:

> The male who reacts sexually and comes to erection upon seeing a streetcar, may merely reflect some early experience in which a streetcar was associated with a desirable sexual partner; and his behavior may be no more difficult to explain than the behavior of the male who reacts at the sight of his wife undressing for bed. There may, however, be more social advantage in the one type of behavior than the other. [I, 646]

Leviticus says (XX, 13, 14): If a man has intercourse with a man as with a woman, they both commit an abomination. They shall be put to death. Kinsey says (I, 661): that the difference between heterosexuality and homosexuality exists ". . . only because society demands that there be a particular choice in the matter, and does not so often dictate one's choice of food or of clothing." The difference, then, is of a level comparable to the choice between mashed potatoes or French-fried, between single-breasted or double.

Titus (II, 5) tells us to teach young women to be chaste.

Kinsey (II, 115, 266, 327, 328, 330) indicates that young women should be encouraged to fornicate prior to marriage because it will teach them to adjust to various types of males; it will contribute to their other non-sexual relationships and to their emotional capacities in a more effective way than if they do not fornicate before marriage, and, Kinsey warns, if they do remain chaste this ". . . may lead to inhibitions which damage the capacity to respond so much that they may persist after years of marriage . . . if, indeed, they are ever dissipated."[4]

Leviticus says (XX, 10): If a man commits adultery with his neighbour's wife, both adulterer and adulteress shall be put to death.

Kinsey (I, II) stresses throughout both volumes that adultery is morally normal. His contention that this and other forms of sexual behavior were normal rested on the frequency of their practice. This is *statistical morality,** which puts the stamp of

---

*On the very day I wrote this satirical reference to statistical morality, a serious reference to it from the Soviet *Literary Gazette* appeared

215

morality on anything which is frequently done. By such criteria the slaughter of Jews in Nazi Germany or the Kulaks in Stalinist Russia would be moral.

Soon sociologists and psychologists were contending that adultery is a good thing; it helps to hold a marriage together.

Scientism Delivers Us from Science

Scientistic contentions such as Kinsey's lead the people to reject religious law, and they also lead us to reject documented findings based on clinical research. Such findings indicate that:

> The slow phylogenetic ascent from highly programmed to flexible behavior is nowhere more clearly delineated than in the evolution of sexual behavior. The center of copulatory control in male insects is in the ganglia of the abdomen.
> . . .
> The sexual behavior of vertebrates differs from that of insects in being controlled almost wholly by the brain, particularly regions of the cerebral cortex.[6]

Ignoring all of the evidence that indicates that functions which are localized in the cerebral cortex are subject to conscious rather than subconscious control, Kinsey reverses our phylogenetic ascent, making it a descent back to a mammalian level. His criterion for human sexual normality is "usual mammalian behavior," "normal in other anthropoids," "biologic normality," and similar expressions that divorce sex from conscience and the lessons of civilization, as well as from religious law.

Following Kinsey's lead, prominent Yale anthropologist George Peter Murdock soon pushed us further down the evolu-

---

stressing that since more births were needed in the USSR, the government should encourage illegitimacy by subsidizing it, saying:

> We prize maiden honor and woman's dignity. We consider the stable family to be not merely the best but the only serious and respected relationship between people who love each other. But tell me, what is to be done about the statistics? Morality should not stand in the way of human happiness.[5]

216

tionary scale, asserting that premarital chastity has no scientific value and proffering five advantages (and no disadvantages) in encouraging youths to let their glands be their guides.[7]

Despite much evidence that demonstrated Kinsey's failure to reach valid scientific conclusions, academicians and others eagerly spread his scientistic doctrine which reduced the sexual activity and beliefs of humanity to an animal level; to products of glandular drives and subconscious conditioning over which we have not only no control, but no awareness. Kinsey's conclusions were taught as scientific truth in many college courses; lawyers proposed that we revise all laws related to sex; many clergymen applauded them, some even proposing that we revise our designation of historical epochs, changing B.C. and A.D. to B.K. and A.K. A college student named Hugh Hefner wrote a sociology term paper in which he eulogized Kinsey's work and went on, as publisher of *Playboy*, to publicize it. In 1960 a fictional take-off on the Kinsey report, called *The Chapman Report* (Irving Wallace), became a runaway best-seller. By 1960, though, the descriptions of adultery and homosexuality that had provided people with sexual titillation in the Kinsey report were insufficient to stir excitement, so *The Chapman Report* had to resort to more extreme items—gang sex and sex with the dead —for kickers! By 1960 a novel devoted entirely to sex with the dead, *The Necrophiles*, appeared.

A nationwide program of sex education, SIECUS (Sex Information and Educational Council of the United States) was established in 1964, and now spreads its sexual doctrine to hundreds of thousands of children each year. SIECUS doctrine, purportedly scientific but actually following Kinsey's scientistic bias very closely, was expressed by a president of the organization, David Mace:

> The simple fact is that through most of our history in Western Christendom we have based our standards of sexual behavior on premises that are now totally insupportable —on the folklore of the ancient Hebrews and on the musings of medieval monks, concepts that are simply obsolete. [*Sexology*, April, 1968]

This former president of SIECUS fails even to mention that our sexual codes, in addition to their religious background, are the distillate of thousands of years of an historical experience shared by every civilization that ever existed.

Also highly publicized and erroneously believed to provide validated scientific answers about socially significant areas of sexual behavior were two books by Dr. William Masters and Virginia Johnson.[8] The first was a restrained and reasonably objective description of neurological responses which occurred during sexual activity as measured by electrodes placed on various parts of the body; the second, a how-to-do-it book telling people how to overcome sexual inadequacies. Dr. Masters has said that the second book would not have been nearly as well received had people not been led to believe from the first book that his findings were soberly scientific. In fancying himself a crusader-as-scientist, Dr. Masters follows in the two-hundred-year-old footsteps of the philosophes. Having measured sex, he proposes to master it.

Of all forms of sexual behavior that Kinsey declared to be normal, the violation he most stressed as being normal was homosexuality. Why this was so, I do not know, but his findings relating to homosexual activity were the most misleading, and the most grossly exaggerated, while his efforts to prove the normality of such behavior necessitated the most tortuous reasoning.

Even before the Kinsey report was published, liberals had ceased calling homosexuality a sin, and the intellectually fashionable designation was "sickness"—something which, like mumps, couldn't be helped. A controllable spiritual weakness had been sublimated to an uncontrollable secular ailment caused by heredity or conditioning. Kinsey's semantic contribution was to cure the ailment by designating it "normal."

The notion that homosexuality is normal was strongly encouraged by the oft-quoted Kinsey contention that 37 percent of adult males have homosexual experience. This high percentage led to ready application of the concept of statistical morality although most, by far, of the homosexual experiences included in it were incidental (one experience of masturbation in the presence of another person of the same sex would qualify for inclusion) and exceptional acts by persons with an otherwise lifelong

218

record of heterosexuality. Only 2 to 3 percent of his sample showed a continuing pattern of homosexuality, and considering that his sample was extremely biased to favor the inclusion of homosexuals, a reasonable figure for male homosexuality as the characteristic lifetime sexual outlet would be somewhere around 1 percent *at the time the study was made.*

But such aspects of human behavior often involve a self-fulfilling prophecy. Once homosexual behavior acquired scientific approval as a normal way of life it, like all other violations of the codes of sexual conduct, increased rapidly. So Kinsey's figures, grossly exaggerated at the time, might later become accurate.

As homosexuality increased rapidly, Orwell's Reversal became operative to change it from normal to better than normal. By 1951 D. W. Cory, author of *The Homosexual in America,* claimed that homosexuality:

> . . . must inevitably play a progressive role in the scheme of things. It will broaden the base for freedom of thought and communication, will be a banner-bearer in the struggle for liberalization of our sexual conventions, and will be a pillar of strength in the defense of our threatened democracy.[9]

A survey of homosexual attitudes conducted by the Committee on Public Health of the New York Academy of Medicine in 1964 found that organized homosexuals:

> . . . would have it believed that homosexuality is not just an acceptable way of life, but rather a desirable, noble, preferable way of life. For one thing, they claim that it is the perfect answer to the problem of the population explosion.[10]

An interesting aspect of the change which elevated homosexuality from "sickness" to normal was the action taken by the American Psychiatric Association (APA) in 1973. Since 1950, homosexuality had been categorized as a mental illness by the APA, but in 1973 a majority of the members who responded to a mailed questionnaire voted to eliminate homosexuality as a mental disorder. Now *that's* medical science in action! All we now need to cure cancer is to get enough doctors to vote that it isn't a sickness! One factor affecting this response was a letter, distributed to all APA members prior to the vote and signed by five prominent psychiatrists, urging that homosexuality no longer be called a mental illness. This letter, it was later learned, was composed and distributed by the National Gay Task Force.

By 1967 a symposium of ninety Episcopalian priests agreed that homosexual acts between consenting adults were "morally neutral" and might even be a good thing. Homosexual churches were established, and by 1977 an avowed lesbian was ordained an Episcopal priest. In Britain, *Gay News* published a poem by Professor James Kirkup which depicted a Roman centurion having sexual relations with the body of the crucified Christ.

In 1977 singer Anita Bryant led a movement to repeal a Dade County (Miami) ordinance which granted homosexuals equal rights, objecting principally to one of the privileges granted by the ordinance—the "right" of practicing homosexuals to teach in public schools. Among those who laughed her efforts to scorn was Dr. Mary S. Calderone, the president of the Sex Information and Education Council of the U.S., who described Miss Bryant's objections as ravings that conflicted with research, as a triumph of ignorance over scientific fact, as unnecessary fears and irrational hates, as witch-hunting, hate-mongering tactics, and as un-Christian zealotry.[11]

The Wages of Non-Sin

In addition to much ancillary evidence which supports its findings, a study of *Sexual Behavior in the 1970s* concluded that while all forms of formerly proscribed sexual activities had increased greatly since the fifties, the change was not uniform —"In general, the more strongly an activity had been taboo, the greater the magnitude of the change." The most dramatic changes ". . . are those that have occurred in the formerly all-but-unmentionable oral-genital acts (which, incidentally, are still classified as punishable 'crimes against nature' in the statutes of most of our states)." Respondents generally were much more permissive in their attitudes toward all forms of sexual activity than people were in the past. "Kinky" sex (sado-masochism) becomes ever more common.[12]

Despite increasing numbers of scientistic studies of sexual behavior, psychiatric counselling, and widespread sex-education programs, the predicted improvement in marital adjustment, decrease in divorce, decline in illegitimacy, and reduction of venereal disease has failed to occur.

Illegitimate births, which were supposed to be virtually eliminated by sex education, by more effective and more readily available contraceptives, and by easily accessible abortions, went steadily upward from 142,000 in 1950 to 448,000 in 1975. And, in addition, we had 1,115,000 legal abortions in 1976, many of which would otherwise have been illegitimate births. Illegitimate births as a percentage of all births rose from 4 percent to 13 percent during the same interval. In 1975, in Washington, D. C. ("Showcase of the Nation"), there were more illegitimate births than legitimate, and more abortions than births.

Despite more readily available and more effective protective devices and widespread sex education, gonorrhea not only became epidemic, but a new strain of gonococci, highly resistant to penicillin and other antibiotics, developed and spread.

As for the improvements in marital life which were supposed to follow upon the new knowledge and the increased sex education: people are postponing marriage longer and longer, more people refuse to become married; the average duration of marriage is shorter; and divorce rates have more than doubled since 1960.

But perhaps as we descend in our sexual practices not only to Kinsey's prescribed mammalian level, but below it, there is hope for the future. For our birth rate is already below the level needed to replace us, and should this long-term trend continue, we shall solve not only our sexual problems but all other problems of human life—by eliminating people!

Down from the Tower, into the Streets

The conception of man which eliminates evil and which glorifies individuation (Do your own thing) above socially responsible behavior while lowering sexual and other aspects of human

221

life to a duckbilled platypus level soon spread from its pseudo-scientific source to permeate novels, movies, and magazines. By the 1970s pornography, an expectable if not an inevitable extension of scientistic interpretations of sex, had become a two-billion-dollar enterprise.

This is not to say that prior to the pseudo-scientific fortification which sheltered pornography from attack, novels avoided all reference to sex. A few American writers such as Henry Miller (*Tropic of Cancer, Tropic of Capricorn*) wrote sexually explicit books, but they were published abroad and had to be smuggled into the United States. Most of the "racy" novels, such as those of F. Scott Fitzgerald, Vima Delmar, and others, referred to sex only obliquely, not physiologically. Fitzgerald's *Tender Is the Night* even had an incestual motif, but it was treated in the classic Greek Oedipal manner, instead of the irresponsible Freudian manner.

The goal of fictional depiction of human life was expressed in the Nobel Prize, which was to be awarded to the author of the most outstanding work of an *idealistic* tendency; and the Pulitzer Prize, to be awarded only for novels which exemplified the "highest standards of American manners and manhood." Plays were to promote good morals and good taste; biography must teach "unselfish and patriotic service to the people."

Such ideals quickly evaporated in a pattern of increasing explicitness; increasing animalization of all forms of sexual behavior. Webster Schott, reviewing two novels about homosexuals, observed that the homosexual assault on United States fiction began sometime around 1945 in the postwar fiction of Truman Capote, Paul Bowles, Carson McCullers, and others.[13] But most of those earlier references were suggestive, oblique, while by the late sixties in many novels the author's portrayal is explicit, physiological. The synopsis of one of the novels included in the latter group (Hubert Selby, Jr.'s *Last Exit to Brooklyn*, a best-seller in 1965) describes the opening episode in which a gang, having crippled a young soldier, stands around him in a circle, methodically kicking in his face, ribs, and crotch.[14] Selby proceeds to fulfill the promise of his opening scene by describing the details "of mayhem, homosexual violence, back-alley girls, and mass fornication of a feeble-minded slut."

222

I indicated above that as the shock appeal of references to pre-marital sex and adultery dissipated, more extreme forms of sex such as homosexuality, gang bangs, and necrophilia had to be described in order to stir the prurience of a jaded public. An additional facet of the change was that any single form of sexual behavior, no matter how violently at variance with moral codes, no longer sufficed, so perversions had to be multiplied, much as bets at a race track are parlayed.

One illustration of this phenomenon should suffice for all but those with the strongest stomachs and the weakest minds. *The Last of the Southern Winds* by David Loovis appeared in 1960 as a forgettable novel with a cast of uncharacters headed (for want of a better word) by Jake Romano, cruelly disabled (a technical literary expression meaning deballed) by an old football (get it?) injury. His wife Melanie is a dangerously destructive paranoid. In the restaurant which Jake owns and calls a café, the waitresses, Betty and Jenny, are lovers (fornicate with each other); likewise Kent and Robin, the waiters. Renee, the bar singer, is a nymphomaniac (screws everybody); Art, the pianist, is a heroin subscriber (an addict who plays a piano with several keys missing); Henri, the chef, lives (fornicates) with a fourteen-year-old waif; and Eddie, the caretaker (janitor), is harmlessly mad. For some reason, I feel drawn toward Eddie!

In an attempt to stem the flood of sludge which was engulfing us, the Supreme Court, in 1957, ruled that published material was obscene and could be banned from distribution if "to the average person, applying contemporary community standards, the dominant theme of the material taken as a whole appeals to prurient interests." This was a reasonable criterion, serving to decrease the flow somewhat, and it had the further advantage (to those of conservative persuasion) in that the issue was properly returned to community standards and prudent judgment. But it was not permitted to stand, and in 1966 the Court ruled that material was not obscene unless it was "utterly without redeeming social value."

Please forgive me as I indicate the implications of such a ruling by setting myself up as an expert on judging if published materials have redeeming social value. I grew up in poverty, in the anthracite regions, during the depression of the thirties, and I well remember the cartoon booklets we bought from under the counter in poolrooms. By flipping the pages you could see the cartoon figures perform sexual acts. And I remember the deep discussions we had as to whether there was more social significance in Jiggs screwing Maggie or Tilly the Toiler screwing everybody. I tell you, we were really interested in social values in my youth.

We were also artistically motivated, and sometimes played hooky so we could see a burlesque show. Not that we had a prurient interest in the strippers or the bumps and grinds but because we were enthralled with burlesque as a "peoples' art form."

Some "redeeming social value" can be culled from anything, of course, but it did salve the conscience of people who should have known better, as it encouraged them to feel that their fine sensibilities found artistic expression where others found only smut. What should have been a definitive rebuttal to such views appeared in the form of a novel called *Naked Came the Stranger* (1968) by Penelope Ashe. *Naked* became a praised bestseller and continued to sell well after it was revealed that it was a total fake. There was no Penelope Ashe; the book was written by several editors and reporters under the guidance of a newspaper columnist who directed his collaborators to put an unremitting emphasis on sex; the only restriction being that any excellent writing would be blue-penciled. The point was to write as badly as possible, cutting out all words of more than three syllables, all symbolism, most character descriptions, and all references to nature, but to include enough perversions to suit a wide readership.

In 1973 the Supreme Court ruled that local juries should decide questions of obscenity, and while thus returning the issue to local decision was a desirable move, and while laws relating to pornography may be necessary, the basic fault, as with all moral issues, lies primarily in an evasion of responsibility by parents, teachers, professors, editors, clergy, and people in general who refuse to acknowledge their own blame, having been cowed into refusing to call smut what it is and failing to take a firm social stand against it.

This issue was pointed up in a 1963 case in which Justice J. Erwin Shapiro of the New York State Supreme Court dismissed indictments against several book distributors charged with sell-

224

ing obscene literature, saying that even though the books in question were: poor writings, bad in taste, profane, offensive, disgusting, and plain unvarnished trash, with no redeeming social value and with fully 90 percent of each book filled with lurid descriptions of sexual activities both hetero- and homosexual, insufficient detail to act as an erotic stimulus to those so inclined, the indictments should be dismissed because the books did not transgress the

> present critical point in the compromise between candor and shame at which the community has arrived.[15]

In 1970, the report of a Commission on Obscenity and Pornography appointed by President Lyndon B. Johnson in 1967 used scientistic evidence to reach its conclusion that neither federal, state, nor local legislation should interfere with the right of adults who wish to read, obtain, or view explicit sexual materials. A majority of the commission did, however, recommend legislative regulations on the sale of sexual materials to young persons without the consent of their parents.

Two members of the commission who were professors of sociology (Otto N. Larson of the University of Washington and Marvin E. Wolfgang of the University of Pennsylvania), basing their decision on surveys which could not possibly have been scientific, dissented from the majority finding, saying that all federal, state, and local statutes that prohibit the sale, exhibition, or other distribution of "obscene" material should be repealed; that there be no statutory restrictions on obscenity or pornography for anyone.

These sociologists, in standard Orwellian fashion, contended that there was no substantial evidence to show that exposure of juveniles to pornography is harmful. "There may even be beneficial effects, if for no other reason than the encouragement of open discussion about sex between parents and children relatively early in young lives."[16]

In a delightfully appropriate sequel, within a short time after publication of the report, an enterprising publisher and editor deleted much of its textual material, replacing it with photographs of heterosexuality, homosexuality, sodomy, and bestiality; titled their product *The Illustrated Presidential Re-*

port of the Commission on Obscenity and Pornography; and, charging $12.50 per copy contrasted with the $5.50 per copy for the pictureless version, quickly sold more than 100,000 copies. This publisher and editor received prison sentences, and two others associated with this imaginative enterprise were also convicted and placed on probation.[17]

A question: Why was it a criminal offense to do what the commission itself recommended?

An answer: The report of the commission was published by Bantam as a *New York Times* book. Adolph Ochs, founder of the dynasty which controls the *New York Times*, when questioned about the propriety of some of the material he published, said: "When a tabloid prints it, that's smut. When the *Times* prints it, that's sociology." How prescient was the late Mr. Ochs!

While the recommendations of the sociologist members of the commission did not immediately result in the insertion of copies of *Hustler* in children's Wheaties, nor in the tooth fairy leaving a subscription to *Gay News* under their pillows, magazines such as *Lollitots, Naughty Horny Imps,* and *Child Discipline* soon appeared, showing children performing sex acts with adults and with other children, and 8-mm films showing children engaged in fellatio, intercourse, and rape were offered for sale.

Although now outdated and (in terms of what has since happened) seeming to recall the innocent simplicity of a bygone day, Edmund Fuller, in his *Man in Modern Fiction,* contended that writers of the 1950s such as Norman Mailer, James Jones, Tennessee Williams, and Paul Bowles promoted and glorified an image of man as a depraved, immoral creature. Fuller traced the development which led to this debasement of the conception of man as beginning with the vogue of the lovable bums—a romanticizing of the scalawag; then Saroyan and Steinbeck developed the lovable bums into "the beautiful little people"—which meant the shiftless, the drunk, and the amoral.[18] If one failed to love these non-characters, one was, by implication, a self-righteous bigot.

As the idealization of the lovable bums faded, out of the shadows emerged the genial rapist, the jolly slasher, the fun-loving dope pusher. Fuller contended that the identification with the degraded which was involved in these portrayals was more often self-pity than compassion. Such writers pretended to subscribe to the bromide: "To understand all is to forgive all"; but actually, said Fuller, they did not understand all—they *devalued* all. "They do not forgive all. They do not forgive anything. They say there is nothing to forgive. They take murder, rape, perversion and say, belligerently, 'What's wrong with it?' " The relativistic, behavioristic standards of ethics in such novels, he says, is the inversion of good and bad.

Similar inversion of morals occurred in magazines, movies, and stage presentations and are now so common that they need no dwelling on except for brief mention of some aspects of this descent to the mammalian level through the medium affecting more people than the others, the movies.

As with novels, the pretense was made that sexually explicit movies represented new, daringly realistic art forms, and for years the dirtiest movies were shown in "Art" theaters. As I look at today's neighborhood movie directory in the "Weekend Guide to Entertainment," I see that Art Holiday Theater has as its feature *The Jade Pussycat,* which has the distinction of being not merely X-rated but XXX-rated. This classic of artistic social significance is described as "a new highly erotic porno film, in color, that reaches an erotic crescendo unmatched in the annals of adult films."

William Zinsser, in the *Atlantic,* brings out the sociopolitical significance of a movie called *Cara Theresa* (Cara being a peasant girl who discovers her true self by engaging in sixteen sexual acts—including one on a motorcycle, one in a crowded bus, and one with a goat) in an interview with the director, Carlo Fugati. Far from being a dirty movie, *Cara Theresa* was, insisted Fugati, a political statement with Theresa representing integrity pillaged by the soulless forces of bourgeois materialism, Nixonian imperialism, and the military-industrial complex. "I decided to show the girl having sex in a wide variety of unorthodox situations to make the point that the masses don't have to be smothered by middle-class conventions."[19]

The sex act with the goat is not bestiality, it is loneliness. The scene where Cara fornicates on the floor of a crowded bus is saying, says director Fugati, ". . . there are not enough buses." Anyone who sees it as other than a plea for more buses is sick.

Time (April 5, 1976) outlines the film *Sweet Movie* as featuring a striptease for children, intercourse plus murder on a bed

227

of sugar, a band of rollicking adults who vomit, defecate, and urinate on one another. Its director says the film is socially beneficial.

Even some extreme liberals objected to the movie *Snuff*, which, among other artistic items, shows a woman being held down while her hands and feet are sliced off; she is split lengthwise, throat to bowels, and her intestinal tubing is triumphantly removed. Such protests faded, however, when it was learned that the sexual murder was faked. Reviewer John Leonard (*New York Times*, February 27, 1976) protested that even though the murder was counterfeit it should have nothing to do with the fact that murder as sexual entertainment is pornographic.

Our cycle is not yet quite impervious. Banned in 1966 was a Swedish film (*491*) which depicts a Christ-figure (Kristes) as providing shelter for juvenile delinquents who engage in sodomy and fellatio and force a prostitute to fornicate with a dog. Also, in 1976, many British citizens objected to a Danish director who wished to make a pornographic film of Christ in England. We must, it seems, be patient for just a brief spell for our cycle of sinless sex to be complete.

In Freud's Service, Perfect Freedom

Although the behavioristic conception of a form of man who is so denatured as to be limitlessly conditionable has widely infiltrated popular as well as academic beliefs, the psychoanalytic interpretation of man and morality has been even more pervasive and more effective in inverting our standards of civility and morality.

There is much evidence to support Professor Rieff's contention, described in Chapter 9, that Freud's influence in the mass media and the college classroom is greater than that of any other modern thinker. But Professor Rieff's reiterated claim that Freud was a scientist is simply absurd, as anyone with even the slightest comprehension of the requirements for scientific investigation can see. Having touched on this issue earlier, I shall not go into detail here to point out that not only has no single aspect of Freudian doctrine ever been scientifically validated—nor in the very nature of the case can it be—but Freud himself admitted, and others observed, that he faked his evidence.

In 1897 Freud wrote a letter in which he admitted that the childhood sexual experiences of his female patients with their fathers, the "factual" evidence on which his hypothesis rested, had never occurred.[20] He had either invented these happenings from his own sexual fantasizing or his patients, anxious to satisfy this man who endlessly importuned them to tell him about their father's sexual advances, finally, regardless of fact, told him what he wanted to hear. Finally he realized:

> ... the awful truth that most—not all—of the seductions in childhood which his patients had revealed, and about which he had built his whole theory of hysteria, had never occurred.

Once aware that the evidence on which his hypotheses rested was mostly a figment of his imagination, Freud said he would gladly have given up the whole thing but he persevered because he could not then begin anew at anything else. Such is the stuff which makes intellectual history!

Even Freud's most devoted disciples admitted that Freud would record patients' statements which were demonstrably false if they fitted into his ideology but refuse to record true statements which conflicted with his convictions.

So much for the "scientific" validity of the conceptions of man which we rely on to replace religious and civilized "myths."

But Professor Rieff is correct in asserting that Freud tried to "expose the whole rotten empire of the family" and to smash the past. He also contended that to be religious is to be sick.

In his lectures on psychoanalysis, Freud proclaimed magistrally:

> ... we have found it impossible to give our support to conventional sexual morality or to approve highly of the means by which society attempts to arrange the practical problems of sexuality in life. We can demonstrate with ease that what the world calls its code of morals demands more sacrifices than it is worth, and that its behaviour is neither dictated by honesty nor instituted with wisdom.[21]

Freud's conception of man never had any scientific validity, and the evidence supporting it has always been superficial. The only intellectually interesting aspects of his doctrine are (a) why he was so obsessed with inverting moral standards and (b) why others, intelligent enough to know better, accept his views as scientific truth.

After intensive analysis of Freud's motivation, J. M. Cuddihy contends that the core of psychoanalytic interpretation, the "Oedipus Complex," is a "universalization of his father's social humiliation." Freud recounts that his father, as a child, had been told by *his* father of an incident in which a Christian had knocked off his cap and ordered him off the sidewalk. Freud's grandfather had meekly accepted this degrading insult, and this humility concerned Freud so much that, according to Cuddihy, it led him (subconsciously, of course) "to transform a misfortune of history into a universalist science of man."[22] Cuddihy's interpretation, obviously, is not scientific and can no more be proved than Freudian doctrine itself can be validated.

To disprove any doctrine is virtually impossible, and the possibility remains that Freudian doctrine does embody some truths about mankind. It is, however, the burden of those who make claims to scientific validity (such as Professor Rieff) to substantiate them, and this has never been done, nor even seriously attempted. Disciples of Freud and believers in his doctrine must accept it as an ideology—visionary theorizing which becomes a closed circle of belief, impervious to contrary evidence. Those who wonder why it expanded and became popular need only remind themselves that ideologies, like bureaucracies, once established, need no sensible reason for their continuance and growth.

It is this ideology—this circle of unverified belief—which has, according to Professor Richard La Piere, demolished the Judaeo-Christian ethic in America.[23] If our moral values are being abolished, and with them the middle class (bourgeoisie) in which they found their firmest support, credit (or blame) ". . . goes to Freud more than any other single man." The middle class is destroying itself, contends Professor La Piere, because it accepts the contra-bourgeois values sanctioned by the Freudian doctrine of man.

Freudian doctrine seeped into anthropology, sociology, psychology, psychiatry (where for a long time it virtually monopolized the interpretation of mental disorder), political science, history, and many other academic studies as well as into novels, plays, and other sources of dissemination. A large part of the appeal lay in Freud's furious rejection of religion, which fitted so nicely into the historical anticlericalism of liberalism, and in Freud's apparently scientific support for the tendency of liberals to be biased in favor of an upside-down version of the values of society.

Thus, where Americans generally were proud (and sometimes, I fear, boastful) of our Puritan heritage, anthropologist Ruth Benedict endeared herself to liberal professors by contending that our Puritan forebears ". . . were the psychoneurotics of New England."[24] And, she threatened, should we insist on maintaining our moral standards and adhere to our conventions, we shall all go mad because "the psychopathic toll that such a motivation exacts is evident in every institution for mental diseases in our country."

Psychoanalysts have interpreted virtually every aspect of human life, and no matter how diverse the subject matter or contrary the facts—Newton's Laws of Motion or Santa Claus—they always come to the same conclusion: perverted sexual desire causes everything. This uniformity of interpretation of such an enormous and disparate variety of effects could (possibly) attest to an actual causal connection, or it could (more likely) indicate a circle of belief which closes itself against outside reality—an ideology. A few examples may illustrate the breadth of coverage of this uniform interpretation.

Freud inveighed strongly against religion, calling it a sickness. In 1946, Rabbi Joshua Liebman, in his *Peace of Mind,* warned his readers that the repression necessitated by religious injunctions that man refrain from sin is "responsible for much of the grief, illness, and anxiety that lash the soul of modern man." Those who do refuse to accede to the temptation to sin ". . . transform themselves into self-torturing masochists or intolerant fanatics." After paying his deference to Freud's Oedipus Complex and to the anthropological "truth" that each culture must create its own God-idea rather than rely upon outworn tradition, Rabbi Liebman proceeds to the proposal that climaxes his theme—that we need a new Ten Commandments of which

231

the first shall be: "Thou shalt not be afraid of thy hidden impulses."[25]

At a far, if not opposite, extreme we have a psychoanalytic interpretation of Isaac Newton.[26] We are informed that Newton's optical experiments were made because he, voyeristically, wished to enjoy intimate visual experiences with his mother; and his laws of motion—likely the greatest discovery in the history of science—were merely an attempt to assuage his feelings of insecurity (engendered by the death of his father and remarriage of his mother) by creating a closed system to shelter him.

In another "scientific" psychoanalytic study, we are told that the Industrial Revolution occurred when post-Copernican man, distraught because he was no longer the center of the universe, felt obliged to fashion substitute phalluses in the form of levers, pistons, bombs, and torpedoes. "What but the greatest orgasm ever seen on earth was the atomic bomb explosion?" The steam engine invented by James Watt was a "phallus to end all others."[27]

We have similar interpretations of Moses, Michelangelo, Leonardo da Vinci, Joan of Arc, Napoleon, John Wilkes Booth, Adolf Hitler, General George Armstrong Custer, President Nixon, Senator Barry Goldwater, and many other prominent people.

The cause of war? Simple. The Japanese attacked Pearl Harbor because they were toilet-trained at too early an age. This "scientific" interpretation was so widely publicized that it was called The Scott Tissue Theory of History. Why did the post-World War II Russians accept the tyranny of Stalin? Easy. Anthropologist Dr. Margaret Mead, later to hold the most prestigious scientific office in America, explained that the Russians love tyranny because they are wrapped in swaddling clothes during infancy. Because they are wrapped in swaddling clothes during infancy, they grow up to fear their natural impulses and hence they seek the protection of an authoritarian state.[28] Any other questions?

As for Santa Claus, Dr. Brock Chisholm, psychiatrist and director general of the World Health Organization, explains that:

There is no sound psychological reason that I know of for children not enjoying the Santa myth as long as they know it is not true.

You see, you tell your child that there is a Santa. When he wonderingly asks you "Is there really a Santa?" you tell him definitively: "There is no Santa." Clear?

If you do tell your child there is a Santa, Dr. Chisholm warns:

> . . . the child's whole relation with reality and whole ability to think clearly in terms of cause and effect have been seriously damaged or permanently destroyed. He will have learned that to think in relation to the evidence of his own eyes leads only to confusion and fear. The fear is engendered by a very real insecurity produced when evidence is presented to the child that he cannot trust his own parents.
> Naturally and inevitably any intelligent child who believes in Santa will be afraid of the dark. He may, because of shame in relation to his fear, conceal that fear from his parents.

An explanatory note to parents: If your child is *afraid of the dark*, it is because you told him about Santa. If your child is *not afraid of the dark*, it is because you told him about Santa. Any questions?

Dr. Chisholm further explains that most parents tell their children about Santa because they want to retain their own infantile satisfactions but others do it "because they have an unconscious antagonism to children and a real necessity to frighten them."

If there are no other questions, I have one. "With people like Dr. Brock Chisholm directing it, I wonder what the World Health Organization is like?"

Perhaps you have rejected your infantile satisfactions and, having no unconscious antagonism toward children, you don't tell anyone about Santa or believe in any other myths. Your interests are cerebrally above and beyond the mythological; you play chess.

Several persons have psychoanalytically interpreted why

people play chess, but one example, *Idle Passion,* by Alexander Cockburn, will indicate the depths of your depravity and should cause all chess players to upset the board, smash all the pieces into fragments, and rush out to proclaim to everyone: "There *is* a Santa Claus!"[29]

Chess obviously (to Cockburn, at least) represents the classical Oedipal situation.[30] The Queen is the mother and the King is both the father and the boy's penis in the phallic stage. The etiquette which requires abstention from touching any of the pieces is a taboo against masturbation and homosexuality. Chess, originally invented to cure the madness of Babylonian King Merodach (who chopped up the body of his father Nebuchadnezzar into three hundred pieces), has as its aim the murder of the father with the help of the mother and is a paranoid, anal-sadistic, dance of death. Checkmate?

In De Quincy's Mirror

In his essay, "On Murder Considered As One of the Fine Arts" (1827), Thomas De Quincey, conservative, rigid moralist and sturdy Tory, strongly opposed murder because he feared that once a person indulges himself in murder, "very soon he comes to think little of robbing; from robbery he comes next to drinking and thence to Sabbath-breaking." Ultimately the downward path may descend to the uttermost depths of incivility and procrastination. We should be wary of embarking on such paths in these "pursy times [when] virtue itself of vice must pardon beg."

While conservatives would stress dangers which are associated with the loss of clarity of definition of our manners and morals brought about by psychoanalytic interpretations and Orwellian techniques, liberals would minimize the risks we take in following these trends and would stress, instead, their beneficial effects.

Liberal Vision—Twin Faceted

Given a conception of man whose malleability opens a path to perfectibility through conditioning, liberals envision a future in which man who has no guilt will live in a society where there is no want, where we need no grace to attain our glory.

One facet of their vision involves emancipation of the personality. Once freed from the "heavy weight of the dead hand of the past" and from religious dogma and superstitious supernaturalism, personalities will attain full bloom in their flowering.

The Skinners, Kinseys, and Freuds seem to have proved that our earlier codes of behavior were based on myth and perpetuated by bigots. The supposed scientific proof of anthropologists holds that since there are hundreds of human cultures, with differing and sometimes diametrically opposite codes of behavior, it is an expression of ethnocentric small-mindedness to contend that ours is better than any of the others. This anthropological doctrine of *cultural relativism* makes all codes of equal worth. Only our *cultural conditioning*—a subconscious process over which we have neither awareness nor control—deludes us into believing that our codes are preferable to those of the Kwakiutl.

One criterion for good moral codes, according to the Freuds and Kinseys in their modern version of Jeremy Bentham's felicific calculus, is hedonistic—do they produce more pleasure than pain. The second criterion, according to Skinnerian behaviorists, also goes back to Bentham, this time to his Utilitarianism, according to which doctrine our principal goal, in relation to our moral codes, is to adapt them to technological developments. It is our failure to keep our codes adjusted to changed environmental conditions that produces many of our social problems according to the *cultural lag* hypothesis developed by sociologist W. F. Ogburn.[31] Social problems are produced when two correlated parts of a culture change at unequal speeds. Since technological changes are many and rapid while moral codes are relatively stable and slow to change, many of our most serious problems arise, so this interpretation holds, because we do not change our moral standards sufficiently often and fast; the re-

235

sulting lag creating an imbalance in social development with its consequent problems.

In relation to pre-marital sex, for example, supporters of the cultural lag doctrine would concede that injunctions against such practices made good utilitarian sense in the past because of risks of pregnancy and dangers of venereal disease. Now, with more effective contraceptives more readily available, the risks of pregnancy are vanishing and sex education plus penicillin has minimized the effects of venereal disease to the point where once-sensible injunctions against pre-marital sex are now anachronistic.

If opponents argue that the facts leading to such a conclusion are wrong, pointing out that despite more than a million abortions a year the rate of illegitimate births has gone up, not down, and citing the new strains of gonorrhea which aggravate our failure to contain the epidemic spread of venereal disease, liberals would admit that these are undesirable, but would contend that they are transient effects that will remedy themselves in the new society that will arise when we adopt the new morality.

The New Morality

Liberals would contend that the changes in manners and morals that are consequent to an acceptance of their view of man do not constitute an abandonment of morality. Such change, they insist, involves the replacement of a once useful but now outmoded set of moral standards with a new set, one much better adapted to the needs of a new age. During the transition between the obsolete old and the utilitarian new there will be some unfortunate side-effects such as increases in crime, venereal disease, illegitimacy, and such, but these are transitional, and will dissipate when the new morality is absorbed into our minds as well as incorporated into our social structure.

Items included in the new morality vary, but the following list is, I believe, representative of their nature:

Social justice
A living wage

236

Social security
Socialized medicine
Good housing for all
Education for all
Racial equality
Internationalism
Pacificism

In accordance with the doctrine of cultural lag, as conditions change, some of these items would change. At present, for instance, many would add sexual equality—with some adding homosexual equality as well as equality between the sexes. Since many workers now receive six or more dollars an hour in addition to generous fringe benefits, pleas for a living wage have neither the humanitarian nor—more importantly—the political appeal they once had, and this item might be dropped or, more likely, replaced by ever-higher federally imposed minimum wages.

Whatever the details of the listing, the inclusion of these items as moral imperatives indicates a revolution in the concept of morality. Increasingly, a moral stance involves support of (this being moral) or opposition to (immoral) a grouping of socio-political programs, while character is relegated to a secondary if not unimportant role. Morality, as Burke put it, no longer involves men, but measures.

This shift in the conception of morality from judgment of the behavior of individuals in terms of their response to spiritual and social responsibilities to one in which the criteria increasingly become the acceptance or rejection of socio-political programs was clearly enunciated by President Lyndon B. Johnson during his campaign for election in 1964. As background, several instances of questionable activities were associated with Johnson's incumbency. One prominent member of his administration, Walter Jenkins, was arrested in a public toilet, charged with homosexual practices; another, Bobby Baker, a long-time protégé of Senator Johnson, was charged with using his high political connection as a lever for financial gain; a third, Billie Sol Estes, was alleged to have avoided arrest for massive misappropriation of funds from the Commodity Credit Corporation through high-level political influence. Senator Goldwater was

237

President Johnson's opponent, and in one of President Johnson's campaign speeches he enunciated his belief that one's stance relating to socio-political programs is a better measure of morality than one's personal behavior. He said:

> . . . while Mr. Goldwater is talking about Bobby Baker, Walter Jenkins and Billie Sol Estes, we want to talk about urban renewal, low income housing. We are going to talk about area redevelopment. We are going to talk about aid to education.[32]

Both President Johnson and his running-mate, Hubert H. Humphrey, implied that Senator Goldwater's attitude toward race and civil rights was in itself a form of public immorality. By referring to Senator Goldwater's *attitude* toward race and civil rights as a form of *public* immorality, candidates Johnson and Humphrey brought out another nuance of the new morality. Factually, Senator Goldwater's voting record in favor of civil rights legislation was appreciably better than Johnson's (as senator) had been, so, not being able to charge their opponent with immoral or less moral acts, he is charged with having an immoral *attitude*. Note also that the charge is *public* immorality.

In his autobiographical *The Vantage Point*, President Johnson described his program designed to produce The Great Society (a designation previously used as the title of Fabian Socialist Graham Wallas' 1914 book, dedicated to Walter Lippmann, and describing how the Fabians would create the socialist state) as including a War on Poverty, greater educational opportunities for all, medical care for the elderly, and more public housing.[33]

On the day following President Johnson's elevation of "public morality" above personal morality, the Reverend Dr. John C. Bennett, president of Union Theological Seminary, issued a statement signed by thirty prominent clergymen publicly protesting Senator Goldwater's references to the twice-arrested Walter Jenkins, saying that arrests for moral violations, which at worst involved "human weakness," should not be permitted to obscure:

238

... moral issues related to public life—moral issues such as the full civil rights of all citizens, the shameful squalor and poverty in our cities and the danger of nuclear war.[34]

In 1965, a large majority of some two hundred Protestant ministers meeting at the Harvard Divinity School went on record as accepting as *articles of faith* (my emphasis) responsibility for equal rights, the war on poverty, and slum housing, better education, Medicare, school integration, the reduction of international tensions, and the consolidation of peace in all corners of the globe.[35]

In 1967, the United Presbyterian Church in the USA made social action an official part of basic church doctrine, at the same time rejecting any thought that the Bible is "inerrant." Spelled out, the social action included most of the items which I had described fifteen years previously as the new morality.

In 1968 the World Council of Churches, meeting at Upsala, Sweden, called for revolutionary action to promote a similar political program.

In 1976, in the "Boston Affirmations," prominent clergymen proclaimed that "the transforming reality of God's reign" now included sexual equality in addition to the usual new morality items, and, imperialistically, annexed the social sciences to the kingdom where God reigns.[36] Those who question their secular socio-political programs are described as the spiritually blind who have chosen an existence where "sin rules, liberation is frustrated, covenant is broken, prophecy is stilled, wisdom is betrayed, and the church is transmuted into a club for self- or transcendental awareness."

While others see a rising level of lawlessness and licentiousness eroding the clear outline of our quiet shores and swamping the very ground on which we stand, liberals discern new headwaters feeding a freshening stream to relieve us of our stagnation.

We are not abandoning morality; we are replacing obsolete conventions with a morality that is suited to our modern needs. What prudes call licentiousness is emancipation—expressions of personalities freed from the stultifying effects of outmoded puritanism. Lawlessness is only a temporary ripple which will calm itself as we accept the beneficence of our new dispensation and

239

cross the frontier into the great society where we need no grace to attain our glory.

Conservatives, ideally at least, would not adamantly oppose the socio-political programs which constitute the substance of the new morality. (Indeed, it was the late Senator Robert Taft, aptly called Mr. Conservative, who first proposed a Federal housing program.) But conservatives would not accept espousal of or opposition to a socio-political program as a crucial test of morality. William Graham Sumner of Yale, first professor to teach sociology in America, stated the relationship between such programs and morality most succinctly.

In an essay entitled "The Forgotten Man," Sumner contended that for A to compel B to do something for C ordinarily did not involve morality on the part of either A, B, or C. The As, Sumner pointed out, are usually politicians who introduce such programs in order to get votes. There is nothing *immoral* about politicians doing things to get votes because that is what politicians do. But there is usually nothing *moral* about the act, either. To introduce and to promote such legislation is neither moral nor immoral; it has nothing to do with morality; it is amoral.[37]

The Cs who receive money or other benefits from such legislation similarly are, in this context, amoral. Old people who receive pensions or free medical care are not, by virtue of taking such largess, moral. Nor are they, or the farmers who receive price-supports, or the welfare recipients, immoral. All are amoral.

B is the forgotten man. He is the taxpayer who, either directly or indirectly, pays for all of these programs while the A politicians get reelected and the C recipients receive the largess which B provides. While the Bs should get much more credit than they do, they are not moral either. Being compelled to do what they do, they have not exercised the willed choice which is an essential ingredient of morality. While conservatives might agree that many of these programs are humanitarian, perhaps economically desirable, or needed for any of many possible reasons, they would argue that in most instances neither the politicians who promote (or oppose) them, nor the recipients of the largess which they endow, nor the forgotten taxpayer who pays for all of them, is moral.

Conservatives would insist that neither the espousal nor the opposition to socio-political programs ordinarily involves morality. (There are, of course, some cases in which politicians have taken a moral stance in relation to such programs, but these instances are so few that they underline the principle rather than negate it.)

Morality, in the conservative purview, is personal, not the public espousal of or opposition to a socio-political program; it is men, not measures; it must involve willed choice in which man, tempted to do otherwise and with opportunity to do otherwise, makes sacrifice to do what is morally right.

Chapter 10. References and Notes

1. Albert Deutsch, "The Sex Habits of American Men," *Harpers*, December 1947.

2. Alfred C. Kinsey, Wardell B. Pomeroy, and Clyde E. Martin, *Sexual Behavior in the Human Male* (Philadelphia: W. B. Saunders Co., 1948).

3. A. H. Hobbs and Richard D. Lambert, "An Evaluation of 'Sexual Behavior in the Human Male,' " *The American Journal of Psychiatry*, 1948. A critical analysis of Kinsey's second volume, *Sexual Behavior in the Human Female* (1953), appeared in *The American Journal of Psychiatry* under the title "Professor Kinsey: His Facts and His Fantasy," in 1954.

4. Alfred C. Kinsey, Wardell B. Pomeroy, Clyde E. Martin, Paul H. Gebhard, *Sexual Behavior in the Human Female* (Philadelphia: W. B. Saunders Co., 1953), p. 121.

5. Seth Mydaus, "Soviets Encourage Unwed Motherhood," *Philadelphia Evening Bulletin*, August 8, 1977.

6. Edward O. Wilson, *Sociobiology*, (Cambridge, Mass.: Harvard University Press, 1975), p. 157.

7. *Time*, February 13, 1950.

8. William Masters and Virginia Johnson, *Human Sexual Response* (Boston: Little, Brown, 1966); and *Human Sexual Inadequacy* (Boston: Little, Brown, 1970).

9. D. W. Cory, *The Homosexual in America* (New York: Greenberg, 1951), p. 235.

10. Robert Trumbull, "Homosexuals Proud of Deviancy, Medical Academy Study Finds," *New York Times*, May 19, 1964.

11. Letter to *New York Times*, June 15, 1977.

12. Morton Hunt, *Sexual Behavior in the 1970s* (Chicago: Playboy Press, 1974), p. 197.

13. Webster Schott, *New York Times Book Review*, January 14, 1968.

14. John Ciardi, *Saturday Review*, April 3, 1965, p. 12.

15. " 'Trashy' Novels Upheld By Judge," *New York Times*, September 10, 1963.

16. *The Report of the Commission on Obscenity and Pornography*, (New York: Bantam, 1970), p. 447.

17. *Time*, "The Kingdom and the Cabbage," August 15, 1977.

18. Edmund Fuller, *Man in Modern Fiction* (New York: Vintage Books, 1958). As reviewed in *Time*, June 2, 1958, pp. 43–44.

19. William Zinsser, "Cara Theresa," *Atlantic*, August 1973.

20. Ernest Jones, *The Life and Work of Sigmund Freud* (New York: Anchor Books, 1963), pp. 168–170, 370.

21. Sigmund Freud, *A General Introduction to Psychoanalysis* (New York: Permabooks, 1958), p. 441.

22. J. M. Cuddihy, *The Ordeal of Civility* (New York: Basic Books, 1974), pp. 63, 135.

23. Richard La Piere, *The Freudian Ethic* (New York: Duell, Sloan and Pearce, 1959) pp. 184–5.

24. Ruth Benedict, *Patterns of Culture* (Boston: Houghton, Mifflin, 1934), pp. 238–236.

25. J. L. Liebman, *Peace of Mind* (New York: Simon and Schuster, 1946), pp. 26–28, 129, 174, 202–203.

26. Frank E. Manuel, *A Portrait of Isaac Newton* (Cambridge, Mass.: Harvard University Press, 1968).

27. Ferdinand Lundberg and Marynia F. Farnum, *Modern Woman: The Lost Sex* (New York: Harper and Row 1947) pp. 84–85.

28. "Reds' Tyrant Bias Laid to Babyhood," *New York Times*, September 23, 1951.

29. June Bingham, "Santa and the Debate Over Him Go On and On," *New York Times Magazine*, December 18, 1949.

30. Alexander Cockburn, *Idle Passion*, (New York: Simon and Schuster, 1975). As described in *Time*, February 17, 1975.

31. W. F. Ogburn, *Social Change* (New York: Viking, 1922).

32. *New York Times*, October 29, 1964.

33. Lyndon Baines Johnson, *The Vantage Point* (New York: Holt, Rinehart and Winston, 1971).

34. *Philadelphia Bulletin*, October 30, 1964.

35. M. S. Handler, "Clergymen Clash on Role in Major National Issues," *New York Times*, February 21, 1965.

36. Kenneth A. Briggs, "Theologians Plead for Social Activism," *New York Times*, January 6, 1976.

37. W. G. Sumner, *The Forgotten Man and Other Essays* (1883) (New Haven, Conn.: Yale University Press, 1919).

PART IV

What Manner of Man?

Man Is Moral Choice

As Beacons To guide us, the twin facets of the liberal vision may be the reference points we need to steer us safely into a happy future in which man who has no guilt lives in a society where there is no want—where we need no grace to attain our glory. For while it is true that no science can surely predict that the light of this liberal vision will change the winter of our discontent into glorious summer, the vision is fueled by much enlightened evidence and many are warmed by its glow.

Conservatives cannot scientifically negate the promise of this vision, and those who complain about it may do so from sour-grapes envy, stereotyped conventionality, or stubborn wrongheadedness. Mine own complaints center on the conception of man which is incorporate in it; my contention being that the secular, seeming-scientific absolution from sin, guilt, and conscientious responsibility which it invokes is, however desirable its goal, merely a modern manifestation of man's ceaseless quest to solve his problems through miracle, mystery, and authority. For if there is anything which characterizes man more surely than his capacity for moral choice it is his unending search for ways to evade his responsibility to choose—the responsibility which is the essence of his birthright.

In *The Grand Inquisitor*, Dostoevsky describes man's efforts to evade the only freedom his nature permits by shifting his responsibility for moral choice over to the Church, endowing it with spiritual powers of miracle, mystery, and authority. Prior to sloughing his responsibility onto the Church, man insisted on creating a variety of omnipotent and omniscient gods who made his choices for him and when, during the eighteenth century, he demolished The Heavenly City of Saint Augustine, he immediately replaced it with "scientific" secular utopias. As Becker astutely observed: "They [the eighteenth-century philosophes] had only given another form and a new name to the object of worship: having denatured God, they deified nature."[1]

Earlier, I described how the authoritarian pronouncements of scientists led us to believe in their miraculous formulas that would mysteriously perfect our children, conditioning them to be anything we desired. I went on to describe how we rejected the absurdities of regimented, stop-watch conditioning only to embrace the mysterious miracles of neurosis-preventing permissiveness. We threw off the yoke of hereditary determinism only to thrust ourselves into the cobweb of environmental determinism. We proclaimed our scientific progress as we replaced the concept of hereditary "bad seeds" with the even more mysterious, totally unidentifiable Freudian "id." We accounted it an advancement when we substituted cultural relativism for manifest destiny, and we preened ourselves on our intellectual sophistication when we replaced our xenophobia with xenophilia. And some intellectuals now eagerly grasp the extreme, unproved and unprovable claims of sociobiology to replace the extreme, unproved and unprovable claims of cultural conditioning and psychoanalysis.

Smugly, we ridicule the ancients who examined the entrails of animals to foretell their future as we study the predictions of demographers, economists, and political scientists while waiting for our psychoanalyst to inform us what his analysis of our id forebodes. We smirk when we read of the cargo cultists of New Guinea who since the end of World War II have centered most hopes for their future and much of their time and effort to bringing back the Big Birds which once showered so much wealth upon them. Being mandated to Australia in 1964, they insisted that their taxes be placed in escrow to create a fund sufficient to entice the master of the Big Birds, President Lyndon B. Johnson, to become their supreme chief, thus assuring the return of the Big Birds with all their glorious bounty. Their

248

effort failed because, accepting his promise that he would bring us the Great Society, we elected him our headman.

Convinced that the formulas of science provide an escape from personal responsibility but not a solution to our problems and that the socio-political programs which constitute the New Morality are no substitute for morality, conservatives would insist that morality must involve willed choice by individuals. It involves men, not measures; persons, not programs.

The Nature of Moral Choice

Moral choice must involve temptation to do otherwise, opportunity to do otherwise, and it must entail self-sacrifice. These must be consonant with order and continuity within a society which permits others to express their integrity as persons through exercise of *their* capacity for moral choice. Acts performed under compulsion are not moral; nor is bovine conventionality.

In *Aeropagitica,* John Milton described the necessary ingredient of temptation in moral choice, saying: "He that can apprehend and consider vice with all her baits and seeming pleasures, and yet abstain, and yet distinguish, and yet prefer that which is truly better, he is the true warfaring Christian. I cannot praise a fugitive and cloistered virtue, unexercised and unbreathed, that never sallies out and sees her adversary . . . that virtue is but a youngling in the contemplation of evil and knows not the utmost that vice promises to her followers . . . it is but a blank virtue, not a pure."

Those sheltered by their environment or by their estate—those immunized by age (from sexual desire), protected by wealth (from the temptation to steal), or otherwise insulated from temptation—do not earn moral credit for abstention which on the part of others would require sacrifice.

It is vainglorious to assume moral worth by being fiscally honest or sexually pure if never confronted with opportunity to violate the codes which govern such conduct.

Morality, in this meaning, is not an absolute; it entails a set of circumstances that requires judgment and involves uncertainty. Judgments will, with legitimacy, differ and one never knows whether his seeming moral stance was prompted by fear or pride rather than character.

William Golding, in *The Spire*, describes a priest who devotes his entire adult life, living in poverty and sacrificing his health, to erect a magnificent spire on his church, only to wonder: Did I do it for the glory of God, or for the glory of me? In 1971, Daniel Ellsburg stole secret files from the Pentagon and distributed them to newspapers. He was convinced that he did it to expose the futility of fighting in Vietnam; but others might judge his act as grandstanding rather than moral. Similarly, a newscaster, Daniel Schorr, illegally obtained documents from a Senate committee investigating the CIA and FBI and gave them to a newspaper. A case could be made that he (being subsequently dismissed from his position) engaged in a moral act or it could be argued that his behavior was unethical and self-centered as well as illegal.

Brave though they undoubtedly were, willing to sacrifice their lives as well as their professional honor—having taken a pledge of loyalty to their Führer—the German officers, led by Claus von Stauffenberg, who tried to assassinate Hitler in 1944, thereby ending the war and freeing their country from regimented tyranny, must still have wondered, despite their personal courage and their virtuous goal, if selfish hopes for a resurgent Wehrmacht were also instrumental in their otherwise noble attempt.

One dissatisfying aspect of this conception of personal morality is the lack of certainty implicit in it and the need for judgment by others as well as by oneself; judgments which, with reason, can differ. An even greater difficulty associated with belief in personal morality is the effort to raise its tenets from a level of dogmatic assertiveness to intellectual credibility.

Functional Complementarity

To make an intellectually credible case that in the relationship between his selfish drives and the codes of civilized conduct man has the capacity to discriminate—to select or reject alternative courses of behavior—and that he is, in consequence, a positive factor in this relationship between his emotional urges and the social controls and a responsible agent in the self-society matrix, two hurdles must be surmounted.

To assimilate the conception of man as a responsible moral agent, it is necessary to modify our customary ways of thinking in these two respects: (1) we must open our minds to the possibility of a different way of conceiving of cause and effect; and (2) we must realize that in human responses, elements which are separately antagonistic may function together so as to complement each other.

1. The Causal Nexus

Our favorite manner of thinking involves straight-line cause-and-effect; or, more properly, we like to believe that our thinking is primarily governed by such simple, direct connections. Hence we say that a person becomes a criminal because he has criminal instincts, or because he has an extra chromosome, or because he is poor, or because he is unemployed, or because he is mentally sick or has complexes. We are convinced that we become angry when confronted with injustice or prejudice or if someone strikes us—and so it goes as we neatly pinpoint a specific thing which, we are convinced, caused our response.

In doing so, we conveniently overlook the complexities involved in most human relations. No instinct for stealing hubcaps or stereos exists; most people with an extra chromosome do not become criminals, nor do most poor people (our crime rate was much lower during the depression of the thirties than it was during subsequent intervals of high income and low unemployment).

Few of us vent our wrath against injustice or prejudice if they enhance our fortunes. If someone strikes us we may become angry, be he smaller and weaker, but be he bigger and stronger we may transmute our ire into apology for being in his way. If the blow be in fun during playful sparring it is forgot, and if it be the love-tap of an adored one, the gush aroused is not one of anger.

It is no distortion of evidence nor neglect of experience to say that most of our responses to the behavior of others, be they love or hate, admiration or contempt, fear or rage, obedience or

251

rebellion, courage or cowardice, involve an evaluation of a situation rather than reaction to a specific stimulus which gives rise to a specific effect.

Particularly in relation to moral responses are we tempted to believe that they involve straight-line cause-and-effect. Our response, we are certain, is caused by heredity, or it is caused by the environment. Since we were not at all involved in the determination of the genetic combinations which constitute our hereditary endowment, it is unfair to say that we are responsible for what they produce. Blame our parents, if blame is warranted, and let them, in turn, blame their parents. We deserve no credit if the act is morally good; no blame if it is reprehensible. Nor should we be praised or blamed if our behavior is caused by environmental factors produced by circumstances over which we had no control—of which we were not even aware. And our behavior, we are sure, must be *either* the result of heredity *or* the result of the environment. How could it be else? Even if it be a combination of factors from heredity and environment, since we control neither we are still absolved of responsibility.

So long as we accept the premise that our behavior is the terminus of a straight line which connects it to either heredity or environment or to a combination of both, it is senseless to ascribe personal responsibility. Only if moral behavior characteristically involves our interpretation of a situation instead of fixed, mechanical cause-effect, is a path cleared for an interpretation which does involve personal responsibility.

A conservative interpretation of morality would involve circular causality—a causal nexus—in place of straight-line cause-and-effect. All responses to moral issues involve at least the environment, upper brain (cortical) levels, lower brain (hypothalamic) levels, muscles, and glands. Such responses can be initiated, facilitated, or inhibited by any of these elements—by muscular reactions, glandular (particularly endocrinological) influences, mental coordination and mental imagery, and external stimuli—among which are moral codes. Though a tendency to respond is initiated, it does not result in socially significant behavior unless it is facilitated by all of the other elements. (Most of the many thousands of stimuli which impinge upon us each day fail to elicit any meaningful response.) An initiated factor does not become a causal factor if the process is inhibited by any of the elements involved in human responses to social situations. Reactions to sexual stimuli illustrate how behavior can be interpreted in terms of a causal nexus.

A tendency toward sexual response can be initiated by the environment; on the cortical level of the brain; on the hypothalamic level of the brain; by glandular functioning or by muscular activity. Many things in today's environment—books, magazines, advertising, movies, plays, television programs (practically everything, it seems!) can serve as initiating factors for a sexual response. Independently, or in conjunction with such stimuli, cortical fantasies can serve to initiate a response, as can emotional urges in the hypothalamus arising from glandular functioning, or muscular friction on sexually sensitive areas of our bodies.

Once initiated, the tendency to respond may result in sexual behavior or it may not, depending on whether it is facilitated on all the necessary levels or whether it is inhibited. Many factors may inhibit the response: environmental circumstances in the form of the intrusion of others; the pressures of work; the phone ringing; someone turning on the lights; children yelling—as they invariably do—for a glass of water; a policeman shining his spotlight in the car; any of these or many other environmental happenings may interfere with the process to abort the initiated factor. Or, the glands may not be functional: a sprained back or a headache (which invariably occurs on those rare occasions when the children don't yell for a glass of water) may interfere; and stomach cramps will quickly terminate the most tempestuous passion.

While all of these elements are involved in sexual behavior, the role of the upper brain is the level on which man's capacity for conscious control is centered. On the cortical level of the brain, man has the capacity for abstract thought. By stating this I do not mean that everyone is a potential genius, capable of absorbing the intricacies of higher mathematical reasoning, but only that all humans above the level of imbecility are capable of assimilating simple abstract ideas, such as the concept of a number. Say, for illustration, the number five.

If one can comprehend that "fiveness" exists when one adds two and three, or four and one, and it also is there when one subtracts one from six or three from eight, this is a sufficiently high level of abstraction to give one the potential for moral choice. With even a low level of capacity for abstract principles one can absorb moral precepts as abstractions.

A child need not be taught every possible combination of stealing that is wrong—taught separately that it is wrong to steal fifty cents, seventy-five cents, three dollars and fifteen cents and on through each denomination of coinage and currency; nor need he be drilled specifically that it is wrong to steal from Tom, Margaret, Mary, or Joe. He can grasp the general idea that stealing any amount, from anyone, is wrong. And similarly he can comprehend, as principles, the rightness and wrongness of other forms of moral behavior.

Even on much simpler levels of behavior, and with infrahuman forms of life, the upper brain level, the cortex, exercises control. K. M. Bykov, protégé of Ivan Pavlov and his successor at the Pavlov Institute, summarized the numerous controlled studies of animal conditioning contained in *The Cerebral Cortex and the Internal Organs* by stressing that with man (and in most cases with other higher vertebrates as well) the process of conditioning is not an uncontrollable reflexive reaction, but one that functions under cortical control.[2] Evidence from many controlled studies of conditioning led Bykov to conclude that the cortex, in addition to regulating the internal functioning (glands, muscles, lower brain levels) of the animal so as to adapt the internal milieu to the external (environmental) factors which impinge upon it in order to maintain the animal in a state of equilibrium with its environment, *also, in an active process, changes this environment.* In other words, even with simple reactions among infrahuman animals, the learning process is not one of environmental determinism but a causal nexus in which the functioning of the upper brain (cortical) level can modify the internal functioning of the animal so as to adapt it to environmental changes. The process is not one-way cause-effect but a relationship involving functional complementarity. In this relationship between the environment and the organism the cerebral cortex can inhibit the tendency to respond to initiating stimuli which originate in either the internal organs or in the environment. Bykov concludes his summary by assigning such controlling power to the cerebral cortex.

The starting and regulating cortical mechanisms are the most sensitive adjusters of the responding apparatus not only by changing their activities both qualitatively and quantitatively, but also by changing their time relations. *Stimuli conveyed from the cerebral cortex have a striking capacity for changing the rate of reaction, for establishing the sequence of events, and, if necessary, for inhibiting the course of any process.* [My emphasis]

Even on the animal level, and with simple conditional reactions, the process of response is circular, involving a causal nexus in which the cerebral cortex, as a necessary element, must function to facilitate or to inhibit it; thus determining whether stimuli initiated on other levels become *causes* by facilitating the process to fruition or whether they be extinguished through inhibition.

With humans, the brain has evolved further than it has with other animals to produce an additional development of the cerebral cortex, called the neopallium or neocortex, which makes human mental processes, such as those involved in moral choice, distinctively different from those of other animals. This form of neurological development is described thus:

A comparative study of structural and functional differentiation in the cerebral cortex throughout the mammalian series, including man, shows clearly that as the cortex increases in expanse it also undergoes regional differentiation in consequence of which more and more cortical areas can be mapped out on the basis of structural differences. These structural differences are not without functional significance; consequently *new cortical areas may in a very real sense be regarded as new cortical organs.* Many of the cortical areas mapped out in the human cortex have no counterpart in any of the lower mammals. The human cortex, therefore, should not be regarded merely as a quantitative multiplication of the animal cortex, but it possesses functional capacities, particularly in the psychic realm, which are not represented in any of the lower mammals.[3] [My emphasis]

It is commonly assumed that the most recently evolved level of the brain, the neocortex, functions primarily in relation to intelligence, but substantial evidence indicates that this development—which makes possible man's chiefest distinction—functions primarily in relation to morality and prudent judgment.[4]

In 1963, a review of the effects of brain surgery, conducted by the Squibb Institute for Medical Research, concluded that the severing of connections between the frontal cortical lobe and the rest of the brain involved in a form of brain surgery called prefrontal lobotomy resulted not primarily in loss of intelligence but in loss of foresight, mature judgment, tactfulness, and self-control, resulting in poor judgment and loss of moral standards. Previously, Freeman and Watts, in their *Psychosurgery,* came to a like conclusion, and in *The History of Psychiatry,* Alexander and Selesnick concluded that surgery that deprived brain functioning of the influence of the more highly developed parts of the cortex caused loss of ambition, tact, self-respect, and empathy with others. Gustav Eckstein, in *The Body Has a Head,* pointing out that while decrease in intelligence resulting from prefrontal lobotomies is only temporary, loss of a sense of propriety is permanent; concluding that "the frontal lobes piece together those delicate shades that some have thought to be a man's soul, the headiest distillate of his mind." Carl Sagan, describing the evolutionary development of the various levels of the brain in *The Dragons of Eden,* similarly describes the frontal lobes of the topmost level as the area where our mental processes enable us to anticipate the future and, as a result, they are also the sites of concern and the locales of worry. While the transsection of these lobes during prefrontal lobotomy does reduce anxiety, it also reduces the patient's capacity to be human, for the price we pay for anticipation of the future is conscientious concern about it.

Since numerous controlled studies of the conditioning of vertebrate animals indicates (as described by Bykov and others) that the cortex of the brain regulates the conditioning process, influencing not only the rate of procedure and its rhythm, but determining whether the process occurs at all, it seems reasonable to contend that human behavior associated with moral choice, being infinitely more complex, is not a simple matter of cause-effect hereditary or environmental determinism but a process in which stimuli, whether initiated in the environment, upper brain, lower brain, glands, or muscles, can be either facili-

256

tated or inhibited by neocortical functioning; thus brought to fruition in the form of significant behavior, or extinguished by conscious control.

The term *homeostasis* has long been used to describe the manner in which the brain coordinates glandular activity so as to maintain functional dynamic balance. In like manner it seems reasonable to suppose that the higher levels of our brain strive to coordinate stimuli from the external environment, including efforts to make meaningful patterns of the moral codes: *that homeostasis functions in relation to the external social environment as well as in relation to the internal milieu of the body.*

A further implication would be that these higher brain levels can coordinate the stimuli from internal drives with external stimuli (including, of course, moral imperatives) into patterns which are meaningful in terms of both, fusing the internal homeostasis with the external into intellectually satisfying, emotionally gratifying, socially responsible behavior.

True, the complexity of the mental processes involved in human behavior is such that patterns which alleviate internal tensions resulting from glandular and muscular functioning may conflict with the rules which are necessary for human society to function, or cultural patterns may be so narrow and rigid that they frustrate balanced functioning of the internal milieu. Exemplifying the first condition would be situations, now so very common, in which we rationalize unbridled lust or unchained brutishness. The second condition would occur when arbitrary conventions are so restrictive as to prohibit all expressions of glandular or muscular urges without, as an alternative, allowing for compensating spiritual outlets.

Or, the patterns may be crazily unbalanced in relation to both internal imperatives and social necessities, thus producing alcoholism, drug addition, or mental imbalance.

Thus the mental hurdle of straight-line cause-and-effect thinking in which man's moral behavior is mechanistically determined to a degree that absolves him of responsibility can be surmounted if we accept the possibility that the thought processes associated with moral behavior operate as a causal nexus in which potential stimuli, no matter where initiated, can be facilitated or inhibited on the neocortical levels of the brain.

By combining this concept of a causal nexus with an extension of the principle of internal homeostasis to include a propensity to make moral sense out of the environment, we attain intellectual credibility for a conception of morality in which man's responsibility rests on his capacity to choose.

Through the functioning of our neocortex we have the capacity to decide, when reacting to either external or internal stimuli, whether they fit into a pattern of moral behavior (which everyone above the level of imbecility develops at an early age without any special education in the matter) or not. If we decide that the stimuli do fit into the pattern, we should incorporate them and thus facilitate the process into socially acceptable conduct. Should we decide that the stimuli are such that they cannot be fitted into what we know to be right, we should (though often we do not), by rejection, inhibit them from further development. Obviously, to refuse to choose is also choice. If we do not actively inhibit impulses which conflict with what we know to be morally right, our refusal to do so constitutes immorality.

2. Functional Complementarity

The second mental hurdle which needs be surmounted in order to present an intellectually credible hypothesis that man is a morally responsible agent has to do with the relationship between our internal selfish urges (whether innate or acquired) and society's rules for conduct. This relationship, expressed in the ancient quip that everything which gives us pleasure is either illegal, immoral, or fattening, is one in which society's rules seem to be antagonistic to our "natural" desires for pleasure. The codes and precepts which constitute the social controls consist in large measure of "Thou Shalt Nots" and "Don'ts" which conflict with the full and immediate satisfaction of our individual desires and are easy to ridicule as arbitrary conventions made up by old men who hate to see anyone have the fun they had when they were young. So the problem is one of reconciling two aspects of our behavior which are—or seem to be—antagonistic to each other. Again, the issue seems to be one of either-or. Either we submit to the moral injunctions of society by forsaking pleasure, or we submit to our desires by violating the social

258

codes through acts which are illegal or immoral, uncivil, or vulgar.

Antagonisms Become Complementary

An hypothesis that man is morally responsible must show that processes which in their separate functioning are antagonistic (such as our urges for personal pleasure *versus* the social rules for conduct) can, in their combined functioning, complement each other. Things that are separately antagonistic can function together so as to complement each other. This process is one of *functional complementarity.*

In another source I have given examples that show how separately antagonistic muscles combine in their functioning to complement each other and make possible such processes as breathing and walking.[5] Many, perhaps most, forms of glandular functioning also conform to this principle, and the separately antagonistic levels of the brain—the primitive emotional urges from the hypothalamic level, affecting and being affected by the patterns of civility and morality on the neocortical level—combine in their functioning and complement each other to produce our mental processes.

Since my purpose is only to indicate the credibility of a way of thinking that allows for the possibility that separately antagonistic elements can, in their combined functioning, complement each other, rather than presenting a lengthy recital of examples, I shall here describe only one such process.

For us to function at all, sugar (glucose) is essential. One set of endocrine glands, the adrenals, functions to elevate blood-sugar levels; another set, the Islets of Langerhans, produces insulin which tends to lower blood-sugar levels. Though these glands, in their separate functioning, are antagonistic in relation to the determination of the level of our blood-sugar, in their combined functioning they complement each other to maintain a proper balance of glucose within the system.

Please consider how this pattern of functional complementarity—a pattern certainly involved in our mental as well as in our physical processes, and likely, also, in most physical and chemical processes—contrasts with our usual cause-effect interpretations. In our usual thinking, once we became convinced that sugar is essential to our very existence, we would "reason" that anything which is conducive to an increase in this vital element is good; while anything which tends to decrease it is bad. Therefore: adrenals are good; Islets of Langerhans are bad and should be removed.

To pursue such ways of thinking to absurdity—which we ofttimes do—we might extend our "rationality" to conclude that since expiration of the "evil" Islets of Langerhans would result in our death rather than in bouncier health, we might reason: If the Islets of Langerhans are essential to our very life, and if those conflicting adrenals nullify the noble efforts of these necessary glands, we should act to prevent such interference by the adrenals—preferably through an amendment to the Constitution! Of course, both of these sets of glands must function so as to produce the homeostatic balance that is essential to our existence.

If the muscular, glandular, and mental functioning which produces our behavior characteristically involves a process wherein the parts which separately act antagonistically combine on a higher level of function to complement each other, then it is intellectually credible (though requiring an inferential jump) to contend that the rules of morality, in our social living, complement our selfish urges.

A simple example of alternative courses of behavior which might occur in response to natural urges can be found in one of the circumstances associated with adolescence. Among the many changes which take place during this phase of our growth is a rapid development of musculature, particularly pronounced among males. Characteristically, as an organism develops new capacities there is an urge to use them, and the tendency of male adolescents to exult in their newly acquired musculature may express itself independently of the social controls by preening before a mirror, by doing push-ups, or jogging, or weight-lifting. But more gratification is found, it seems, in using one's muscles competitively with others, and primal urges tempt youths to fight each other, there being much pleasure in beating up another person. But there is risk that the beater become the beatee and have his head covered with contusions instead of filled with pride.

To avoid such risk, and yet obtain the gratification of using one's muscles on another person, youths can, by violating the social codes, beat up on small children or old people, and this happens more often than we like to admit. Recent accounts tell of teen-agers who "like to beat up kids" beating a two-year-old and throwing him off a roof to his death; of four others who spent a week beating, burning and raping an eighty-four-year-old woman; of three youths who beat and raped two sisters, age seven and nine, then threw the seven-year-old off a roof to her death while the nine-year-old escaped. Another youth, discharged from a mental hospital as cured, raped and beat to death a seven-year-old; another raped and beat to death a ninety-two-year-old woman; and other youths stoned to death a sixty-five-year-old fisherman. Many hundreds of such cases occur each year, and there is little doubt that these youths derived satisfaction from behavior which, while antagonistic to the social controls, is at the same time a pleasurable outlet for natural urges.

Or such urges could be met by stealing a football and a tape recorder with crowd noises dubbed in and running up and down a football field, spurred by synthetic cheers, and making touchdown after touchdown all by one's self. Tiring of this one could put a hoop two feet off the ground and drop in basket after basket, outscoring even the greatest professional basketball player.

Fortunately, youths have not yet reached such a state of affairs as Anthony Burgess depicted in *A Clockwork Orange;* and most youths find their outlets through football, basketball, baseball, or other competitive sports where performance is governed by precise rules to determine what is fair and what is not. Rewards are not won easily as they are through narcissistic exhibitionism or brutishness, but they may be more fulfilling.

Similarly, in the broader areas of life, the sacrifice involved in renouncing the pleasure of immediate satisfaction of our desires may be outweighed by a feeling of gratification which is earned by blending what we feel the urge to do with what we know we *ought* to do. This feeling, though postponed, uncertain of attainment, and always partial, contributes to our character —our sense of integrity with the social life which is necessary for civilization to exist.

The contention that man is moral choice rests on an hypothesis which acknowledges that much immediate pleasure may be had by satisfying our desires independently of the social controls or contrary to them, but it holds that most people, during the course of a lifetime, will come closer to fulfilling their sense of self-respect, their integrity as responsible persons, by accepting such codes of behavior as complementary to our desires rather than antagonistic to them. Some premises on which this hypothesis rests follow.

Premises for Man Is Moral Choice

1. Man must live in society. Being weak and slow, with inadequate physical equipment for use as effective weapons, he cannot survive except in company with his fellows. We need not assume an "instinct of gregariousness" nor posit some form of social contract; his banding together would evolve out of experience.

2. Society, in its nature, means some sort of rules. We can reasonably argue about the kind of rules and the manner and degree of their enforcement, but not about the fact of their necessity. Forms and processes must be established to determine what belongs to whom and who has this responsibility or that.

3. While the necessity for some kind of social rules is axiomatic, their nature is debatable. Liberals, abetted by many anthropologists, would argue that there is no sound basis for selecting any particular set of rules from the hundreds of sets which have been formulated independently of each other. But an hypothesis of moral responsibility would be premised on a belief that general patterns lie beneath this surface diversity. Most students of morality have reached this conclusion, and Will and Ariel Durant, in a summary of their ten-volume study of intellectual history, describe the difference between these liberal-scientistic contentions and broader intellectual views:

> A little knowledge of history stresses the variability of moral codes, and concludes that they differ in time and place, and sometimes contradict each other. A larger knowl-

edge stresses the universality of moral codes and concludes to their necessity.[6]

Rather than willy-nilly accept as moral codes the often happenstance practices which garrulous tribesmen convey in pidgin to anthropologists who are oblivious to the nuances of the language and ignorant of the ethos of the culture, conservatives would try to probe beneath the details of cultural difference in an effort to ascertain those principles of morality which have been shared by all civilizations.

In Deuteronomy (Chapter XXV:5–10) it is written that Moses conveyed to the Hebrews how, when a brother dies without leaving a son, his widow shall have intercourse with his brother and he shall take her in marriage to perpetuate his dead brother's name. If the brother refuses, the widow shall go up to him in the presence of the elders, pull the sandal off his foot, spit in his face, and declare: "Thus we requite the man who will not build up his brother's family." And his family shall be known in Israel as the House of the Unsandalled Man.

This practice, which was not only permitted, but actively sanctioned by law and custom, might well be interpreted by an outsider as an outlet for lasciviousness or proof that the Hebrews were polygamous rather than monogamous. Actually, the principle which underlies the practice is that of social responsibility, which governed other multiple marriages (such as the sororate) as well as this practice: the levirate.

The moral principle beneath these and other diverse practices would be that sexual relationships must be governed by social responsibility. Monogamy is the rule, but multiple marriages, where they contribute toward fulfillment of a social obligation, are permitted; sometimes even required.

Such interpretation of morality would also hold that violations of moral codes would be judged according to the degree of violation rather than in absolute terms of all-or-none. In *Sexuality and Homosexuality* Arno Karlen relates the manner in which Saint Thomas Aquinas described the degree of sinfulness involved in sexual acts.[7] Sexual pleasure felt during a dream would involve no sin because the capacity for judgment is dormant. The degree of sinfulness is a function of the extent of departure from socially responsible, heterosexual naturalness,

263

progressing in severity from masturbation, to oral and anal heterosexual acts, through homosexual sodomy to bestiality. All these are wrong in that the natural result of sexual activity, procreation, is prevented. Masturbation prevents this natural result by omitting the partner, and in oral and anal heterosexual activity, the proper species and proper partners are involved but the wrong holes are used. Homosexuality joins the proper species but the wrong sex and the wrong holes, while bestiality involves the wrong species.

4. Such moral codes are not merely arbitrary customs nor transitory conventions to be thrown on a scrap heap with each change in technology or style, much as we change the models of automobiles. If the basic premises are valid, such codes are an integral aspect of human functioning; as natural as our glandular drives. They are intrinsic to any civilized milieu as is air to a bird; water to a fish. Though they seem antagonistic to our glandular urges, they function to complement them and thus constitute an integral aspect of human environment.

5. Individual differences must be taken into consideration in an evaluation of human choices. Differences in the strength of glandular drives—depending on age and sex as well as heredity—all should be taken into consideration in an assessment of behavior. The double standard of sexual morality for males and females rested on a belief, now unfashionable but not disproved, that male sexual hormones are qualitatively as well as quantitatively different from female.

6. Differences in environmental factors which make moral choice easier or more difficult should also temper our judgment without, however, leading us to accept the "sociological" assumption that culture is a monolith, imposing itself with equal and irresistible force upon all of us. We should remember that man reacts to culture as he interprets it; not as it objectively is. Differences in the interpretation of the same cultural forces are obvious when the blind are contrasted with the sighted; the color-blind with those sensitive to delicate shadings; the deaf with those of acute hearing; the tone-deaf with those who have "an ear for music." Differences of age and sex, fortune and temperament affect our interpretation of culture. We select or reject among the thousands of environmental influences which impinge upon us each day, and our behavioral environment is

264

one in which, reciprocally, we affect what our culture is as well as it affecting what we are.

And in all this interplay we strive to make moral sense of our external environment as we filter its stimuli through the neocortex in much the same fashion as the brain tries to keep our internal environment in homeostatic balance. Perhaps this is why children raised under either strict discipline or permissively can commonly adjust to social living, while children brought up under circumstances in which the same act is sometimes rewarded, sometimes ignored, and sometimes brutally punished with a degree of inconsistency that hinders the formation of a sensible pattern of appropriate behavior, commonly become social misfits.

A Need for Prudent Judgment

In discussing the process of complementarity, wherein phenomena which separately produce antagonistic responses combine in their functioning to complement each other, I speculated that, on learning that the adrenals tend to raise the level of the sugar which is so essential to our functioning while insulin tends to lower it, we might be tempted to feel that the adrenals are "good" and should be encouraged into hyperactivity while the "evil," interfering Islets of Langerhans should be squelched if not extirpated. We may tend to have a similar either-or, good-bad reaction if we accept the reasoning embodied in the hypothesis of functional complementarity and conclude that since the social controls are essential to civilized life and since our individual desires lead us to act contrary to our mores we should drastically reenforce our rules and put strong dampers on individual desire.

In our present circumstances those who become increasingly skeptical that the socio-political programs that constitute the essence of the New Morality will, in fact, create the Great Society that, through cultural determinism, will find its greatness reflected by goodly men—those who see the unabated growth of crime and perversion not as a passing side-effect of a transition to a better life but as a deepening swamp of iniquity—such as these are tempted to grasp at

265

any support which promises to stay our further sinking.

Our readiest and surest support would seem to be firmer laws, fiercely enforced. On the surface, such recourse would seem to comply with Edmund Burke's admonition that if people refuse to govern themselves from within, they will be governed from without, a process strikingly conveyed in *Cabaret*, the movie made from Christopher Isherwood's "Sally Bowles." As increasingly grosser forms of sexual degradation are performed on the stage of the cabaret, its mirrored walls reflect increasing numbers of brown-shirted Nazis in the audience, forecasting the total regimentation which would follow the total licentiousness. But Burke saw such external formal controls not as a goal of conservatism but as an undesirable—though perhaps inevitable —alternative to it.

Though traditionalists might seek refuge behind rigid formal controls, philosophic conservatives would sense the danger of following such a course to its extreme: dangers comparable, though obverse, to those found in our current permissiveness. The comforting dream of an obedient society where people can safely walk the streets at night, where trains run on time, where streets are clean and flies no longer pester is now a nightmare filled with mountains of corpses and rent by the shrieks of spirits tortured by Communism, Nazism, and Fascism.

Our conceit would tempt us to believe that we are immune to such excesses but in *Eichmann in Jerusalem*, Hannah Arendt convincingly argued that most people could descend to the depths of cruelty that many Germans did under Hitler[8], and in support of her view, Stanley Milgram describes a series of studies which lend credible support to the notion that our potential for cruelty or other forms of evil is always just barely beneath our fragile veneer of civilized decency.[9] In these studies, college students from Princeton and Yale and persons from diverse occupations and different countries (South Africa, West Germany, and Italy) participated in what they believed to be an experiment in learning.

The experimenter, a professorial, scientific-seeming figure, explains to the participant that he is to act as a "teacher" in an experiment designed to measure the effect of punishment on learning. Another participant, the "learner," is strapped to a chair and told to learn a list of paired words. Whenever the learner makes an error he will receive an electric shock. The "shocks," of increasing intensity, are administered by the "teacher," who is quite unaware that the impressive shock machine is a fake and that the "learner" is an actor who receives no shocks at all.

As the "teacher" administers "shocks" of increasing intensity, the "learner" feigns an expression of pain, begs to be released from the experiment, and screams in pretended agony. When the worried "teacher" asks whether he should continue, the authority figure insists that he do so. The fundamental lesson of the study was that:

> . . . ordinary people, simply doing their jobs, and without any particular hostility on their part, can become agents in a terrible destructive process. Moreover, even when the destructive effects of their work become patently clear, and they are asked to carry out actions incompatible with fundamental standards of morality, relatively few people have the resources needed to resist authority.

Our temptation to impose rigid controls, to use great force to restrain the excesses of permissive behavior, needs tempering by an awareness that the human potential for evil can veer too sharply and go too far in this direction also. A good case can be made to justify tightened controls at the present, but such action should be limited by an understanding that it must be reined by prudent judgment and that, though necessary, it is an undesirable substitute for control from within, which should always be the principal focus of our concern and our efforts. As Burke said, "It is better to cherish virtue and humanity, by leaving much to free will, even with some loss to the object, than to attempt to make men mere machines and instruments of a political benevolence."

While the horrors of the regimentation which culminates in the extremes of control have been properly publicized, the equivalent horrors of the obverse—the anarchy which is an extension of uncontrolled permissiveness—are commonly glossed over, or perverted in De Quincey's fashion. The rampant crime, drug addiction, sexual perversion, and degradation associated with the expansion and loss of definition of our codes of conduct have not, by far, yet reached their full measure. In a manner similar to that in which the horrors of regimentation can be identified by names such as Stalin, Hitler, or Mussolini, the horrors of unbridled permissiveness can be identified with Charles Milles Manson, Weathermen, and Baader-Meinhof.

Peer-Group Pressures

Inside the blood-spattered house in the Hollywood hills was the body of Sharon Marie Polansky, a.k.a. Sharon Tate, 26, who had been an astonishingly beautiful woman with a statuesque figure and a face of great delicacy. She had died of sixteen stab wounds of the chest and back, penetrating the heart, lungs, and liver, causing massive hemorrhage. A fork, jabbed far into her pregnant body, caused one of the wounds.

Thomas John Kummer, a.k.a. Jay Sebring, 35, hair stylist and head of Sebring International Corporation, had been stabbed seven times and shot once.

Abigail Anne Folger, 25, heiress to the Folger coffee fortune, had been stabbed twenty-eight times.

Wojiciech "Voytek" Frykowski, 32, who had been living with Abigail Folger, had been shot twice, struck over the head thirteen times with a blunt instrument, and stabbed fifty-one times.

In a car in the driveway was the body of Steven Earl Parent, 18, who had been shot four times.

On the door of the house, written in Sharon Tate's blood, was the word "PIG."

On the following night, August 10, 1969, Leno LaBianca, 44, head of a chain of Los Angeles supermarkets, and his wife Rosemary, 38, were found murdered in their home. His hands had been tied behind his back, a lamp cord was knotted around his neck, a carving fork protruded from his stomach and in addition to numerous stab wounds, the word "WAR" had been carved on his flesh. Mrs. La Bianca had been stabbed so many times that no one tried to count her wounds.

On one wall, written in blood, was "DEATH TO PIGS," and on another, "RISE." On the refrigerator door, written in blood, was "HEALTER [sic] SKELTER."

268

These and other murders were done by young white persons who were members of a group called Charles Manson's Family. Manson himself was an amoral, megalomaniacal thug who changed his name from Charles Milles Manson to Charles Willis Manson so he could say "Charles' will is man's son," meaning that his will was that of the Son of Man.[10] He boasted that he had earned the highest award given to members of the cult of Scientology; he had spent much of his life in prison; at the time of the murders he was on probation on the recommendation of a psychiatrist; and he had repeatedly violated parole without being returned to prison.

Though permissiveness in the judicial system was a factor in the numerous senseless murders performed by Manson and his followers, to me the most significant aspect of the situation was the readiness with which his followers—middle-class, mostly well-educated girls—totally abandoned all restraints of civilized living.

"Squeaky" was the daughter of an aeronautical engineer; "Sandy" a college dropout whose father was a stockbroker; "Katie" had been a Bluebird, a Campfire Girl, a member of her church choir and a student at a Jesuit college; "Lulu" had been a homecoming princess in high school; "Brenda" was the daughter of a designer of missile guidance systems; and "Gypsy," an accomplished violinist, had lived with her psychologist stepfather before running away to join Manson's Family.

Living in the isolation of an abandoned ranch, they sloughed off civilized restraints almost as quickly as they dispensed with their patronyms. They engaged publicly as well as privately in all possible sexual combinations; male-female, female-female, male-male, intercourse, cunnilungus, fellatio, and sodomy to destroy not only sexual inhibitions but all inhibitions. One thirteen-year-old girl's initiation into The Family consisted of her being sodomized by Manson while the others watched. Manson also "went down on" a young boy to show the others that he had rid himself of all inhibitions.

Total sexual licentiousness expunged the deepest of their self- as well as socially-imposed restraints, and in a short time these middle-class females would eat garbage, defecate and urinate in public, and do vicious senseless murder without the slightest compunction.

But man does not function directionless in a vacuum, and having smashed their former guideposts to behavior they eagerly grasped for new ones which they found by accepting Manson's contention that he was the Son of God; that the British rock group, The Beatles, in their recording of *Helter Skelter*, proved that a racial war was about to begin; that the blacks would win the war but, being untrained in leadership, they would appoint Manson their leader. Manson convinced his otherwise directionless followers that if they would murder enough whites, brutally and otherwise senselessly, blacks would be blamed and in retaliation whites would begin the racial Armageddon which would result in Charley becoming King of the World!

This process whereby the reunuciation of historically tested mores finds its resulting vacuum occupied by worse than savagery (on which stingy nature imposes restraints not felt by those who live in affluence) is not at all restricted to members of Charles Manson's Family. When the Weatherman faction split from the Students for a Democratic Society in 1969, they formed collectives in which they isolated themselves—much as Manson's Family had done—by barricading their houses, putting double locks on every door and chicken wire over the windows to protect themselves from imaginary bombs thrown by illusionary enemies. In fashion similar to Manson, they created ideologies and tried to expunge all aspects of "bourgeois" mores and folkways.[11] Clothes were strewn everywhere, food rotted, toilets jammed, and cockroaches paraded. They vandalized graveyards to destroy respect for the dead and, most importantly perhaps, they compelled everyone to be sexually promiscuous.

Weatherperson leader Bernadine Dohrn praised the Manson Family murderers of pregnant Sharon Tate, saying "Dig it! First they killed those pigs, then they ate dinner in the same room and shoved a fork into Tate's stomach! Wild!" Others grinned in approval of her description.

Members of the Weatherman faction as well as other observers describe the process that quickly converted well-to-do college-educated youths into fanatic infra-animals as centering around the smashing of conventions in general but with especial emphasis on the destruction of all standards of sexual behavior; prohibiting personalized sexual relationships and ridiculing privacy.[12]

270

The similarities between the rapid transition of civilized youths into sub-bestiality found in Manson's Family and the Weatherman (Weathermen, Weatherperson, Weatherbureau) faction of SDS are also found in West Germany's Baader-Meinhof gang, organized during the late 1960s by children of successful parents (Andreas Baader's father was an historian; Ulrike Meinhof's an art historian) who, despite their many murders and widespread destruction, found many "sympathizers among intellectuals and 'knee-jerk' liberals (as they are called in America)."[13]

While danger of stultifying regimentation is always present, the destructive desire to smash all rules and to descend to a subhuman level also lurks just beneath our civilized facade, and we need constantly to exercise prudent judgment to steer a safe course between them.

Creative Evolution

Additional intellectual support for the conception of man as an active, and thereby responsible, factor in moral choice comes from the concept of creative evolution, described as long ago as 1906 by Henri Bergson.[14] Bergson argued that in man, evolution developed a being who is intrinsically endowed with the power to go further in the direction that evolution brought him if he chooses to exercise that power.

This concept of creative evolution was revived in 1949 by Sir Arthur Keith with his *A New Theory of Human Evolution*,[15] and none has delineated the nature of the concept and its implications more clearly than G. G. Simpson in *The Meaning of Evolution*.

Man has risen, not fallen. He can choose to develop his capacities as the highest animal and to try to rise still further, or he can choose otherwise. The choice is his responsibility, and his alone. There is no automatism that will carry him upward without choice or effort and there is no trend solely in the right direction. Evolution has no purpose; man must supply this for himself.

It is fundamental in all this that responsibility is rooted in the true nature of man. It has arisen from and is inherent

271

in his evolutionary history and status. Responsibility is something that he has just because he is human, and not something that he can choose to accept or to refuse. It cannot be rejected or unconditionally handed over to others. The attempt to do this is ethically wrong, and the responsibility, to the extent that it is possible and proper, involves continuing responsibility for the actions of the delegate. In the last analysis, personal responsibility is nondelegable.[16]

Support for the belief in active responsibility for moral choice can be garnered from many other areas, such as Lloyd Morgan's conception of "emergent evolution," Wolfgang Kohler's principles of "configurationism" and "Gestalt," from concepts such as "holism" developed by Jean Piaget and expanded by Lawrence Kohlberg to explain the moral development of children, and otherwhere, but since such compilations of evidence can never constitute irrefutable scientific proof such piling up would soon become an exercise in pedantry which says nothing more, really, than can be found in the Bible.

Genesis

The Book of Genesis is the true and original birthplace of all theology.[17] It contains those ideas of God and Man, of righteousness and judgment, of failure and hope, which are presupposed through the rest of the Old Testament and which prepare the way for the mission of Christ.

God, having made man from the dust, told him "You may eat from every tree in the garden, but not from the tree of the knowledge of good and evil."

Eve, created by God from Adam and warned by Adam not to eat of the tree of the knowledge of good and evil, yet succumbed to the temptation of the serpent's promise that ". . . your eyes shall be opened and ye shall be as gods, knowing good and evil." Having eaten of the fruit of the tree of the knowledge of good and evil their conscience led them to clothe themselves and to hide from the Lord God. And the Lord God condemned the woman to bring forth her children in sorrow and ". . . thy desire shall be thy husband, and he shall rule over thee."

And unto Adam he said, Because thou hast hearkened unto the voice of thy wife, and hast eaten of the tree of which I commanded thee, saying, Thou shalt not eat of it: cursed is the ground for thy sake; in sorrow shalt thou eat of it all the days of thy life.

And the Lord God said that Adam the man "is become one of us, to know good and evil: and now, lest he put forth his hand and take also of the tree of life, and eat, and live for ever" the Lord God sent him out of the garden of Eden to till the ground from whence he was taken.

And in the dictionary of the Bible which is dedicated To The Most High and Mighty Prince James, we learn that the Fall denotes the first entrance of sin into the world, and we are advised that "The story which is there told should probably be regarded as allegory rather than as literal history."

This description of the Fall continues by saying that at a certain point in the history of the race man's development took a (wrong) turn in which man consciously set himself to act in opposition to the will of his Creator; a deliberate act of self-assertion which is handed on from one generation to another.

The Bible Dictionary describes conscience as:

The Christian belief that we are born with a natural capacity to distinguish between right and wrong. . . . We have the faculty by means of which we can pass judgment on our own conduct, either approving or condemning it, so anticipating the divine judgment on it. . . . The possession of it at once makes us responsible human beings. Like other faculties it needs to be trained, and may be deadened through misuse.

And we are further told that this and other parables convey to the hearer truth exactly in proportion to his faith and intelligence; that the application may be infinitely varied in every age and circumstance; and that the meaning grows and deepens by the lessons of history and the teaching of science. And so we see that the Bible foretells of "emergence," "creative evolution," "Gestalten," "holism," "functional complementarity" and all else involved in the conception that when man evolved to the point where he obtained the neocortical capacity to comprehend

273

as abstractions the ideas of right and wrong, he then set himself apart from the simple life of animals that lack such capacity and became uniquely identifiable as a creature of moral choice.

Perhaps President Abraham Lincoln, in his Gettysburg Address (1863), would have been better advised to have given the complete reference to the phrase ". . . of the people, by the people, for the people." Originally, this reference was to the first English Bible, the 1384 Wycliffe translation, and reads: "This Bible is for the Government of the People, by the People, and for the People."

So this interpretation of man in which he has the capacity to discriminate, to select or reject among the impulses from his internal glands and from the environment, and to choose to fit his responses in conformity with the codes of civilized conduct, or independent of them, or in opposition to them, finds support from religion as well as from clinical results and other findings, and I take it to be of considerable significance that creative writers throughout all of history have also, almost without exception, assumed the presence of man's innate potential for good or evil and have taken conscious moral choice to be the highest expression of his nature.

Self-Love and Social Be the Same

Plato (in the Phaedrus myth) described man's soul as a composite which his higher nature was as a superb white steed needing only a gentle word for guidance, while his lower self was as a dark nag, crooked and lumbering, shag-eared and deaf, needing strong restraint.

In *Paradiso*, Dante described man's capacity to will as the greatest gift which God bestowed, prized highest, and limited to creatures which have intelligence. As Dorothy L. Sayers advises us in her introduction to *The Divine Comedy*, in reading Dante "We must abandon any idea that we are the slaves of chance, or environment, or our subconscious; any vague notion that good and evil are merely relative terms, or that conduct and opinion do not really matter. . . . We must try to believe that man's will is free, that he can consciously exercise choice, and that his choice can be decisive to all eternity."[18]

274

Even the "scientific" Bacon, in his *New Organon*, declares, unscientifically but soundly, that "It was the ambitious and proud desire of moral knowledge to judge of good and evil, to the end that man may revolt from God and give laws to himself, which was the form and manner of the temptation."[19]

And blind, glorious Milton saw Christ as the image of the possibility for humans, in their limited way, to harmonize flesh and spirit, body and soul, saying that He left it in man's power, voluntarily exercised, not in fate or necessity, for man to find his freedom to rise from the imposition of strict laws to free acceptance of Grace—meantime warning, as did Burke, that the loss of their inner freedom would deprive them of their outward liberty.

Newton's discovery of the laws of motion was so awesome in its implications and so deceptively simple in formulation that many eighteenth-century intellectuals believed that their most precious possession, their penchant for abstract rationalization, would earn them similar acclaim if they applied a similar technique to the study of man. Their Baconian assumptions convinced them that new methods of analysis would transmute their mediocrity into genius which would create similarly profound, equally provable, and comparably simple laws of human behavior. Unhappily, their rejection of moral sentiment and neglect of human experience unbalanced their judgment, tempting them to ignore or deny their failures, to plagiarize science in order to justify their conceit, and to glorify dessicated intellect as the apex of human attainment. Unable to discover legitimate scientific theories of human behavior, their conception of man rigidified into today's scientistic formulas which hold that malleable man is nothing but the passive product of environmental conditioning.

But other philosophers of the time, now mostly ignored, maintained that man's innate nature included a moral sense capable of developing into conscience; that such moral sense was a uniquely human attribute; and that conscience actively interacts with rationality in a process of functional complementarity to produce the prudent judgement which Edmund Burke and Thomas Jefferson proclaimed as the highest attribute of mankind.

Anthony Ashley Cooper, 3rd Earl of Shaftesbury, is credited[20] with developing (in 1711) the concept of an innate moral sense existing in the very constitution of the human mind which complements reason to produce prudent judgement.

Francis Hutcheson (1694–1746) based his system of moral philosophy on his conviction that we have an inborn moral sense which[21] ". . . from its very nature appears to be designed for regulating and controlling all our powers." Rationalism plays a contributory but secondary role in producing those "right actions" which ". . . promote the general welfare of mankind." Reason alone cannot produce such virtuous acts because "Reason of itself is utterly impotent in this particular" and must find its support in morality, the active principle ". . . which nature has made universal in the whole species." "Even the rudest of mankind shew such notions, and young minds are rather more moved with *moral forms* than others."[22]

Though we see many references, usually disparaging and often erroneous, to Adam Smith's 1776 *Inquiry into the Nature and Causes of the Wealth of Nations*, his 1759 *The Theory of Moral Sentiments*[23] is commonly ignored. As David Hume did also, Smith patterned his thinking after the precedent of Francis Hutcheson and throughout his analysis of morality he stressed the innate nature of a conscience which is the highest secular tribunal for judging the acts of mankind, man's primary motivation being ". . . the love of what is honourable and noble, of the grandeur, and dignity, and superiority of our own characters." "It is not in being rich that truth and justice would rejoice, but in being trusted and believed," and that ". . . by acting according to the dictates of our moral faculties, we necessarily pursue the most effectual means for promoting the happiness of mankind. . . ."

With disciplined enthusiasm, Thomas Reid[24] insisted that, far from being the puppet of either his heredity or environment, man is an active agent, able to distinguish between right and wrong and ". . . capable of acting from motives of a higher nature." The ". . . active powers of man make so important a part of his constitution, and distinguish him so eminently from his fellow animals, they deserve no less to be the subject of philosophical disquisition than his intellectual powers." We should acknowledge, Reid says, ". . . that to act properly is much more valuable than to think justly or reason acutely." Quite carried

276

away by his zeal, he contends that the system of morals which shape the conscience of every human creature may ". . . be compared to the laws of motion in the natural world."

For centuries our literature has been replete with this same message: man has the capacity to choose the direction he will take. Aleksandr Solzhenitsyn repeats it, saying:

> The most important part of our freedom, inner freedom, is always subject to our will. If we surrender it to corruption, we do not deserve to be called human.[25]

To round out this partial recital of intellectual support for the contention that man's uniqueness lies in his capacity for moral choice, Carl Sagan, describing the metaphor of the Garden of Eden in his sprightly account of the evolution of the human brain, fixes this capacity, as I did earlier, in the neocortex, saying:

> It is interesting that it is not the getting of *any* sort of knowledge that God has forbidden, but, specifically, the knowledge of the difference between good and evil—that is, abstract and moral judgments, which, if they reside anywhere, reside in the neocortex.[26]

We Shall Be Moral . . . Only Not Yet

With abundant sacred as well as secular evidence to support the concept of personal moral responsibility, why, throughout history, have we stubbornly refused to acknowledge that most human fault ". . . is not in our stars, but in ourselves"?

In the theodicy which is *The Brothers Karamazov*, Dostoevsky's parable of *The Grand Inquisitor*[27] portrays the central issue of man's fate not as rationality or irrationality, as the conceit of shallower minds leads them to believe*—but freedom

---

*In fearless defence of the Supreme Court, for years I have breached the "wall of separation between church and state" by asking thousands of students why God drove Adam and Eve from the Garden of Eden. Of those who believe they know, more than eight of ten confidently assert that it was because they ate the fruit of the *Tree of Knowledge.*

of choice and its consequences: the painful uphill struggle on the lonely unmarked road which is man's search for his essential meaning. It is much more comfortable to assume that our rationality is the end, not the beginning, of our search, and so today instead of crawling into the sanctuary of the Church with its miracle, mystery, and authority, we grovel in our classrooms before a scientistic priesthood which entwines us in similar bonds.

"Nothing has ever been more unsupportable for a man and a human society than freedom." After all, even Saint Augustine hedged his plea to God for the strength to practice chastity and continence, saying: ". . . only not yet."

Chapter 11. References and Notes

1. Carl Becker, *The Heavenly City of the Eighteenth-Century Philosophers*, (New Haven, Conn.: Yale University Press, 1932), p. 63.

2. K. M. Bykov, *The Cerebral Cortex and the Internal Organs*, trans. W. Horsley Gantt (New York: Chemical Pub. Co., 1957), p. 240.

3. A. Kuntz, *A Textbook of Neuro-Anatomy* 5th ed. (Philadelphia: Lea & Febiger, 1950), p. 430.

4. Zola P. Horovitz, *Function of the Brain* (New Brunswich, N.J.: Squibb Institute for Medical Research, 1963), p. 6; W. Freeman and J. W. Watts, *Psychosurgery* (Springfield, Ill.: Charles C. Thomas, 1950), p. 29; F. G. Alexander and Sheldon T. Selesnick, *The History of Psychiatry* (New York: Harper and Row, 1966), p. 285; Gustav Eckstein, *The Body Has a Head* (New York: Harper and Row, 1970), p. 650; Carl Sagan, *The Dragons of Eden* (New York: Random House, 1977), p. 71.

5. A. H. Hobbs, "The Hypothesis of Reciprocal Complementarity," *The American Journal of Psychiatry*, (1960), pp. 54–58.

6. Will and Ariel Durant, *The Lessons of History* (New York: Simon and Schuster, 1968), p. 37.

7. Arno Karlen, *Sexuality and Homosexuality* (New York: W. W. Norton, 1970), p. 76.

8. Hannah Arendt, *Eichmann in Jerusalem* (New York: Viking Press, 1963).

9. Stanley Milgram, *Obedience to Authority* (New York: Harper and Row, 1974), pp. 3–5, 6.

10. Vincent Bugliosi with Curt Gentry, *Helter Skelter* (New York: W. W. Norton, 1974), p. 235.

11. Thomas Powers, *The Making of a Terrorist* (Boston: Houghton Mifflin, 1971), Quoted in *Philadelphia Bulletin*, September 16, 1970.

12. Susan Stern, *With the Weathermen: The Personal Journal of a Revolutionary Woman* (New York: Doubleday, 1975).

13. Ralph Dahrendorf, "Baader-Meinhof—How Come? What's Next?" *New York Times*, October 20, 1977.

14. John Passmore, *The Perfectibility of Man* (New York: Charles Scribner's Sons, 1970), pp. 242–243.

15. Arthur Keith, *A New Theory of Human Evolution* (New York: Philosophical Library, 1949).

16. G. G. Simpson, *The Meaning of Evolution* (New York: New American Library, A Mentor Book, 1951), pp. 134–5, 161.

17. *King James Bible Dictionary.*

18. Dante, *The Comedy of Dante Alighieri, Cantica I, Hell (L'Inferno)*, trans. Dorothy L. Sayers (Baltimore: Penguin Books, 1960), pp. 10, 11.

19. Francis Bacon, *The New Organon*, ed. Fulton H. Anderson, Bobbs-Merrill, (Indianapolis: 1960) p. 15.

20. Thomas Fowler, *Shaftesbury and Hutcheson*, Sampson, Low, Marston, Searle and Rivington, London, 1882, pp. 81–82.

21. Same source, pp. 185, 192, 225.

22. William T. Blackstone, *Francis Hutcheson and Contemporary Ethical Theory*, U. of Georgia Press, Athens 1965, p. 24.

23. Adam Smith, *The Theory of Moral Sentiments*, 12th edition, B. Chapman, Glasgow, Scotland, 1809, p. 133ff, p. 189, pp. 26–27.

24. Thomas Reid, *Essays on the Intellectual Powers of the Human Mind*, Thomas Tegg, London, 1827, pp. 440–441, p. 623.

25. Aleksandr Solzhenitsyn, ed., *From Under the Rubble* (Boston: Little, Brown, 1974), p. 25.

26. Carl Sagan, *The Dragons of Eden* (New York: Random House, 1977), p. 93.

27. Fyodor Dostoevsky, *The Grand Inquisitor*, trans. Ralph E. Matlaw (New York: E. P. Dutton, 1960), pp. xx, xxi.

Chapter 12

Ills the Spirit Is Heir To

It Is The elixir of the gods; and whether it is designated *aqua vitae, akavit, uisge beatha, usquebaugh,* whiskey, or *eau de vie,* mere mortals refer to it as *the water of life.*

In a rare exception to his customary invective, H. L. Mencken once drooled that the wedding of *genievre* and vermouth was the closest America ever came to producing a sonnet.

It is Demon Rum; it is the devil's helper; it is the servant of Satan; and a barrel of whiskey contains:

> A barrel of crime, a barrel of groans,
> A barrel of orphans' most pitiful moans;
> A barrel of serpents that hiss as they pass,
> That glow from the liquor in the bead of the glass
> A barrel of falsehoods, a barrel of cries,
> That fall from the maniac's lips as he dies.[1]

Such maledictions distort the role of drinking as much as the euphemisms which precede them, for regardless of the demonstrated harm done through abusive consumption of alcohol, contrary to dire warnings of parents and clergy, in violation of informal complaints and formal prohibitions, and in every clime and throughout all time alcohol has been drunk by members of most human groups, whether religious or pagan, civilized or primitive.

282

We drink to speed the passing of the old year and to welcome the new; to wish long life to the new-born and peace to the new-dead; to warm the cockles of our heart and to relax our wrinkled brow; to proclaim our joy in victory and to drown the sorrow of defeat; to commune with the Lord and to shake hands with the devil.

Yet no matter how customary the consumption of spirits nor how commonly even excessive drinking is tolerated on a New Year's Eve, a Mardi Gras, or a victory celebration, no matter if there be no formal (legal) prohibitions at all, the informal controls of custom set limits to excessive breaches of propriety even during drunkenness, and we would ridicule anyone who continued to celebrate New Year's Eve on into July.

Both Flesh and the Spirit

In titling this chapter "Ills the Spirit Is Heir To" I do not imply that the problems of alcoholism are totally spiritual—they likely involve material as well as spiritual phenomena. Nor, by any means do I imply this problem is a psychosomatic one in which mental processes alone produce the behavioral manifestation of the troubled condition.

In Chapter 4 I described how philosophers of the eighteenth century, awed by the elegant simplicity and mathematical precision of Newton's laws of motion, became entranced by the delusion that they would soon develop similar simple and precise laws to explain, with unbiased objectivity, all human behavior and social events. In Chapter 7 I outlined the manner in which this eighteenth-century scientistic delusion, through proponents such as B. F. Skinner, not only still influences our beliefs about man and society, but more and more nearly determines them. Throughout my analysis of the moral nature of man I have stressed that such scientistic conceptions of man must, by their very nature, reduce him to a totally malleable, easily conditioned, glob of protoplasm. In Chapter 11 I argued in favor of an alternative conception of man; one in which his inborn potential for evil as well as for good limits his malleabilty, while endowing him with the capability of consciously willed moral choice.

283

Are Combined Through a Causal Nexus

To illustrate how the abstract principles of complementaritly apply to actual behavior, I shall show that both the effects of the consumption of alcohol as well as the problem condition called alcoholism can be understood by interpreting them in terms of the circular process of a causal nexus rather than through customary straight-line cause-and-effect. These problem conditions, like other social responses, involve the environment, upper brain (cortical) levels, lower brain (hypothalamic) levels, muscles, and glands, and they can be initiated, facilitated, or inhibited by any of the elements involved in the process. Though a tendency toward human response may be initiated on any of these levels, such a tendency does not eventuate in socially significant behavior unless it is facilitated by all of the other elements of the causal nexus.

To stress man's capacity to be an active element in his moral choices is not to deny the role of physiological or other material factors in alcoholism but to focus attention on the upper brain levels where man's capacity for conscious control is centered and where moral precepts have developed into a pattern that makes social sense. Man can choose to make this non-material (spiritual in the dichotomy of flesh and the spirit) level either an inhibitor or a facilitator in respect to tendencies to drink or to control a condition of problem drinking.

Functional Complementarity

In human behavior, the consumption of alcohol acts *as both a stimulant and a depressant*, producing contrary effects that cannot be explained by simple cause-and-effect but which can be reasonably interpreted in terms of a causal nexus.

Much evidence supports the contention that the consumption of alcohol depresses neurological functioning, even to the degree that death will result if a very large amount (say a quart of 100-proof bourbon) is consumed in a short (say an hour) interval of time.

Yet history and ordinary observation abundantly demonstrate that social and psychological responses are stimulated by drinking. Such stimulation, in further contradiction to simple cause-and-effect interpretations, takes a variety of forms and varies to a degree which bears no constant relationship to the amount consumed. Responses to drinking vary from giggling gaiety to "crying in your beer." Some drinkers become friendly and others withdraw or become hostile; some people, after a few drinks, begin roisterously to "swing from the chandeliers," while others decorously swallow drink after drink with no observable effect until, perhaps, they fall flat on their faces when they try to stand up.

How can one explain this seeming paradox of simultaneous neurological depression and psychological as well as social stimulation? How explain the wide range in variety and degree of stimulation from the same quantity of alcohol? Why does the same "cause" in the form of the consumption of a given quantity of alcohol have contrary effects not only on different people but on the same person at different times?

Many such apparent paradoxes, some of them seemingly flat contradictions in terms of cause-effect, could be listed, but only a few will be analyzed in order to support the contention that explanations in terms of a causal nexus provide more satisfying answers than those which are based on cause-effect. In addition to alcohol being a stimulant at the same time that it is a depressant, it is strange that[2]:

1. The consumption of alcohol commonly increases sexual desire, but detracts from sexual performance;

2. The effects of drinking are physiological and neurological, but they are just as truly psychological and social;

3. Alcohol is not in any high degree physiologically addictive, but many people become habitual drinkers;

4. A person who hasn't had a drink for years can still be called an alcoholic, while most people who drink regularly are not alcoholics;

5. Chronic alcoholism may be a medical condition as well as a psychological state of mind, but it is most successfully treated as a moral problem;

6. The most highly trained and skillful psychiatrists usually fail in their attempts to treat chronic alcoholics, but an uneducated skid-row bum may contribute vital help in treatment.

These and other seeming paradoxes associated with the

consumption of alcohol can be resolved if we accept the premise that our brain is an evolutionary product. Areas which control different functions (muscles, sight, smell, hearing, analytic process, speech, and the patterning of the proprieties and moral imperatives) evolved over millions of years and as they evolved the differing—and often antagonistic—functions which they fulfill became organized into homeostatic balance through functional complementarity.

Thus we have learned to inhibit many of the urges for emotional behavior (fear, rage, sex) which arise from their center in the hypothalamus if they fail to fit into the patterns of the moral codes which are centered in the neocortex. We learn, not quite intuitively but certainly with very little formal education, the differing balances of emotionality and propriety which are appropriate to a funeral service in contrast to a football game; to office work contrasted to vacation play. Drinking changes this balance by increasing the component of emotionality in our behavior.

The depressant effect of alcohol is selective, acting first on the most recently developed and most sensitively delicate neurological connections,[3] and causing them to lose some of their integrational and inhibitory capacity. With these ordinarily inhibitory neocortical functions weakened, impulses toward emotional expression from the phylogenetically older hypothalamic areas, while unchanged in an absolute sense, become relatively stronger in the functional relationship.

Depending upon his characteristic temperament and his mood of the moment, the drinker becomes gay or gloomy, friendly or hostile, argumentative or amorous to a degree which exceeds his sober responses. Varying degrees of increased emotional responsiveness also depend on the consistency and cohesiveness of the patterns of social controls in the mind of the drinker, the rate of absorption of alcohol into the blood stream, and the social situation.

Alcohol is absorbed more rapidly if the stomach is empty or if the drink is effervescent—thus the "lift" of the relaxing ("I needed that!") drink before dinner or the quick sentimentality which bubbles up from champagne. This increase of the emotional component in our responses is useful as a relaxing change of pace, and likely is associated with the heavy drinking so

286

commonly found among novelists that F. Scott Fitzgerald called it "the writer's vice." Some of the more prominent writers affected by it include Fitzgerald, Eugene O'Neill, Sinclair Lewis, John Steinbeck, William Faulkner, Edgar Allan Poe, Dylan Thomas, Winston Churchill, John O'Hara, Thomas Wolfe, Brendan Behan (who once went on a diet in which he "restricted" his daily alcoholic intake to two quarts of whiskey plus an unlimited quantity of ale!), Jack London, and many others. Ernest Hemingway recounts a day of drinking with a jai-alai player in 1943 Cuba during which they drank sixteen frozen daiquiris apiece, each containing four ounces of Bacardi rum, after which he worked all night and ". . . never felt better."[4]

While such increased emotional component might contribute moderately to creative writers, it would likely handicap mathematicians.

In drinking, any increased creativity would constitute only a passing phase. As more alcohol is absorbed, and as time passes, the depressant effect spreads to phylogenetically older levels of the brain, affecting first the finer degrees of coordination, then hampering gross muscular control. As speech and visual centers of the brain are affected, speech becomes slurred and the vision blurred. Drinkers dribble, glasses are knocked over, unsteadiness becomes weaving, weaving becomes staggering, and the safety valve of sleep or passing out prevents the effects of excessive consumption from interfering with the brain centers which control breathing and heart rhythm.

Lechery: Alcohol Provokes and Unprovokes

Ogden Nash described the relationship between drinking and sex by saying that "Candy is dandy / But liquor is quicker" —later adding "Pot is not" to his doggerel. But Shakespeare (in *Macbeth*) offers a more apt description of this relationship. When Macduff asks the Porter to describe the three things which the hungover Porter said drink provokes, he responds,

> Marry, sir, nose-painting, sleep, and urine.
> Lechery, sir, it provokes, and unprovokes;
> it provokes the desire, but it takes away

the performance.

Thus, while the depressed neocortical functioning weakens governance of the proprieties relating to sexual behavior thus relatively increasing sexual urges, heavy drinking makes performance more frantic than effective as the functioning of brain centers controlling the muscular coordination essential to sexual activity is depressed.

To ignore the complexities and subtleties of functional complementarity by describing the effects of drinking "scientifically"—that is, as a quantifiable straight-line effect of the consumption of specified quantities of alcohol—though widely quoted and used as the basis of tests for drunken driving, is arbitrary and dogmatic rather than intellectually informative.

Getting Drunk by Formula

Directly or indirectly, all tests for drunken driving seem to have their source in "The Definition of an Intoxicating Beverage," published in 1955 from the Laboratory of Applied Psychology, Yale University.[5] The author, an associate professor of applied physiology at Yale, summarized his conclusions thus:

On the basis of studies in which alcohol intoxication as judged by clinical criteria was correlated with tissue concentrations of alcohol, the conclusion is reached that intoxication occurs when there is an alcohol concentration of 0.15 percent or more in the blood. Any beverage having a sufficiently high alcohol content to produce such a concentration, considering the normal human capacity for fluid consumption, is then considered an intoxicating beverage.

Dr. Greenberg, the author, then states that approximately four ounces of alcohol must be ingested in order to attain a concentration of 0.15 percent in the blood. Since pure alcohol is too strong to drink, and since alcohol is oxidized at the rate of one-half ounce each hour, the formula for getting drunk on 100-proof distilled spirits (whiskey, bourbon, gin) is 8 + H; that is, 8 ounces of 100-proof (50 percent alcohol) spirits plus one additional ounce for each hour of drinking. Anyone who drinks fewer than 12 ounces of 100-proof spirits during a four-hour interval of drinking is, therefore, not intoxicated. According to similar formulas, anyone who drinks less than 52 ounces (approximately 1½ quarts) of wine during an evening is not drunk, and to become intoxicated by drinking beer requires the consumption (the formula being 80 + 10H) of at least 120 ounces of 3.7 percent beer. Dr. Greenberg insists that since the consumption of such a quantity of beer is "physiologically unnatural," *beer is not an intoxicating beverage.* He makes this astonishing statement three times in his article.

Thus do "scientific" findings conflict with common sense, fact, and, perhaps, personal experience. Since the only variable which is taken into consideration in deriving these formulas is bodily weight (the basis being 160 pounds), any man, woman, or child, without any drinking experience, and allowing only for differences in weight, can drink up to eleven ounces of 100-proof spirits or 51 ounces of 20-proof wine, or 119 ounces of 3.7 percent beer without being intoxicated, and nobody in the entire history of mankind, according to Dr. Greenberg, even got drunk on beer!

Based on such patently absurd formulas we assume that the effects of the consumption of alcohol have now been quantified and instruments such as alcometers, drunkometers, intoximeters, and breathalysers are used to determine liability for arrest for drunken driving. Since the motor skills and judgment necessary to drive sensibly vary widely from person to person and since the effects of drinking also vary widely on the basis of experience, age, metabolism, and many factors other than weight, it would make more sense to test motor coordination and reaction rather than to measure (and these instruments are far from exact) the content of alcohol in the blood.

Contrary to assertions such as the above, there is no quantified formula for becoming intoxicated. In addition to weight as a variable, many others: drinking experience, age, sex, metabolism, health, and state of mind must be taken into consideration together with the social context in which the drinking occurs. The effects of drinking are a function of social situations and cultural values, as well as of personal and psychological factors. To determine ability to drive we need tests and judgment based on much more than the percentage of alcohol in the blood in its relationship to differences in weight.

The Problem of Alcoholism

Our temptation to eliminate all differences between people by fitting them into seemingly quantified formulas derived by pseudoscientific techniques dominates our interpretation not only of the effects of drinking but, more importantly, it governs our approach to the problem condition of chronic alcoholism.

Our zeal to reduce human behavior to simple scientistic formulas, measurable by instruments, is not entirely the fault of writers who claim that they have discovered "The Definition of an Intoxicating Beverage" based on "clinical criteria" which "scientists" have used to "provide an objective measurement— a biochemical fingerprint . . ." of intoxication. Despite author Greenberg's inclusion of some of the many social and psychological aspects of drinking, and his recognition that small amounts of alcohol, far less than those necessary to produce 0.15 percent in the blood, do adversely affect sensory perception and discrimination, reaction time, physical coordination, and judgment, he does overemphasize the biochemical factor to justify the quantification and the formulas which we have so eagerly incorporated into law. Such arbitrary exclusion of not only some but most, of the factors associated with the effects of alcohol consumption is another illustration of Sir Arthur Eddington's "fishnet fallacy." The misleading nature of such quantification of qualitative complexities is further compounded because the term he attempts to define, "intoxication," is itself inappropriate.[6]

Greek warriors tipped the arrows for their bows (toxon) into a poisonous substance designated *toxikon*, which became the Latin word *(toxikum)* for any poison, and the verb is *intoxico*. To intoxicate means to poison, and intoxication would mean that the condition of the subject was caused by poison. While some hosts jocularly invite their guests to "name their poison," and while the metabolism of alcohol does involve a toxic (acetaldehyde) phase, the first usage is only a cornball colloquialism, and the toxic acetaldehyde is so quickly converted into non-toxic acetic acid that it is a perversion of meaning to call alcohol an intoxicant.

"Intoxication" is a nice-nelly pedanticism, not a meaningful

290

descriptive term. Much more meaningful, in their richly aged, well-soaked connotations, are drunk, sloshed, blotto, loaded, obfuscated, stinko, snozzled, plastered, stoned, stewed, crocked, or higher than a kite. None of these, however, has been "scientifically" defined.

We have been similarly misled by scientistic claims and by authoritarian pronouncements into believing that the problem condition of alcoholism has been scientifically defined and perhaps quantified. An alcoholic, we are told, is someone who drinks on three or more days of the week. Such quantification conveniently ignores the many people who drink seven days a week without significant adverse effects. We are told that an alcoholic is someone who drinks more than a quart of distilled spirits a week—a description which would include many responsible and some famous people, while numerous skid-row bums with impeccable credentials as alcoholics drink much less, though perhaps more steadily.

And we are told (by the same Dr. Leon Greenberg who produced the scientistic definition of an intoxicating beverage) that alcoholism is the result of precisely twelve steps. Under the prestigious aegis of the National Council on Alcoholism these steps, inevitably leading "down the ladder" to alcoholism, entail[7]:

- The social drink, where most people stop and you don't.
- The blackout: you can't remember what happened the night before.
- You drink more than your friends do and liquor means more to you.
- You continue to drink more than you mean to; the intended two drinks after work turns into six.
- You begin inventing excuses for drinking (a cold, fatigue, etc.).
- You start taking eye-openers before breakfast.
- You begin to drink alone.
- You start going on benders or prolonged drinking bouts.
- You are tortured by remorse in your sober moments, but only briefly. Then you resume drinking more heavily than ever.
- You develop anxiety over your ability to obtain liquor and begin hiding bottles around the house.

- You finally realize you are an alcoholic, perhaps because of a traffic accident or a bad fall on the stairs.
- You decide whether to turn yourself over to a doctor for treatment or give up and drink yourself to death.

One is likely to feel that he has learned much about the nature of alcoholism and its cause as he reads about these twelve steps that lead down this rungless ladder because they are described as being scientifically derived and presented authoritatively by the National Council on Alcoholism. One's credulity in this precise quantification of these steps might, however, be shaken were he aware that similar "scientific" findings, from similarly authoritative sources (in this instance, the Director of the Section on Alcoholic Studies at Yale and chairman of the Connecticut Commission on Alcoholism and by a research specialist on alcoholism for the World Health Organization[8]), conclude that there are sixteen, not twelve, steps which lead down this roundless ladder to alcoholism.

The major fault in such purportedly scientific conclusions is not their pretensions to quantification but their behavioral nature. The supposed steps which lead to alcoholism were discovered not through clinical research nor scientific investigation; they were learned through commonplace observation, which may or may not be correct.

Though it happened many years ago, I vividly recall reading a temperance tract when I was a child. A colored painting in front of the book showed a straw-hatted, bright-eyed, pink-cheeked country lad, while one at the end of the tract in equally vivid but now depressive color showed, lying in a filthy gutter clutching an empty whiskey bottle, a bleary-eyed, ashen-cheeked besotted bum with his sweat-stained hat askew on his grease-matted head. On the pages between these graphic contrasts I learned how bright-eyed, pink-cheeked, straw-hatted country boys took their steps down the primrose path (the primrose path to alcoholism preceded the rungless ladder) to reach the gutters in which they, bleary-eyed, ashen-cheeked, besotted bums would lie.

Salt was the cause! Our country cherub began his descent by sprinkling salt on his food; then he began to add dashes of pepper; soon his jaded taste buds demanded stronger stimulation. Catsup led to mustard and mustard to hard cider as he raced, pell-mell and unstoppable, down the primrose path till he stumbled drunkenly into the gutter.

Even as a child—perhaps because I was already addicted to chili sauce—I was skeptical about the notion that salt led to spiced food and thus to alcoholism, suspecting—then and now—that it was the change from straw hat to felt that started the unstoppable slide.

As with all behavioral interpretations, this supposedly scientific proof that there are twelve (fourteen, sixteen—or seventy-six if you prefer) steps which lead to alcoholism describes only commonplaces and explains little. Nowhere in such interpretation is it explained *why* some people take all of these steps to become alcoholics while the vast majority of people who take one, or even several, do not. It describes *what* sometimes happens but neither explains why it happens in those cases where it does, nor why the vast majority of social drinkers never become alcoholics.

The final step, "You decide whether to turn yourself over to a doctor for treatment or give up and drink yourself to death," is another sensible-sounding but specious interpretation of alcoholism; a viewpoint which is widely publicized by the Federal government in placards which proclaim "Alcoholism is a Sickness—It can be Cured." Neither of these assertions has been proved.

As with criminals, drug addicts, the mentally unbalanced, even with those whose opinions differ from ours, we are tempted to evade the complexities of causation and to excuse defects of character which may be involved by saying that their reprehensible—or, perhaps, just different—behavior is caused by being "sick."

While it is forgiveable for a person to indulge in such colloquial faddishness, it is less than responsible for the government to deceive people by propagating this dubious assumption. I shall consider this question—whether or not the term sickness is the appropriate metaphor for such conditions—in some detail in my analysis of mental imbalance, but for the moment I limit myself to the proposition that if, by sickness, we mean a condition which is essentially physiological, a condition, further, which can be diagnosed from specific symptoms which are clearly defined if not quantified, and readily and universally recognized if not measurable by instruments,* then alcoholism is not a sickness; and the use of this designation to refer to it is primarily an attempt to exculpate alcoholics from their personal guilt in evading their social responsibilities.

The twin of this assertion that alcoholism is a sickness and can be cured is likewise contradictory to the weight of available evidence. While, in 1964, Arthur H. Cain claimed in *The Cured Alcoholic* that he had developed a form of treatment which enabled alcoholics to return to moderate drinking instead of—as with Alcoholics Anonymous—being restricted to lifelong abstinence, Cain's evidence rested on only seven (of ninety-three) cases in which alcoholics were able to return to moderate drinking, and this modest proportion, coupled with extreme latitude in the interpretation of the condition we call alcoholism, make his findings less than convincing.[9]

In 1976 similar claims—that some alcoholics could safely return to normal drinking—were made on the basis of studies sponsored by the United States Public Health Service and published by the Rand Corporation, but these studies were premised on an assumption that alcoholism is due primarily if not entirely to social conditioning, which in the nature of the case is unproveable, and which also conflicts with clinical findings that brain chemicals such as tetrahydropapaveroline (THP) may induce alcoholism and remain in the brain to reestablish the condition of the post-withdrawal abstainer returns to any form of drinking.[10] For many reasons it is premature to say that THP or any other specific chemical causes alcoholism or that brain chemicals necessitate abstention after treatment; but such findings do indicate a reasonable likelihood that chemical factors as well as neurological, psychological, and social factors are involved in the syndrome which is alcoholism—making dubious the claims that it can be cured.

A basic issue which underlies all assumptions about the etiology, diagnosis, or cure of alcoholism is the question of its

---

*The National Council on Alcoholism asserts "that only one in 300 physicians can accurately diagnose alcoholism [since] there is no single symptom, laboratory test or physical sign which is in itself specifically diagnostic of alcoholism."

definition. As I indicated earlier, most of the terms we use so glibly have never been clearly defined, and most of our disputes are about names, names which may or may not bear a close relationship to the things they are supposed to designate. If this contention is essentially correct, and if even terms such as life and death lack clear definition—if, indeed, the most basic and elemental particles and forces within the atom itself are a confused jumble of undefined unknowns—it is passing bold to say that undefined conditions such as alcoholism are caused specifically by this or that and should be treated thus or so on the basis of their hypostatized cause.

Despite many efforts to define alcoholism in terms of the frequency of drinking or the amount, or to reduce its complexities to simple social or psychological conditioning or to chemical determinism, no clear definition yet exists and all descriptions (which, lacking clear definition, we must use) are so loose as to encourage wide variations of interpretation."

In fairly recent years such descriptions—often miscalled definitions—increasingly interpret alcoholism as a condition in which a person's drinking seriously interferes with social responsibilities. A 1957 description is:

> The medical definition of an alcoholic, as distinguished from a social drinker, is one whose drinking harmfully and definitely interferes with one or more of his important life activities. He may lose time from work due to drinking, or the quality of his work may suffer, or his home life harmony may be disrupted, or he may so speak and generally conduct himself that his reputation and relationships with others suffer.[12]

Believing as I do in the importance of social rules in human affairs, I approve of this writer's description of an alcoholic as one whose drinking—regardless of frequency or quantity—definitely interferes with one or more of his important life activities; but his statement is too broad, too much a catchall to constitute a proper definition, and it certainly is not a *medical* definition. Time lost from work, a decline in the quality of work, disharmony in one's home life, and obnoxious behavior may occur to teetotalers as well as drinkers, and when they do occur to people who drink, factors other than drink may be the cause.

A 1978 description is prefaced by a statement describing the problems involved in defining alcoholism and the changing nature of definitions, then asserts that an acceptable definition for this last quarter of the twentieth century is:

> ... *an alcoholic is an individual who uses alcohol to such an extent, and in such a way, that it interferes with his personal, social, or occupational behavior.* This is obviously a psychosocial definition, since it does not talk of blood alcohol levels, medical problems or quantities of alcohol consumed. It does not say the alcoholic is suffering from an illness. It just says that when alcohol mucks up a person's life in any way, let's call him an alcoholic and see if the problem can't at least be reduced.[13]

My own interpretation, first described in 1960, is:

> Chronic alcoholism exists when the essentially social nature of drinking is subordinated to the consumption of alcohol as an excuse to evade social responsibilities.[14]

Such social responsibilities include, for most of us, occupational as well as familial ones. Instead of drinking to depress the functioning of the neocortical pattern of mores and proprieties moderately and temporarily, an alcoholic attempts to extinguish them permanently. Drinking, a practice meant to be a means to an end by temporarily reducing the social imperative in the self-society matrix, becomes a *self*-ish end in itself.

In terms of functional complementarity, an alcoholic distorts the homeostatic equilibrium between his personal emotional urges and the social controls. Subconsciously, he is aware of this distortion and feels a sense of guilt which, usually, he vehemently denies. But social guiltiness is evidenced by gulping and sneaking drinks and by far-fetched rationalizations. He drinks, he tells anyone who will listen, because of the lousy boss he has on his lousy job where he works his lousy ass off to feed his lousy wife and lousy kids because of the lousy inflation caused by those lousy businessmen who drink three-martini lunches. And he also drinks, he nonstoppably continues, because

296

of the lousy state of the country where the lousy bastards on relief piss away our taxes on booze, etc., etc., etc.

At parties, he graciously offers to serve as "Mother's Little Helper," insisting that the hostess charm the guests while he mixes the drinks. Whereupon he proceeds to pour one for guest A and one for himself, one for guest B and one for himself, one for guest C and, having worked so hard, a double for himself.

He may become a closet drinker, then engage in solitary drinking. His subconscious awareness of social guilt leads to "blackouts" which expunge disgraceful drunken acts from his memory. During hangovers, metabolism has drained off the depressant effects of alcohol from the neocortical levels of the brain, but these depressant effects still hamper the functioning of the lower brain levels. Relatively, therefore, the social conscience is more active than usual, giving rise to acute but undefined feelings of guilt and unshaped smothering fears. Soon or late an alcoholic learns to "stroke the hair of the dog that bit him" by taking a drink to alleviate his hangover. This practice makes good neurological and physiological sense but bad psychological habituation. The efficacy of this homeopathic remedy probably results from the caloric content of alcohol giving a quick lift of needed energy, while its depressant effect on neocortical functioning stills the shrill inchoate shrieks of guilt by temporarily reducing the disparity between the hyperactive neocortical levels and the hypoactive lower brain levels. Obviously, the drunk "reasons," if one drink makes him feel 10 percent better, two will make him feel 20 percent better, etc., etc., etc.

In describing these practices which indicate that alcoholism is characterized by an imbalance in the homeostatic relationship between the social controls and self-desires, I do not imply that this is a simple cause-effect pattern in which selfishness causes alcoholism; nor should one infer that such practices are inevitable or universal—certainly not to the degree implied in assertions that twelve (or sixteen) steps lead, unstoppably, to alcoholism. I do contend that this phenomenon is involved in alcoholism, and I stress it because it is in this relationship that the potentiality for conscious control over the process exists.

Old Treatments for Alcoholism

Be of good cheer, ye who despair of a cure for alcoholism, for here is one that has been aged by more than a century and derived from a truly formidable source. In *The Artist's Guide and Mechanic's Own Book, Embracing the Portion of Chemistry Applicable to the Mechanic Arts with Abstracts of Electricity, Galvanism, Magnetism, Pneumatics, Optics, Astronomy and Mechanical Philosophy; Also Mechanical Exercises in Iron, Steel, Lead, Zinc, Copper, and Tin Soldering and a Variety of Useful Receipts; Extending to Every Profession and Occupation of Life: Particularly Dyeing Silk, Woollen, Cotton and Leather* (Boston, 1857), author James Pilkington informs us how:

To cure those who are too much addicted to drinking wine

Put in a sufficient quantity of wine, three or four large eels, which leave there till quite dead. Give that wine to the person you want to reform, and he or she will be so much disgusted with wine, that though they formerly made use of it, they will not have an aversion to it.

Should eels be unavailable, or should you prefer a more recent cure, more precisely attuned to the "scientific" practices of today, consider the advantages of converting the alcoholic into a morphine addict. By 1889 it had been "proved" that opium ". . . is less inimical to healthy life than alcohol; that it calms instead of exciting the baser passions and hence is less productive of acts of violence and crime."[15] Statistics had proved that the substitution of morphine addiction for alcohol addiction brought about peacefulness and quiet to many disturbed and distracted homes; kept the head of the family out of the gutter and out of the lock-up and kept him from neglect of his affairs. Besides all these advantages, a morphine habit could be supported on five cents a day while an alcoholic might spend as much as twenty-five cents a day.

But what was to be done when later experience showed that the effects of morphine addiction were, despite the contrary claims of our 1889 author, worse than the effects of alcohol addiction?

Not to worry, folks, your indefatigable scientists soon produced a new drug, *the heroic drug*, which would cure addiction to morphine and other opiates. While this new "wonder drug" cure produced addiction in a few cases, medical scientists assured skeptics that:

> . . . all observers are agreed, however, that none of the patients suffer in any way from this habituation, and that none of the symptoms which are so characteristic of chronic morphinism have ever been observed . . . a large number of the reports refer to the fact that the same dose may be used for a long time without any habituation.[16]

This new "heroic drug" cure for morphine addiction was heroin!

But not to worry, folks, a new wonder drug, methadone, discovered during World War II, is now being used as a substitute for heroin. Methadone came into fairly widespread use in government-supported clinics about 1970, and by 1973, 2,933 new methadone addicts were added to the 13,050 additional persons who became addicted to heroin in that year! An accurate count of drug addicts is difficult to ascertain, and the index often used as an indirect (and grisly) measure of addiction is the number of deaths attributed to use of drugs. While deaths attributed to heroin declined in the early 1970s, deaths from methadone—either alone, or in conjunction with other drugs—increased so rapidly that total drug deaths did not decrease at all.

I refer to the infusion of the stinking effluvium and the circulation of the nauseous detritus of decaying eels into wine to indicate that such therapy was essentially no different than modern "scientific" attempts to threat alcoholics through negative conditioning. I similarly cite the persistent failure and the frequent danger in attempts to treat this and other such human failings through drugs. With both types of examples my criticism of such practices is based on the manner in which they treat the alcoholic as though he were a puppet to be subconsciously manipulated into changing the direction of his life. Both approaches fail to respect the potential of alcoholics and other drug addicts to exercise their own power to choose; to reassert their own damaged character as a significant element in their treatment.

Old Eels in New Bottles

One modern form of drug treatment of alcoholism takes advantage of the process in which alcohol, during its metabolism, is converted into a toxic substance, acetaldehyde. In the ordinary course of events, this toxic acetaldehyde is almost immediately converted into nontoxic acetic acid. But if a drug such as Antabuse interferes with this process, the acetaldehyde is not further metabolized and it accumulates. Severe headaches, nausea, vomiting, and difficulty in breathing result from even moderate consumption of alcohol when acetaldehyde is in one's system, and alcoholics are persuaded to take disulfiram (Antabuse) daily to discourage drinking. As for the effects of such Draconian therapy, studies indicate that "It's a good theory, but there are no good data to support it."[17] Within two or three days after an alcoholic discontinues the treatment he can—and often does—resume drinking without any of the toxic reactions, and those who continue to take Antabuse would likely have stopped drinking anyway.

Another version of attempts to treat alcoholism through a process of negative conditioning involves giving the alcoholic an electric shock whenever he picks up an alcoholic drink;[18] and the most exotic of these efforts to treat alcoholism through negative conditioning involves an injection of curare, which prevents the alcoholic from breathing by paralyzing his muscles. "The paralysis lasts for sixty to ninety seconds. It is so terrifying it convinces him he is going to die."[19] And, may I say, no wonder!

This last form of therapy illustrates the pernicious influence which scientism has on our beliefs about human beings. With the source identified as *Science Services*, and designated as a new *cure* for alcoholism, five references to science occur in six column-inches of newsprint to create respect for practices which readers would otherwise find amusing or, in its potential for serious injury, shocking.

All of these approaches (Antabuse, electric shock, curare) are premised on an assumption that alcoholism is the product of positive conditioning. Implicitly if not explicitly, it is assumed that a person becomes an alcoholic because, subconsciously, he has formed strong conditioned connections between the pleasures associated with drinking and the drinking itself. Since, in such assumption, the condition was created subconsciously, it can be eliminated by substituting negative subconscious connections—violent headaches, nausea, electric shocks, paralysis which prevents breathing—with drinking.

Such approaches reduce human beings to less-than-conscious automatons, ignoring their potential for restoration of their lost character through conscious choice. If the rationalization for drinking is on the conscious cortical level, such subcortical modifications are usually few and temporary. The chief difference between the dead eels in the wine and these modern treatments is that the real stink of the eels is replaced by the fake aura of science.

Benzodiazepine drugs such as Librium and Valium were widely publicized as effective agents in the treatment of both acute and chronic alcoholism, but when Librium was administered to some alcoholics and chemically inert placebos were administered to others under double-blind conditions (in which neither the patient nor the doctor knew whether the patient received the drug or an inert placebo) only minor differences in results were found.[20] Most of the effects from administering Librium to alcoholics were psychological, not chemical. Administration of Valium to rats who were induced into alcohol habituation tended to *strengthen* the habituation rather than to weaken it.[21] Valium itself is sometimes called dehydrated gin, and some workers in the area of drug abuse believe it to be the number-one drug of abuse in the United States.

Treatment of Alcoholism Through the Social Controls

In addition to substituting one drug addiction for another, as in the past we substituted morphine for alcohol, then heroin for morphine, then methadone for heroin, and now, in some instances, Valium for alcohol; or progressing in the techniques of negative conditioning from the temporary nausea arising from the stench of dead eels to the risk of death through electric shock or curare, other approaches to the treatment of alcoholism exist, and some of them have at least the virtue of recognizing the area where the problem lies—the relationship between personal desires and those rules which regulate our living together in society, the social controls.

Some of the rules which together constitute the social controls are *formal*, and such are incorporated into laws which are enforced by the courts through instruments such as police, jails, and prisons (now correctional institutions). While every complex society needs such formal controls in order to function, it is part of conservative doctrine to believe that the *informal social controls*, those which are incorporated into the sense of propriety and in the human conscience, whether codified into laws or not, are even more important than the necessary formal controls; for no matter how strict the written laws may be, they will not be effectively obeyed unless they are re-enforced by the convictions of the citizenry. Thus, as indicated earlier, the number of divorces in the United States could be reduced to one-third or less merely by strictly enforcing existing legal codes. This feeling that the informal controls are more important than the formal controls in the functioning of a representative republic finds its cogent expression in Edmund Burke's aphorism that if we refuse to govern ourselves from within, we thereby permit our passions to be our fetters, and we shall increasingly be ruled from without. Man should rely on his fellows' capacity for innate control, even though it be at some loss.

Certainly our attempt to control the problems of drinking through the formal controls in the form of the Eighteenth Amendment to the Constitution was ineffective. Smuggling, bootlegging, illegal stills, bathtub gin, homemade wine, and prescription alcohol produced alcoholic beverages in quantities so sufficient that anyone who wanted to drink had no difficulty in obtaining booze. Violations of the National Enforcing (Volstead) Act were so numerous and so flagrant that Americans soon realized that many members of the police and of other enforcing agencies were conniving with bootleggers. And though the amendment itself, in prohibiting the manufacture, transporta-

302

tion, sale, and importation of intoxicating beverages did not make it illegal to drink, they knew that when they bought bootleg booze they were abetting violation of the law.

Apparently few people stopped drinking because of prohibition, and it is likely that some people, feeling that the government went too far in imposing such formal controls on their private lives, spitefully drank to show their defiance. Few persons would now contend that formal controls such as the National Prohibition Act of 1919 solved, or even appreciably alleviated, problems associated with drinking.

At an opposite extreme, there are those who argue that the abuses associated with the consumption of alcohol arise from its "forbidden fruit" appeals. They say that if we would only remove all formal prohibitions and rid ourselves of all informal inhibitions relating to its use, people would enjoy drinking in social moderation, without problems. In pursuit of this objective, the Federal government spent a million dollars in 1967 in a National Institute of Mental Health study that concluded that we could best combat alcoholism by encouraging liquor advertisements which showed alcohol being consumed by the whole family, including children, in a family setting; urged that alcoholic beverages be made available to young persons at church gatherings; and so forth.

Now, perhaps there is something edifying rather than amusing in envisioning a bucolic picnic setting wherein an idyllic family of Mommy, Daddy, and all the kiddies are getting roundly smashed together, maybe under a caption "The Family That Guzzles Together Nuzzles Together," or a church youth choir hiccupping its way through "Show Me the Way to Go Home" instead of "Onward Christian Soldiers," but before we stagger further into a nationwide program of "Booze Belongs—Tipple Together," it might be well to see what has happened in societies where virtually all inhibitions have been removed from drinking.

France is the country which is usually thought of as prototypically one in which removal of inhibitions as well as prohibitions against drinking has produced only moderate and social drinking. But "Alcoholism kills more people in France than in all the other major Western industrialized countries together," according to the World Health Organization.[22] French

303

death rates (per 100,000) from alcoholism in 1965 were 12, contrasted with 1.4 for the United States and only 0.1 for England and Wales, and her 34.2 death rate for cirrhosis of the liver was the highest in the world.

After World War II, Japan, where historically most people restricted their drinking to ritualistic enhancement of their appreciation of Shinto festivals, cherry blossoms, births or marriages, took off their informal injunctions against even excessive drinking to the degree that Dr. Hiroaki Kono, Japan's leading expert on alcoholism, says that the Japanese are now "the most permissive people in the world as regards alcohol,"[23] and it is estimated that some 3,000,000 problem drinkers and alcoholics constitute a fourfold increase since World War II. Consumption of alcoholic beverages increased from 934 million gallons in 1965 to 1,549 million in 1977, and the Japanese equivalent of Alcoholics Anonymous now has 50,000 members.

Advocates of the new morality lead us to believe that when we have fully adopted their socio-political programs which guarantee economic security, socialized medicine, subsidized housing, and universal education, alcoholism, together with other forms of drug addiction, crime, divorce, and mental disorder, will markedly decrease if they do not disappear, but the Soviet Union ranks first in the world in consumption of distilled spirits per person of drinking age (over 15).[24] *Literaturnaya Rossiya*, official publication of the Russian Republic's Writer's Union, describes drunkenness as the Soviet's most persistent and fastest worsening social problem.[25] Attempts to attribute rampant alcoholism to a carry-over of conditioning from Tsarist days, once persuasive, are absurdities after sixty years of Communist rule, and youths who have spent their entire lives under Communism are turning to excessive drinking more than their elders ever did. Attempts by the state to impose formal controls in the form of prohibitive prices, rigid restrictions on sales and other regulations on alcohol have all failed.

Similar though not so extreme conditions apply in Sweden, which, though now described as an illustration of the way in which the New Morality degenerates into *The New Totalitarianism*, for many years (and still in the romantic imaginings of many liberals) was portrayed as the ideal society, possessing all of the virtues of socialism, but none of the restrictions of regi-

304

mentation.[26] A recent survey found that about 85 percent of the ninth-graders in Stockholm drink beer, and seven out of ten fifteen-year-olds have been drunk.[27]

Whether old or new, eels or curare, morphine or Valium, the "scientific" psychological or drug treatments of alcoholism do not, according to available evidence, significantly affect the long-term likelihood of remedying the condition, though acceptance of formal treatment—which involves a consciously willed choice—does somewhat (25 percent abstinent six months after treatment compared with 16 percent among persons who were not in a formal program) increase chances of improvement.[28] Whether they attempt to stonewall the problem within the confines of rigid formal controls or romantically rely upon man's innate goodness to assure moderation, social programs have failed. Removal of the informal controls has failed to reduce, and sometimes has exacerbated, problems of alcoholic consumption. Likewise, the rosy promise that adoption of the New Morality would free us from such problems remains unfulfilled.

Serenity, Courage, Wisdom

Born in Vermont of middle-class parents, William Griffith Wilson was a bright but unstable youth who dropped out of college after his father's drinking dissolved his parents' marriage. Moving to New York City after he married, he became a brilliant securities analyst, but both his work and his marriage suffered from his excessive drinking, which involved binges as well as drunkenness.

He stopped drinking in 1934 when he joined the First Century Christian Fellowship (later called the Moral Rearmament Movement or Oxford Group), and his resolve to stop was also strengthened by William James' *Varieties of Religious Experience*. In 1935, following an extremely disappointing loss in a stockholders' proxy fight over control of a factory in Akron, Ohio, William Wilson was about to drown his sorrow in booze but he postponed his urge to get drunk while he tried to locate someone who was a member of the Oxford Group. He persevered through a complicated series of difficulties and finally arranged a meeting with Dr. Robert Holbrook Smith, a prominent

305

surgeon of Akron, and, like Mr. Wilson, an alcoholic whose drinking had interfered with his career. A long talk between these two total strangers, from different cities and different occupations, with nothing in common but their passion for alcohol and a concern about what it was doing to their families, their work, and their self-respect is described by the biographer of Bill W. (as William Wilson came to be called by members of Alcoholics Anonymous).[29]

> For Bill it had been a unique, wondrous and totally engrossing experience. After admitting his deep need to share his problems with another drunk, he had not felt the slightest desire to preach or in any way judge the other man. With a sense of incredible freedom, relief and, yes, joy, he'd felt the two of them growing closer, their talk becoming a mutual thing, and he knew they had both felt this. Two drunks had found a new, mysterious and loving kind of communication, a new language of the heart.

Gradually, with exasperating slowness, "Bill W." and "Doctor Bob" shared their experiences with others, and as time passed drunks joined together to discuss their problem and by 1939 they began to refer to themselves as members of Alcoholics Anonymous. In 1937 the co-founders had appealed to John D. Rockefeller for a donation to assist in organizing and spreading the movement, but he, either as an indication of his foresight or an expression of his stinginess, turned them down.

By word-of-mouth, simply, without the aura of science, the trappings of research or the pseudo-jargon of pedantry, and without governmental sponsorship or aid, Alcoholics Anonymous spread until there are now some 25,000 groups throughout the world and almost a million members. After A.A. was established, William Wilson's wife founded Al-Anon for wives of alcoholics and Alateen for their children.

In contrast to a maximum of 25 percent who continue to be abstinent six months after psychological forms of treatment, a 1968 survey of 11,355 members of A.A. indicated that 41 percent stopped drinking immediately upon joining A.A., an additional 23 percent stopped within a year after joining, and a further 18 percent (for a cumulative 82 percent) stopped drinking within two to five years of participation. Thirty-eight percent of the respondents had maintained their abstention for up to a year; an additional 33 percent had maintained abstention for up to five years, and a further 13 percent had abstained from drinking for up to ten years.[30] More recent surveys indicate similarly high rates of abstention.

The A.A. treatment that helps such high percentages of alcoholics to gain control over their vice involves twelve steps.[31]

1. We admitted we were powerless over alcohol—that our lives had become unmanageable.

2. We came to believe that a Power greater than ourselves could restore us to sanity.

3. Made a decision to turn our will and our lives over to the care of *God as we understood Him* (i.e., non-sectarian, but spiritual).

4. Made a searching and fearless moral inventory of ourselves.

5. Admitted to God, to ourselves and to another human being the exact nature of our wrongs.

6. Were entirely ready to have God remove all these defects of character.

7. Humbly asked Him to remove our shortcomings.

8. Made a list of all persons we had harmed, and became willing to make amends to them all.

9. Made direct amends to such people wherever possible, except when to do so would injure them or others.

10. Continued to take personal inventory and when we were wrong, promptly admitted it.

11. Sought through prayer and meditation to improve our conscious contact with *God as we understood Him,* praying only for knowledge of His will for us and the power to carry that out.

12. Having had a spiritual awakening as a result of these

307

steps, we tried to carry this message to alcoholics and to practice these principles in all our affairs.

The non-sectarian spiritual appeal made by members of Alcoholics Anonymous is:

God grant me the serenity to accept the things I cannot change, the courage to change the things I can, and the wisdom to know the difference.

Essentially, the process that enables an alcoholic to cope with his weakness involves an admission to others, and especially to himself, that he has a weakness—not a sickness— which, whatever the cause, is his responsibility. It is his existential weakness, and he must not blame his heredity, the slums, his toilet training, the insufficiency of untrammelled affection in his childhood, the threat of nuclear holocaust, his onerous job, or his nagging wife for it. This self-admission of personal responsibility should be accepted without any mental reservations.

He recognizes that drinking has a different effect on him than it has on most other people. Ideally, he should not become a zealous advocate of universal prohibition. Other people can drink moderately and still fulfill their social responsibilities. He cannot. For him, the social controls relating to drinking must be tightened to a degree far beyond that necessary for other people, and this tightening must be self-imposed on a day-to-day basis. To "swear off the stuff forever" which any drunk will readily (and frequently) do for his priest, his boss, his wife, or his children, is a grand gesture, but he knows it is an empty one; his resolution must be reaffirmed every day of his life. This resolution must be internalized and self-imposed. No playing games like smashing all the bottles of liquor, refusing to serve liquor to his guests, or avoiding association with people who drink, or moving to a "dry" community. He must know that no matter what he does there always will be ways to find liquor and his surcease is to be found not in the external physical removal of temptation but the internal psychic (spiritual) control of it.

His conscious, willful choice is essentially internalized, but his resolve receives the comfortable help of his fellow alcoholics

—his sponsors who pledge to help him through any crisis when he feels that he cannot control his desire for booze by himself. In the stereotypical situation, when the alcoholic calls upon one of his sponsors to help him through a crisis which he cannot cope with alone, he and his sponsor sit and talk, drinking coffee and smoking cigarettes until the crisis passes.*

This support from members of his peer group is vital, and in a limited sense one might say that Alcoholics Anonymous is a society within a society in which its specialized controls, akin to those which bind the members of some cults and fraternal organizations, constitute a bond which is stronger than, and sometimes conflicts with, the bonds formed under the more permissive controls of the larger society. Some dispute as to the effectiveness of A.A. treatment has been based on this contingency, critics saying that members need their association with the group as a crutch; that they may be weaned from the bottle but not from the group. This inability to function effectively without leaning on the peer group as a crutch is, when it exists, a worthwhile trade-off, I should say.

Such peer-group dependence seems to be more common and a significantly deeper limitation of the effectiveness of Synanaon, an organization for the treatment of drug addicts patterned after the way A.A. practices the treatment of alcoholics. But a contributing factor to the continuing dependence of Synanon members on their group is the lack of any spiritual element in Synanon procedure. By relying solely on secular, intimate but external peer-group bonds, members lack the personally internalized fortification provided by spiritual support. Members of Alcoholics Anonymous who combine internal spiritual fortification with secular peer-group support seem to attain a greater degree of integrity and independence.

The importance of this spiritual factor is obvious in the Twelve Steps, and it was emphasized in a letter which psycholo-

*Some years ago it occurred to me that an organization analagous to Alcoholics Anonymous might be formed to help people who want to stop smoking and can't do it on their own. Calling itself Nicotinic Nobodys, when a member felt he needed someone to help him avoid lighting a cigarette, he would call in his sponsor and the two would sit and talk and get drunk together.

gist C. G. Jung wrote to William Wilson.[32] After stating his conviction that the craving of an alcoholic for secular spirits in alcohol has its spiritual analog in a search for wholeness, Jung expressed the desirability of combining spiritual and secular support in our lives, saying:

> I am strongly convinced that the evil principle prevailing in this world leads the unrecognized spiritual need into perdition, if it is not counteracted either by real religious insight or by the protective wall of human community. An ordinary man, not protected by an action from above and isolated in society, cannot resist the power of evil, which is called very aptly, the Devil.

Alcoholics Anonymous is not a panacea for the problems associated with drinking, and its effectiveness is certainly not demonstrable through scientific proof. There is no clear-cut definition of alcoholism, and there is no established set of symptoms which confirm its presence or absence with certainty. All assertions of cures for alcoholism must be questioned as to whether the cured condition was actually alcoholism to begin with. Questions arising from such lack of clear definition and uncertainty of the symptoms must be added to those which relate to the meaning of cure (Is the substitution of one form of drug addiction for another a cure?) and, since many alcoholics have occasional dry periods, the issue of the duration of abstinence must be considered.

With A.A. there is no pretense of cure. Though the participant abstains from drinking, he is still considered to be an alcoholic—a "dry alcoholic."

From an intellectual point of view, Alcoholics Anonymous is also unsatisfying because the treatment is not premised upon any hypotheses about the basic causes of the condition, resting instead on the assumption that whatever the cause or causes may be, correction of the condition depends upon the alcoholic consciously accepting his personal responsibility for it.

Though the weight of evidence—non-scientific though it be —strongly indicates that treatment of alcoholism through Alcoholics Anonymous is far more effective than any other approach, intellectuals generally, and academicians particularly, either ignore, minimize, or ridicule its effectiveness because its premises involve an assumption that man, through a conscious act of will, can control significant aspects of his life.

The commitment of academicians to supposedly scientific procedure with predictability as its most convincing test requires their allegiance to the concept of a degree of subconscious conditioning which leaves little room in their credo for conscious moral choice. Though the spiritual aspects of A.A. procedure are nonsectarian, these also dissuade many academicians from approval. Their secular scientism is reenforced by the historical anticlericalism of liberalism, which prejudices them from giving Alcoholics Anonymous the credit it deserves, and their romantic conception of the innate goodness of man still leads them to believe, despite much evidence to the contrary, that attainment of their visionary New Morality will eliminate the problems of alcoholism when their socio-political programs remedy the materialistic conditions which, they are convinced, cause such "deviance."

As education, books, magazines, television, churches, and politicians continue to indoctrinate people into believing that their ideas and their behavior are the product of subconscious conditioning and psychoanalytic mechanisms; that neither they nor others are responsible for human behavior; that in our helplessness we can neither develop our character nor correct our defects and that alcoholism is a sickness which can be readily cured by psychological or chemical nostrums, alcoholism continues to increase. Though physiological, neurological, and quite possibly hereditary factors are involved in alcoholism, the spiritual aspect—our power to control it through conscious act of will—is also involved. But such choice is less difficult when fortified by peer-group empathy and comforted by spiritual guidance; buttresses to the will which are now being dismantled by rampant individuation, secular cynicism, scientistic propaganda which promises easy cures, and doctrines of personal irresponsibility. As these spread, problems associated with the consumption of alcohol increase, reflected in increases in alcoholism, alcoholic psychoses, deaths attributed to alcohol, a rapidly increasing percentage of addiction among females, and more drinking to excess at ever younger ages, with the percentage of

311

students who became drunk while still in high school increasing from 19 percent in 1957 to 45 percent in 1977, while the age at which the first drink was taken declined from 13.6 in 1965 to 12.9 in 1975.[33]

Chapter 12. References and Notes

1. *A Temperance Tract* (Monroe, N.C.: Earl A. Cook, n.d.)

2. A. H. Hobbs, "The Consumption of Alcohol and the Hypothesis of Reciprocal Complementarity," *The American Journal of Psychiatry*, (1960), pp. 228–233.

3. Ray Oakley, ed., *Drugs, Society, and Human Behavior* (St. Louis: C. V. Mosby Co., 1978), p. 144.

4. "Hemingway Letters Reproach Critics," *New York Times*, March 9, 1972.

5. Leon A. Greenberg, Ph.D., "The Definition of an Intoxicating Beverage," *Quarterly Journal of Studies on Alcohol*, June 1955.

6. Wilfred Funk, *Word Origins* (New York: Grosset and Dunlap, 1950), p. 171.

7. Harry Ferguson, "Alcoholism: The Slow Revision of Life Toward Drinking, Drinking, Drinking," *Philadelphia Evening Bulletin*, September 27, 1963.

8. Professor Selden D. Bacon, "New Light on Alcoholism," *New York Times Magazine*, February 9, 1958.

9. Arthur H. Cain, *The Cured Alcoholic* (New York: The John Day Company, 1964).

10. R. D. Myers and C. L. Melchior, "Alcohol Drinking: Abnormal Intake Caused by Tetrahydropapaveroline in Brain," *Science*, April 29, 1977.

11. Jane E. Brody, "Ways to Detect Alcoholism Set," *New York Times,* August 2, 1972.

12. Harry R. Lipton, *Medical Psychological Aspects of Alcoholism* (Atlanta: Peachtree Sanitarium, 1957), p. 1.

13. Ray Oakley, ed., *Drugs, Society, and Human Behavior,* p. 152.

14. A. H. Hobbs, "The Consumption of Alcohol," p. 231.

15. J. R. Black, "Advantages of Substituting the Morphia Habit for the Incurable Alcoholic," *The Cincinnati Lancet Clinic,* 1889. In Ray Oakley, ed., *Drugs, Society, and Human Behavior,* p. 307.

16. M. Manges, "A Second Report on the Therapeutics of Heroin," *New York Medical Journal,* 1900. In Ray Oakley, ed., *Drugs, Society and Human Behavior,* p. 308.

17. F. Baekeland, L. Lundwell, B. Kissin, and T. Shanahan, "Correlates of Outcome in Disulfiram Treatment of Alcoholism," *Journal of Nervous and Mental Disease,* 1971. In Ray Oakley, ed., *Drugs, Society, and Human Behavior,* p. 158.

18. "Wired Highballs Shock Alcoholics," *New York Times,* February 2, 1966.

19. "Doctors Introduce Terror in Attempt to Cure Alcoholism," *New York Times,* June 23, 1963.

20. "Placebos Found to Aid Alcoholics," *New York Times,* February 7, 1965.

21. "Diazepam Maintenance of Alcohol Preference During Alcohol Withdrawal," *Science,* October 21, 1977.

22. "France Tops Survey for Alcoholic Deaths," *New York Times,* April 13, 1969.

23. "Drinking As a Way of Life," *Time,* May 22, 1978.

24. Vladimir G. Treml, in *Journal of Studies on Alcohol,* reported in *New York Times* by Israel Shenker, under heading, "Moonshine Is Helping Soviet Tipplers to Top the World," June 24, 1975.

25. Christopher S. Wren, "Alcoholism Seen As Soviet Scourge," *New York Times,* February 11, 1974.

26. Roland Huntford, *The New Totalitarians* (Briarcliff Manor, N.Y.: Stein and Day, 1972).

27. "Most Students Drink, Swedish Survey Shows," *Philadelphia Evening Bulletin,* December 22, 1975.

28. C. D. Emrick, "A review of psychologically oriented

treatment of alcoholism. II. The relative approaches and the effectiveness of treatment versus no treatment," *Quarterly Journal of Studies on Alcohol,* (1975).

29. Robert Thomsen, *Bill W.* (New York: Harper and Row, 1975), p. 238.

30. "Alcoholics Group Reports 41% Stop Habit on Joining," *New York Times,* September 20, 1968.

31. A. A. (a pamphlet), Alcoholics Anonymous Pub. Co., Box 459, Grand Central Annex, New York City.

32. Robert Thomsen, *Bill W.,* pp. 362–363.

33. *Institute of Alcohol Abuse, New York Times,* March 25, 1977.

Chapter 13

Which Way Lies Madness?

EIGHT SANE PEOPLE, by faking a few symptoms of mental imbalance, gained admission to twelve different mental hospitals. In all twelve instances, these pseudo-patients were admitted when they complained that they heard voices saying "empty," "hollow," and "thud." Beyond alleging these symptoms and disguising their identity, they presented all aspects of their life truthfully—no aspect being in any way pathological— and immediately upon admission they ceased simulating any symptoms of abnormality. In eleven instances the faked symptoms resulted in a diagnosis of schizophrenia, while in the twelfth instance the same faked symptoms were diagnosed as a manic-depressive psychosis.

Throughout hospital stays which averaged nineteen days, and despite there being no evidence of mental imbalance in their entire prior lives and (except for the one recital of faked symptoms to get admitted) exhibiting perfectly normal behavior during their entire hospital stay, no member of any hospital staff recognized that these pseudo-patients were sane, though thirty-five of the patients did.

Once a diagnosis was made, all evidence, whether from the person's past life or his present behavior, was twisted so as to fit into the diagnosis. One pseudo-patient, who had a close relationship to his mother as a child and was friendly with his father during adolescence; whose relationship with his wife was, except

316

for infrequent spats, close and warm, had his life-history described thus:

> This white 39-year-old male . . . manifests a long history of considerable ambivalence in close relationships, which begins in early childhood. A warm relationship with his mother cools during his adolescence. A distant relationship to his father is described as becoming very intense. Affective stability is absent. His attempts to control emotionality with his wife and children are punctuated by angry outbursts and, in the case of the children, spankings. And while he says he has several good friends, one senses considerable ambivalence embedded in those relationships also.
> . . .

A psychiatric diagnostician, once having labelled this sane person schizophrenic, must distort whatever the person says to fit it into the diagnosis and seem to confirm it. Without sensible warrant, and inappropriately, he inserts pejorative "buzz" words such as ambivalence (twice) and the totally unjustified "affective stability is absent" into a description of normal relationships. Such gratuitous interjections of concepts taken from purported definitions of schizophrenia, while rejecting the facts of normal living in order to arrive at a contrary interpretation which, "one senses," enable psychiatrists to distort the most banal of normal statements into the rantings of a psychotic.

Despite identical symptoms and uniform diagnoses, the treatment applied to these pseudo-patients involved a variety of differing drugs, but of the 2,100 pills which were administered, only two were actually swallowed; most others being flushed down the toilet.

Despite overwhelming evidence that these people were sane, no psychiatrist would admit it, and all, when released, were labeled as "schizophrenic, in remission." That is, the psychiatrists insisted that the demonstrably sane person was not only insane when he faked his way into admission, but always; not only insane while in the hospital; but also insane when he was discharged and likely always would be insane.

In a follow-up test, the opposite to having sane people admitted to a mental hospital was tried. The staff of a hospital was acquainted with what had happened in the experiment and informed that sometime within three months one or more pseudo-patients would attempt to be admitted to their hospital. Though no pseudo-patient ever actually presented himself for admission, forty-one of 193 applicants who were actually insane were judged to be sane by members of the admissions staff.

In conformity with Sir Arthur Eddington's "fishnet fallacy," psychiatrists see what they want to see, not what is there, and Professor Rosenhan, who conceived and conducted these imaginative tests of psychiatric diagnostic ability, concluded that psychiatrists cannot distinguish between the sane and insane in psychiatric hospitals and that we should dispense with all psychiatric labels, these being at best useless, and at worst, harmful and misleading. He generalizes about the state of knowledge in what is often called the "science" of psychiatry by saying that:

> Whenever the ratio of what is known to what needs to be known approaches zero, we tend to invent "knowledge" and assume that we understand more than we actually do.[1]

Such difficulty in distinguishing between sane and insane; such distortion of facts to make them fit into the preconceptions which are involved in psychiatric diagnosis; such stubborn refusal to admit error; such mechanical administration of drugs to patients who are so completely depersonalized by the treatment that hypostatized psychiatric categories are being treated instead of people—these and many other serious weaknesses in modern psychiatry do not prove that nothing is known about mental imbalance, that the profession of psychiatry is stagnant, or that its practitioners are callous.

Neurological and endocrinological research is constantly producing a great amount of new information about brain and glandular functioning; the erroneous nature of earlier information is being exposed; fallacies of previous hypotheses are being revealed; intriguing new hypotheses are being tested and many practitioners of psychiatry demonstrate, I am quite sure, a deep and conscientious concern for their patients as persons and an intelligent and sensitive awareness that their practice is not a science but an art.

318

Despite such an accretion of new information, such admission of the erroneous nature of old information, and such rejection of earlier hypotheses and postulation of new ones, the impression conveyed by psychiatrists, especially by those who are psychoanalytically oriented, is grossly misleading. Not all, of course, but many of the practitioners and most of the popularizers of the psychiatric arts try to persuade us that psychiatric diagnosis and treatment involve scientific procedures based on validated scientific theories. A public which has been indoctrinated to accept scientific findings as precisely correct, permanently true, and irrefutable, is led to believe that psychiatrists possess the absolute truth about mental imbalance and practice scientific therapeutic techniques which cure it. This, of course, is not at all the state of this necessary but uncertain art.

This delusion to which most people succumb has many ramifications but I shall limit my analysis of it to those effects of this delusive belief which tend to denigrate human beings by eliminating from psychiatric interpretations consideration of man's potential to make moral choices.

All Criminals Are Innocent Until Certified Insane

There is no overall (generic) definition of the condition which I have referred to as mental imbalance. Whatever it is in actuality, this condition has been variously designated as mental disease, mental illness, mental derangement, mental disorder, madness, lunacy, crazy, mental imbalance, insanity, and by colloquialisms too numerous to list.

One of these terms, "insanity," once clearly delineated those who were justifiably exempt from the usual penalties invoked for violations of the law. Today this same term, its once-clear meaning now distorted, permits virtually anyone to violate any law without guilt or punishment.

Daniel M'Naghten was convinced, for reasons which made sense only within his unbalanced mind, that Sir Robert Peel, Prime Minister of England, was mucking up his life. To bring an end to this imagined harassment, in 1843 he shot and killed a man he believed to be Sir Robert but who in fact was Edward Drummond, a secretary. He was found to be "not guilty, on the ground of insanity," and for the remainder of his life M'Naghten was confined to an asylum for the insane.

Central to this interpretation of "not guilty on the ground of insanity" was evidence which convincingly demonstrated that M'Naghten was completely unaware that there was anything wrong with what he had done: he made no attempt to hide the fact that he had killed a man; no attempt to flee or otherwise avoid apprehension or arrest. Evidentially, M'Naghten was unaware that he had done any evil, and since guilt for perpetrating an offense against society implies awareness that the act was wrong—wrong, that is, in the judgment of society—he was not guilty. He was not guilty in the same sense that common law decreed a child of fewer than seven years to be not guilty of his crimes; not guilty in the same sense that evolutionary infrahumans, prior to developing the capacity to comprehend moral principles and to make moral choices could not, in their Eden, be guilty of sin. M'Naghten, due to improper functioning of his mental processes, lacked knowledge of good and evil in relation to his act. He could not be guilty of criminal wrongdoing because guilt implies knowledge of the difference between right and wrong and also implies a capability to make willful choices. This relationship between improper mental functioning and responsibility for criminal acts implicit in what came to be known as the M'Naghten Rule is thus in substantial accord with the conception that Man Is Moral Choice. But the capacity for moral choice as the criterion for criminal responsibility has now been abandoned.

Those who made a profession of studying the mentally unbalanced were once termed alienists to signify their focus on the alienation of persons from society. This term, "alienation," did not have the same meaning as the word does in Communist jargon, but had connotations of an attempt to treat those who were estranged or alienated from society through improper mental functioning.

As alienists became psychiatrists with pretensions to scientific certitude, the M'Naghten Rule for determining those who are exempt from the usual penalties provided by law was superseded in an increasing number of jurisdictions by the Freeman Rule, recommended in the Model Penal Code of the American Law Institute. *Freeman* provides:

A person is not responsible for criminal conduct if at the time of such conduct as a result of mental disease or defect he lacks substantial capacity either to appreciate the wrongfulness of his conduct or to conform his conduct to the requirements of law.

While *Freeman* does refer, as did *M'Naghten,* to lack of capacity to appreciate the wrongfulness of his conduct, it would seem sensible for a defense attorney to ignore this aspect of the interpretation and focus his efforts to attain a verdict of "not guilty, by virtue of insanity" by arguing that the accused "lacked substantial capacity to conform his conduct to the requirements of law" when he committed the crime.

Assuming that it has been established that the accused *did commit the crime,* this act in itself would seem to be factual proof that he lacked the capacity to obey the law. Having established this, one must then show that this lack of capacity to conform to the law (which has been proved by his commission of the crime) was the result of mental disease or defect.

Unless this mental condition were *paresis,* resulting from neurological damage done by syphilis, or the result of arterial malfunction, it would be impossible to prove mental *disease* as the cause, because in the context of available knowledge, this is a misleading and inappropriate term. But nobody is perfect, and certainly no mind functions perfectly. Mental defects in the form of mistakes, memory lapses, illusions and delusions affect us all to prove that we all have mental defects, so no one is now responsible for his criminal conduct!

Use of the insanity defense for acquittal in the state of New York rose from fifty-three cases during 1965–71 to 225 cases during 1971–76,[2] and some psychiatrists carry the Freeman Rule to its senseless but logical conclusion, contending that:

> The assertion that serious criminal behavior and repeated episodes of physical violence aren't mental illness is bullshit.[3]

The relationship between psychiatry and legal process which began with the M'Naghten decision has become ever more intertwined, and as the M'Naghten Rule was distorted into the

Freeman Rule the Rule of Psychiatry now threatens to replace the Rule of Law.[4] Sirhan B. Sirhan admitted killing Senator Robert F. Kennedy in 1968, giving as his reason Senator Kennedy's pledge as a presidential candidate to supply increasing numbers of fighter planes and tanks to Israel. Sirhan, reasonably enough, considered this pledge to be a threat to Mid-Eastern Arabs and felt that he had performed an ethnic patriotic service in murdering Senator Kennedy.

Dr. Martin M. Schorr, a psychologist who served as an expert witness for the defense in Sirhan's trial, asserted that a series of technical (Rorschach) tests proved that this interpretation was wrong; that Sirhan was a paranoid personality with tendencies toward schizophrenia and hypomania, who had killed Senator Kennedy only because the senator was a substitute (surrogate) for Sirhan's father, the person Sirhan really wanted to kill. Dr. Schorr presented a detailed description of the way in which this oedipal drive was the real cause of the murder, Sirhan being not guilty because he could not be held responsible for the "instinctual demands for his father's death and the realization that killing his father is not socially acceptable." Thus, it was oedipally inevitable, and in no sense the fault of Sirhan, that he found "a symbolic replica of his father in the form of Kennedy" and killed him.

The prosecution was hesitant to challenge such "scientific" evidence until a spectator at the trial recognized some of the phrasing Dr. Schorr used to describe Sirhan's uncontrollable oedipal motivation and informed them of its source. It was then shown that Dr. Schorr, without acknowledging the source, had taken his statements from *Casebook of a Crime Psychiatrist*, by Dr. James A. Brussel. Dr. Schorr's verbatim quotations about Sirhan B. Sirhan's motivation in murdering Senator Kennedy because the senator was a "symbolic replica" of the father whom he really wanted to murder but feared to because patricide, as it was so delicately put, "is not socially acceptable," actually related to an entirely different set of circumstances which involved the murder of a *woman*, Mrs. Mary Nerich.

Dr. Schorr refused to admit either his plagiarism or the lack of relevance of his interpretation but fortunately the jury rejected his interpretation as well as refusing to accept conten-

322

tions of the defense that Sirhan's unhappy childhood in the slums caused the killing, and found Sirhan guilty.

Vincent Bugliosi, Deputy District Attorney who conducted the prosecution of Charles Manson and his followers in the Sharon Tate and La Bianca murders is convinced that these callous but sane murderers would have been acquitted if California had not retained the M'Naghten Rule for insanity. Mr. Bugliosi stresses that "It is not enough, however, that he personally believe his acts were not wrong. Were this so, every man would be a law unto himself." Were this so, a man could rape several women and evade criminal punishment by saying "I don't think it's wrong to rape."[5]

The clincher is whether he knows that society thinks his actions are wrong. If he does, then he cannot be legally insane. Any deliberate acts to avoid detection, such as cutting telephone wires, eradicating prints, changing identities, disposing of incriminating evidence—constitute circumstantial evidence that the defendant knows society views his acts as wrong.

Manson and his followers were, fortunately, convicted and so, too, was Arthur Bremer, despite appeal to the Freeman Rule by psychoanalyst chairman of the Psychiatry Department at the University of Maryland Medical School, Dr. Eugene Brady, who asserted as his professional diagnosis that Bremer:

... lacked both the capacity to appreciate the criminality of his conduct or conform his conduct to the requirements of the law.

when he deliberately attempted to murder presidential candidate, Governor George Wallace.

The delay and complications which psychiatric testimony has introduced into juridical procedure was indicated in the trial of David R. Berkowitz, confessed murderer of six people, publicized as the "Son of Sam" killer. In August, 1977, two court-appointed psychiatrists found Berkowitz mentally unfit to stand trial, and in October, conceding that Berkowitz was aware of the charges against him and "He understands that by society's standards his acts were criminal," they reiterated their contention that he was not mentally capable of standing trial because "he could not assist in his own defense and suffered from paranoia." In February of 1978 the same two court-appointed psychiatrists found—apparently due to history's fastest recovery from paranoia—that he *was fit* to stand trial. In May, three judges were to sentence Berkowitz on the basis of his plea of guilt, but the accused created a disturbance in the courtroom. The three judges then postponed sentencing pending further psychiatric examinations by additional psychiatrists, their tests to be added to the dozens of tests he already had.

If additional tests showed confessed murderer Berkowitz not competent to stand trial, his sentencing for the murders would be postponed until he was competent. If sentenced to prison, he would be examined by a prison psychiatrist. If he was found mentally unbalanced, the Department of Correctional Services would have to request a judge to appoint two independent psychiatrists. If these found him unbalanced, he would be sent to an institution for the criminally insane. Some murderers then recover their sanity very quickly and are released. Fortunately, in June, 1978, three judges sentenced confessed "Son of Sam" killer, David Berkowitz, to a total of 315 years, 240 based on a series of consecutive sentences and 75 on the basis of concurrent sentences. Mr. Berkowitz will now be given a psychiatric examination to determine whether he should be remanded to a mental hospital for the criminally insane or to a correctional institution. Despite sentences which total 315 years, he will be eligible for parole in 25 years.[*]

At least one professional criminal, Garrett Brock Trapnell (his father a graduate of Annapolis and his mother a graduate of Radcliffe), has made a career out of hoodwinking judges with psychiatric jabberwocky to make a burlesque of the judicial system.[6] Early in his career, when arrested for a series of armed robberies, Trapnell was told by his lawyer that he had a choice of getting a ten- to twenty-year prison sentence or pleading not guilty by reason of insanity. During the year he spent in a

[*]In July, 1978, the convicted Berkowitz was again found "mentally ill" and transferred from the custody of the Department of Correctional Services to the Department of Mental Hygiene.

mental hospital, Trapnell studied psychiatry to refine his insanity defense and created an imaginary Gregg Ross to be the Mr. Hyde to his Dr. Jekyll in what he proudly terms "paranoid schizophrenia." "Gregg Ross" commits the crime but then he submerges, so it would be unfair to punish the emergent Gary Trapnell for what Ross has done. In a long and profitable criminal career, Trapnell has been often arrested but, he says, "I have committed all of these crimes, and have never gotten a number for any of them. It's the fallacy of your legal system."

Thus "insanity," a term which once had a sensible purpose in delineating those who were justifiably exempt from the usual penalties imposed by law because they lacked capacity to be aware of wrongdoing, has now become a nonsensical impediment to justice. Such lack of clarity obscures the meaning of all the generic terms associated with mental imbalance, but the misunderstanding associated with one of them, mental disease, and its connotation that this condition is analogous to physical sickness, in particular creates misunderstanding.

Is Sickness the Root Metaphor?

Even more than we are tempted to exculpate alcholics, dope addicts, gamblers, criminals, homosexuals, and others from social responsibilities by calling them sick, we are constrained to liken mental imbalance to physical illness. Though a few psychiatrists, such as Thomas Szasz, insist that the condition is psychosocial and ethical rather than medical, most psychiatrists believe pathological criteria such as illusions, delusions and hallucinations "are as valid as the pathological criteria used in the diagnosis of physical conditions."[7]

Most symptoms of physical illness (temperature, blood count, blood pressure), however, have been quantified and are measurable by instruments, while the symptoms of mental imbalance are qualitative and so vague that they give rise to a wide variety of interpretation. Psychiatrists have tried to meet this difficulty by increasing the number of symptoms, so that now there are, for example, literally hundreds of phobias, each of which is supposedly symptomatic of mental imbalance.

Having mentioned phobias, I should be giving in to my

hypengyophobia were I to shun my responsibility and cravenly submit to my *graphophobia* by failing to write about them. My *ergophobia* (or perhaps it is my *ponophobia*) tempts me to shy away from such work and my *phonemophobia* blocks me from thinking about such complex scientific symptoms, so I shall describe a few of them in simple boy-meets-girl language.

John met Mary, and when he overcame his *gyneophobic* fear of women in general and his *parthenophobic* fear of virgins in particular, she bravely responded by quelling her *androphobic* fear of men, though her *anthophobic* fear of flowers almost caused her to break off their relationship when John gave her some posies. Their mutual support helped them to overcome their *gamophobic* fear of marriage, and courageously surmounting *hagiophobia, hierophobia* and *homilophobia,* they were wed in a church.

Patience and several psychiatrists helped them to still their *coitophobic* and *erotophobic* fears of sex and though Mary's *hematophobia* made thoughts of birth repulsive, they had a child—fortunately not twins, because both suffered from *didymophobia.*

Obsession with their numerous phobias made John and Mary concerned that they might be *pantophobic,* and thus fear everything, but they consoled themselves by timorously observing that it was better to acknowledge their fears of being afraid in a forthrightly *phobophobic* way than to try to conceal it in *phobophobophobia.* Besides, it being the 13th, their qualms likely reflected their *triskaidekaphobia,* so they suppressed their *dementophobic* and *lyssophobic* fear of insanity.

It is possible that this explosion in the number of symptoms of mental imbalance indicates a great increase in tested knowledge which reflects itself in more specificity and precision in psychiatric symptomatology, but it is also possible that it is a frantic effort analogous to those Ptolemaists who tried to justify their incorrect geocentric hypothesis of the universe by hypostatizing cycles within epicycles within cycles. A more recent illustration of such frantic effort to build support for an untenable hypothesis was the multiplication of instincts in an attempt to explain each type of human behavior as being the result of a specific instinct. The jerrybuilt superstructures of both of these

326

earlier attempts ultimately collapsed upon their shaky foundations.

In addition to numerous other factors which differentiate the symptoms of mental imbalance from those of physical sickness, the symptoms of mental imbalance fail to delineate the boundaries between normality and abnormality as clearly as do those of physical sickness. Since all of us make illusive mistakes in our perceptions of what we see or hear, and have delusive ideas about ourselves and the world—most of us, as children, even having indulged in imaginary fantasizing which could easily be designated as hallucinatory—it is difficult to determine the point at which these normal mistakes of mental functioning become symptomatic of mental disorder.

One conception of mental disorder, derived from Freud and still dominating psychiatric theorizing, is that a continuum stretches between an hypostatized point designated normality and another one called abnormality. Since all people have experiences which could be designated illusions, delusions, phobias and other symptoms—since everyone's mental processes function imperfectly—no one is precisely normal. Everyone lies somewhere along the continuum between normality and abnormality and therefore is at least somewhat abnormal. The difference between normality and abnormality is a quantitative difference, not a qualitative one; a difference of degree rather than of kind. Bluntly: Everyone is at least a little bit crazy, but some are crazier than others. Illustrative of this view is a contention by the president of the American Institute for Psychoanalysis that most Americans have either schizoid or manic-depressive personalities and 9,999 persons out of every 10,000 are abnormal.[8]

Another view, with profoundly different implications, is the conception that, in conformity with its etymological roots, normality is *not a point, but an area.* Within the boundaries of this area a line which represented a hypothetical center could be drawn, yet behavior which was off this center line but within the area should be called eccentric or idiosyncratic but not abnormal. This conception would be concordant with physiological interpretations. While we commonly say that our *normal* bodily temperature is 98.6, a medical diagnostician would not say we are sick and rush us into an intensive care unit if he found it to be 98.8. Since our temperature varies with the hour of the day and other

327

factors and since some people have a characteristically higher or lower reading than others, we really mean that 98.6 is an *average* temperature and any reading within a degree or two of this average is within an acceptable range of normality. Blood pressure, glucose levels, cholesterol, triglyceride, and numerous other tests also use the concept of normality as an area rather than a precise point.

This conception of normality as an area rather than a point would allow a wide variety of differences in human behavior to be viewed as normal. Though eccentrically different, such behavior would not be considered indicative of mental imbalance, or even of "deviance." To accept this conception of normality as an area does not, however, solve the difficulties one encounters in defining mental imbalance because authorities differ as to where the boundaries of normal behavior lie.

Alexander Pope wondered who shall decide when doctors disagree, and sometimes medical diagnoses do conflict, but most physical sickness can be quickly and uniformly diagnosed. With mental imbalance ignorance about the nature of the overall condition conjoins with vague and qualitative symptoms to make diagnosis uncertain and often idiosyncratic. Such difficulties are further compounded because the categories of mental imbalance have no clear definition and differ from time to time and place to place.

Most widespread and most difficult to treat among the functional psychoses is schizophrenia, and a description of some of the complexities associated with attempts to define this category of mental imbalance will serve to indicate diagnostic difficulties in general.

A popular view of schizophrenia, encouraged, I fear, by some psychiatrists, is that it is a split personality, a conception fictionally portrayed in Robert Louis Balfour Stevenson's *Dr. Jekyll and Mr. Hyde.* Such a notion of a split personality makes good melodrama but bad etymology because *persona* indicated a mask worn by an actor and indeed our personalities, our social front, our façades, are various masks which we change constantly to suit the changing circumstances we encounter. Everyone has several personality masks, so this lyric description is of little diagnostic help, particularly if we remember that the condition, which is now called schizophrenia, has in other times been designated: Dementia Praecox, Discordant Psychosis, and Intrapsychic Ataxia. Stevenson's root metaphor in his melodrama was more likely the intrinsic duality of man's nature—his potential for evil as well as for good—than the masks which we put on and take off.

A description which is approximately in accord with that of the *Diagnostic and Statistical Manual* of the American Psychiatric Association is found in a book devoted solely to this category of mental disorder and titled *Chronic Schizophrenia*. Described as a "multidimensional conceptual model," schizophrenia is described as:

> The schizophrenic reaction is regarded as a disorder of adaptation discernable by psychiatric methods in terms of the patients' disabilities to engage in interpersonal relations, disorders of thinking, dissociation of affect, bizarre motility and speech patterns, and variations in the clinical course. The reaction may be temporary, recurrent, or permanent. It is regarded as an adaptive process available to every member of the human species. The schizophrenic reaction, furthermore, is capable of various degrees of reversibility or irreversibility.[9]

The writers of this description include numerous ideas and likely some of these ideas would help one to diagnose schizophrenia, but note how their statements lack certainty, quantification, and precision. They use the passive voice to convey abstracted omniscience which they do not possess; they describe reactions which are supposed to indicate the condition but then add: ". . . and variations in the clinical course," indicating that they may be present or they may not be present. To say that a schizophrenic reaction may be temporary, recurrent or permanent, and that it may improve or not is to cover all contingencies without explaining any of them. A statement that schizophrenia "is available to every member of the human species" has a fine democratic ring to it, but is a flight from reality because the evidence is overwhelmingly to the contrary.

With such loose, catchall descriptions, it is small wonder that eleven of twelve sane people were diagnosed as schizophrenic on the basis of a few faked symptoms, and small wonder that

"... the less skilled the psychiatrist, the more often the diagnosis of schizophrenia."[10]

The USSR, unwittingly, to be sure, has contributed a definitive rebuttal to the notion that mental imbalance is a sickness diagnosable into clearly identified categories through specific, universally recognized symptoms by creating "sluggish schizophrenia" which has no symptoms at all!

This unintended revelation of the intellectual bankruptcy and scientific sterility of a doctrine was surpassed only by the adulation accorded T. D. Lysenko's absurd dogma of environmental determinism thirty years ago.

In 1948, academician T. D. Lysenko read an extensive report at the annual session of the V. I. Lenin Academy of Agricultural Science, the crux being:

> Heredity is the effect of a concentration of the influences of conditions of the external environment, assimilated by organisms in a sequence of preceding generations.[11]

Implied in Lysenko's claims is the contention that scientists, by controlling environmental conditions, can change the hereditary endowment of animals (including man) as well as plants so as to determine what their inherited characteristics in the future will be. In short: scientists can create the perfect man.

Such doctrines fitted snugly into the economic determinism which is the principal Marxian expression of environmental determinism, so Lysenko's colleagues in the Academy listened to him with the respect which, under a dictatorship, must be paid to official dogma, but with little interest since they recognized his contentions as a rehash of the eighteenth-century doctrines of Jean Baptiste Lamarck. So extreme were Lysenko's claims that his fanatic extension of Lamarckian doctrine (comparable to current contentions that identical replicas of a human being have been produced through cloning) would have been ridiculed had he not, at the end of his report, asserted that in the future his doctrine would be the only one which would be accepted as scientific, that it would have the full support of the Party and the government, and I. V. Stalin would personally see that no other doctrine competed with it. After announcing this dictum he received "tremendous applause" and the Praesidium of the Academy of Sciences, USSR, soon afterward wrote to "Comrade I.V. Stalin"

> The Praesidium of the Academy of Sciences promises you, dear Iosif Vissarionavich, and through you, our Party and Government, determinedly to rectify the errors we permitted, to reorganize the work of the Division of Biological Sciences and its institutes, and to develop biological science in a true materialistic Michurinist [environmental deterministic] direction.

But we learned little from this demonstration of the slavishness with which scientists will kowtow to dictates of authority in support of patently absurd doctrines. Under the Nazis, German scientists supported equally absurd doctrines about creating a master race through breeding. While the extremist hereditary doctrines of the Nazis were appropriately ridiculed and totally discarded, our social scientists still give respectful hearing to equally extreme forms of environmental determinism. It is, therefore, optimistic as well as premature to assume that the absurdities of symptomless sluggish schizophrenia will raise the questions about psychiatric hypotheses in general which they should. Here is a description of this condition from Dr. Daniil Lunts of the Serbsky Institute, USSR:

> Sluggish schizophrenia is not characterized by such extreme psychopathic manifestations as hallucination or delirium. The illness progresses at the same time that the person retains his normal ability to work, his intellectual capacity and his usual behavior.[12]

This symptomless category "sluggish schizophrenia" is applied most frequently to those who question the Communist establishment. Once diagnosed as such, they are remanded to psychiatric prisons because they have "paranoid delusions of reforming society or reorganization of the state apparatus" or they express "opinions of a moralizing character."[13] Succinctly: Anyone who criticizes the communist bureaucracy is crazy.

Sensing a growing danger, the American Civil Liberties Union has issued a pamphlet which protests the manner in which

331

the rights of people are violated when courts remand them to institutions on the basis of fallible psychiatric diagnosis, pointing out that agreement on such diagnoses is only slightly better than random chance, while diagnostic agreement on a specific functional mental condition ("schizophrenic reaction, paranoid type") occurs only 40 percent of the time; they also question whether the psychiatric treatment received in such institutions is as beneficial as similar treatment administered outside the hospitals or no treatment at all.[14]

Psychiatrist Thomas Szasz began many years ago to attack (in *The Myth of Mental Illness*[15] and other works) the delusion that mental imbalance is closely analogous to physical illness and, like it, can be specifically diagnosed by clearly identified—though not quantified nor measurable by instruments—symptoms which are universally recognized. But the popularity of the myth of mental illness continues, and perhaps its pervasiveness can now be attributed to mental inertia (*phonemophobia?*) as it persists despite reasonable evidence to the contrary.

After a lifetime career of studying and, as director of The Menninger Foundation, treating mental imbalance, Dr. Karl Menninger summed up his doubts about the sickness metaphor by proposing:

> ... that all the names so solemnly applied to various classical forms and stages and aspects of mental illness in various individuals be discarded.[16]

Specifically, his lifetime of study led him to conclude that our knowledge of mental illness is so limited that the terms we use to describe it are more misleading than helpful.

> Now I not only believe that no such disease as schizophrenia can be clearly defined or identified or proved to exist, but I also hold that there is no such thing as a psychosis or a neurosis. My point is that no one can satisfactorily define these terms in a way which the rest of us can accept, so that if we use the terms we involve ourselves in confusion because we are all, or nearly all, talking about different things. It is like a Russian, a South African, a Swiss, an American, and a South Sea Islander talking about freedom.

Also, Dr. William Glasser recommended in 1965 that we dispense with "... the common psychiatric labels, such as neurosis and psychosis, which tend to categorize and stereotype people."[17] D. L. Rosenhan reached a similar conclusion as a result of his findings about the fallibilities of diagnosis which he described in "On Being Sane in Insane Places," saying:

> ... psychological categorization of mental illness is useless at best and downright harmful, misleading, and pejorative at worst. Psychiatric diagnoses ... are in the minds of the observers and are not valid summaries of characteristics displayed by the observed.

In 1978 M. L. Gross reported that the American Psychiatric Association is currently planning to eliminate totally the classification of neurosis from the next (1979) edition of its official diagnostic manual.[18] It is proposed that the term *neuroses*, with its Freudian connotations of an emanation squeezed out of a mythic unconscious by sexual repression, be replaced by the term *anxiety*. Together with author Gross, I feel such a change to be salutary, anxiety being a concomitant of our higher evolutionary development. Anxiety is a manifestation of our necessary concern about fulfilling our responsibilities. Though anxiety, when uncontrolled and undefined, can mushroom to cloud our thoughts and confuse our purposes, such *abnormal* manifestation could be redirected through consciously willed redefinition helped, perhaps, by trained guidance and spiritual comfort.

Confusion between the psychic-spiritual and the physical with its associated misapplication of terms, which occurs in relation to mental imbalance, has historical precedent in that prior to the discovery of effective treatments for physical sicknesses they were attributed, first, to the wrath of gods, then to psychic phenomena. Susan Sontag has perceptively described how, during the sixteenth century, it was believed that a happy man would not get the plague, and how, for many years, tuberculosis was thought to be caused by frustrated passion generated through sexual repression.[19] This belief persisted until a specific cure was found. Since no specific cure for cancer has yet been discovered, some still contend that it is caused by the inhibitions and frustrations associated with repressed sexual passion.

As absence of effective treatment for physical diseases led to the creation of psychic metaphors to explain them, so absence of effective treatment for psychic imbalance tempts us to accept the sickness metaphor whereby it can be cured by more potent pills or sharper knives.

If the sickness metaphor is inappropriate and the symptomotology ineffective, a description of mental imbalance similar to that of alcoholism might be helpful as a reference point.

A person is mentally abnormal when the improper functioning of his mental processes significantly limits his effectiveness in meeting his social responsibilities.

It was likely in accord with this conception of mental disorder as an imbalance between one's self interest and his concern about his social obligations that psychiatrists were earlier called alienists who tried to remedy their patients' estrangement, or alienation, from society.

To replace the sickness metaphor with a description of failure to meet social responsibilities may provide a more meaningful orientation, though it constitutes neither an explanation nor a cure for mental imbalance.

Since there is increasing dispute about which generic term is correct, how it should be defined, whether the sickness metaphor is appropriate, and whether it is possible to attain a clearly defined symptomatology from which universally agreed-upon categories can be induced, it would be astounding for anyone to pretend that we know the causes of mental imbalance.

Despite such great ignorance (or perhaps because of it) for many years we were absolutely convinced that science had revealed the causes and discovered the treatment for mental imbalance. Many scientists told us that all problems associated with mental imbalance would be alleviated if not totally eradicated when we stopped treating individual patients and concentrated on changing society because *society is the patient.*

Society Is the Patient

The Communist Revolution completely eliminated manic-depressive psychoses from the USSR. Such surprising information was conveyed to millions of sociology students through their textbooks which, they were repeatedly assured, were scientific and therefore true. They were told how the head of the American Hygiene Association, after visiting several mental institutions in Russia had, on informing the Commissar-in-charge that he had seen no cases of manic-depressive psychoses, been told that since the revolution, there were no cases of manic-depressive psychosis in Russia! This amazing finding was presented as unarguable, verified fact. What had likely happened was that this particular diagnostic designation had, for one reason or another, been discarded, a change similar to the one where U.S. Navy doctors, reluctant to fill out the numerous forms that were required whenever they diagnosed a case of influenza began to call it catarrhal fever. Or, perhaps, under the gray dullness of Communist bureaucracy, manic-depressives ceased to experience their manic phases.

With hammering insistence, sociological and psychiatric "scientists" led us to believe that our overly competitive society was a "sick society,"[20] a "schizophrenic society." "Sick individuals were produced by sick families in a sick society" and differences between rates of insanity were due to the character of the culture. Science, we were told, had proved that we should look upon *Society As the Patient*.[21]

Not only was our present sick society causing mental sickness but our tradition was one in which we approved of the mentally sick while we persecuted the sane. From the more than a million copies of anthropologist Ruth Benedict's *Patterns of Culture*[22] which were sold, mostly to college students whose professors had recommended or required it, one learned that of the three primitive groups which she studied, the compulsively competitive but fearful society (the Dobu of New Guinea) were schizophrenic; the highly competitive Kwakiutl of the Pacific Northwest (whose parallelism to our society was painfully obvious) were overbearing, megalomaniacal paranoids with delusions of grandeur—as, she more than implied, so were we—and

335

only the helpful, friendly, unsuspicious, cooperative Zuni, lovingly sketched as prototypical socialists by Dr. Benedict, were normal, even taking care to prevent their children from developing an Oedipus Complex.

Since our society is a replica of that of the megalomaniacal paranoid Kwakiutl, it is no wonder that our competitive society takes a psychopathic toll that "is evident in every institution for mental diseases in our country."

Our craziness came down to us from the psychopathic Puritans, for "it is they, not the confused and tormented women they put to death as witches, who were the psychoneurotics of Puritan New England."

What evidence did sociologists and other social scientists possess to give them warrant to indoctrinate millions of people into a belief that science had proved that mental disease—as they insisted on naming it—was caused by social conditions and could be remedied by reshaping society in a collectivistic mold?

In 1939 the prototype for the many sociological studies which were to follow was made in Chicago, and showed that the rate of mental disorder increased steadily as living conditions changed from the best (suburban type) environment to the worst (slum) environment.[23] Many sociology textbooks indicated that the average rate of insanity increased from "under 70.0" to "more than 150.0," being more than doubled when the worst environment is compared with the best. Since these textbooks claimed to be scientific, millions of students were convinced that such studies constituted scientific proof that slums cause insanity in much the same way as they had been indoctrinated with the belief that slums cause crime. The remedy for insanity was obvious: slum clearance and public housing provided by a beneficent government would alleviate the problem.

There are many and serious fallacies in assuming such a conclusion because this study and all the similar ones which followed it contained numerous faults, but another look at the increase in rates of insanity which seems so impressive when stated in the way it is above—and as it is stated in the sociology textbooks—should suffice to show the absence of significance in such findings. The base for this rate is 100,000 persons, meaning that the difference is not a difference between 70.0 and 150.0, but between .0007 and .0015, a difference of .08 percent, meaning

336

that the difference between the best and worst environments would have to be multiplied by twelve before it would amount to even 1 percent! When an investigator finds a difference of only one-twelfth of 1 percent in a study which was not done under controlled circumstances and which relates to a qualitative phenomenon which has never been defined, there is one obvious thing to do—ignore the findings. Such findings were not ignored, however; they were widely publicized as constituting scientific proof that the cause and—inferentially—the cure for mental imbalance is solely environmental.

This unbridgeable gap between their evidence and their conclusions tempts one to feel that the social scientists of today are similar to the eighteenth-century philosophes who preceded them in that they are more concerned with changing the world than in understanding it, and are unwilling or unable to learn anything from evidence (or lack of it) which cannot be incorporated into their ideology.

While they showered honors and awards upon B. F. Skinner because he seemed—incorrectly, to be sure—to follow and improve upon Pavlov's conditioning hypotheses, and they widely reported the case of the dog "John" who had been conditioned to be neurotic in the Pavlov Institute, they refused to modify their belief when it turned out that "John" had not been conditioned into his acrophobic fear of heights; he had sensibly learned to distrust the trainer who sometimes fed him when he responded appropriately but at other times crazily gave him an electric shock. They praised Ivan Petrovich for his magnificent contributions to the study of conditioning, but neglected to inform their students that Pavlov insisted that *his findings did not apply to man.* Far from contending that all dogs were equally susceptible to neurotic reactions, Pavlov stressed[24] that some dogs responded with nervous upsets after a single stimulation; some required several stimulations, and some dogs never did respond despite numerous repetitions of the test situation. Pavlov's interpretation was that the factor which caused dogs to react differently in respect to neurotic responses was individual difference in the degree of their innate balance.

> . . . neuroses can be obtained without difficulty only in an animal in which there is normally no requisite balance be-

tween the elementary phenomena of nervous activity . . .
between the processes of excitation and inhibition.

Such differences are obviously innate, not environmental.

As the 1939 Chicago study constituted the prototype for studies which attempted to show that mental imbalance was caused by the environment, F. J. Kallmann's twin-index studies were prototypes for numerous studies which find that heredity is also a causal factor, and evidentially a stronger one.[25] Though not rigorously scientific, the relevant variables are controlled much better in these studies and the findings range to more than 80 percent concordance in contrast to the difference of only one-twelfth of 1 percent in the prototype study which assertedly proved environmental determinism.

Despite extremely strong evidence that heredity is a major factor in psychoses and very weak evidence in support of environment as a causal factor, twenty years after Kallmann's evidence was published and subsequent to the publication of similar studies which supported his findings, in a summary[26] dealing with the causes and development (etiology) of schizophrenia all but two of the contributors stressed environmental causation, and one of these two which referred to genotypic factors did so in an acrimonious criticism of Kallmann's studies.

A summary of studies dealing with the same topic in 1970[27] pointed out that much evidence indicated that the child of a schizophrenic parent was fifteen times more likely to be schizophrenic than a person selected from the population at large and that monozygotic (formed from the fertilization of a single egg, and popularly called identical) twins are four times more likely to be concordant (if one member of the set has it, the other will have it also) than dizygotic twins (which, being conceived by the fertilization of two separate eggs by two sperm, have an hereditary relation no closer than non-twins). Various combinations of heredity and environment all indicated that heredity was a much more potent factor than environment. Though such evidence presented "insurmountable difficulties for adherents of environmental theories," many academicians still refused to accept it.

A definitive rebuttal to the "slums cause mental imbalance" contention which so many still cling to summarizes the influence of low social status and bad environmental surroundings by saying:

> Social deprivation and pressure experienced by children and adults in the lowest social stratum are not severe enough to produce self-perpetuating psychological disorder in otherwise normal human beings.[28]

The reviewer of this book in *Science* took this flat statement to mean:

> ... *there is no such thing as environmentally produced personality defects and, therefore, symptoms that persist in the absence of stress situations ... are of genetic origin.*[29]

Though much evidence supports the view that heredity is a more significant causal factor in mental imbalance than environment, for one to contend that heredity causes schizophrenia as such would be, for many reasons, neither scientifically nor specifically justified. Available evidence would point to the likelihood that if a factor related to schizophrenia is inherited it takes the form of a *predisposition* (probably, I should suppose, an imbalance in endocrine function) toward that direction. An environmental *precipitating* factor (shock, accident, illness) must conjoin with such a predisposing factor to produce the pathological condition. It would be analogous to a predisposition toward diabetes (associated with unbalanced functioning of the adrenal glands and the Islets of Langerhans) which, though potential, can be prevented from coming to fruition by appropriate diet.

Such an interpretation would be resisted by scientistic liberals because the environment is something they can control, while heredity is a factor which they cannot. These liberals would also object to the individual differences in the homeostatic balance of nerve function which Pavlov alluded to, and to probable individual differences in glandular functioning. Such individual differences do not fit into the scientistic assumption that all men are equally malleable, nor into the romantic premise that man's innate goodness will govern

339

his behavior once the bad environmental factors are corrected.

Psychoanalyst, Heal Thyself

In an unceasing search for ways to evade our responsibilities we found in Freudian psychoanalysis a gentle path into lotus land. As a way to satisfy our yearning for miracle, mystery and authority, psychoanalysis was without compeer; it was perfect, rounded, symmetrical, complete.* Here these Dostoevskian ingredients were so smoothly blended in a palatable mixture that we swallowed it without ruminating.

In the cure we found the miracles we sought. In this radical therapy, we were told, the analysand himself probed to the very roots of his mental difficulties and once their tangled web was exposed to the light of this wondrous doctrine, his complexes withered away and his neuroses shrank to nothingness. He was now free of all sexual repression. All this came about merely by revealing his dreams and his inmost thoughts to an analyst. True, it was not quite so miraculous as *scientology*, a close kin to psychoanalysis, developed by science-fiction writer L. Ron Hubbard—which promised to create a perfect mind for the $4.50 price of *Dianetics*—but scientology was handicapped because Hubbard was literate and his "engrams" made etymological sense, while the rootless neologisms, awkward phrasing, and syntactical mishmash of Freud's writing enhanced its appeal by adding the zest of obscurantism to psychoanalysis.

Nothing could be more thrillingly mysterious than the undifferentiated, undefinable *id* (Is it es or is it Esdras—or perhaps Esau?); unlocatable in anatomy, endocrinology, or neurology. Truly it boggles the mind.

Authority was personified by the analyst, who knew all and told nothing, who responded to every question by asking one himself; and who used "non-directive" therapy to compel the analysand to say what the analyst wanted to hear. The President of the American Institute of Psychoanalysis describes his use of "non-directive" therapy thus[30]:

*Mark Twain's way of describing a swindle.

During therapy [if a patient] would say, "Oh, I had a bad thought—I thought my parents were dying," I would tell him to get out of my office—that I had no time for patients who wanted to be saints. He had to learn to accept his "bad" feelings and not apologize for them.

When he would say, "Gee, I saw a girl I'd like to sleep with," then I saw a guy who wanted to be a real person and I would treat him with utmost warmth.

This enticing interweave of miracle, mystery, and authority was combined with claims to scientific validity which persisted despite the spurious evidence on which psychoanalysis rested and the fact that Freud reported only what fitted into his ideology. The mixture was so appealing that clinical psychologists in 1960 acclaimed Freud as the most influential psychologist of the century, and its popularity justified Professor Rieff's declaration[31] that "Freud's intellectual influence is greater than that of any other modern thinker."

Thousands of articles in magazines and newspapers and millions of copies of hundreds of books told people not only how to raise their children, what to think and do about sex and marriage and how to understand and cure alcoholism, drug addiction, mental disorder and allergies, but what to do about education, how to reform criminals, and what causes wars. It offered "scientific" answers to just about every question which man has ever asked about himself, mankind, society, history, religion, art and chess. People accepted such answers because they believed that they had been arrived at by scientific method—which they were not—and because they thought that psychoanalysis was a validated cure for mental imbalance—which it is not.

Much evidence shows that psychoanalytic interpretations are devoid of scientific validity, and all evidence which has been obtained by methods which involve even a moderate degree of objectivity shows that psychoanalytic therapy is less effective than no therapy at all.

Spontaneous remission is a significant factor in the improvement or cure of most forms of functional mental disorder. In the same manner that a cold will run its course and we recover our health independently of any treatment, so "personality disorders" and most forms of neuroses will run their course and

341

our innate resiliency will restore itself without the administration of any formal treatment in about 60 percent of the cases. Spontaneous remission limits the duration of even psychoses in about 20 percent of the cases. Therefore, unless a given form of treatment results in more than 60 percent of the cases involving neuroses or higher than 20 percent of the cases involving psychoses, we have no certainty that the therapy does any good at all.

In 1953, the American Psychoanalytic Association requested its members to record the number of patients who were markedly improved or cured after undergoing psychoanalytic therapy. No objective criteria of improvement or cure need be met; the analyst's unverified opinion sufficed as evidence. By 1958, even with such generous latitude in interpretation, only 27 percent[32] of some 3000 patients, some 75 percent of whom suffered from only neuroses or "personality disturbance" were reported to be markedly improved or cured, a rate of success far lower than would occur without any treatment at all.

The most thorough inquiry into the effectiveness of psychoanalytic therapy appeared in 1977 in *The Scientific Credibility of Freud's Theories and Therapy*.[33] Though the authors emphasize that they restricted the sources for their analysis to studies which have scientific credibility, they apply the term " 'scientific' . . . to any study in which observations had been gathered according to rules more exacting than 'This is what I personally witnessed or experienced.' " Such a criterion is far removed from the controlled observation of quantified and stable phenomena verified through exact prediction which rigid scientific procedure requires. Their criterion would endow flying saucers, shared illusions, delusions, common tastes, and practically everything else which two or more people agree on with scientific credibility. Their elaboration of this criterion is likewise a fishnet with extremely large holes. This very leaky interpretation of science is coupled to the authors' evident desire to reach favorable conclusions about the effectiveness of psychoanalytic therapy but they nonetheless conclude that:

> . . . there is at present no justification for a patient to assume that he will achieve a greater degree of improvement in a therapy called psychoanalysis than in a therapy

342

given another label such as analytically oriented, client-centered, or behavioral. There is virtually no evidence that psychoanalysis generally results in more long-lasting or profound patient change than other therapies.

They could find no clear or consistent evidence to support the contention of psychoanalysts that their treatment, by probing down to and then dissipating the root cause of neuroses, brought about a complete cure while other therapies were only palliative, partial, and temporary. Several studies found that patients "cured" by psychoanalysis still had unresolved neurotic conflicts years later. They also found that as high as 40 percent of patients with borderline psychoses were *worse* after psychoanalytic treatment than they had been before.

With this record of the ineffectiveness of the therapy and with a theoretical rationale which is a parody* rather than an example of scientific procedure, why did psychoanalysis become so popular? Why did so many people, most of the exceedingly

*As I previously indicated, Freud admitted that the supposed childhood seductions on which he based his whole theory of hysteria were merely figments of his imagination and Ernest Jones, his sympathetic biographer, revealed how Freud failed to report information he received from his patients in addition to reporting things about them which were not true. In Fisher and Greenberg's evaluation of psychoanalytic therapy they present a definition, ostensibly scientific, of the Oedipus Complex, a fundamental premise on which the elaborate superstructure of psychoanalytic interpretation rests very heavily. The Oedipus Complex, as commonly interpreted, involves the universal desire of all boys between the ages of four and six to kill their fathers so they can have sex with their mothers. Here, according to psychoanalytic interpretation, are some situations which prove that a boy wants to kill his father: ". . . if the child gives Daddy a good-night hug and insists that he, rather than Mummy, tuck him in, this behavior may also confirm our original hypothesis. His desire to have father put him to bed rather than mother could be the result of a fearful state, *i.e.*, as long as the father is with him the little boy can be sure the father is not doing anything to harm him. On the other hand, or also simultaneously, it may be an act of aggression toward the father in that it separates him from the mother for the time being. Or yet again, it may be because the little boy fears that if the mother puts him to bed her seductive powers will prove too much for him. . . ."[34]

educated and some of them moderately intelligent, lustfully embrace Freudian doctrine?

Undoubtedly one factor in its acceptance was the borrowed prestige of science, and another was its sex appeal. In earlier years there was considerable novelty and shock appeal in chanting this daring litany to erode away the Victorian fetters which cultural conditioning had forged upon our natural sexual urges. And when it was first introduced, a recital of Freudian doctrine gained one membership in an elitist intellectual avant-garde whose mental processes were superficial rather than deep, circumlocutory rather than direct, polysyllabic rather than pragmatic. Its sex appeal explains why it was even more popular than Scientology, the difference being comparable, on a lesser level, to the widespread acclaim which greeted the first Kinsey volume and the much lesser notice paid to the similarly extreme scientistic attack on other than sexual values by B. F. Skinner.

Those who contend that the acceptance of psychoanalytic doctrine and its acclaim arose from an appreciation of Freud's genius would find it extremely difficult to justify this contention to anyone who is intelligent, literate, and reasonably objective. They would need to explain (among other things) why they do not accept with equal credulity Freud's evaluation of cocaine and numerology.

Freud called cocaine a "magical drug" which he prescribed as a harmless substitute for morphine and which he himself took "regularly against depression and against indigestion, and with the most brilliant success" to relieve his neurotic symptoms.[35] As Freud conveyed to his closest friend Wilhelm Fliess the admission that the childhood seductions on which he built his whole theory of hysteria had never occurred, Fliess conveyed to Freud his enthusiasm for numerology. Fliess believed that males function in terms of twenty-three-day cycles while females have twenty-eight-day cycles. From these periodicities, Fliess claimed he could predict when life crises would occur; when one would be happy, when in despair. Freud was an enthusiastic disciple of this numerology; convinced that he would die at age $28+23$; describing the onset of his son's illness as $5 \times 28^2 - 10 \times 23^3$; and awarding the accolade "Kepler of Biology" upon Fliess.

In addition to its appeal as an excuse to demolish traditional standards of sexual behavior and to rip away all the "decent drapery" which had clothed the subject, the conception of man inherent in psychoanalytic doctrine has much appeal to scientistic liberals. As Richard La Piere describes the Freudian ethic, it:

> ... presupposes that man is by inherent nature weak, uncertain, and incapable of self-reliance and that he must, therefore, be provided by society with the security that is his greatest need.[36]

A Remedy Without a Cure

Twenty-five years ago, the most competent statisticians, armed with full knowledge of the trends in mental imbalance, would have "scientifically" proved that by 1978 there would be some 1,000,000 patients under treatment for mental disorder in public and private hospitals. Instead, there are less than 200,000; many fewer than the 632,000 in 1955, less than half the 518,000 there were in 1945, and fewer than the 268,000 there were in 1923, when such records were first compiled on a nationwide basis.

The number of patients in public and private hospitals under treatment for mental disorder was generally accepted as being an index of the total amount of mental disorder within the society. This index number, when divided by each 100,000 persons in the total population, gives a rate of mental disorder which compensates for population growth. The trend in this rate of mental disorder increased steadily throughout our entire history. True, there were fluctuations within the trend, as when, in conjunction with the World War II draft, examinations revealed cases of mental disorder which otherwise would, for a time at least, have escaped recording. Additionally, some persons who were predisposed toward mental imbalance were precipitated into a recordable diagnosis by wartime conditions, and probably a small percentage of the cases which were recorded in this upward fluctuation included persons without predisposition who became mentally unbalanced when undergoing severe combat conditions so often that their natural resiliency had insufficient leeway to reassert itself—a situation which is called the "Old Sergeant's Syndrome."

345

After this fluctuation peaked, the rate declined, but even after this drop it was substantially higher (384 patients per 100,000 population) than the 359 it had been in 1940. In all, the record showed that the trend, decade by decade, moved inexorably upward, steadily (except for fluctuations) increasing from a rate of 242 in 1923 to 392 in 1955 while the number of patients being treated for mental disorder rose from 268,000 to 632,000. Psychiatrists had tried to explain away this increase, attributing it to increased acceptance of hospitalization by the public, educational programs which made people aware of what the symptoms were, increased urbanization, increasing competitiveness in society, and other factors. But by the early 1950s rising concern led to demands for a crash Federal program for the construction of new hospitals to house the expected flood of mental patients. Had we responded to these demands we should now have five times the hospital space we need for in-patient care.

A general lesson to be learned from the enormous error in this projection is an awareness that scientific prediction is impossible in social matters, and every projection, being in its very nature premised on past trends or current conditions, is subject to great error if significant new variables arise.

One might suppose that psychiatrists would have advised statisticians of the possibilities of such new variables, but they did not and could not have done so because the drug treatment which constituted the intrusive variable came from outside the profession and had no relationship to psychiatric research or with any treatment they believed to be effective.

A folk medicine which had been used in India for centuries was the source of Reserpine, the pilot drug. In the mid-thirties two Indian chemists, believing that chemical analysis would prove that the supposed calming (ataraxic) effect of snakeroot (Rauwolfia Serpentina) was empty folklore, discovered to their surprise that a derivative of the plant, Reserpine, did possess significant capabilities to calm people.[37] Only by a series of far-fetched coincidences was it introduced as a treatment for mental disorder in America in the early fifties. Chlorpromazine (Thorazine) which followed Reserpine (Serpasil) was accidentally discovered in a French commercial laboratory while looking for a new antihistamine to use as a palliative for colds.

346

A variety of some thirteen phenothiazines followed Reserpine and Chlorpromazine to a degree that hundreds of thousands who would otherwise be in-patients can now be treated on an out-patient basis. Hundreds of controlled, double-blind tests in which neither the patient nor the psychiatrist knows whether an inert placebo or the drug is being administered to the patient, and comparisons of the efficacy of phenothiazines versus other forms of therapeutic techniques in a variety of combinations, all indicate that these drugs reduce symptoms more effectively than any other treatment.

Since we now have, for the first time in our history, a way to treat seriously disordered mental patients so as to reduce, steadily and markedly, the index which we always relied upon to measure the amount of this condition in the general population, we might be tempted to proclaim that we are well on the way toward curing the problem of mental imbalance in America. Unfortunately, despite the great improvements contributed by drug treatment, it is neither a cure for the patient nor a solution to the general problem.

While the number of in-patients has declined steadily since 1955, the number of out-patient-care episodes has risen, and continues to rise, at a disturbingly high rate, increasing from 379,000 in 1955 to 1,071,000 in 1965 and 4,618,000 in 1975.

While phenothiazines are demonstrably more effective than placebos or any other therapeutic technique, a relapse rate of 75 percent or higher occurs within a year after discontinuance of the treatment.[38]

Studies of the adjustment of patients released from mental hospitals by both the National Institute for Mental Health and the Veterans Administration found that most (89 percent) released patients functioned less well in the community than the average person of their general social level and many still had symptoms of psychopathology; that less than 15 percent of the patients who had been hospitalized for schizophrenia for any appreciable time ever functioned in a completely normal way.

Before we acclaim the downward trend of in-patients as a sign that our problems of mental imbalance are decreasing, we should mute our applause with an awareness that the open palm of venality shoves many of them out the hospital door and into the community. Most mental hospitals are operated by state or

347

local communities, and current estimates are that costs involve some $20,000 per patient per year. If patients are put out of the hospitals the Federal government, through its Supplemental Security Income program, foots most of the bill. While the beneficial effects of drug treatment on patients must be hedged with qualifications, their financial benefit for some politicians is unqualified.

Politicians in the USSR also exploit these drugs for their own advantage rather than to help the patient. Political dissidents incarcerated for "sluggish schizophrenia," which has no symptoms, are given symptoms by abusive administration of these drugs. By overdosage, side-effects such as emotional indifference, reduction of motor activity (akinesia), hypotension, impotence, and excessive gain in weight combine to[39]:

> ... wear down the dissenter and neutralize his "reformist" thinking, his social dangerousness . . . and make the full-scale recantation which is the KGB's prime goal.

Though the drug treatment of mental imbalance alleviates some symptoms of psychosis more effectively than any previous therapeutic technique, it is not a cure. While the benefits from its use far exceed the harm done by its abuse, Communist bureaucrats have already set a precedent for calculated abusive usage of phenothiazines (and more potent drugs such as Halperidol) which recalls to a skeptical mind what happened when morphine was prescribed as a cure for alcoholism, heroin acclaimed as the heroic drug which would cure morphine addiction (unless one preferred Freud's cocaine prescription), and now Methadone prescribed for heroin addiction. Such precedent makes one wonder if our current "remedy" might itself become a problem.

Mental Imbalance As a Causal Nexus

Most forms of treatment for mental imbalance are based on a doctrine which denigrates man because they ignore his potential to make moral choices. The psychoanalytic premise that man is governed by dank undescribable forces of which he has nei-

348

ther awareness nor control is conjoined with a treatment which indoctrinates him into believing that moral standards are merely conventional falsehoods, deludes him into believing that he has discovered this himself, and substitutes an ideological fairyland for a pragmatically effective social order. Phenothiazines (our more potent pills) are administered to categories, not people, as were the less potent insulin, metrazol, and electric convulsive shock treatments. Our "sharper knives" were used to perform lobotomies which made zombies out of people.

I now venture a possible alternative, one in which man's capacity for moral choice can be a factor in the process. Being quite aware of the many complexities involved in mental imbalance, I wish to stress the speculative nature of what follows, and to caution readers that it is offered as an hypothesis which might be worthwhile to take into consideration rather than a prescription to be applied.

In this hypothesis, mental imbalance would be interpreted in terms of a causal nexus involving the environment, the cortical levels of the brain, lower brain levels, glands and muscles. An initiating factor could have its source on any of these levels but, for simplicity, and because much evidence indicates that heredity is a significant factor in the etiology of psychoses, let us suppose that a person inherits overactive adrenal glands.

Such hyperactivity could produce an excess of epinephrine (adrenaline) in the blood. This hormone is characteristically associated with "flight or fight" emotions of fear or rage. An excess activates the sympathetic nervous system and our heart pumps more blood into the brain and muscles; systolic blood pressure goes up; our blood sugar level is elevated; the blood clots more rapidly and other changes occur to help us cope with emergency. The excessive epinephrine would not of itself cause us to fight or flee but would prepare us to do so more effectively. Such excess apparently produces a state of anxiety which the cortical level of the brain must interpret in the context of environmental circumstances to decide whether to be aggressive or fearful.

Another hormone, norepinephrine (noradrenaline), is also secreted by the same inner (medulla) portion of the adrenals which secretes epinephrine. Though also released in conjunction with stress, it tends to sustain the blood pressure which the

349

epinephrine pushes up, and generally moderates the functions which epinephrine excites. The apparently antagonistic functions performed by epinephrine and norepinephrine could be conceived as functional complementarity in coping with stress.

"Under certain conditions epinephrine also acts to promote the release of adrenocorticotrophine (ACTH) from the anterior lobe of the pituitary, with a consequent release of adrenal corticoids and a gearing of the body for more prolonged adjustment to stress."[40]

ACTH induces an outpouring of hormones from the outer (cortex) part of the adrenals, which secretes cortisone, steroids and other hormones. If stress is prolonged, the adrenals increase in size and sustain a high production of these corticosteroid hormones.

Some of the hormones from the outer (cortical) portion of the adrenals serve to modify the effects of the emergency mobilization induced by epinephrine from the inner (medulla) portion of the adrenals.

In accordance with the concept of functional complementarity, we have here seeming antagonisms between hormones produced in the inner portion of the adrenal glands and between these hormones and those produced in the outer portion of the glands, together with a reciprocal relationship between the adrenal glands and the pituitary combining so that the sympathetic (emotional-emergency) nervous system will dominate over the *parasympathetic* nervous system (which, in routine functioning, regulates digestion and other aspects of our ordinary metabolism) to cope with stress. With most persons this change in the balance of factors involved in homeostatic functioning would be temporary. They would calm down when the crisis passed and ordinary parasympathetic functioning would again dominate over stressful sympathetic reactions.

But suppose that through heredity or otherwise, either the balance is lacking or resiliency is lost. There are many ways in which this could, hypothetically at least, happen. Production of epinephrine might be so excessive as to nullify the moderating effects of norepinephrine, or deficient production of norepinephrine might make normal production of epinephrine relatively excessive and thereby produce imbalance. In several possible combinations, the balance between hormones produced in the

350

core of the adrenals and those produced by the cortex might be upset. The reciprocal relationship between the pituitary and the adrenal cortex might malfunction in several ways,* or deficiencies in neurotransmitters such as acetylcholine might hamper the functioning of the normal parasympathetic nervous system so that the stressful sympathetic system becomes relatively hyperactive.

Any of these or numerous other chemical relationships could become unbalanced, to produce an internal stress reaction though no stressful situation exists in the external environment. Since the cortical level of the brain is our only source for the conscious explanation of things, messages (likely in the form of changed chemical combinations in the blood) are sent upstairs for an explanation as to why our internal environment is in a state of emotional stress.

In a manner which we have all experienced, the cortical level is likely, for a time at least, to inhibit these signals when, after traversing the lower brain levels, they reach it. When walking alone through the woods at night, we may start in fear as a ghostly hand grasps at us but we calm ourselves as we realize that it is but a branch in a breeze. If we are about to shriek in terror when we waken to see a burglar crouched and about to spring upon us we inhibit our response as we realize that what we saw were the clothes we threw over the back of a chair; and we speedily return from our Walter Mitty deeds of derring-do when our wives remind us to take out the garbage.

But if the stressful reaction persists in the internal environment the cortex may reinterpret the external environment so as to attain homeostatic balance between these two aspects of its functioning. It will create imagined situations in the external environment to justify the chemical imbalance which prepares us to respond to primal fear or rage. We develop obsessive fears about nuclear holocaust, the FBI, the CIA, or our fondness for chess, or become enraged at our chosen Sir Robert Peel.

Now a balance has been attained; environmental conditions have been created to justify our internal push toward fear or

*Years ago, when injections of cortisone were prescribed to relieve the pain and inflammation of arthritis, some patients developed illusions, hallucinations, and other symptoms of mental imbalance.

351

rage. The cortical factor which had been an inhibitor, preventing the initiating stress factor from becoming significant behavior, is now a facilitator. The circle is completed, the ideology is logic-tight. Anyone trying to break into it through reason merely proves that he is part of the plot. Reason, that weak inconstant evolutionary newcomer, cannot vanquish the primal fears on which our very survival has always depended.

Drugs, however, can break into this circle. Chlorpromazine and other phenothiazines and more recently discovered butyrophenones and dibenzadiazepines are anti-adrenergic; that is, they create reactions opposite to those of epinephrine. They reduce input into the reticular system which controls cortical arousal[41] and the cortex, its stimuli no longer impelling it to respond, is neutralized.[42] Belligerency, hostility, agitation, hallucination, confused ideas, and other symptoms decrease to a degree that patients can function outside the strict regimen of a hospital.

Harold E. Himwich elucidated a conceptualization of mental imbalance some twenty years ago, hypothesizing that Reserpine, by depressing the sympathetic activity of the hypothalamus, decreased the effects of the sympathetic nervous system (emotionality) on the cortex, contending that: "The diminution in reactivity of the organism probably influences the quantity or intensity of the emotional impact on the cortex."[43]

Once such drug treatment has reduced the emotional imperative which urges the cortex to compensate for the internal stress by finding delusions, hallucinations, or other symptoms in the environment, the cortex changes from a facilitating factor to a neutral one in the causal nexus. The next step is to attempt to convert it again into an inhibitor. With the shriek of the primal emotional imperative now muted, the patient can be appealed to through "eclectic" psychotherapy, eclectic meaning to elect or pick whichever persuasive argument seems most likely to restore the patient's capability to function appropriately in the community.

Those who believe in man's capacity for conscious moral choice would direct their appeal to self-respect within a context of social responsibility. Thomas Szasz objects to *The Myth of Mental Illness* not only because physical sickness is an inappropriate metaphor, but because "by assigning to an external

352

source (the illness) the blame for antisocial behavior," we undermine "the principle of personal responsibility, upon which a democratic political system is necessarily based."[44]

Viktor Frankl, basing his *Logotherapeutic* approach on his experiences and observations in the Nazi concentration camp at Auschwitz, tries ". . . to make the patient fully aware of his own responsibilities; and therefore it must leave to him the option for what, to what or to whom, he understands himself to be responsible." Criticizing the psychoanalytic approach not only for its "pan-sexualism," but for its "pan-determinism," by which Dr. Frankl means its view of man which disregards his capacity to take a stand, no matter how harsh conditions are, he insists that man is not simply the product of conditioning, ". . . man is ultimately self-determining."

> What he becomes—within the limits of endowment and environment—he has made out of himself. In the concentration camps, for example, in this living laboratory and on this testing ground we watched and witnessed some of our comrades behave like swine while others behaved like saints. Man has both potentialities within himself; which one is actualized depends on decisions but not on conditions.[45]

Similarly, Dr. William Glasser's *Reality Therapy* replaces Freud's stress on sex and aggression by an emphasis on relatedness and respect in which patients are persuaded to face the issue of the morality of behavior, to recognize that their moral standards are not, as Freudians insist, too high, but too low; that they do have the capacity to do what is responsible and right.

Persuasive evidence of the desirability of stressing the self-respect and social responsibilities of mentally unbalanced persons can, I think, be derived from the treatment for hysteria. Strecker, Ebaugh, and Ewalt emphasize two things characteristic of hysteria: (1) some form of gain is commonly derived from a display of hysteric symptoms; and (2) under wartime circumstances, hysteria spreads contagiously.[46]

Traditionally, the element of potential gain was eliminated from this "disease of the womb" by defining the situation for the hysteric by a slap in the face. Refusing to learn through such crude and unscientific precedent, hysterics and other psychoneurotics were removed from combat, hospitalized, and released from military service during World War II, and in 1943 more men were discharged because of psychiatric reasons than were inducted, one out of ten being taken out of combat because of mental disorder. Some twenty years later, under the more onerous conditions of Vietnam combat, the loss rate was reduced to one man in 100.

After World War II, it was learned that the incidence of disabling neurosis among German troops retreating from the advancing Russians *decreased* despite extremely bad physical conditions, great danger, and shattered morale. German soldiers knew that if they gave in to their hysteric fears the Russians would kill them. With the possible gain replaced by certain death, neurotic breakdowns decreased dramatically.

Learning from such experience, troops who broke down with "combat fatigue" during the Korean conflict were not discharged, sent to rear-echelon hospitals, or rewarded with R and R (rest and recreation) leave but treated at the front lines with the attitude that they were not sick and were expected to be back in action within a day or two. Under this changed approach 80 to 90 percent returned to combat and only a few broke down again.[47]

This procedure, which took the prospect of gain out of neurotic breakdown while insisting that the person face up to his responsibilities, was employed with even greater success in Vietnam. What was emphasized was not global abstractions of patriotism, saving the world for democracy or from communism, the American Way, the Four Freedoms, or Mom's Apple Pie, but responsibility to his microcosm: his squad, his tank crew. Brigadier General Spurgeon Neel, chief medical officer in Vietnam, reported that when fairly but firmly confronted with such responsibility, most servicemen were ready and willing to return to combat after twenty-four to thirty-six hours of rest.[48]

Such procedure sounds unscientific, cold, inhumane, almost cruel, but apparently it is therapeutically effective because recovery rates are quicker and more complete than treatment which encourages the person to evade his responsibilities. Guilt associated with such evasion is more likely to persist, prolonging the condition and delaying if not preventing recovery.

The argument which I have developed in this chapter is that

mental imbalance is not analogous to physical sickness; it is a psychic (spiritual) and social condition in which a person, due to improper mental functioning, fails to meet his social responsibilities. In a manner analogous to the imbalance in glandular functioning which upsets the homeostatic equilibrium of internal functioning, his obsession with his imaginary symptoms upsets the equilibrium between self-interest and social obligation.

If such be so, part of therapy should be concerned with encouraging the patient to restore his fractured ego by recognizing its role in the process and building up his self-respect through recognizing and accepting his social obligations.

This interpretation is, of course, similar to that of Alcoholics Anonymous, and a parallel group, Neurotics Anonymous,[49] was founded in 1964 by Grover Boydston who patterned it, including the spiritual factor, after A.A. I am sorry that I know of no data to indicate its degree of success.

Chapter 13. References and Notes

1. D. L. Rosenhan, "On Being Sane in Insane Places," *Science*, January 19, 1973.

2. "The Criminal Insanity Defense Is Placed on Trial in New York," *Science*, March 10, 1978.

3. "Patuxent: Controversial Prison Clings to Belief in Rehabilitation," *Science*, February 10, 1978.

4. Thomas S. Szasz, "Subversion of the Rule of Law," *National Review*, March 12, 1968.

5. Vincent Bugliosi, with Curt Gentry, *Helter Skelter: The True Story of the Manson Murders* (New York: W. W. Norton, 1974), p. 439.

6. Robert Lindsey, *New York Times*, January 18, 1973, p. 43.

7. David Mechanic, *Mental Health and Social Policy* (Englewood Cliffs, N.J.: Prentice-Hall, 1969), p. 17.

8. Nancy Greenberg, *Philadelphia Evening Bulletin*, November 8, 1974, p. 26.

9. Lawrence Appleby, Jordan M. Scher, and John Cumming, *Chronic Schizophrenia* (New York: The Free Press, 1960), p. 3.

10. David Mechanic, *Mental Health and Social Policy*, p. 15.

11. Conway Zirkle, *Death of a Science in Russia* (Philadel-

phia: University of Pennsylvania Press, 1949), pp. 126, 283–285.

12. Ludmilla Thorne, "Inside Russia's Psychiatric Jails," *New York Times Magazine*, June 12, 1977.

13. Sidney Bloch and Peter Reddaway, *Psychiatric Terror* (New York: Basic Books, 1977), p. 247.

14. Bruce J. Ennis and Richard Emery, *The Rights of Mental Patients*, (New York: Avon Books, 1978).

15. Thomas Szasz, *The Myth of Mental Illness* (New York: Hoeber-Harper, 1961).

16. Karl Menninger (with Martin Mayman and Paul Pruyser), *The Vital Balance* (New York: Viking Press, 1963), p. 9; and in *Chronic Schizophrenia*, by Lawrence Appleby and others (above), p. 55.

17. William Glasser, *Reality Therapy* (New York: Harper and Row, 1965), p. 15.

18. M. L. Gross, *The Psychological Society* (New York: Random House, 1978), p. 321.

19. Susan Sontag, "Illness as Metaphor," *New York Review of Books*, three articles, January 26, 1978, February 2, 1978, February 9, 1978.

20. A. H. Hobbs, *The Claims of Sociology* (Harrisburg, Pa.: The Stackpole Co., 1951), p. 58, p. 26.

21. Lawrence K. Frank, *Society As the Patient* (New Brunswick, N.J.: Rutgers U. Press, 1945).

22. Ruth Benedict, *Patterns of Culture* (New York: New American Library, 1960), pp. 236, 238.

23. R. E. L. Faris and H. W. Dunham, *Mental Disorders in Urban Areas* (Chicago: University of Chicago Press, 1939).

24. I. P. Pavlov, *Psychopathology and Psychiatry* (New York: Foreign Languages Pub. House, n. d.), pp. 190, 248.

25. F. J. Kallmann, "The Genetic Theory of Schizophrenia," *The American Journal of Psychiatry* 1946; *The Genetics of Schizophrenia* (Locust Valley, NY: J. J. Augustin Co., 1938); *Heredity in Health and Mental Disorder* (New York: W.W. Norton, 1953).

26. Seymour Kessler, "The Etiological Question in Mental Illness," a review of *The Transmission of Schizophrenia*, ed. David Rosenthal and Seymour S. Kety (New York: Pergamon

Press, 1968). In *Science,* September 26, 1969.

27. Leonard L. Heston, "The Genetics of Schizophrenic and Schizoid Disease," *Science,* January 16, 1970.

28. Bruce P. Dohrenwend and Barbara Snell Dohrenwend, *Social Status and Psychological Disorder* (New York: Wiley-Interscience, 1969), p. 125.

29. R. Jay Turner, review of *Social Status and Psychological Disorder* (above), *Science,* March 6, 1970.

30. Nancy Greenberg, interview with Dr. Isaac Rubin, *Philadelphia Evening Bulletin,* November 8, 1974.

31. Philip Rieff, *Freud: The Mind of the Moralist* (New York: Anchor Books, 1961); preface.

32. James V. McConnell, *Understanding Human Behavior* (New York: Holt, Rinehart and Winston, 1977), p. 587.

33. Seymour Fisher and Roger P. Greenberg, *The Scientific Credibility of Freud's Theories and Therapy* (New York: Basic Books, 1977), pp. 15, 341, 338.

34. S. Escalona, "Problems in Psycho-Analytic Research," *International Journal of Psycho-Analysis,* 1952, p. 16. In Fisher and Greenberg (above), pp. 16–17.

35. Martin L. Gross, *The Psychological Society* (New York: Random House, 1978), pp. 234–241.

36. Richard La Piere, *The Freudian Ethic* (New York: Duell, Sloan and Pearce, 1959), p. 285.

37. Mike Gorman, *Every Other Bed* (Mountain View, CA: World Pub. Co., 1956), p. 90.

38. Ray Oakley, ed., *Drugs, Society, and Human Behavior* (St. Louis: C. V. Mosby Co., 1978), pp. 254, 255.

39. Sidney Bloch and Peter Reddaway, *Psychiatric Terror* (New York: Basic Books, 1977), p. 209.

40. Edward O. Wilson, *Sociobiology* (Cambridge, Mass.: Harvard University Press, 1975), p. 253. (Professor Wilson's description of these interrelations is the best I've seen, and I've followed it in this section.)

41. Ray Oakley, ed., *Drugs, Society, and Human Behavior,* p. 257.

42. John M. Davis, "Efficacy of Tranquilizing and Antidepressant Drugs," *Archives of General Psychiatry,* December 1965, p. 565.

43. H. E. Himwich, "Psychopharmalogic Drugs," *Science,* January 10, 1958, p. 12.

44. Thomas Szasz (above), pp. 296, 297.

45. Viktor Frankl, *Man's Search for Meaning: An Introduction to Logotherapy* (Boston: Beacon Press, 1959), pp. 111, 136–7.

46. E. A. Strecker, F. G. Ebaugh, and J. R. Ewalt, *Practical Clinical Psychiatry* 6th ed. (Philadelphia: The Blakiston Co., 1948), pp. 46–52.

47. Pierre C. Fraley, "Battle-Line Psychiatry Seen As Aid in Treating Mental Ills," *Philadelphia Evening Bulletin,* January 6, 1955.

48. B. Drummond Ayres, Jr., "Combat Fatigue in Vietnam Rare," *New York Times,* May 4, 1969.

49. "Now It's Neurotics Anonymous," *Time,* March 2, 1970.

Chapter 14

The Twain Met

IT IS THIRTY *years since the Lammas-eve when Romeo and Juliet wed, and it is three o' the morn. Uncertain fingers of pale green light from the dying moon enhance the darkness they do not touch. Wine sloshing in his belly causes Romeo to stagger into a chamber pot, spilling its ample substance to soil his boots and spread its stench throughout the bedroom. He shouts at sleeping Juliet.*

ROM. Why in blue-blazin' hell can't you leave on some friggin' lights for me when I get home? Do you think your moonface lights up the room? Do you think the sun rises and sets on you? Do you think you're J.C.?

Juliet stops snoring, snorts loudly, and wakens. Her pasta has formed more symmetric distribution than Romeo's pot; her well-rounded belly being nicely balanced by a steato-pygic rear. Her moustache, the merest hint of a downy sugges- tion on that earlier Lammas-eve, now gives sharp contrast to her cheeks, left ashen when youth's fire burned out. She opens her "fairest stars of heaven" to reveal the twin red moons of Mars. She speaks.

JUL. Romeo? *Romeo!!* Where in hell have you been, you bastard?

ROM. Come on, now, Juley, don't call me a bastard, *you're* the one who told me to forget I had a father. Remember how you said I'd smell like a rose even if I wasn't Romeo?

JUL. Smell like a rose! That's a good one—*you* smell like a rose? You *stink;* you smell like the dregs of a wine cask. You think you're a Romeo? Hah! You're an old lech, that's what *you* are, baying like a dog at the moon every time you smell a young bitch in heat. I *know*, you cradle snatcher, I was a baby when you took advantage of me. Now you stay out all night sniffin' after chicks young enough to be your damned granddaughters.

ROM. Yappity-yappity! You talk but you don't say anything. Just keep it up, you devil. *His voice softens and he pleads.* Just give me some lovin' at home and I'll stop roaming around. Give me some lovin' and I'll be a new man. *He touches her cheek.*

JUL. Take your crummy hands off me, you lech. Do you think I got round heels? Do you think I'm gonna roll over on my back every time you snap your fat fingers? Don't you know I always have the curse at the change of the moon? Now shut up and go to sleep and dream about it; do I have to tell you a thousand times?

ROM. I'm climbing the walls! You're killing me! This is no dream, it's a damned nightmare. What do you think I am; your pigeon? You stifle me!

JUL. Boy, I can't wait till daylight to get away from you and out of this stinkin' rat-trap.

W.S. VIA PRINCE. Never was a story of more woe than this of Juliet and her Romeo.

This caricature of the dialogue which took place in Capulet's orchard when Juliet was thirteen is, in a heavyhanded way, designed to show the transient nature of romance.

It is quite possible that this view was also intended by Shakespeare—that *Romeo and Juliet* was written not to immortalize romance but to mortalize it by further telescoping its always temporary nature into a few days—all that were needed for passionate rashness to produce senseless tragedy.

The larger issue is whether the romantic conception of man, of itself, can bind male and female to each other with sufficient cohesiveness to constitute the basic unit that is required for the perpetuation of every society.

Romance, as the term is ordinarily used, differs in detail from the romantic conception of man but it involves basically the same phenomenon—the innate goodness of man. In romance this innate goodness is found in a relationship between two

361

people. Each not only admits, but insists on his own faults, but is certain-sure that all of them will vanish under the influence of the relationship between the two.

This feeling is a sentiment, generally called love, which is aroused by a blocked striving toward another person. What we repeatedly forget is that the essence of this romanticism is produced by the blockage and dissipates once the blockage is removed. While it is blocked, the sentiment engenders idealization of the other. The motivation for the sentiment is largely sexual but not entirely so. Significantly involved also is ego striving—a desire to convey to another those aspects of our feelings which propriety ordinarily bars from expression. Release of these feelings to a sympathetic other results in euphoria. It is a unique relationship with the only person in the whole world who understands the *real* you.

When we think of the great romances of myth and history we realize that most of them were unrequited loves; existing only so long as the striving toward the other was blocked.

How began this enigma, this mirage which is real only when at a distance? Some have it that Pandora started it all when Zeus, having created her from clay, commissioned Hermes to present her as a gift to Epimetheus, brother to Prometheus.[1] Prometheus, who already had offended Zeus by giving fire to mankind, warned his brother to accept no gift from Zeus, but yet Epimetheus took her to wife. Enraged by Prometheus' additional challenge to his authority, Zeus had him chained naked to a pillar in the mountains, where a vulture tore at his liver all day.

Prometheus warned Epimetheus not to permit Pandora to open the box in which the Spites of Old Age, Sickness, Insanity, Vice, and Passion were imprisoned, but foolish Pandora permitted the Spites to escape to plague mankind unto death were it not for one, Delusive Hope, which keeps us from our own extinction.

Some prefer the companion story in which Archangel Michael, having put Adam upon the earth, made Eve his Pandora to release trouble upon the world by tempting Adam to eat the forbidden fruit of the tree of the knowledge of good and evil.

In other myths, Pygmalion, his yearning for Aphrodite spurned, then detested the faults which nature has given women and created a marble statue which came to life as Galatea.

362

Apollo, struck with Cupid's golden arrow, is aroused to passion which Daphne, having been struck by the blunt arrow which repels love, rejects.[2] Thus blocked also were the short-lived Pyramus and Thisbe, Orpheus and the lost Eurydice, and the halcyon days of perfect peace are tribute to a drowned, dead love, not a living.

In Beatrice Dante saw Heaven's glory, the earthly vessel which held divine experience, only because he viewed her from afar.[3] Merlin, once entrapped by Vivien, soon realized that she had changed from his imagined Heaven to a tongue-raging Hell. Elaine, the maid of Astolat, died of her unrequited love for Sir Lancelot of the Lake and in doing so was fortunate in that she did not live to see her noble knight ignobly transform the perfect circle of Camelot into a sordid triangle by his adulterous affair with King Arthur's wife. And after Lancelot and Guinevere had unblocked their pent-up passion in deed as well as word, they were "silent once more." And how long would Cyrano have shared in the laughs about his nose once he and Roxanne were wed?

Many authors of fiction practice as well as preach the blocked striving of unrequited love which is romance. Jonathan Swift felt it for Esther Johnson ("Stella"), while Hester Vanhomrigh ("Vanessa") felt it for him; bachelor Ivan Turgenev felt a lifelong attraction to Pauline Vardot, though she was wedded and constant to another; and the odes of Samuel Taylor Coleridge were inspired by Mary Evans rather than Sara Fricker, his wife. Percy Shelley, in addition to his other numerous and complicated affairs, idealized, afar from the convent in which her parents kept her, Emilia Viviani, "a divine presence in a place divine." Lord Byron (in "Don Juan," 74) noted that sighs were "deeper for suppression" and stolen glances "sweeter for the theft."

Ernest Dowson, when he "cried for madder music and for stronger wine," was breaking his heart for the daughter of the owner of an Italian eating house.[4] William Butler Yeats yearned deeply from a distance for his Maude Gonne though he abhorred her radical ideas, believing that "in custom and in ceremony are innocence and beauty born." George Bernard Shaw carried on his "pleasantest and most enduring of all courtships" with Ellen Terry for many years—but only through correspondence. Despite his "lifelong horror of women," T.S. Eliot conducted for many years a courtship by correspondence with Emily Hale, leading only "towards the door we never opened." Franz Kafka also "spent most of his passion on postage stamps," and his attempt to place Felice Bauer on a pedestal was patterned after Pygmalion's creation of Galatea.

Romantic Love

It seems reasonable to contend that we cannot have a human society without people, and until such time as the techniques of cloning are perfected to produce replicas of humans asexually, some process must be found to assure that relationships between males and females are such that sufficient children are born and cared for to keep society going. When the romantic conviction that man is innately good modifies itself into romatic love wherein two people believe that their flawed selves have formed a unique combination of perfect goodness, we have a desirable adjunct to such a process but not the necessary whole of it.

The sentiment of romantic love which is aroused by a blocked yearning for another person generates idealization and passionate emotion. While the motivation is partly sexual it is not completely so, including also deep desires to reveal aspects of ourselves which are barred from expression in our usual social relationships. We all nurture wishes, hopes, fears, poetic feelings, and other sentiments which our own shyness or conventional proprieties ordinarily suppress. We are told that we should be grown-up; we should be dignified; don't wear your heart on your sleeve; don't be a sissy; don't be Mickey Mouse; and "it isn't done," so often that when we find a sympathetic audience to unburden ourselves of these feelings we rise to a state of euphoria.

Our life becomes bigger than a double-decker ice-cream cone with a cherry on top, more luscious than a coconut-coated, chocolate-covered, jelly-filled doughnut for breakfast, more exciting than the first sleigh ride down hill or the first "no-hands" on a bicycle, more gratifying than Santa Claus coming down the chimney with the Bunny Rabbit in his sack. It's the night before the Sunday School picnic on the Fourth of July with parades and bands and firecrackers and runaway horses. It is a fraternity house party that goes on forever while everyone is having his third martini, and it's midnight on New Year's Eve in Times Square on VE Day. All the girls in chiffon dresses have snow in their hair which shines in the full moon of springtime as we dream of children who will always be four years old on Christmas morning.

Such idealization and the euphoria does indeed change reality; each lover becomes more interested, kinder, less selfish, more considerate of the other, but the changed behavior is not enough to fulfill the idealization. We rely upon fantasy to complete the picture of the other that we hold in our imagination—a picture for which sensory confirmation may be lacking or even contradictory. The "dream girl" who is kind, beautiful, gracious, passionate—but only for sexy you—fun-loving, considerate, charming, sensitive, emotionally stable, yielding, firm, agreeable, knows her own mind, bright—but ready to learn from you —needs considerable help in her creation. As does the handsome, brave, loyal, true, generous, gallant, considerate, honest, courteous boy.

Since sensory data fail to substantiate the idealization— though a trim ankle is proof of charm; giggles are a guarantee of wit; stubbornness is assurance of pride; and six cents worth of perfume is greater proof of sexual desire than a gallon of pheromone—it must find its confirmation in an "inner essence" or "spirituality." The "spirituality" is an endeavor to elevate the self-interest of Eros to agape or caritas, a fellowship in the love of Christ expressing itself as secular love, self-given without calculation of cost or gain; or love spiritualized to its perfection. Thus Dante's Beatrice, *the fairest among women,* is also the "Spouse of Lebanon," the Bride of God, transcending thereby the romantic passion which is but an assertion of the personal will. And thus the idealized other becomes Goethe's eternal feminine which draws us upward.

In their representations of the female beloved, both Dante and Goethe attempted to combine Eros with caritas and agape, to etherialize love for the secular female into an analogue of the perfect gift, once given, beloved Christ. Many others have wondered if these forms of love can be blended or if they are, for

365

mortal man in earthly life, discrete, each unique unto itself, parallel estrangement. This yearning to combine the love of person and the love of God may be man's glory; equally it may be his mirage, Delusive Hope.

Would Dante have renounced the cool and reasoned guidance of Vergil to have untouched Beatrice lead him upward had she been touched? Would Goethe have chosen the eternal feminine to lead him upward had she been substantial female?

Of such things we know not, and cannot know.

The "inner essence" can be seen only by looking deep and long into the eyes of the loved one. Since insensitive outsiders cannot see all of the special qualities which the idealized beloved possesses, their company is avoided and their opinion (which sometimes boorishly mistakes spirituality for far-sightedness) shunned. Lovers cherish their own private jokes, their secret codes and glances, and they create the perfect formula which guarantees that their romantic love will last forever.

1. Each of us will keep our independence. We are not going to destroy this precious individuality which made us love each other. You, husband, will have a night out each week to do as you wish, and we will have separate vacations—if we wish; but I'll never want to be away from you, my own little pootsie-pie.

2. We will never let our friends interfere. If those bums you pal around with want to go to the ball game and drink beer or play poker 'till all hours of the morning, you'll tell them you'd rather stay home with me, won't you, honeypot?

3. We'll never let the in-laws interfere—especially your mother; she always sticks her nose into everything.

4. We'll never separate if we are still angry (who could ever be angry with you, silly?). We'll talk things out like the civilized, intelligent people we are.

5. If one of us is angry, the other will stay calm (actually, this is one of the most irritating things in life, but it sounds very mature to say it).

6. Neither of us will boss the other. We'll have a fifty-fifty arrangement, share and share alike.

7. If we ever fall out of love we'll separate as friends because your happiness is all that matters, and though I want you more than anything else in the world, I'd rather give you up than know you are unhappy.

Evermore Fades the Dream

Gradually, imperceptibly and above all, unadmittedly, the glamorous thrill of the union dissipates; the air oozes out of their pink balloon and it drifts back to earth. They "get the stars out of their eyes," stop moongazing and daydreaming and get their feet on the ground.

The tiresome repetition of their soul searching and the interminable recital of their dreams blunts the enthusiasm of response, and their innermost feelings become once again suppressed. Their rationale for this retreat back into their own shell is that now they "understand" each other and have no need to rehash such childish feelings. Their mutually shared jokes are worn threadbare; their cute mannerisms have become irritating; their expressions of endearment are reduced to rituals which even they recognize as banal. They try to ward off encroaching boredom by seeking the outside company which they once shunned.

The real and potent pressures of social interchange between ordinary people and everyday living bring the romancers back to the realities which are themselves. All the world loves a lover, but for heaven's sake get over it and get back to normal. None is easier to ridicule than the sincere and sentimental swain. None is easier to persuade that she must "stop making a fool of herself over that man" than the woman who receives this advice, and receives this advice, and receives this advice from her oh-so-solicitous sisters.

"Down to earth" sexual humor gnaws at the pedestals which held aloof their tenderness till they crumble in a realization that what they considered preciously unique is gutter-common. Expressions of deepest emotion become parrot phrases as though the repetition of "I love you" a certain number of times per day guaranteed the continuance of the sentiment which once, unsaid, conveyed the deepest meaning they had ever felt. Her casual pecks which pass for kisses are now litmus tests for alcohol on his breath.

Increasingly imperative demands from their temporarily subordinated egos pry their loose-bound selves further apart. Come hell or high water, he's going to read the paper at the dining table; he doesn't give a damn what she says, if he wants a night out with the guys he's going to take it, and if he feels like having a few drinks after work she's not going to stop him. . . . She becomes irritated and weary of being mauled, and he remembers how she once sighed at what she now calls "mauling," and marvels at the precision with which her headaches fit into the intervals between her menstrual periods which, like measles, are one week coming, one week here, and one week going. Doesn't he understand how much trouble it is to fix one's hair after it has been all mussed? Does he *have* to leave his ashes in his saucer, and why doesn't he talk with her about what he does at the office instead of watching the Superbowl?

This is not to say that either is selfish or unfeeling, only to indicate that as the ties which bound their suppressed egos weaken, the centripetal force of ego-centricism reasserts itself. An excellent portrayal of understandable self-interest in relations between husband and wife is in John P. Marquand's *Sincerely, Willis Wayde.*[5]

Willis, self-made and with a lower middle-class background, is married to Sylvia, patrician daughter of a Harvard professor. Willis has just achieved a height of business success and an amount of acclaim far beyond his most hopeful dreams. He skips from cloud to cloud as he hurries home to tell wife Sylvia so she will share his elation.

She responds to his exuberant "Yoo-hoo, honey, I'm home" by asking "Is that you, Willis?" To his quip "No, it's the president of the Aluminium Corporation of America," she somberly tells him to come out to the kitchen and help her or they won't have any supper. It turns out that the maid has quit and Sylvia's preoccupation with unaccustomed chores makes her quite oblivious to Willis' enthusiasm. Somewhat deflated, Willis suggests that she drop everything and he will tell her the news he is bursting with while they dine out.

They can't dine out. Why not? She has to get supper for the baby's nurse. Why can't the nurse get her own supper? Because —Sylvia is now quite impatient at Willis' inability to comprehend the significance of important differences in status—she's a *trained* nurse, not a practical nurse. When Willis quips that anyway Sylvia won't have to cook the (breast-fed) baby's supper, Sylvia snidely tells him not to joke about such things.

368

When the now repeatedly rebuffed Willis suggests a cocktail to celebrate, Sylvia wonders what there is to celebrate. He tells her some of the great news but she doesn't respond except to say that she'd better not have a cocktail. Why not? *You know* I breast-feed the baby. The baby, says Willis, Ha! Ha! won't get drunk. Frigid silence. As Willis prepares his martini she ridicules the NEWLY APPOINTED FIRST VICE-PRESIDENT OF HARCOURT ASSOCIATES, WITH STOCK OPTIONS WHO JUST A FEW HOURS AGO MADE A VERY IMPORTANT SPEECH WHICH RECEIVED A STANDING OVATION by saying that he looks like an old maid making a pot of tea.

When Willis tries to tell her the remainder of the good news Sylvia says that she is "dying to hear it," but couldn't he tell her in the kitchen while she prepares supper for the nurse—we wouldn't want her to get cross, would we? Why, Willis wonders, now somewhat querulous, is it more important to have the nurse's supper ready exactly on schedule than for Sylvia to spend just a few minutes to hear about the greatest success he has ever had.

Well, Sylvia snaps with acerbity, if he absolutely must have *a big business conference* with her *right now* when the maid has left her in such a mess and the nurse must have her supper, he should, *by all means Mr. First Vice-President,* just you sit yourself right down and she will (looking at her watch) listen to whatever is more important than their baby's supper.

Leadenly stomping out of the house, Willis goes to his club, returning a few hours later to apologize.

Egocentricism such as this is a normal human attribute. It is an aspect of a life in which there are no friends, lovers, or enemies; only interests, and as other interests coincide or conflict with our own we give them names and faces and call them friend or lover or enemy; but they will remain such only until our interests or theirs change.

Many refuse to recognize such harsh facts of life and blame the loss of romance on a person, a particular incident, or an especial set of circumstances; quite often becoming bitter toward life in general because of their loss. But some mature as they grow older and, though the realization that all the shiny unmarred days that never were will never be brings sadness, they leave their Enchanted Cottage, the world which was their own private world, feeling " 'tis better to have loved and lost . . ." as they face the reality of a man's world and a woman's world forged together by necessity and held together by complementarity. They now live together as husband and wife—precisely so.

Delightful though the romantic relationship is, its necessarily short-lived nature and the fragility of the bonds which hold it together make it only an adjunct to the lasting and substantial process that must exist to assure that enough children are born and cared for to keep society going.

Many things in the past—the dictates of the Church; a spiritual aura which enhaloed marriage; rigid formal controls imposed by the State relating to marriage, divorce, adultery, fornication, and homosexuality; and informal controls in the form of people's attitudes about the family—conjoined with romantic attraction to constitute the pragmatically effective institution which is essential for the perpetuation of civilized life.

Churches sanctioned marriage as a sacrament and either frowned upon divorce and birth control or dogmatically prohibited them. Where divorce was permitted, remarriage was often forbidden. Secular laws totally prohibited divorce or were so constrictive as to make it extremely difficult to obtain, and sexual practices outside the bonds of matrimony (adultery, fornication, sodomy, homosexuality) were not only immoral but criminal.

Even more important than such formal controls were informal controls, spiritual as well as secular, which shaped the climate of opinion about this essential process. Marriages were made in heaven and were to last until death did them part. People took seriously the religious admonition to increase and multiply. Girls were cautioned to be chaste and trained to be helpmates. Boys aspired to be men who were the head of the household. Old maids were ridiculed and bachelors were regarded with at least faint suspicion. Childless couples were pitied only if it were crystal clear and certain-sure that it wasn't their fault that they didn't have children. When divorce occurred both parties were commonly excommunicated from the Church, ostracized from proper society, and no matter what the grounds or to whom the divorce was granted, the blame was likely to fall on the erstwhile wife. In the early 1920s the temper of the times

370

was such that all of the films of the most popular "matinee idol" of the time (Francis X. Bushman, I believe) were withdrawn from circulation because he had divorced his wife. His producer felt, with good reason, that the American public would be outraged by being asked to pay their good money to see such a scoundrel.

There were failures (runaway husbands, informal separations), there was inequity (especially in respect to wives), and there was much else about the process which could be criticized from a rationalistic viewpoint, but by-and-large the institution performed its functions effectively until scientism created a different climate of opinion.

From Institution to Individuation

Rationalistic liberals, convinced that they were dedicated to quantitative scientific analysis of social institutions, could do naught else but ridicule quintessentially qualitative romantic attraction. Since the test of scientific validity is prediction and the predictability of social processes requires that all humans, male or female, must be totally and equally malleable, the sex differences implicit in the institutionalized husband-wife relationship had to be explained away.

Since rationalistic liberals are not really scientists, but pseudo-scientists who attain their appearance of objectivity by holding our social values upside down, they acquired intellectual stature as realistic truth-seekers by attacking marital as well as sexual rules.

And since, for reasons which I earlier described, these rationalistic liberals dominated the informational media as well as education, in a comparatively short time they have been able to substitute individuation for the institution of marriage.

Dr. Margaret Mead's 1935 *Sex and Temperament in Three Primitive Societies* was a potent scientistic influence in persuading people that all of the temperamental and emotional differences between males and females are created through cultural conditioning.[6] Dr. Mead, you may recall, together with Dr. Ruth Benedict (*Patterns of Culture*), were the most influential of all anthropologists in convincing us that none of our beliefs

are sensibly based on conscious, discriminating rational processes, experiences, or history, but that all of our attitudes,
sentiments, and patterns of thought arise to the conscious level
through cultural conditioning which we subconsciously absorb.
She was also included among those "scientists" who proved that
the aggressive post World War II imperialistic expansion of
Soviet Russia was caused because they had subconscious memo-
ries that their ancestors were swaddled during infancy.

Both Benedict and Mead were disciples of Dr. Franz Boas,
who criticized our effective monogamous form of family structure by contrasting it with the Communist form.

> The efforts to force man into absolute monogamy have
> never been successful and the tendency of our times is to
> recognize this. The increasing ease of divorce which has
> been carried furthest in Mexico and Russia is proof of this.[7]

In citing the ease of divorce in Russia, Boas permitted his
dislike for monogamy and his enthusiasm for cultural relativism
to nullify the evidence of civilized history. In selecting Russia as
an example of the ideal of the future society in which divorce
would be readily granted, he was fooled by a temporary situation during which divorces were free and were granted at the
request of either husband or wife, with no questions asked as to
why the divorce was wanted and without the spouse even being
informed. This freedom soon developed into a chaotic situation
in which the larger cities had more divorces than marriages.
Within a few years the laws governing divorce in Russia were
so tightened that they were more restrictive than ours.

Both Benedict and Mead were indoctrinated by Boas into
believing that cultural anthropology is a science, and his anti-
heredity, cultural determinism bias also rubbed off on his disciples.

In *Sex and Temperament,* Dr. Mead claimed that in New
Guinea, within a one-hundred-mile area she had found three
societies which had three distinctively different sets of masculine and feminine roles. In one of them, the Mundugumor, the
roles were similar to those in our traditional patriarchal family
arrangement. The male was the dominant, assertive family head
and breadwinner while the submissive, meek wife cared for the

372

children and did the household chores. In a second society, the Arapesh, the roles are those which Dr. Mead obviously favored, being archetypical of those which should exist in the Democratic Family which sociologists soon began to stress as the ideal arrangement. Arapesh men as well as women were maternal toward their children and feminine in temperament. Arapesh were cooperative, unaggressive, and responsive to the needs of others. One can't help but think that if we could only combine the temperament and traits of Dr. Mead's Arapesh with those of Dr. Benedict's idyllic Zuni most human problems would be solved.

It is with reluctance that we leave these fine folk, the Arapesh, to survey the near-by Tchambuli, where the sex roles are the reverse of those in our culture. It is the Tchambuli women, not the men, who are outgoing, breezy, brisk, and hearty; who manage all the business affairs[8] and work in cooperative groups. Women have charge of all valuables, and are businesslike and competent. Shunning adornment themselves as being unwomanly, they dress up the children—and the males. It is the Tchambuli girls who are bright, open, and free, while the boys are jealous and catty. Tchambuli men idle away their time with painting, gossip, and temper tantrums arising out of their rivalrous jealousies.

All of these remarkable differences were presented as being scientifically proved fact. Sales of the book flourished; its findings were cited in sociological and psychological as well as anthropological textbooks; and its popularity held up so that twenty-eight years after its first publication a new edition was brought out.

Dr. Mead proclaimed that her doctrine of cultural conditioning had triumphed over all attempts to attribute significant differences between male and female temperaments to heredity or conscious decision, saying "The battle which we once had to fight with the whole battery at our command . . . is now won."[9]

Dr. Reo Fortune, who worked with Dr. Mead in their study of the three New Guinea societies, disavowed her interpretation of their joint field data saying, for example, that Arapesh males and females do not have the same temperament, citing in support of his view an Arapesh proverb, "Men's hearts are different; women's hearts are different." Effeminate men, said Fortune, are assigned to inferior social status among the Arapesh.

One thing which puzzled me about the catty, chintzy Tcham-buli men is that they were headhunters, and (for some reason I wot not of) I find it difficult to envision an effeminate headhunter! But Dr. Mead's interpretation that all significant attitudinal and temperamental differences (and all of the mannerisms and customs which are the behavioral manifestations of such differences) between male and female are caused by cultural conditioning fitted so snugly into the rationalistic conception of malleable man-woman that it quickly became entrenched as the conventional wisdom and students were indoctrinated with it.*

Dr. Mead's accomplishments were hailed as being the greatest of any woman since Madame Curie; her contributions to the doctrine of environmental determinism—more extreme, even, than those of Academician T.R. Lysenko—were rewarded by appointment to the highest office in scientific organizations, and her 1939 proclamation that the doctrine of cultural determinism had banished hereditary factors from consideration as a significant element in temperamental and attitudinal differences between male and female (together with all of the mannerisms and customs which are the behavior manifestation of such differences) was fulfilled.

The conviction that all such differences between the sexes were either happenstance conventional quirks or the result of an ages-old male plot quickly expressed itself in demands for sexual equality, and unisex hair, dress, and speech.†

In his prescient *1984*, George Orwell forsaw that "who controls the language controls the people," and the language which Big Brother used to control the people of *1984* was "newspeak."

*The author of a widely used college textbook on marriage, who wishes to remain anonymous, recently informed me that his publishers strongly object to the inclusion of any reference to hereditary differences between males and females.
†During the late 1960s as I stood on a walkway outside an airport at dusk I heard three skycaps arguing about the gender of a long-haired, nondescript clothed human figure in the distance. One said it was a boy, but another was equally sure it was a girl. After these two had argued "Boy," "No, girl!" "Boy!" "Girl!" for a while the third interjected "It's a Taint." "What's a Taint?" the others asked. " 'Taint one and 'Taint the other!" guffawed the end-man.

Now as liberal doctrine persuades us to evolve from the subordination of women into equality between the sexes—this interval quite possibly being only an hiatus which precedes their superordination when Big Sister will use Sispeak to womanipulate our womanifold thoughts, we insert chairperson for chairman, congressone for congressman, genkind for mankind, ve vis and ver for he and she, and herstorectomy for hysterectomy.[10]

As Orwell foresaw, we shall likely proceed from bitcherizing the language to rewriting herstory so tomorrow's pupils will learn that Washington was first in the hearts of his countrypersons.

In 1978, displayed in a public school in Long Island City were paintings by thirteen women artists, the collection designed to be a replica of Michelangelo's "Creation of Adam" in the Sistine Chapel.[11] The contemporary version is called the Sister Chapel. God of course is a woman, no longer enhaloed by spiritual glow but by the realistic sun. "Womanhero" is tattooed on the woman who replaces David. Womanhero uses the Virgin Mary's veil as the sling and the world as the shot to slay Goliath. Prophetically posed alongside is cowboy [oops!] hatted Bella Abzug ready to replace the Lady Goddess at the drop of a gender. Michelangelo, I believe, is resting quite peacefully.

One linguistic abuse associated with the agitation for equal rights which, perhaps pettishly, annoys me is that it is almost always referred to as a *feminist* movement. Since erasure of the demarkations between masculine and feminine roles is one of the main purposes of this activity, to designate it a *feminist* movement would seem misleading if not oxymoronic. And in this girlila war to womancipate the sexes, to refer to point-women such as Bella Abzug as *feminist* puts a desperate strain on the credulity of mortal person.

Scientistic doctrines which persuaded people that there are few if any significant innate differences between the sexes weakened the patriarchal role-relationships of husbands and wives, and these are now rapidly giving way to other arrangements, variously designated as the Companionship Family, the Democratic Family, the Egalitarian Family, and the Fifty-fifty Family. Religious, spiritual, and social functions which the institution of the family was designed to fulfill are now minimized as marriage is looked upon as a source of companionship between equals, a

375

secular arrangement designed to emancipate the personalities and to facilitate convenient sex.

As liberals exploited scientistic claims such as Dr. Mead's to change the role-relationships between husbands and wives, they also exploited scientistic claims about the nature of sexual activity to further weaken the family, their stubborn foe in a struggle to rationalize society.

Previously, I described how Freud, from a conceptual approach, set out to "expose the whole rotten empire of the family" and opposed traditional standards of sexual morality, claiming that he could easily prove that such standards do more harm than good. Professor Kinsey, from a behavioral approach, convinced many people that, whereas the Bible and history opposed pre-marital sex and adultery, his "scientific" discoveries had proved them to be helpful to marriage. In defiance of evidence from endocrinology and history some of Kinsey's claims (such as his assertion that the female sex drive exceeds that of males) were even more extreme than those of Dr. Mead.

Freudian premises and Kinsey's scientific claims, together with those of Masters and Johnson, are used by SIECUS (Sex Information and Education Council of the United States) to indoctrinate youths into believing that any form of sexual behavior by anybody, with anybody, at any time, under any circumstances is acceptable. Pleasure is the sole purpose of sex and the only harm done by indiscriminate promiscuity is venereal disease or pregnancy. SIECUS does not directly recommend promiscuity to children who study in their sex education programs; but, following the example set by Freud and Kinsey, they ridicule the old standards out of effectual existence, thus depriving such children of all guides to sexual behavior except the desire to seek from it as much pleasure as they can get while avoiding the unpleasantness of pregnancy and venereal disease.

By avoiding open advocacy of promiscuity, sex education programs can slough off charges that they actively encourage immorality. In dismissing charges that their programs are immoral, proponents of sex education are technically correct; they are not *immoral* but *amoral,* in the same way that their doctrine is *ahistorical, ascientific,* and *agnostic.* Though these proponents of sex education—in relation to standards which govern sexual behavior, most sex programs *indoctrinate*

376

rather than educate—are technically correct in asserting that they do not actively advocate immorality, their assertions are very misleading.

In Chapter 10, I cited the manner in which officers and advisers to SIECUS persistently ridicule Judaeo-Christian standards of sexual behavior together with all those handed down as part of the heritage of Western civilization, saying that such premises, derived as they are from the "folklore of the ancient Hebrews and the musings of medieval monks," should not be accepted as guides. Also (in Chapter 10) I indicated how the president of SIECUS described the arguments of those who objected to homosexuals teaching children in public schools as ravings which conflicted with research, as a triumph of ignorance over scientific fact, as indicative of unnecessary fear and irrational hate, as witch-hunting, hate-mongering tactics, and un-Christian zealotry.

In that they do not openly advocate promiscuity, programs of sex education technically avoid charges of being immoral, but by denigrating all tested standards of sexual behavior they leave youths without stabilizers or compass to help them steer through the sexual cross-currents they will encounter and thus promote wreckage which could be avoided.

> If we grant the inescapable fact—the imperative nature of the male sex drive in youth—then the SIECUS amoral emphasis on sexual behavior actually creates a situation analogous to releasing the brakes on a car parked on a steep hill and, watching it as it careens downhill to its destruction, protesting that it's not your fault, you didn't push it.[12]

That the ostensibly neutral presentation of sex education is actually "neutral for" promiscuity and "neutral against" chastity was evidenced in a 1978 conference on sex held in Atlanta, Georgia, and attended by 1,200 teen-agers and 500 adult counselors.[13]

A group moderator "who tried to lead the teen-agers into an acceptance of the possibility of pre-marital sex," when repeatedly met with "you don't need to know about that if you don't mess around," concluded that ". . . the Judaeo-Christian ethic is the greatest contributor to pregnancy that I run into." A Unitarian Church counselor, describing the advantages and disadvantages of different contraceptives, was taken aback when a girl member of her group asked "Why do it in the first place?"

Thus the temporary but lovely strands of romance that held male and female together are frayed by scientistic indoctrination in which agape and caritas as well are rationalized into limbo. Now Eros, denuded of her social and spiritual connotations and freed from her romantic association, becomes lust.

As the growth of secular concerns pushed spiritual awe into smaller and remoter areas of our thoughts, the authoritarian strength of church-enforced marital bonds weakened. This attenuation, too drastic to be repaired by the fragile ties of romantic love, left the institution of the family wobbling on uncertain premises. Scientism rushed into the breach with a vast armamentarium to reconstruct relationships between the sexes so that the twain would now meet on the grounds of rationalistic liberalism.

1. Since no significant differences in temperament, emotionality, or sex drive exist, all relations between the sexes must henceforth be based on equality. Therefore, all customs, laws, and language premised on or connoting such differences must be abolished.

2. The purpose of marriage is the fulfillment of the personalities of two individuals. Religious sanctions are not needed for such fulfillment, social obligations interfere with it, and spiritual sentiments are irrelevant to it. If the marriage ceases to contribute toward personality fulfillment—if the relationship is no longer a meaningful one for either partner—divorce is not only acceptable but desirable.

3. The purpose of sex is pleasure. Sex education is needed to teach youths to pursue this pleasure sooner, more frequently, more openly, and without guilt. It is needed also to teach them how to avoid the principal harm done by sex—having a baby. They are taught, without acknowledgment of its source in George Orwell's *Animal Farm*, that while all forms of sexual behavior are equal, those forms which pervert its natural purposes are more equal than those which conform to it.

Especially among educated people, these scientistic-based liberal doctrines about sex and marriage now constitute the

378

conventional wisdom. Such convictions are fostered by courses in preparation for marriage, sex education programs supported by many millions of dollars in Federal funds, and marital adjustment training. Textbooks, trade books, and thousands of authoritative articles written by overnight scientific experts inform us of the latest How-to-Do-It Sexual Techniques, Sixty Surefire Secrets of Seduction, and How to Be Happy Though Married. Marriage counselors proffer their Number-One formula: How to Avoid Divorce, and when it fails they eagerly offer their Number-Two formula: How to Adjust After Divorce.

Contraceptives more effective, more readily available, and more widely used than anyone would have conceived possible a few decades ago are virtually forced upon youths.

The Vision of Companionship

We were told that these new scientific approaches would be of great benefit. Sex would be more psychically fulfilling as well as more frequent and more pleasurable. Sex would not be promiscuous, but restricted to "meaningful" relationships—unfortunately the meaning of "meaningful" was not defined, nor was the duration of the relationship specified; so a "slam-bam," so long as it was accompanied by "thank you, ma'am," might qualify. Since many neuroses, we were told, were caused by repression of our sexual urges, mental health would improve once sex was brought out into the open—out of the poolroom into the schoolroom.

Sexual experience before marriage ("You wouldn't buy a pair of shoes without trying them on, would you?") together with frank sexual discussions between spouses would improve marital adjustment. As we loosened the grip of "the heavy weight of the dead hand of the past" by getting rid of the archaic social and religious fetters that bound people to the institution of the family, the free association of egalitarian companionship would produce happier marriages.

Children would be had only if and when they were wanted.

The Reality: Promiscuity

A survey published in 1978 indicated that sexual activity among teen-age females increased by more than 30 percent between 1971 and 1976.[14] Despite an increase of more than 100 percent in the use of contraceptives, premarital pregnancies increased by more than 30 percent, and 45 percent of such pregnancies were terminated by abortion, compared to 33 percent five years earlier. While 50 percent of the 1971 teen-agers married after they became pregnant, by 1976, 67 percent chose abortion or illegitimate births rather than marriage.

United States Census figures—which are far from complete on such matters—indicate that illegitimate births increased from 89,500 in 1940 to 448,000 in 1975. Between 1950 and 1975 the percentage of all births which were illegitimate increased from 3.9 to 14.2, and the increase was greatest among teens; their rate going from 22.5 percent of all illegitimacies in 1950 to 41 percent of the total in 1975.

Since 74 percent of all legal abortions are performed on the unmarried, the increase in abortions (from 193,000 in 1970 to 1,115,000 in 1976) adds appreciably to the percentage of conceptions which take place outside the bonds of matrimony. In all of our larger cities more conceptions now take place outside of marriage than within it, and (as previously indicated) in Washington, D.C., both illegitimate births and abortions separately exceed the number of legitimate births. Put another way, two-thirds of the children conceived in our nation's capital are illegitimate. Most abortions as well as most illegitimate births occur to teen-agers who, on average, have had more exposure to sex education and other aspects of rationalistic-liberal sexual doctrines than older persons.

The promise that sex education would reduce the amount of illegitimacy is not at all borne out by fact; to the contrary, the climate of amoral opinion associated with such programs is accompanied by huge increases in promiscuity, illegitimacy, abortion, and venereal disease. Gonorrhea increased from 236,000 new cases reported in 1955 to more than a million reported in 1975, and since many cases of gonorrhea go unreported, it is estimated that the total number of cases of gonorrhea is now in excess of three million. To aggravate this epidemic, new strains of gonorrhea, stubbornly resistant to formerly effective treatment (penicillin) have now developed and are spreading.

As scientism strips romance as well as agape and caritas from Eros to reduce sexual attraction to lust, not only does promiscuity with its attendant illegitimacy, abortion, and venereal disease increase, but those sexual practices which were most severely condemned in the Judaeo-Christian code and throughout the history of Western civilization increase fastest. The stronger the taboo, the greater the magnitude of change.[15]

Ancillary evidence as well as numerous surveys indicate especially large increases in perverse forms of sex (oral-genital, masochism, sadism, homosexuality) in which satisfaction of sexual desire is sought through activities which are totally dissociated from the natural purpose of sex—reproduction. Most such practices are dissociated also from anatomical and muscular movements that are natural to sexual performance. It is no accident that the historically customary form—the now ridiculed "missionary position" (the man upstairs)—makes pragmatic sense while many of the currently popular forms make no more anatomical sense than trying to scratch your ear with your elbow.

An interesting recent development, plausible but as yet without sufficient verification to warrant credibility, is a decline in sexual desire. At the 1978 national convention of the American Association of Sex Educators, Counselors, and Therapists, it was reported that "a lack of [sexual] desire" seemed to be the prime problem with at least 50 percent of their patients. More and more this lack of sexual desire is found among young people, males and females in their twenties and thirties.[16]

Such a decline in sexual desire, if confirmed, might follow from the "realistic" approach used in sex education. When denuded of spiritual sentiment, romantic appeal, and its aura of mystery, sex becomes manipulation of those parts of human plumbing which are used for the excretion of wastes. Sewers may be essential, but they are not the stuff that dreams are made on.

The Reality: Marriages Down, Divorce Up

As is the case with many listings of figures, those for marriage rates are deceptive. At present our marriage rates are inflated because: (1) the exceptionally large number of babies born following World War II now constitutes a bulge in those age groups where the highest percentage of marriages occur, and (2) our divorce rate is extremely high. Since four out of five persons who are divorced remarry, this large number of divorces, in apparently paradoxical fashion, inflates the marriage rate. One reason why our current marriage rate will decline further in coming years is that the babies born from 1960 onward are comparatively few in number—many fewer than were born during the post-war baby boom—and will soon constitute a dent rather than a bulge in the age groups where the highest percentage of marriages occurs.

When we eliminate the inflationary factor of the remarriage of divorced persons and consider only the trend in the rate of first marriages, we see that these declined from the post-war peak of 143 marriages per 1,000 single women aged 14–44 to 112 by 1960, and went down to 99 in 1976.

Another indication of the decreasing desire to marry is found in the postponement of marriage. Between 1960 and 1977 the proportion of all women 20 to 24 years old who had never married increased by more than one-half: from 28 percent to 45 percent. Among men of the same age group, the percentage who had never married increased from 53 to 64 percent during the same period. Also indicative of increasing reluctance to marry, males in 1977 postponed getting married for a year longer than those who married in 1974.

Current estimates indicate that some two million men and women are now living together though not married (an 83 percent increase since 1970), a practice which was once called "living in sin" but would now likely be referred to as "demonstrating the emancipation of their personalities."

As we are increasingly influenced by the rationalistic liberal conception of sex, love, and marriage, these acids of modernity dissolve more and more marriages, and do it ever more quickly. The 393,000 divorces of 1960 increased to 708,000 by 1970 and to 1,077,000 in 1976, while the rate (per 1,000 population) of divorce went from 2.2 to 5.0, more than doubling in the decade 1965–1975. This increase of more than 100 percent was almost three times as large as the 34 percent increase from 1960 to 1970. As with all of the factors associated with the decline of the family institution—promiscuity, illegitimacy, abortion, "shacking-up," and avoiding marriage—divorces are most common among younger people; those whose generation was the first to grow up in this rationalistic climate of opinion. Most of the increase in divorce has been among younger couples, with their divorce experience far exceeding that of older adults when they were of a comparable age. If present trends are to continue, some 40 percent of the marriages now being formed will end in divorce.

In addition to increases in divorce, marital separations are increasing, with the increase again being greatest among younger couples. In addition to an increase from 5.0 percent divorced in 1970 to 8.8 percent in 1976, separations increased during the same period from 3.8 percent to 5.1 percent. Among the youngest group, those aged 25–34, the percentage of marriages broken by either separation or divorce jumped from less than 9 percent in 1970 to 14 percent in 1976. Among blacks 25–34 who had ever been married, 34 percent of the marriages had been broken by either divorce (13.4 percent) or separation (21.0 percent) in 1976.

No More Problems Because No More People

In 1960 there were 4,307,000 births in the United States and 1,708,000 deaths to give us a natural increase of 2,599,000 persons. By 1976 the number of births had decreased to 3,163,000 while deaths increased to 1,914,000 to reduce our increase in population to 1,249,000—less than half the increase of 1960. During this same interval, the birthrate (number of births per 1,000 people) declined from 24.1 to 14.7, and the rate of natural increase dropped from 14.4 in 1960 to 5.8 in 1976. Our rate of natural increase in 1976 was the lowest in our history, lower even than the 7.5 it had been in 1935 when the depression-induced downward fluctuation prompted "scientific" population experts (demographers) to predict that the population of the United States would never be more than 143,000,000 (it was 218,000,000 in 1978), and that this peak of 143,000,000 would be reached in 1955, after which our population would forever decline.

To those who are unaware that demographic forecasts are not scientific and that ideology is a significant influence in making them, it must seem strange that such dire predictions were made in 1935 while even lower rates today not only fail to elicit warnings of impending population decline but are interpreted as a favorable development. A reason for these quite opposite reactions to what is ostensibly the same phenomenon (the current one, in fact, is a more ominous portent for our future) is that the earlier decline could be blamed on failure of the capitalist economic system—a favorite subject of liberal criticism—while the current decline is portrayed in the most favorable way possible because it is associated with practices which accord with liberal doctrine.

This optimistic interpretation of population trends is still fostered even though the intrinsic rate of natural increase—the rate at which the population will grow (or decline) if birthrates at specific ages remain unchanged—has, since 1972, consistently indicated that our population will decline in the future. These data provide much more substantial evidence of a future decline than did the 1935 data.

The intrinsic rate of natural increase/decrease is based on an assumption that birthrates at specific ages will remain the same in the future as they are today, but in fact birthrates—especially the birthrates of younger people—have been declining rapidly, are now declining rapidly, and will almost certainly continue to decline rapidly in the future. Therefore, absolute declines in our population will likely be even more drastic than current projections indicate.

Among younger married women (aged 20–24), those who remained childless increased from 24 percent in 1960 to 43 percent in 1977, while childlessness among married women aged 25–29 increased from 13 to 22 percent, but there were no such increases in choosing to remain childless among older married women. The most drastic decline in the birthrate, together with the greatest increases in promiscuity and abortion, is among

384

younger people, those brought up in a climate of opinion dominated by rationalistic liberal doctrine. This sharp increase in refusal to accept the responsibility for bearing and rearing children among younger people will, if it continues, bring about a population decline earlier and more drastic than is now generally anticipated.

Education, the principal source of the climate of opinion, is also a significant factor in reducing the birthrate: As the number of years of education increases, the number of births decreases. Each 1,000 women between the ages of 35–44 in 1976 who had less than an eighth-grade education had borne 3,496 children, while each 1,000 women who were college graduates had borne only 2,217. Since pressures for people to remain in school at least through high school (at which level the sharp decline in willingness to bear children begins) continue to mount, this factor also will push birthrates downward in the future.

This decline, now slowed and obscured by the large percentage of people in the ages of highest reproductive potential (a result of the post-World War II temporary jump in births), will be accelerated as the much smaller number of children born from 1960 onward becomes the basis for our future population.

The Fifth Horseman

The likelihood of a decreasing population joins with the strange prospect of a society which proclaims its progress while renouncing its will to survive to constitute the design for our future.

Our present circumstances are not at all the same as those of the thirties when the conviction of liberals that private enterprise would be forever unable to cope without federalized economic planning persuaded population experts that individual decisions would never enable Americans to reproduce themselves without social planning. Such bias led them to ignore many basic demographic factors while projecting a temporary downward fluctuation in the birthrate into a portent of population decline in the near future—withal, having the gall to imply that their projection was a scientific prediction.

Nor are the present circumstances the same as those of

post-World War II when a temporary upward fluctuation in birthrates led the clones of the earlier population experts to predict a population explosion so vast that unless we restricted parents to no more than one child we would soon have so many people that everyone would starve.

If we feel any responsibility for perpetuating the rights and privileges which we received in this society as an entailed inheritance, we must now include in our considerations of the future several factors which were not present in the 1935 population projections and which, irresponsibly, were ignored in the many projections of an impending "population explosion" that experts continued to forecast into the seventies. To understand the nature and significance of these new factors, a summary of the major factors which govern population trends will be helpful.

The rate of reproduction in the United States, as well as in all of the other countries of Western European civilization, has declined for more than a century. This trend, of course, is not a smooth downward slope. Fluctuations such as a sharper downturn in births during the thirties depression and the sudden (but expectable) upturn in births after World War II create valleys and peaks, as do fluctuations resulting from epidemics; but all of these are temporary and none has ever changed the basic nature of this long-term downward trend.

Most of our increase in population for more than a century has been brought about, not by any long-lasting upward trend in birthrates, but by declines in the death rate as it decreased even more sharply than the birthrate. In an apparent paradox, most of our growth in population took place as birthrates were declining, not rising. A flood of immigration to the United States, especially large between 1890 and the 1920s, also contributed substantially to population growth. Immigrants contributed to population growth not only directly, but indirectly also. Children in their large families were for a generation or two imbued with traditional principles of family life, principles which included the desirability of having many children of their own.

These major decreases in the death rate were brought about principally through control of the contagious diseases of infancy and childhood. Such deaths are now so few that no further substantial declines can be made. Our death rate has remained stable for several decades and any declines in the future will be small—miniscule compared with those of the past. Never again can we expect decreases in the death rate to contribute to any significant increase in population or even to compensate for declines in the rate of reproduction.

One of the Four Horsemen of the Apocalypse, Pestilence, no longer plagues us. Another, Death, has been reined in as tightly as he can be by mortal man. Whatever other harm is done by Horseman War, he has seldom inflicted any but passing damage on population trends. If the trend was upward before the war, the fatalities, postponed marriages, and delays in having babies which are associated with war are unlikely to cause any but a transient downward fluctuation followed by an upward fluctuation and then by resumption of the upward trend.

Changes in attitudes associated with war may, however, change the trend. After losing World War II, influenced by American ideas, the Japanese changed their attitudes about the family, began to practice abortion on a large scale, and slowed what had been a rapidly increasing population to a virtual standstill. Faced with a population decline that it pretends cannot happen, America already fantasizes that the third Horseman has galloped away into the mists of antiquity to return no more.

Famine, the fourth Horseman, has never ridden through our land to seriously affect the population. For several decades we have been capable of producing, without any difficulty, more than twice as much food as we can possibly consume. Food production is kept at a lower level and food prices are kept at a high level principally by federalized programs of acreage limitation and target (formerly parity) prices established by Congress.

Production of food in our past, however, did bear a significant relationship to the production of people. Throughout history the inhabitants of large cities have had low birthrates, and their lack of will to reproduce themselves would have been evident had it not been for large-scale migration of rural folk into the cities. In the overall trend of the population, the high rural birthrates of the past acted as a brake on the downward slide in reproduction. However, neither our current downward slide in reproduction nor those of the future will have their effects mitigated by high rural birthrates. In 1935, the 32,000,000 people who lived on farms constituted 25 percent of the total population of the United States, but by 1976 this number had decreased to

8,250,000 people—less than 4 percent of the total population.

The once rampaging beasts of the Four Horsemen of the Apocalypse—War, Famine, Pestilence, and Death—have temporarily been curbed. But we must now ask ourselves what we are to do about the rider whose course will intersect our path to the future. How can we rein the fifth horseman—our lack of will to survive?

How Rein the Pale Horse?

In our earlier conviction the institution of the family was the keystone of the entire social structure. The firmness of our allegiance to it was buttressed by authoritarian dictates of both Church and State, but the core of its effectiveness centered in convictions about the sanctity of marriage and the responsibility to bear children.

As the formal controls of both Church and State became less effective supports for high birthrates, for a time our rapidly declining death rates more than compensated for this decrease to assure continuing high rates of population increase.

The effectiveness of informal pressures, expressed through the reactions of relatives, lifelong friends, and neighbors, was diluted by the anonymity of urban living, in addition to which people who attended school into the college level—especially women—had their grasp of ageless verities sufficiently shaken by transient rationalistic doctrines to encourage them to concoct excuses not to have children. But declines in reproduction in such areas were more than compensated for by the temporary continuation of large-family traditions among immigrants and by in-migration from rural areas where beliefs in having large families also persisted.

Now all of these supporting factors—the formal reenforcement of Church and State; declines in the death rate; waves of immigrants from Europe and in-migrants from rural areas who were still imbued with traditional family convictions; informal spiritual feelings which lifted people into marriage and childbirth; romantic attraction which anesthetized people into them; and social pressures which prodded people into them—have lost their ability to compensate for or to slow our century-old declines in willingness to reproduce.

Most factors which have been associated with reproduction recently—increased anonymity of living; longer education (with especially large increases in the percentage of college-trained women) and, above all, the climate of rationalistic liberalism premised on identical sexes, marriages formed primarily to assist personality development, and hedonistic indoctrination of youths who are taught that they should bear children only when and if they feel it will enhance their personality—such factors now actively encourage further decline.

The romantic conception of the innate goodness of man, expressed through the sentiment of romantic love (which is premised on an assumption that when the deficiencies of one person are wedded to the deficiencies of another person a perfect blend will result) was an ineffective stopgap. Though aided by the considerable help of romantic movies, novels, and nasally sentimental crooners, the gossamer wings of romance were not strong enough to stay the downward trend.

The scientistic conception of man—that he is totally malleable and can be perfected by scientific formulas designed by savants—is expressed through rationalistic liberalism. Through its paradoxical combination of scientism and romanticism, liberalism transmuted malleable man into equal and equally malleable man-woman, and romantically assumed that unisex perfection would be attained through linkage in Companionship, Democratic, Egalitarian, Fifty-fifty Marriage. As prelude to such unisex linkage, sexual repressions were to be expunged through conditioning, called sex education. Since such "repressions" had been inflicted upon us through beliefs about sex which included its romantic, spiritual, religious, and societal connotations, their erasure not only reduced Eros to lust but blurred the relationship between sex and bearing children.

Thus far in our experience the expression of scientism which is conveyed through the rationalistic liberal conception of marriage and sex has been conducive to the further breakdown of the institution of the family instead of its improvement and has accelerated the downward trend in reproduction rather than slowing it.

It is easy to forgive romantics who foster Delusive Hope because their delusion of the innate goodness of man is elevated above the selfish level by their sentimental hope that two can be wed into higher perfection than one. It is not so easy to forgive scientistic authorities when these "scientists" ignore the very evidence on which their claims to expertise rest and use Orwellian techniques in their continuing attempts to control the minds of people.

I earlier described the manner in which Freudians promoted the Delusive Hope that science could free them from all sexual repressions and thereby make their lives happier, their marriages better adjusted, their children safe from neuroses. Later, Professor Kinsey convinced people that premarital sex was desirable for marital adjustment, and sociologists authoritatively claimed that adultery did not weaken marriage but strengthened it. At the same time that such unproved claims were touted as scientific truths, equal evidence which, however, did not fit into rationalistic doctrine—evidence that females derive more pleasure from masturbation than from any other form of sexual outlet—was ignored or minimized. A disturbing implication of this finding is that sex alone cannot hold people together for any appreciable time. Human couples will remain together and reproduce themselves only if sexual desire is supplemented by social pressures or spiritual uplift.

In 1945, in an early example of Orwell's Reversal, a prominent sociologist titled his textbook, *The Family, From Institution to Companionship,* proclaiming in it that sociologists had proved the family to be obsolete and should be abandoned, to be replaced by companionship marriage because the primary purpose of marriage is companionship. He argued that the increasing number of divorces was a good thing because a higher divorce rate proved that the family was abandoning its outmoded traditional values and being remolded around new and better values of equality and companionship.

Even as late as 1976, when postponement of marriage, decreasing percentages of people getting married, and mountainous increases in desertion, divorce, and shacking-up were occurring, an analyst for the United States Bureau of the Census contended that these trends were desirable; that postponement of marriage, refusal to marry, and increasing rates of divorce merely showed that Americans were "being more careful about selecting mates," and therefore "marriages of the future may be more stable than they are now."[17] He implied that scientific studies supported his contention that such factors ". . . should make marriage more viable with more of a chance for success."

All through the sixties and into the seventies, long after the transitory nature of the post-World War II upward fluctuation in births was evident and the long-term downward trend had inexorably reasserted itself, a gaggle of experts "predicted" in media ranging from *Science* to *Esquire* that our population would explode into 250,000,000 by 1975 (it was only 212,700,000); would be 344,000,000 within twenty-one years from now (it will likely be almost 100,000,000 less); and will be 400,000,000 sixty years from now. They claimed that mathematical computations proved there would be at least 1,000,000,000 people in the United States by the twenty-second century.

Just as the rate of population increase was about to resume its long-term decline, the Director of the Population Reference Bureau, Inc., foredoomed that "Our rate of population increase has a disaster potential greater than a nuclear bomb. The only difference is, the fuse is a little longer."*[18]

As late as 1969, an article by a professor of economics in the prestigious journal *Science* warned us that Malthus' fears were about to be "irremediably confirmed,"[19] thereby demonstrating that he did not understand Malthus, was ignorant of our capacity to produce food, and had no comprehension of long-term population trends.

In 1964, the fuse on his nuclear population bomb still burning, Robert C. Cook, president of the Population Reference Bureau, increased its megatonnage to 300,000,000 by year 2000, warning of holocaust unless "Every Tom, Dick and Harry [is taught] the elements of human arithmetic, which many people don't know or won't recognize." (Tom, Dick, and Harry; meet Robert, a new classmate).

In 1967 a Yale University demographer dogmatized that no one had the right to have more than two or three children, because the population explosion (how they loved this inapt expression, together with references to long fuses on nuclear bombs!) threatened "personal freedoms and pleasures."[20] He

*If nuclear bombs had long fuses—which they don't—this one would be not only longer, but wetter.

concluded his exhortation by urging that "contraceptives be readily available to anyone." He was the main speaker at a symposium sponsored by a manufacturer of birth control pills.

Loudest of the quackers was Dr. Paul R. Ehrlich, population expert and director of graduate biology programs at Stanford University, who contended in October of 1969 that the science of ecology proved that an "ecocatastrophe" (an ecocatastrophe is something like what happens when the long fuse on the nuclear people-bomb produces a population explosion) would occur unless everyone limited his family to one child.[21] In November[22] our indefatigable ecocatastrophe forestaller foresaw a time when the United States Government ". . . might have to put sterility drugs in reservoirs and in food shipped to foreign countries."[22] He also recommended that the population of the United States be quickly reduced—he didn't say how—to 150,000,000 people.

Also in 1969, a group of professional population scientists meeting in Aspen, Colorado, criticized President Nixon because he had said that governmental efforts to limit population should not interfere with either religious or personal convictions.[23] These "scientists" said that such efforts to respect the convictions of people constituted "insanity." Whereas in 1964 such experts recommended reducing the number of children to two or three per family, in a few years they were recommending no more than one, and this group recommended zero births by 1976. This goal could be approached, if not attained, by indoctrinating children.

> We have to take children in their earliest years and start implanting some different ideas about the good-life simply constituting getting married and multipying. We have to tell them what a good time the unmarrieds are having.

Two Yale sociologists, testifying before a Congressional Committee on Natural Resources in 1969, said that the present "pervasive emphasis . . . on marriage as the only 'normal' adult status and on childbearing as a lifetime career for women" should be abandoned.[24]

Even twenty years after the sharp but short-lived increase in the birthrate had ceased and the century-old downward trend had resumed at an accelerated rate, zealous experts ignored such obvious realities and proclaimed an exceeding minor upward fluctuation in 1977 as a re-lighting of the fuse on the nuclear population bomb. Demographers siezed upon this petty incident to reaffirm their predictions of an upturn in fertility and to reassert their contention that we must further reduce the birthrate.[25]

As experts they must have known that such fluctuations are always occuring, and should not be interpreted as trends, especially when they are tiny and short-lived—the one they proclaimed as a new trend lasted only a few months, and was easily explainable.

Since the post-World War II upsurge in births began in 1947, by 1977 those included in it were entering their thirtieth year. After the age of thirty, first births entail greater risk for the mother, so likely much of the increase in late 1977 and early 1978 was due to "last chance" births. Similar fluctuations will also occur in the future, and it is the responsibility of demographers to explain, in the absence of good and lasting evidence to the contrary, that they are merely fluctuations, not trends.

It is true that none of these experts went so far in their recommendations to reduce the population as did Jonathan Swift in *A Modest Proposal for Preventing the Children of Poor People in Ireland from Being a Burden to Their Parents or Country, and for Making Them Beneficial to the Public.*

In 1729 Swift parodied "the then familiar benevolent humanitarian [forerunner of the modern sociologist, social worker, economic planner] concerned to correct a social evil by means of a theoretically conceived plan."[26] As you may know, Swift's "modest proposal" for solving the problem of excess Irish children was to sell them to absentee English landlords to be fattened and eaten. Not all children, mind you; only those who were not wanted. This practice, Swift assured his readers, would advance trade, provide funds to raise the remaining infants—if any —and relieve poverty while yet giving pleasure to the rich. Put into practice today, it would save all the money now spent on contraceptives and abortions and eliminate the costs of programs of sex education. In time it would drastically reduce teenage unemployment, vandalism, and criminality. Only culturally conditioned values would impede acceptance of this eminently rational, elegantly simple solution for unwanted children.

Snail Darters, Furbish Lousewords and . . . Oh, Yes! People

Sociological-demographic-ecological-biological-economic "scientific" experts who insist that we use increasingly extreme methods to accelerate our prospective population decline would not, I am quite sure, recommend Jonathan Swift's cannibalism to reduce our population. Nor do I believe that these much-educated, admittedly humanitarian experts would actually implement the proposals of some of their more ardent colleagues and put sterility chemicals into the drinking water and food of people who have more than the approved number of children.

But the authoritarian pronouncements about population growth made by such experts are not verified scientific conclusions; they often conflict with demonstrable facts; they usually ignore historical trends; and they are wrong, drastically wrong, more often than they are right. Nor, of course, do projections such as mine constitute scientific prediction. With both rationalistic liberals and philosophic conservatives all statements made in the future tense are fallible, involving judgments which are strongly influenced by the values of those who make them. Rationalistic liberals are often able to convince themselves that their judgments are value-free, objective, and scientific, while conservatives may obdurately cling to irrelevant conventions of the past, convinced that they are adhering to immutable natural law.

My conservative bias obviously influences my belief that liberal rationalism, which so often is detached from pragmatic realism, probably would not lead to Swiftian solutions but might possibly involve rather strange priorities among values.

Professor Paul Ehrlich, whose book on the dangers of the "population explosion" was a best-seller and who successively insisted that no one should have more than three children, then two, then one, prior to suggesting that sterility chemicals be injected into drinking water and food, joined forces with those people who are active in preserving endangered species. Such people are often referred to as ecological scientists though their activities bear no relation to scientific procedure, and some of the species which they insist on preserving have an ecological relation to mankind only in the same farfetched manner that an acorn dropping on one's head proves that the sky is falling. This alliance between these two groups of rationalists—the advocates of population decline and the aggressive guarantors of the contained existence of endangered species—gave rise to a juxtaposition of value judgments which occurred within a few days of each other in 1978.

The Supreme Court of the United States decreed that, though it would cost millions of dollars and would do economic harm to many people, construction work on a major dam must cease because a three-inch fish called the snail darter might be threatened. Despite this ruling which, in ways I cannot understand, somehow must have preserved the Constitution as well as the snail darter, it was felt that construction on another huge dam (similarly involving millions of dollars and affecting the lives of many people) might possibly be permitted to proceed provided measures were taken which absolutely guaranteed that it would not threaten 512 furbish louseworts. During the same session, the Court permitted the Federal government to continue to subsidize (and thereby encourage) human abortions.

Granted that members of both groups believe themselves to be foresighted as well as humane; granted that those ecological "scientists" can spin thin threads of rationalism to make sympathizers believe that in some manner unfathomable to common folk the great chain of being links both the snail darter and the furbish lousewort significantly to our lives. Granted also that advocates of population decline can make charts of exponential population growth that soar into the stratosphere. Granted these things, is it unreasonable to ask: Where is the hard evidence? Why not tincture abstract idealism with a touch of pragmatic realism? Why not, in sum, use prudent judgment about such issues?

There are some 20,000 species of bees, an additional 14,000 species of ants, 15,000 species of wasps, and more than 2,000 species of termites. If all forms of life—plant as well as animal, micro-organisms as well as macro-organisms—are included, millions of species of organisms exist. New species are constantly evolving while others become extinct. Should we guarantee that all species exist forever? Why? At what cost? Since other citizens must undergo hardship and are compelled to pay the costs of indulging the whims of these rationalistic ecologists, they should be reminded that in ecosystems there are ". . . ectoparasites, meaning that they spend much of their time riding on the backs of their hosts."[27]

Isn't there some confusion about values when a society taxes its citizens to protect snail darters and furbish louseworts while also taxing people so human organisms can be destroyed?

If this downward trend in reproduction not only continues but accelerates, it will be very difficult to slow and perhaps impossible to stop. It was easy to accelerate because liberal rationalistic doctrine appeals to the baser urges of man—his lusts and selfishness. Romanticism having been unable to stop it and rationalism speeding rather than slowing the decline, the possibility remains that conservatism might be effective. But not if the precedent of other countries is followed and we attempt it by a combination of economic conservatism and traditionalist conservatism rather than philosophic conservatism.

Many of the countries of Western European heritage have tried to halt their declining reproductive rate; all used essentially the same technique; all failed. With the exception of Nazi Germany and the USSR, all have relied upon economic bribes to curb the decline. Sweden, though not a combatant in either World War, and a prosperous country, nevertheless was confronted with declining birthrates which it attempted to buoy with: annual allowances for all children under sixteen, no matter how high the parent's income; marriage loans; free prenatal care, hospitalization, delivery and postnatal care; free nurseries for mothers who work; free school lunches; job preference for parents; and rental rebates. Taxes increased very much but the birthrate didn't. Similar programs tried in Belgium, France, and England similarly failed. Fascist Italy tried to combine patriotism with economic incentives without success, but Nazi Germany, using a similar combination, did increase its birth-rate temporarily.

Despite patriotic appeals which include medals and the title of "Mother Heroine" to women who have ten children, in addition to cash awards on the birth of the third child, the Soviet birthrate dropped from 24.9 in 1960 to 18 in 1976. And despite sex education and readily available abortion clinics, illegitimacy is increasing, as is divorce, though marriage counselors are readily available and free. The number of divorces increased from 67,000 in 1950 to 270,000 in 1960 and 861,000 in 1976 (with a smaller population, we had 1,077,000 divorces in 1976). As did the Nazis, the Soviets now openly encourage illegitimacy to bolster the declining birthrate, which would be even lower if the USSR did not include in its population so many rural people.

In most of the Western European countries—Sweden, England, France, Belgium—and the United States with its estimated eight million illegal aliens, heavy immigration now obscures the extent of the decline.

Equitable Complementarity

The husband, sovereign household head, is owed such duty
as a subject owes a prince. Wives who try to boss their liege
will learn that they, unable worms, have lances which are
as straws, and weakness past compare.

I suspect that Katherine was winking gleefully at her sisters as she pulled Petruchio's leg by this pretended subservience and ere long would use her native wiles to make him wish he had never tried to boss her—especially in front of other people.

This paraphrase from *The Taming of the Shrew* is the impression which is often fostered about husband-wife roles in the traditional patriarchal family, and it is true that in religion, law, and custom, women had distinctively different and often secondary if not subservient roles compared to men; but as with most things, we tend to envision the patriarchal past as clear-cut stereotypes which, however, as long as 150 years ago actually were beginning to blur. In 1835 the perceptive observer Alexis de Tocqueville complained that efforts to treat the sexes equally were threatening the social structure.

There are people in Europe who, confounding together
the different characteristics of the sexes, would make man
and woman into beings not only equal but alike. They would

397

give to both the same functions, impose on both the same duties, and grant to both the same rights; they would mix them in all things—their occupations, their pleasures, their business. It may readily be conceived that by thus attempting to make one sex equal to the other, both are degraded, and from so preposterous a medley of the works of nature nothing could ever result but weak men and disorderly women.[28]

Since relations between the sexes based on the romantic conception of man lack sufficient durability to perpetuate the society, and the hedonism promoted by rationalistic liberalism so weakens our will to survive that even extravagant bribes fail to restore it, one is tempted to advise that the twain again be met in the only relationship which assured the continuance of society —the traditional family.

But efforts to restore the traditional family would encounter serious, perhaps insurmountable difficulties, especially in those attempts to reinstitute earlier role-relationships. In the patriarchal family the husband's authority was superior to the wife's, and warrant for his authority was deeply embedded in custom, fortified by religious doctrine as well as clerical decree, and codified into law.

A way of life in which the husband provided for the family's material needs, either directly by hunting, fishing, or farming, or indirectly by hard manual labor in mine or factory while the weaker wife, as helpmate, kept the house and tended the children, also contributed to sharply defined male-female roles which both accepted as God's will and nature's way.

Woman, the weaker vessel, was bound by codes of sexual behavior more rigid and more restrictive than those of man. The sniggering clubhouse jokes about a son who sowed his wild oats contrasted sharply with the wrath of God visiting eternal damnation upon the girl and everlasting disgrace upon the family whose daughter sinned by shamelessly submitting to the lusts of the flesh.

> . . . women [should] adorn themselves in modest apparel, with shamefacedness and sobriety; not with plaited hair, or gold, or pearls or costly array; . . . but with good works

while they "learn in silence, with all subjection," nor usurp authority over the man.

For Adam, the first formed, was not deceived ". . . but the woman being deceived was in the transgression."

Notwithstanding, she shall be saved in childbearing, if they continue in faith and charity and holiness with sobriety. [I Timothy, 2].

"The husband is to the wife as Christ is to the Church. While man has Christ for his Head, woman's head is man." (I Corinthians, 11)

With such distinctively different, clearly delineated roles established for husband and wife, romantic love was not needed to begin the marriage nor to perpetuate it, though affection might develop in the form of an earned equitable respect. It would have been absurd to suppose that mutual interests could bind such disparate natures together in companionship.

Now, however, the reverence which once moved people to respect biblical doctrine and to conform to dictates of the Church has been replaced by secularism; once potent social pressures to marry and, once married, to bear and rear children, have been neutralized if not reversed by hedonism; and scientistic unisex indoctrination has virtually obliterated the once distinct boundaries of husband-wife roles. No more is the hunter home from the hill* and the fisherman home from the sea. Mechanized farming is now a corporate business, and machines do most of the heavy labor in mines and factories. Most jobs can now be performed by women as well as by men, and of the 37,800,000 women in the labor force in 1976, 23,400,000 were women who had been married. Ever-married women who are gainfully employed increased from 32 percent in 1960 to 46 percent in 1976, and among younger married women (aged 20–24), the percentage rose from 32 in 1960 to 57 in 1976. In a majority of today's marriages the roles of husband as provider and wife as helpmate no longer exist; families in which the husband has been the sole provider are rare (only seven out of every hundred), and—except for a few sects—the patriarchal family has become an endangered species.

*With apologies to Robert Louis Stevenson.

Attempts to restore the traditional family with its patriarchal roles, whether they be motivated by nostalgia or fortified by academic persuasion (as is found in Steven Goldberg's creditable endeavor, *The Inevitability of Patriarchy*[29]), are not likely to succeed.

No matter how drastic the need to restore our weakened will to survive, efforts to reconstruct the core of the traditional family, the patriarchal role-relationship, would conflict not only with our rationalistic rejection of biological, historical, and religious precepts and the hedonistic climate of sexual opinion but also with the reality of drastically revised occupational requirements. In addition, we now realize that many of the restrictions on females were unrealistic as well as inequitable.

Beliefs that females lacked the innate capacity for higher education, for public and clerical office, and for professional careers were often based on male self-interest. Conventionality as well as morality rigidified the double standard for sexual behavior. Such considerations make changes in role-relationships sensible as well as equitable. But we need also be aware that such changes (as with all else in life) can be overdone, and if carried to extremes they could convert a cliché into a truism as we throw out the baby as well as the bath water.

Though modification was needed, it is paradoxical that much of the agitation for women's liberation seems to be premised on an assumption that men will adopt the very characteristics which women insist upon discarding: an interest in the home, a nurturing attitude toward children, tenderness, passivity, and delicacy.[30] Some examples of this role-reversal have occurred, but if King Arthur's contention that the thing which "all women crave, and what they most desire" is to "have their will" be true,[31] we may find that as we reject patriarchy we select matriarchy.

The Equal Rights Amendment to the Constitution, like most efforts to change basic factors by passing a law, will, if passed, probably be only a secondary and certainly a negative influence on our survival. Men and women have long had complete equality under the Constitution of the USSR, but this decree has only shifted the bases for job opportunity and status evaluation from sexual criteria to political favoritism. Women comrades now have the right to work eight hours outside the home in addition to doing most of the housework and caring for the children. Understandably, under such circumstances, divorce rates skyrocket and birthrates plummet.

Attempts to return to the traditional family as the basis for restoration of our will to survive would be the focus of traditionalist conservative concern. Philosophic conservatives would hold that while such attempts might reduce the rate of reproductive decline to a slower pace than the frantic one now urged upon us by rationalistic liberalism, another aspect of the condition should receive consideration.

Stressing equity between the sexes rather than equality, and emphasizing the enhancement of sexual differences rather than their diminishment through unisex, philosophic conservatives would view the current situation as a crucial and perhaps final test of our willingness to act on the basis of conscious moral choice—with the burden of such choice resting most heavily upon women.

For the first time in history, unsheltered by the miracle, mystery, and authority of the Church, unpersuaded by convention, uncoerced by social pressures, and uncompelled by the dictates of law, women can consciously control the ultimate issue of secular morality—whether we perpetuate ourselves as a society or rationalize ourselves into extinction.

Chapter 14. References and Notes

1. Robert Graves, *The Greek Myths* (Baltimore: Penguin, 1955), vol. 1, p. 145.

2. Edith Hamilton, *Mythology* (New York: Mentor, 1940), pp. 101–116.

3. Dante, *The Divine Comedy, I: Hell*, trans. Dorothy L. Sayers (Baltimore: Penguin, 1949), pp. 67, 68.

4. *The Norton Anthology of English Literature*, rev. ed. (New York: W.W. Norton, 1968), vol. 2, p. 1405.

5. John P. Marquand, *Sincerely, Willis Wayde* (Boston: Little, Brown, 1955), pp. 350–361.

6. Margaret Mead, *Sex and Temperament in Three Primitive Societies* (New York: Harper and Row, 1935).

7. Franz Boas, *Anthropology and Modern Life* (New York: W.W. Norton, 1928), p. 227.

8. Margaret Mead, *Blackberry Winter: My Earlier Years* (New York: William Morrow, 1972), pp. 214–215.

9. Shirley Lindenbaum, "Reconsiderations," *Human Nature*, May 1978, p. 95.

10. Stefan Kanfer, "Sispeak: A Misguided Attempt to Change Herstory," *Time*, October 23, 1972.

11. Laurie Johnston, "The 'Sister Chapel': A Feminist View of Creation," *New York Times*, January 22, 1978.

12. Albert H. Hobbs, *Seek for Sex Education and You*

Shall Find (New Rochelle, N.Y.: America's Future, 1972). A pamphlet.

13. Wayne King, "Teen-Agers on Sex: Confusion Is Clear," *New York Times*, June 21, 1978.

14. Jane E. Brody, " '76 Survey Finds Teen-Age Pregnancy Up 33% in 5 Years," *New York Times*, January 31, 1978.

15. For example, see: Morton Hunt, *Sexual Behavior in the 1970s* (Chicago: Playboy Press, 1974) or Anthony Pietropinto and Jacqueline Simenauer, *Beyond the Male Myth* (New York: Times Books, 1977).

16. Georgia Dullea, "A Lack of Sexual Desire Emerges As a Contemporary Condition," *New York Times*, May 1, 1978.

17. Ann Blackman, "Don't Write the Obituary for Marriage," *Philadelphia Evening Bulletin*, January 12, 1976.

18. Robert O'Brien, "The Predictable Peril of the American Birth Bomb," *Esquire*, September 1960.

19. Joseph J. Spengler, "Population Problem: In Search of a Solution," *Science*, December 12, 1969.

20. William Borders, "Physicians Chided on Child Bearing," *New York Times*, April 7, 1967.

21. Gary Brooten, "Birth Control Advocate Urges One Child Per Family," *Philadelphia Evening Bulletin*, October 2, 1969.

22. Gladwin Hill, "A Sterility Drug In Food Is Hinted," *New York Times*, November 25, 1969.

23. Gladwin Hill, "Scientists Tell Nixon Adviser Voluntary Birth Control Is Insanity," *New York Times*, September 22, 1969.

24. Luther J. Carter, "The Population Crisis: Rising Concern at Home," *Science*, November 7, 1969.

25. Robert Reinhold, "New Data Show Birth Rate Down, Undercutting Talk of Baby Boom," *New York Times*, June 1, 1978.

26. *The Norton Anthology of English Literature*, vol. 1, p. 1640.

27. Edward O. Wilson, *Sociobiology* (Cambridge, Mass.: Harvard University Press, 1975), p. 373.

28. Alexis de Tocqueville, *Democracy in America* (New York: Vintage Books, 1959), vol. 2, p. 222.

29. Steven Goldberg, *The Inevitability of Patriarchy* (New York: William Morrow, 1973).

30. George F. Gilder, *Sexual Suicide* (New York: New York Times Book Co., 1973).

31. Thomas Bulfinch, *The Age of Chivalry* (New York: David McKay, 1900), p. 65.

Chapter 15

What Manner of Man?

HE SHOULD HAVE been smiling. His eyes should have glowed softly and warmly, perhaps misting a bit at the honor they had bestowed upon him. His mien should have been deferential as he humbly expressed his gratitude to his hosts, and to the land of the free and the home of the brave, the society which had granted him asylum from his persecutors, giving him freedom to express without let or stint his genius for critical analysis.

He should have praised his listeners for their progressiveness in proclaiming more and more rights for ever more people, for codifying such rights into law and providing state-imposed penalties upon those who failed to promote such dictated equality. Had he done this, as he should have, they would have swelled with self-satisfaction at this contrast to the situation of the comrades he had left behind in his regimented homeland.

He should have applauded his audience for having a President who spoke with admitted candor and courage in favor of civil rights in the USSR and who reacted to flagrant violations by restricting visits to that country of several minor bureaucrats.

He should have eulogized those militant ideological former students of this proud university, whose protests contributed toward ending the war in Vietnam.

This former artillery captain should have saluted the society which leads the march toward a peaceful future for united mankind by making so many concessions to reach détente with the USSR, by "normalizing" relations with the People's Republic of China, and by counting among our "most favored nations" more and more Communist countries.

His smile turned wry, he would have heard appreciative chuckles from his urbane audience as he quipped that we had supplanted bad foreign wars with good domestic combat as we fought fierce wars against poverty, launched assaults on unemployment, and sent task forces to mop up slums. All of these tactical exercises being part of the grand strategy which would vanquish those redoubtable bastions of private enterprise from which deviants (murderers, muggers, rapists) sortied to attack the citizenry.

Having been persecuted because of his writing, above all else he should have expressed his awe-struck appreciation for the freedom our press enjoys. He should have lauded the crusading zeal of the reporters whose incessant headlining of a single instance of breaking and entering encouraged Congress to smash The Imperial Presidency.

Perhaps he should have said such things because, until recently, they were what commencement speakers were supposed to say. Now, however, speakers at university commencements are often emissaries from Federal University, come not to praise the minions of their subordinate institutions but to instruct them that standards can best be raised by lowering requirements and fairness attained only by preferential treatment. But he didn't say what he was supposed to.

Aleksandr I. Solzhenitsyn, with tight-lipped seriousness, focused his penetrating gaze upon his Harvard audience, and he said that their most striking feature was their lack of courage.

He told them that the diplomatic détente which they pursued so abjectly was no assurance of peace and that the concessions they made to attain it would lead to betrayal. Moral courage is necessary to fight Communism.

He told them that lack of moral courage rather than an idealistic yearning for peace made us guilty of complicity as our abandonment of responsibilities in Vietnam contributed to the suffering of 30,000,000 people.

He disagreed with the belief that legal rights guarantee

either justice or equity, knowing, as did millions of others who were incarcerated in the Gulag Archipelago because of political dissidence, that the constitution of the USSR legalizes rights by the bushelful. Again, the issue is morality, not legality.

Instead of praising our efforts to eliminate social ills through the socio-political programs which constitute the New Morality he indicated that such attempts are based on an erroneous conception of man, "a humanistic and benevolent concept according to which there is no evil inherent to human nature; the world belongs to mankind, and all the defects of life are caused by wrong social systems which must be corrected."

People of the slack and pusillanimous West, he indicated, should impose more restraints on their behavior rather than seek increased license; they should spend more effort in fulfilling their obligations and less in demanding unearned rights.

Instead of expressing admiration for our free and fearless press, he charged it with inaccuracy, guesswork, rumors, suppositions, immaturity, superficiality, sensationalism, and misleading judgment. Though there is no censorship, the press, he indicated, is not independent. Too often, in both pressroom and classroom, only the current fashion—what I have referred to as the climate of rationalistic liberal opinion—is printed or heard.

He did not refer to Watergate at Harvard, but in 1973, while accusing Western liberals of dual standards of morality in their quick readiness to denounce oppression in rightest countries but reluctance to criticize the Soviet Union, he contended that similar hypocrisy existed in domestic affairs as well, saying that he was "amazed at the hypocritical, clamorous rage displayed by the Democrats" over the Watergate affair.[1]

Bless You, Prison!

A report issued by Tass, Soviet press agency, on February 13, 1974, stated:

> By the decree of the presidium of the USSR Supreme Soviet, A. I. Solzhenitsyn has been stripped of citizenship of the USSR for performing systematically actions that are incompatible with being a citizen of the USSR and detrimen-

tal to the Union of Soviet Socialist Republics and was expelled from the Soviet Union on February 13, 1974.

Solzhenitsyn's family can join him when they deem it necessary. Item ends. . . .

The item ended, but Solzhenitsyn's pointed criticism of the manner in which the State stifles the human spirit did not. He dreaded to leave, partly because he felt that any writer whose roots are pulled out of his native soil soon dries up, and, simply, because he loved Russia. In 1970 his fear of being prevented from returning to his native Russia dissuaded him from going to Stockholm to receive in person his Nobel Prize for Literature.

Born in Kislovodsk in 1918, Aleksandr Isayevich Solzhenitsyn, his father having been killed on the German front prior to his birth, was brought up in Rostov by his mother.[2] Writing was part of his nature, but repeated rejection of his manuscripts discouraged him from pursuing it as a career and he studied mathematics at Rostov University. While in command of an artillery spotting company in East Prussia in 1945 he was arrested, accused of having made "disrespectful remarks about Stalin" in correspondence with a friend. He was sentenced to eight years in a detention camp.

In various detention camps he worked as a miner, bricklayer, and foundryman, all the while composing fictional as well as factual accounts of his thoughts and experiences, mostly by committing ideas and facts to memory. All this he did despite suffering from cancer.

After he served his eight-year sentence, he was exiled for life to southern Kazakhstan. Upon Stalin's death in 1953 some restraints on his freedom were reduced but his health deteriorated so badly that he was soon sent to a cancer clinic, an experience which provided the theme for *The Cancer Ward.*

His citizenship was restored in 1956 and in 1962 Nikita S. Khrushchev permitted publication of his description of conditions in a camp for political prisoners titled *One Day in the Life of Ivan Denisovich.* His nomination for the Lenin Prize for literature was rejected because he failed to distinguish between "honorable and good people" and "criminals and traitors."

Since they could not be printed in the USSR, Solzhenitsyn's works were smuggled out and published, first in Europe, then in the United States. Harassment by Soviet officials became more frequent and more intense, though he appealed to the State for surcease and protested to the National Congress of Soviet Writers. His home was under constant surveillance, his friends were shadowed, his wife was dismissed from her job, and he was barred from residence in Moscow before he was expelled from the USSR.

Solzhenitsyn's conviction that earned inner freedom is the essential goal of human development—an inner freedom which (as he describes so clearly in *The First Circle*[3]) cannot be taken away by imprisonment, forced labor, torture, or harassment— is the distillate of his experience.

> . . . it was only when I lay there on the rotting prison straw that I sensed within myself the first stirrings of good. Gradually it was disclosed to me that the line separating good and evil passes . . . through every human heart—and through all human hearts . . . even within hearts overwhelmed by evil, one small bridgehead of good is retained. And even in the best of all hearts there remains . . . an uprooted small corner of evil.
>
> *It is impossible to expel evil from the world in its entirety, but it is possible to constrict it within each person.*[4] [my emphasis]
>
> "Know thyself!" There is nothing that so aids and assists the awakening of omniscience [conscience?] within us as insistent thoughts about one's own transgressions, errors, mistakes.
>
> . . . And that is why I turn back to the years of my imprisonment and say, sometimes to the astonishment of those about me: *"Bless you, prison!"*

Our Ugly Cousin, Communist Man

Those who listened to Solzhenitsyn at Harvard readily understood and totally agreed with the central theme of most of his writing—his denunciation of the suppression of dissent in the USSR. But they were shocked and bewildered to learn that this fiercely independent man also criticized us—the dwellers in the land of the free and the home of the brave—as being unfree and pusillanimous. Many of them recovered from their shock when *The Washington Post* assured them that Solzhenitsyn's Harvard address was simply based on a misunderstanding of Western society. Perhaps this is so; perhaps Solzhenitsyn does misunderstand Western society, but I take it to be at least equally conceivable that the editorialist of *The Washington Post* did not understand Aleksandr I. Solzhenitsyn.

Most Americans of 1978 were sure that the Soviet conception of man which Solzhenitsyn criticized so stubbornly and so bravely was so diametrically opposite to our beliefs that his admirers gloried in sharing his repugnance. To hear his assertions that the Western conception of man was also—to a lesser degree, but with similar motivation—degrading was, indeed, hurtful.

The Soviet conception of man is not the same as that held by rationalistic liberals of the West, but it is not totally opposite, either. Soviet man is a gross caricature of man as he is conceived in the New Morality of rationalistic liberalism. He is not the twin, but he is an ugly cousin. Now shunned in his brutish maturity, he was a rough but exciting playmate in his youth.

Few Americans and no advocates of the New Morality would object to a government which is designed to give people richer, fuller lives through a growing list of social services—housing, education, and medical care; a government which strives to free man from consuming worry about his livelihood and security.

Such a government also gives "Real—and not merely formal—individual freedom [which is] freedom from want, freedom from the uncertainties of the future. . . . Freedom from want means not only material freedom, it means also spiritual freedom which frees man from oppressive fears, gives him social purpose, optimism, vigor."[5]

In the USSR where all of these material, social, and intellectual freedoms are guaranteed by law there is no dictatorial power because ". . . the people themselves control and direct the development of all forms of social life." All citizens have the right ". . . to express publicly—whether in speech or writing—their views on all matters, to criticize shortcomings in the work of officials, government agencies, economic bodies, directors of industrial plants, etc." These freedoms and rights are guaran-

410

teed by law; legal dictates we are striving toward in the United States, though we have not yet attained such empyrean heights of legalized freedom and justice as were reached in the USSR many years ago. Obviously a society which is the sole trustee of such freedom and equality "... does not allow anyone the freedom to advocate antidemocratic views," and it "prohibits the dissemination of any propaganda for war, racism, national hatred and other such misanthropic ideas."

Potemkin Villages

In view of the abundance of freedoms which the beneficent state showered upon him, such qualifications appeared to be minor, and Soviet man—legally freed from material want, released from oppressive fears for the future, free to express all but misanthropic and antidemocratic ideas, and living in equality which was guaranteed to all—seemed the incarnation of the vision which entranced liberals all over the world. Small wonder that British students chanted "Stalin Is My Darling" and native Stalinists took control of student organizations in America as well as Britain. Perhaps Fabian George Bernard Shaw was a bit extreme when he described Stalin as a charmingly good-humored man, with no malice in him, whose aides were "harmless and beneficent spirits" and then concluded that anyone who interfered with this idyllic system should be shot. And it is understandable that Fabians Beatrice and Sidney Webb, bemused by this heady vision of man totally emancipated by the State, abandoned their earlier romantic conviction that "the state exists for the individual, and the maintenance of his rights is its first duty"; replacing it by societal determinism in which scientific state control could perfect man's totally malleable nature.

On their 1932 visit to Russia they were convinced that the administrators in the Kremlin "... believe in their professed faith, and this professed faith in science." Russia was not, they admitted, a democracy, but was not free thought and speech a mockery of human progress, wrote Beatrice, "unless the common people are taught to think, and inspired to use this knowledge in the interests of their commonwealth?"[6]

Communist bureaucrats were, of course, creating illusory

411

situations for Shaw, the Webbs, and other visitors; using an ages-old technique made notorious by Grigori Aleksandrovich Potemkin, minister to Catherine the Great. To impress his empress when she toured the provinces he administered in 1787, Potemkin constructed fake villages to create the illusion of prosperity, and he ordered the villagers, scrubbed and dressed as never before, to be happy on the day of Catherine's visit.

In *The First Circle*, Solzhenitsyn tells how such Potemkin illusions were used to exploit the gullibility of Western liberals. He describes the visit of Mrs. R_____, an American "widow of the well-known statesman, a perspicacious woman prominent in many good causes, who had done much to defend the rights of man," to a Soviet prison.[7] Knowing of her impending visit, the prison had been cleaned as never before, boards had been taken from the windows to permit the sun to shine where it had never shone before, bars had been painted baby-blue, carpeting put on the floor, pictures on the walls, icon lamps burned before the Virgin Mary, and copies of *Amerika* (the United States counterpart of *USSR*, from which the above description of Soviet man was taken) were placed on a table.

Mrs. R_____ asks about a prisoner who has, in fact, been sentenced to serve ten years because he conversed with an American tourist. The commandant tells her that he was arrested because:

> That man was an active Hitlerite. He worked for the Gestapo. He personally burned down a Russian village, and, if you'll forgive my speaking of such things, raped three Russian peasant girls. The number of children he killed will probably never be known.

Interrupted in her penetrating investigation of "Russian Prisons As They Actually Are" by a Russian Orthodox priest who "accidentally" enters the cell while making his "usual rounds," Mrs. R_____ then requests the commandant to ask the prisoners a question: Did any of them wish to complain to the United Nations?

Instead of asking this question, the commandant brusquely tells the prisoners that he intends to deprive them of the permission to smoke which was granted for the duration of her visit. He then interprets their agitated, angered response:

> They unanimously protest against the serious predica-
> ment of Negroes in America and demand that the Negro
> question be submitted to the United Nations.

Having convinced herself of the falsity of the innuendos spread by hostile people in the West, Mrs. R_____ (told him), "You have a magnificent prison!"

Such illusions fitted snugly into the reformist zeal of liber-als to persuade them that scientific socialism could perfect man. The delusions which they formulated from such contrived illu-sions led them to eulogize Communism in the abstract and to justify the reality of its brutal oppression with euphemistic inter-pretations. Soviet Communists had found it necessary to make minor adjustments in their social engineering; Chinese Commu-nists were perhaps a bit overanxious to complete their agrarian reforms; Ho Chi Minh was the George Washington of Vietnam, and the Cambodian Communists, like Voltaire's Candide, merely wanted to be left alone to tend to their rice paddies without imperialistic interference.

But, Solzhenitsyn's listeners would protest, we are not members of the Communist Party of the USA, most of us no longer idealize Communism as the wave of the future, and Presi-dent Jimmy does protest violations of human rights in the USSR whenever the victims have influential political or media connec-tions in America. As for their disagreement with morality based solely on science, they could point to prototypical liberal Arthur Schlesinger's refusal to accept behavioral scientist B. F. Skin-ner's conception of man as an homunculus devoid of freedom and dignity. They could refer to Berelson and Steiner's reluc-tance to renounce morality and sentiment even though their summary of 1,045 "scientific" studies showed that a majority of the most influential social scientists spend most of their time trying to prove that man is, as the Communists say he is, essen-tially nothing but the creature of his social environment.[8]

Such protest would have some warrant in reflecting liberal rejection of the conception that man has no conscience, no free-dom to choose between good and evil, and no self-respect, though

413

Professor Schlesinger admitted that Professor Skinner had reached such conclusions about man by pursuing the logic of the behavioral science approach to its rational conclusion. Though he admired the intellectual path revealed by the light of science, Professor Schlesinger refused to follow Skinner to its terminus. Many liberals similarly ignore the basic premise (predictability) of a way of thinking which they have extolled since the eighteenth century and, with Professor Schlesinger, are similarly appalled when they see the results which follow from its pursuit. They shield themselves from the logical implications of science by espousing a form of scientistic rationality which illogically combines pseudo-science with the romantic notion of an innately good man whose transient flaws will be remedied as soon as the evils of social and economic competition are eliminated.

So Solzhenitsyn's listeners could, in good conscience, be convinced that they reject Communist Man as firmly as they reject Skinner's Man, and as decidedly as they reject "hard" science as the basis for morality. Their intellectual credibility rests not on such hard science but on the "soft" science expounded by Sigmund Freud, Margaret Mead, Ruth Benedict, and similar pseudo-scientists. By pursuing this course they evade the naked implications of real science while still using its prestigious cloak to adorn the false science which supports the socio-political programs of their New Morality.

Such objections to Solzhenitsyn's criticisms at Harvard would be valid had he accused his listeners of being Communists or Communist sympathizers, but he didn't—he accused them of being pusillanimous, of lacking that inner freedom which he prizes so highly, of lacking sufficient will to resist Communism. Thus the interpretation of the *New York Times* was properly focused in pointing out that Solzhenitsyn's address sharply challenged Enlightenment Man who trusted in the rationality of mankind.

There are obvious and vast differences between the practices of the USSR from which Solzhenitsyn was exiled and those of the United States in which he spoke, but in principle the Communist conception of man and that of rationalistic liberalism are but differing branches of a common lineage.

Both assume that man is highly malleable and easily improvable through socio-political programs. Both stress the ne-

414

cessity to impose external forces upon him for his own good. Both reject the conception of man which I have emphasized and which Solzhenitsyn describes in Part Two of *The Gulag Archipelago:* Man who has as his intrinsic nature an amalgam of potentials for evil as well as good, evil which cannot be expunged by revolution; with man's self-respect, his seldom glory, and perhaps his hope for physical survival as well as spiritual salvation resting in his capacity to constrict the evil within himself by his own effort.

In the United States this choice: to re-form man through socio-political programs or to encourage him to exercise his capacity for moral choice was enunciated almost fifty years ago by Professor Rexford Guy Tugwell, the most influential member of President Franklin Delano Roosevelt's "Brain Trust," as he rationalized that if the economic depression of the thirties ". . . was not a conclusive argument for collectivism, there never would be one."

> Of course if he [President Roosevelt] insisted that character was involved, if a man's morals and those of his family would be impaired by having an assured income regardless of his ability to get and hold a job, and if this was to determine policy, then no real change was possible.[9]

President Roosevelt, the practical politician, at first believed the socio-economic programs proposed by his rationalistic advisers to be unrealistic, much as pragmatic Lenin felt that some of Trotsky's schemes were "intellectualistic formulas that fail to take into account the practical side of the question."[10]

Before his native prudent judgment was overwhelmed by the myriad scientistic "proofs" heaped upon it by his professorial advisers, President Roosevelt said that for the Federal government to guarantee an income to those without work was a precedent which, if continued, would destroy the moral fibre of the recipients:

> The lessons of history, confirmed by the evidence immediately before me, show conclusively that continued dependence upon relief induces a spiritual and moral disintegration fundamentally destructive to the national fibre. To

415

dole out relief in this way is to administer a narcotic, a
subtle destroyer of the human spirit. It is inimical to the
dictates of sound policy. It is in violation of the traditions
of America. Work must be found for able-bodied but desti-
tute workers.

The Federal government must and shall quit this business of relief.[11]

Professor Tugwell convinced the President that such Federal economic programs were more important than personal morality and therefore the Federal government did not "quit this
business of relief"; it expanded relief from a few million per year
to many billions. Tugwell, who had derived his conception of
morality from the hedonistic "felicific calculus" of Jeremy Bentham, warned Roosevelt that our adherence to moral imperatives, though they might seen more virtuous, would cripple us.
Moral imperatives, he argued, must give way to progress, and
Roosevelt's qualms gave way as his actions affirmed his assent.

From this preference for federal "welfare" even if it were
at the expense of personal morality evolved "intellectualistic
formulas that fail to take into account the practical side of the
question" such as the Social Security Act—its concept as well as
the huckstering phrase derived from British socialist Beatrice
Webb—and the Agricultural Adjustment Act, both based on
"scientific" formulas and predictions. Though both of these acts
were drawn up by professors, the formulas were by no means
scientific (for that matter, they were quite irrational) and "predictions" based on them were invariably and egregiously wrong.
To cover up their mistakes and to justify the continued waste of
billions each year on such programs, bureaucrats and politicians
of both parties have practiced deliberate deception upon the
public for decades. Public ethics as well as private morality
decline as we increasingly rely on such programs to improve
mankind.[12]

In *The Best and the Brightest* David Halberstam says of
the chief advisers during the incumbency of President John F.
Kennedy:

. . . if those years had any central theme, if there was
anything that bound the men, their followers and their

416

subordinates together, it was the belief that sheer intelligence and rationality could answer and solve anything.[13]

Exulting in their own rationality, Kennedy and his advisers rationalized that Ho Chi Minh would be similarly rational. He wasn't. And as the Vietnam conflict degenerated into a disgraceful American defeat—

> If the reporters would not write upbeat stories, the Kennedy Administration, facile, particularly good at public relations, would generate its own positive accounts. Thus optimism became a major and deliberate part of the policy; warfare by public relations. High-level Americans were sent over not to learn about Vietnam . . . but to pump up this weak policy. Their speeches and statements had been written for them before they left, full of talk . . . of a victory in sight. . . .
> Vietnamese realities did not matter. . . . More and more effort went into public relations because it was easier to manipulate appearances and statements than it was to affect reality on the ground.

And this, our version of the Potemkin villages, we called Camelot!

In Chapter 10 I described how President Lyndon B. Johnson, in his 1964 campaign against Senator Barry Goldwater, labeled support for his Great Society as "public morality," indicating that this New Morality was superior to personal morality. I told how he and his running mate designated Goldwater's purported *attitude* toward race a form of public immorality. I also recounted that many clergymen so worshipped the socio-political programs of the New Morality that they called for guerilla warfare to attain them. The blood-lust of these unchristian soldiers would have brought an avuncular twinkle to the eye of "Uncle Joe" Stalin.

Advocates of the New Morality will go to extremes to attack those who disagree with their doctrine—as, for example, during this campaign in which Arizona's Senator Goldwater, running on conservative principles, stressed personal morality while incumbent President Johnson indicated that dissidents who refused to support the socio-political programs of the Great Society were

417

immoral. During this campaign editors of respected newspapers accepted full-page ads which questioned the mental stability of conservative Senator Goldwater. These ads were paid for by Ralph Ginsberg, publisher of *Fact* magazine and previous publisher of *Eros,* a magazine so obscene that it was banned from distribution. Subsequent to the appearance of the ad, a summary of the responses of 2,417 psychiatrists (of 12,356 asked for their professional judgment) was reported in *Fact.* Of those responding psychiatrists who gave definitive diagnoses, *none of whom had ever examined Senator Goldwater,* 1,189 said that his mental imbalance disqualified him from public office, diagnosing, for example, that "His public utterances strongly suggest the megalomania of a paranoid personality."[14]

It is true that Senator Goldwater was not forced into a mental institution because of his dissidence, and it is true that the American Psychiatric Association protested this political diagnosis more vehemently than Soviet psychiatrists protest the prostitution of their art by comparable political diagnoses; nonetheless a diagnosis of "public utterances which strongly suggest the megalomania of a paranoid personality" has enough similarity to diagnoses of "sluggish schizophrenia with paranoid delusions of reformism" to indicate that there is some relationship between the ideologies which produce them.

Western intellectuals who express dissent with the doctrine of the New Morality are not imprisoned nor confined to mental institutions, but they have been prevented from speaking at universities; they have been threatened with loss of academic position and denied deserved promotion; they do have difficulty in publishing their works; and if their works *are* published they learn that some editors seem to feel that freedom of the press means that since liberals are assigned to review books written by liberals they should also be assigned to review books written by conservatives.

So while Solzhenitsyn would have been unfair had he accused Western intellectuals of being Communists, or of still being the ardent apologists for Communism that they once were, he could, with reason, indicate that they lacked sufficient courage to acknowledge the implications of their doctrine and that they lacked the will to oppose Communism vigorously because beneath their verbal protests about its practices they sensed

418

that any strong attack on its principles would reflect adversely on their own doctrine.

By the time (1978) that Solzhenitsyn spoke at Harvard the 1840 forecast of another foreign observer, Alexis de Tocqueville, had come to fruition. The "immense and tutelary power"[15] of government now in fact does provide for our security, direct our industry, and regulate the descent of our property. Our dependence on the State has "softened, bent and guided our will" and rendered the "exercise of the free agency of man less useful and less frequent," robbing him of the uses of himself.

The belief which eighteenth-century intellectuals called rational and worshiped because they thought it would lead to glory without grace as it enabled them to transport Saint Augustine's Heavenly City of God into their secular control had failed. It had merely transferred the governance of men by mystery, miracle, and authority from the Church to the State.

The rationalism which they irrationally believed to be science had been exposed as unsubstantial scientism, so lacking in solid evidential support that they would have to fortify it with terror to fulfill their desire to "measure and master" the world. Though they could rationalize such use of terror by others, they lacked the courage to practice it themselves.

The vision wherein soft science creates a soft communal society where brotherhood is guaranteed by law and where man's evil is submerged by the goodness which swells forth as social and economic competition are eliminated is so appealing that it seems boorish to question its premises and pessimistic to be skeptical about its attainment. Philosophic conservatives, however, would doubt that any form of secular society, whether Communistic, softly socialistic, or capitalistic can be perfect in the sense that it will effect the perfectibility of man.

Unperfect Society

Milovan Djilas, born in 1911, was arrested and imprisoned for three years by the Royalist government as a Communist organizer in 1929. During World War II his effectiveness as a guerilla fighter against the Nazis earned him the rank of Partisan General; when the Communist regime was established his ranking in the hierarchy was second only to that of Tito, and he was considered to be Tito's likeliest successor. Despite these honors and this power, and particularly in view of his continuing belief in the principles of communism, he had the considerable courage he needed to criticize its practices. He attacked the ways in which Communist leaders of both the USSR and Yugoslavia, contrary to the principles of communism which they proclaimed, deceived and degraded man. In 1954 he was expelled from the Central Committee of the Communist Party and in 1955 he was tried as a criminal for his "hostile propaganda" and given a suspended sentence. When he publicly criticized the Yugoslav government for its failure to denounce the Soviet invasion of Hungary, he was compelled to serve his sentence—in the same prison where the Royalist government had once committed him because he was an organizer for the Communist Party! In all, Djilas was to serve twelve years in prison as punishment for his dissent.

As Solzhenitsyn had been, Djilas was forbidden to write in prison, but he composed incisive critical analyses of Communist practices—written mostly on toilet paper. In *The New Class* (1957), he described how ruling Communists, instead of creating a perfect society by the abolition of classes, had actually created a new class, the bureaucracy, which replaced the bourgeoisie they had destroyed.

The Unperfect Society expresses Djilas' conviction that while "men must hold both ideas and ideals, they should not regard these as being wholly realizable."[16] Society, he says, is not merely *imperfect*—a designation which would imply that certain improvements might make it perfect—but *unperfect*; in its very nature unperfectible.

Visions of social improvement and humanitarian dreams are necessary to reform society, but whenever such visions are based on doctrinaire hypotheses about man, premised on the belief that they can change human nature, they will either fail or result in tyranny, because ineradicably man is governed by the twin gods of good and evil.

Though philosophical conservatives might admire the liberal vision incorporate in some socio-political programs and approve of some of them on an existential humanitarian basis, they would dispute any doctrinaire assumption that these constitute

420

a New Morality which will change the nature of man. We now need sufficient courage to emerge from the "perpetual childhood" in which the minute and mild strings of the beneficent State cocoons us; enough good sense to recognize that both we and society are unperfect and unperfectible; and sufficient strength of will to accept our individual responsibilities as adults.

Invictus—With Reservations

Conservatives do respect the role of rationality in human thought and they do recognize that social factors influence our behavior. They contend, however, that desiccated rationality needs the leavening of emotion and the tempering of experience to mold it into prudent judgment. Though social factors do influence our behavior, so also do hereditary factors and, conservatives would insist, both influences should be mediated through man's capacity to choose between good and evil.

When rationalized to the degree that it excludes man's capacity for moral choice, social determinism becomes the Gulag Archipelago of the Union of Soviet Socialist Republics. When rationalized to the degree that it excludes man's capacity for moral choice, hereditary determinism becomes the Auschwitz Archipelago of the National Socialist Worker's Party.

The "rational" choice for Aleksandr I. Solzhenitsyn—having already proved his courage by surviving cancer as well as prison camps; having received deserved acclaim as a Nobel Laureate; having heard the accolade of approval from party boss Nikita Khrushchev; loving his native Russia and fearful that his gift for writing would wither if he were expelled from it—was to soften his criticism. But he chose instead to suffer in defense of the dignity of man.

The "rational" choice for Milovan Djilas—having already proved his courage as a Partisan fighter and under imprisonment by Royalists as well as Communists for his convictions—was to soften his criticism, reasoning that when he replaced Tito he would then remedy the evils he denounced. Instead, he applied his conviction that good ends do not justify bad means to himself as well as others. He chose instead to suffer in defense of the dignity of man.

Viktor Frankl, describing his experiences in Nazi concentration camps in *Man's Search for Meaning*, said that the mixture of good and evil which goes through all human beings becomes apparent even at the bottom of the abyss which is laid open by the concentration camp, that "Man *can* preserve a vestige of spiritual freedom, of independence of mind, even in such conditions of psychic and physical stress . . . everything can be taken from a man but one thing: the last of human freedoms—to choose one's attitude in any given set of circumstances, to choose one's way. In the final analysis it becomes clear that the sort of person the prisoner became was the result of an inner decision and not the result of camp influences alone."[17] Frankl concluded that even under the horror of conditions in Nazi concentration camps "any man can . . . decide what shall become of him—mentally and spiritually." He can retain his human dignity.

Langdon Gilkey, an American who was teaching at Yenching University in China, was interned in 1943 by the Japanese and spent two and a half years in a "Civilian Internment Center" in Shantung Province.[18] As a student at Harvard he had been led to reject religion, asking himself: "Why add religious frills to the ethical commitments any unbelieving naturalist can easily avow? Cannot the modern agnostic intellectual be capable by himself of leading a creative and upright life devoted to the moral absolutes of peace in the world and justice in society?"

After graduating from Harvard, influenced by Reinhold Niebuhr, Gilkey renounced such rationalist absolutes in favor of a realistic morality which:

> . . . was not based either on a belief in the overriding goodness of man or even on the possibility of establishing ideal solutions in social history—both of which seemed contradicted by the obvious facts.

During his first month in the internment camp Gilkey returned to "the confident humanism so characteristic of the liberal academic circles in America," convinced that man's ingenuity in dealing with difficult problems made moral and spiritual issues irrelevant. But then he saw that some crises in this desperate situation involved a breakdown in character rather than a breakdown in techniques, revealing a need for moral integrity and self-sacrifice. Such experiences led him to believe that the weakness of humanism was not its reliance upon science and technology, but ". . . its naive and unrealistic faith in the rationality and goodness of the men who wielded these instruments."

Langdon Gilkey summarizes how the realities of life in a Japanese internment camp changed the rational conception of man he had been indoctrinated with at Harvard.

> Our camp experience demonstrated that two things can safely be said about mankind. First, it seemed certain enough that man is immensely creative, ingenious, and courageous in the face of new problems. But it was also equally apparent that under pressure he loves himself and his own more than he will ever admit. Furthermore, both the universality and yet the puzzling "unnaturalness" of this self-love were certainly established by our experience, for men consistently denied the motivations which equally consistently determined their conduct. If men were just plain "good," this self-love would not have been so pervasive in all they did. If, on the other hand, they were just plain "bad," if this self-love were simply "natural" to man, those who acted upon it would not have been so intent to deny its presence and to claim that their acts flowed instead from moral intentions.

Those who exercised their courage to rise above their degrading experiences in prison camps demonstrated that man can retain his self-respect, resisting even the most drastic temptations to relinquish it. Man can rise above the circumstances of even the worst conceivable environment.

Functional Complementarity

More than coincidence led all of these varied inmates to the same conclusion about man—that he is a combination of potentials for evil as well as for good over which he can exercise conscious choice. They rejected the extremes of desiccated ratio-

423

nalism which, whether applied through environmental determinism or hereditary determinism, deprives man of his capacity to choose.

The hypothesis of functional complementarity (described in Chapter 8) is an intellectually credible alternative to the determinism which makes man either a robot programmed by his genes or a puppet dangling on strings manipulated by social engineers.

The mental hurdle of straight-line cause-and-effect rationalism in which man's moral behavior is mechanistically determined to a degree which absolves him of responsibility can be surmounted if we accept the possibility that thought-processes associated with moral behavior operate as a causal nexus in which potential stimuli, no matter where initiated, can be facilitated or inhibited on the neocortical levels of the brain.

Through the functioning of our neocortex we have the capacity to decide, when reacting to either external or internal initiating factors, whether they fit into the pattern of morality or not. If we decide that the initiated factor does fit we should incorporate it into our behavior by facilitating the process. When we realize that the initiating factor cannot be incorporated into what we know to be right, we can and should inhibit it so that it does not become a cause of our behavior. To refuse to choose is also choice. If we do not actively inhibit impulses which conflict with what we know to be morally right, our refusal to do so constitutes immorality.

The second mental hurdle which must be surmounted in order to accept the intellectual credibility of the hypothesis that man is a morally responsible agent has to do with the relationship between our selfish urges (whether innate or acquired) and the moral codes of civilized society. This is a problem of reconciling two factors affecting our behavior which are—or seem to be—antagonistic to each other. Our choice seems: either we submit to the moral injunction and forsake pleasure, or we submit to our desires by violating the social codes through acts which are illegal or immoral, uncivil or vulgar. This hypothesis would hold that, as with so many other things which are separately antagonistic, selfish desires and social codes of conduct complement each other when they function together. Most people, during the course of a lifetime, will come closer to fulfilling their sense of self-respect, their integrity as responsible persons by thinking of such codes as complementary to our desires rather than antagonistic to them.

Since the crucial test of science is predictability, and this hypothesis of functional complementarity is designed to show that man can consciously select or reject stimuli which impinge upon him it obviously cannot be scientifically validated. Its acceptance or rejection will be based mostly on emotional preference. For those who wish to supplement their emotional preference I have indicated some sources from which to draw support: conclusions from reflexologists such as Pavlov and Bykov; evidence from glandular and brain function; the concepts of emergent evolution; the Bible, when interpreted as parable; much of man's historical experience, and current examples such as Solzhenitsyn and Djilas; numerous philosophers; pragmatic evidence from the consumption of alcohol and mental imbalance; and the expression of this theme in our lasting literature.

But perhaps the best evidence in support of the conception that man's nature combines potentials for good and evil over which he can exert conscious control is self-experience. Do you romantically believe yourself to be innately good—free of all faults except those inflicted on you by social or economic competition? Have you pursued the rationality of scientistic environmental determinism far enough to accept yourself as totally malleable, needing a Big Brother "social engineer" to manufacture your attitudes and control your behavior? Or do you believe "that we are born with a natural capacity to distinguish between right and wrong. . . .

"We have the faculty by means of which we can pass judgment on our own conduct, either approving or condemning it. . . . The possession of [this faculty] makes us responsible human beings. Like other faculties it needs to be trained, and may be deadened through misuse." If you believe in this description of man from the Bible dictionary you may further agree (with Alexander Pope) that the proper study of mankind leads us to realize that self-love and social be the same.

A realization that our happiness is best pursued and the greatest good for the greatest number attained when "self-love and social be the same," or when we love our neighbor as ourself should not prompt us into frantic efforts to do things for people

425

which they had best do themselves. As your love for yourself is not narcissism but self-respect, so your love for your neighbor should be respect for him as an end in himself, not as means to an end. As you should condemn yourself for your moral weakness, so you should condemn him. As you deserve punishment for moral violations, so does he. As he respects himself, so he should want responsible control over his affairs. As his interests, wants, attitudes, and abilities differ from yours, so they should be respected if they violate no moral code. As the Declaration indicates, he is equal to all men in that he possesses man's highest faculty—a conscience. So neither your acts nor your laws can give him freedom because true freedom is inner freedom, earned through his own character, molded by his own will.

This conservative conception of man lacks the sentimental appeal of romanticism and is prosaic compared to the visionary utopian promises of rationalism. It requires stern judgments upon ourselves as well as others. The true nature of morality is so uncertain and our motives so complicated that we now insist that the State use its authority to measure our virtue on the inchworm scale of the New Morality as earlier we insisted that the Church use its authority to measure our virtue in terms of its clerical "laws." Despite this disquieting uncertainty and the assurance that we will sometimes make judgments which punish good and reward evil, yet:

> It is better to cherish virtue and humanity, by leaving much to free will, even with some loss to the object, than to attempt to make men mere machines and instruments of a political benevolence.[19]

Thirty-five years ago, George Orwell said that the real problem of the West, having lost our belief in the immortality of the soul, is to find some way to preserve man's ethical and moral values. When we lost our conviction that living the good life on earth would earn us beatific immortality after death, and when the mystery, miracle, and authority of the Church which formalized this spiritual desire was dissipated by scientistic rationalism, the focus of our yearning shifted to the State, believing that its authority could mysteriously perform the miracle of eradicating evil from man's nature.

426

Western liberals, lacking the intellectual rigor to pursue their assumptions to their logical conclusions, and lacking the physical courage to put into practice the rigid controls which are necessary to force man to fit into the mold of their social engineering, capriciously endowed him with romantic innate goodness. They believed that their socio-political programs would gently elicit this goodness by eliminating the only things which cause badness—social and economic competition.

This heady vision is now blurred and fading. As Solzhenitsyn at Harvard pointed out, ". . . the materialism which is farthest Left always ends up being stronger, more attractive, and finally, victorious, because it is *more consistent*" (my emphasis). Liberalism, he went on to say, is displaced by radicalism, radicalism surrenders to socialism, and ". . . socialism never could resist communism."

Without Christianity, the glorified humanism of the Enlightenment is reduced to "ossified" rationalistic formulas rigidified into social dogmatism.

The zeal to make man good through such rationalistic formulas ignores Jefferson's contention that:

> Morals were too essential to the happiness of man to be risked on the incertain combinations of the head. She [nature] laid their foundation therefore in sentiment, not in science.[20]

And they pervert Burke's aphorism that:

> The lines of morality are not like the ideal lines of mathematics. They admit of exceptions; they demand modifications. [They are] not made by the process of logic, but by the rule of prudence.[21]

Only Not Yet; Not Me

During the 1964 presidential campaign, conservative Goldwater's manager said he would resign if the Senator made one more speech like one he had recently given. The subject had been the Social Security Act, and Goldwater had described some of its fraudulent aspects. What he said was true, and his criticism could have been much stronger. But the speech was given to an audience composed largely of retired people who would get more from Social Security than they had paid into it. Such people agree that federal handouts must be reduced—but not yet; not theirs.

During the 1976 presidential campaign the conservative candidate for vice-president strongly discouraged federal handouts, but when he returned to his role as a senator after his candidacy was defeated, he strongly encouraged increased federal handouts for the farmers of his state. Most of his rural constituents thought federal handouts were scandalous and should be stopped—but not yet; not theirs.

In 1977 conservative citizens of New Jersey voted approval of a new state income tax. The choice had been either an increase in the sales tax or the new income tax and the approval came from retired people whose purchases were taxed, but whose incomes were mostly tax-exempt. During their working lives most of them likely railed against all income taxes and would have vigorously opposed a new one—but not now.

Businessmen extol the glory of free enterprise and excoriate federal regulations which restrict it—but they gratefully accept regulations which help them.

Thus agreement on the principle that Big Brother government restricts our freedom is nullified by practices which embody an Orwellian truism: Regulations which benefit others are bad; those which benefit me are good.

The beneficent government which has softened, bent and guided our will to render the free agency of man less useful is not an abstraction. We created it, we perpetuate it, we alone can diminish it. It is our enemy—it is us.

Intellectuals—those who shape the thoughts of others—will find it difficult to reshape their own thinking: to admit that much of it has rigidified into "ossified formulas" of the Enlightenment; to absorb the realization that his capacity for moral choice rather than his ability to rationalize is man's highest attribute; to acknowledge that their precious scientism is not real science and has likely done mankind more harm than good; to decrease their attempts to measure and master the world and to increase their efforts to understand it.

People will find it difficult to reject the seeming certitude of

428

science and the superficial clarity of rationalism which offers them Utopia Tomorrow for their society and Painless Panaceas for their conscience. They will be upset by the proposal that they relinquish their pleasant nostrums and their guaranteed effort-less progress for the guilt of conscience, the hard choices of fallible judgment, and for little, unsure reward. They will yearn to remain in the cocoon of perpetual childhood in which scientism and the beneficent State has encased them; they will resent the restraints on personal behavior demanded by conscience and resist shouldering the social obligations appropriate to adult-hood. Many will rather cling to the delusion of unearned rights conferred by an authority which can readily take them away than strive for the only freedom they can ever attain, the inner freedom which is subject to our will. "If we surrender it to corruption, we do not deserve to be called human."[22]

The difficulties in deciding to accept our responsibility for moral choice are so many that the burden of them is intolerable. Under such circumstances rationalistic methodology suggests that we petition our elected representatives to select an ad hoc committee to peruse appropriate findings of behavioral science to determine the probabilities of a viable alternative to this deci-sion-making process.

Chapter 15. References and Notes

1. Theodore Shabad, "Solzhenitsyn Assails Liberals in West," *New York Times*, September 12, 1973.

2. Israel Shenker, "Dissident Russian Writer in Exile," *New York Times*, February 14, 1974.

3. Aleksandr I. Solzhenitsyn, *The First Circle* (New York: Harper and Row, 1968).

4. Aleksandr I. Solzhenitsyn, *The Gulag Archipelago, Two* (New York: Harper and Row, 1975), pp. 615–617.

5. Vasili Tugarinov, "The Individual and Society Under Socialism," *USSR*, June 1961, p. 23.

6. C. Northcote Parkinson, *Left Luggage* (Boston: Houghton-Mifflin, 1967), p. 94.

7. Aleksandr I. Solzhenitsyn, *The First Circle*, pp. 332–337.

8. Bernard Berelson and Gary A. Steiner, *Human Behavior: An Inventory of Scientific Findings* (New York: Harcourt, Brace and World, 1964), p. 666.

9. Rexford Guy Tugwell, *The Brains Trust* (New York: Viking Press, 1968), pp. 408–9.

10. Edmund Wilson, *To The Finland Station* (New York: Doubleday Anchor, 1953), p. 443.

11. Raymond Moley, *The First New Deal* (New York: Harcourt Brace and World, 1966), pp. 279–280.

12. A. H. Hobbs, *The Vision and The Constant Star* (New Canaan, Conn.: Long House, 1956), pp. 129–146.

13. David Halberstam, *The Best and the Brightest* (Greenwich, Conn.: Fawcett, 1972), pp. 57, 255.

14. "The Couch and the Stump," *Time*, October 9, 1964.

15. Alexis de Tocqueville, *Democracy in America*, vol. 2 (New York: Vintage Books, 1960) pp. 336–337.

16. Milovan Djilas, *The Unperfect Society: Beyond the New Class* (New York: Harcourt Brace and World, 1969), pp. 4–5.

17. Viktor Frankl, *Man's Search for Meaning* (Boston: Beacon Press, 1959), p. 65.

18. Langdon Gilkey, *Shantung Compound* (New York: Harper and Row, 1966), pp. 72, 75, 232.

19. Edmund Burke, *Reflections on the Revolution in France*, pp. 149–150.

20. Garry Wills, *Inventing America*, p. 187.

21. Edmund Burke, *An Appeal from the New to the Old Whigs, 1791*, in Peter Viereck, *Conservatism* (New York: D. van Nostrand, 1956), p. 30.

22. Aleksandr Solzhenitsyn, ed., *From Under the Rubble* (Boston: Little, Brown, 1974), p. 25.

Index

433

438

441

Rationalistic scientism, 24; Coleridge's rejection of, 97; effect of, on writers, 199–200; as faith, 53–55; and man, 12; and philosophical conservatism, 14; sociology as, 56–57; Woodrow Wilson on, 59

Reade, Winwood, 136

Reality Therapy (Glasser), 353

Reason, 100; Paine on, 88; society governed by, 89–90

"Redeeming social value," 223–24

Reed, John, 90

Reflections on the Revolution in France (Burke), 83, 88, 91, 93

Reich, Charles A., 154

Reid, Thomas, 276–77

Reisman, David, 192

Religion: and democratic republics, 13; of enlightenment, 54; and morality, 12–14; and politics, Burke on, 86; and science, Paine on, 90–91; science as replacement for, 187; scientism and, 195

Republic (Plato), 37, 156

Reserpine, 346, 352

Responsibility, moral or social, 262–63; and alcoholism, 295–96; 308; and evolution, 271–72; and mental imbalance, 334, 352–53, 354

Reynolds, Sir Joshua, 67

Rieff, Philip, 180, 228, 229, 341

Right(s): conservative view of human, 184; natural, 84, 88; to pursuit of happiness, 105–6

Rights of Man (Paine), 88, 89, 90–91, 96

Roberts, Catherine, 24

Rockefeller, John D., 306

Romance, 361–70

Romanticism: maturation of, into conservatism, 97–99; Melville's view of, 95n; rise of, 64–71, 76–77; and scientistic rationalism, 150, 152; and student rebellion of sixties, 144, 149, 150, 154–56, 160, 163–64; Voltaire's critique of, 82–83.

Romeo and Juliet (Shakespeare), 361

Roosevelt, Franklin D., 193–94, 415–16

Root, E. Merrill, 196

Rosenhan, D.L., 318, 333

Rousseau, Jean-Jacques, 26, 66–67, 68, 72, 75, 83, 97

Rousseau and Revolution (Will and Ariel Durant), 65

Rudd, Mark, 155, 160

Russell, Bertrand, 151, 174–75

Rutherford, Lord Ernest, 117

Sagan, Carl, 256, 277

Saint-Simon, Duc de, 145

Salinger, J.D., 187–88, 199

Saroyan, William, 226

Savio, Mario, 145

Sayers, Dorothy L., 274

Schizophrenia, 328–30, 338–39; "Sluggish," 330, 331, 348

Schlesinger, Arthur, Jr., 168–69, 413, 414

Schopenhauer, Arthur, 16

Schorr, Daniel, 250

Schorr, Dr. Martin M., 322

Schott, Webster, 222

Science: books on nature of, 196–97; contemporary physical, 117–18; eighteenth-century critique of, 80–82; as human behavior, 131–32; and human values, 199–200; vs. morality, 87; and religion, Paine on, 90–91; soft definitions of, 125–26; term broadened by Newton, 49; term, connotation of, 117. *See also* Scientific method

Science, 391

Science is a Sacred Cow (Standen), 196

Science: The Glorious Entertainment (Barzun), 196

Scientific Credibility of Freud's Theories and Therapy, The (Fisher and Greenberg), 342–43

Scientific method or procedure, 119–22; applied to man, 22–24, 138; defi-

442

443

Weizenbaum, Joseph, 133n–34n
"Welfare clause," 104, 106, 108
Wells, H.G., 151
What Is to Be Done? (Cherny-shevsky), 100, 187
Wheeler, Dr. John A., 117
Whitehead, Alfred North, 47, 53, 119
Williams, Tennessee, 226
Wills, Garry, 105, 106
Wilson, E.O., 29–30
Wilson, William Griffith, 305–6, 310
Wilson, Woodrow, 59

Wolfgang, Marvin E., 225
Wollstonecraft, Mary, 68, 69–70, 75, 97
Wordsworth, William, 97–98
World Council of Churches, 239
World Hypotheses (Pepper), 197
Wundt, Wilhelm, 58

Yeats, William Butler, 363

Zinsser, William, 227
Zosimus, Pope, 39

445